D1265623

Knowledge and Decisions

KNOWLEDGE

AND

DECISIONS

Thomas Sowell

Basic Books, Inc., Publishers

NEW YORK

Library of Congress Cataloging in Publication Data

Sowell, Thomas, 1930–
  Knowledge and decisions.

  Includes bibliographical references and index.
  1. Decision-making. 2. Reality. 3. Knowledge, Theory of.
  4. Civilization, Modern. I. Title.
  HM73.S69   301.15′54   79-7347
  ISBN: 0-465-03736-4

'80 by Basic Books, Inc.
nited States of America
by Vincent Torre
7 6 5 4 3 2 1

Man is no Aristotelian god contemplating all existence at one glance.
—Walter Lippmann

CONTENTS

ACKNOWLEDGMENTS

The debts to be acknowledged in the writing of this book are so numerous and varied that any listing must be partial, and accompanied by apologies to those not mentioned.

Intellectually, this book is a product of an odyssey of the mind that goes back more than three decades. Those from whom I gleaned particular insights have ranged across the philosophic spectrum, from Karl Marx to Milton Friedman, and the fields have ranged from biology to law. If one writing contributed more than any other to the framework within which this work developed, it would be an essay entitled "The Use of Knowledge in Society," published in the *American Economic Review* of September 1945, and written by F. A. Hayek, later to become a Nobel Laureate in economics. In this plain and apparently simple essay was a deeply penetrating insight into the way societies function and malfunction, and clues as to why they are so often and so profoundly misunderstood.

The immediate environment within which the research for this book began was the Center for Advanced Study in the Behavioral Sciences, in Stanford, California, where I was a fellow in 1976–77. Preparatory planning for this work was begun during 1974–76, when generous grants from the American Enterprise Institute in Washington, D. C., and the Hoover Institution at Stanford University permitted me the time needed for reflections and reconsiderations. Several months in residence as a Senior Fellow at the Hoover Institution in 1977 enabled me to complete the research begun at the Center for Advanced Study and to proceed with the writing.

The person with whom I discussed this book most during its writing was Mary M. Ash, an attorney in Palo Alto, California. Her legal mind was helpful in her critiques not only of the discussions of law but also of material throughout the book. Her friendship and encouragement sustained my efforts and my spirits.

A two-day conference in 1978 at the Center for Law and Economics at the University of Miami was organized around a paper of mine on legal issues, and provided an invaluable experience in confronting leading scholars in law, economics, and political science with the ideas that form the foundation of this book. The generous support of the Liberty Fund in Indianapolis, Indiana, made possible this gathering of distinguished scholars from all parts of

Acknowledgments

the country, and the generous permission of Professor Henry G. Manne, Director of the Center for Law and Economics, has made possible the incorporation of that paper into this book. Other discussions of the book's evolving themes were held at the University of California at Berkeley, Wesleyan University in Connecticut, the University of Maryland, and San Jose State University in California. I learned something from all of them.

The support, enthusiasm, tact, helpfulness, and wisdom of my editor, Midge Decter, have been of inestimable value during what seemed like interminable years of writing, and in smoothing what can be a rocky road between the manuscript and the finished book. All the good things I had heard about her proved to be true, and I am pleased to hereby amend my long-standing belief that the only good editor is a dead editor. (A couple of other possible exceptions also come to mind.)

These contributors are only the tip of the iceberg. Many librarians, colleagues, secretaries—and especially the marvelous staff at the Center for Advanced Study—have helped me along the way.

In the end, however, after all the influences, aiders and abettors, responsibility for all conclusions and errors is mine.

THOMAS SOWELL
University of California, Los Angeles
May 9, 1979

Part I

SOCIAL

INSTITUTIONS

Chapter I

The Role of Knowledge

Ideas are everywhere, but knowledge is rare. Even a so-called "knowledge-able" person usually has solid knowledge only within some special area, representing a tiny fraction of the whole spectrum of human concerns. Humorist Will Rogers said, "Everybody is ignorant, only on different subjects."

How does an ignorant world perform intricate functions requiring enormous knowledge? These intricate functions include not only such scientific feats as air travel and space exploration, but also the complex economic processes which bring a slice of bread and a piece of butter to your plate at breakfast. Anyone who has studied the actual process by which everyday food items are planned, produced, and distributed knows that the complexity staggers the mind. Many highly intelligent and highly trained people spend a lifetime studying it, and learning more all the time. Among those who speculate financially in such commodities, economic disaster is commonplace, even after they have spent years studying the market. In short, individually we know so pathetically little, and yet socially we use a range and complexity of knowledge that would confound a computer. The question is not only how given institutions (including whole societies) manage to do this, but how various institutions (and societies) differ in the manner and effectiveness with which they do it—and what do the historic and continuing *changes* in the way they function portend for the future?

We shall begin with the *production* of knowledge—with the process by which ideas are filtered and transformed into recognized knowledge, having the force to guide decisions. Then we shall consider the *application* of knowledge in economic, legal, social, and political institutions. And finally, we shall consider the evolution of institutions, attitudes, and beliefs, and the way all these affect our ability to produce and apply knowledge in the future.

IDEAS

Physicists have determined that even the most solid and heavy mass of matter we see is mostly empty space. But at the submicroscopic level, specks of matter scattered through a vast emptiness have such incredible density and weight, and are linked to one another by such powerful forces, that together they produce all the properties of concrete, cast iron and solid rock. In much the same way, specks of knowledge are scattered through a vast emptiness of ignorance, and everything depends upon how solid the individual specks of knowledge are, and on how powerfully linked and coordinated they are with one another. The vast spaces of ignorance do not prevent the specks of knowledge from forming a solid structure, though sufficient *misunderstanding* can disintegrate it in much the same way that radioactive atomic structures can disintegrate (uranium into lead) or even explode.

Ideas, as the raw material from which knowledge is produced, exist in superabundance, but that makes the production of knowledge more difficult rather than easier. Many ideas—probably most—will have to be discarded somewhere in the process of producing authenticated knowledge. Authentication is as important as the raw information itself, and the manner and speed of the authentication process can be crucial: the surprise attack on Pearl Harbor succeeded despite the fact that knowledge of the impending attack had reached the War Department in Washington hours before it occurred. Still the bombing caught Pearl Harbor by surprise because the information had not yet passed through the authentication process established by the military institutions. Whatever the merits or demerits of those institutions as they existed on December 7, 1941, it is clear that any military organization must have *some* authentication process, or else any unverified idea that enters the system has the potential to set off a war. More recently, a flock of Canadian geese set off the American warning system to detect incoming nuclear missiles, and only subsequent authentication procedures prevented a "retaliatory" nuclear strike which could have ended in World War III.

Various kinds of ideas can be classified by their relationship to the authentication process. There are ideas systematically prepared for authentication ("theories"), ideas not derived from any systematic process ("visions"), ideas

4

which could not survive any reasonable authentication process ("illusions"), ideas which exempt themselves from any authentication process ("myths"), ideas which have already passed authentication processes ("facts"), as well as ideas known to have failed—or certain to fail—such processes ("falsehoods"—both mistakes and lies).

While these various kinds of ideas are conceptually different, in reality a given notion may evolve or metamorphose through several of these states. For example, we may start with a general impression of how and why certain things happen the way they do, without having any real evidence or any logically structured argument about it. But after we begin with such a vision, we may proceed to systematically determine that *if* this vision is correct, *then* certain empirical consequences will be observable under the proper conditions. The "vision" has led to a "theory." The proper conditions may be created in a laboratory or observed in history or otherwise constructed or discovered, and the validity and certainty of the results may be more or less open to criticism. The important point here is simply to distinguish such *systematic* authentication procedures from decisions based on consensus, emotions, or traditions.

On the continuum of human thinking, at one end is pure science; at the other end pure myth. One is sustained entirely by *systematic* logical procedures, the other by *consensual* verification by contemporaries, by their predecessors represented through prevailing traditions, or by posterity for those who expect historic vindication. The crucial distinction is one of procedures, *not* of end results. Science is no more certain to be correct than is myth. Many scientific theories have been proven wrong by scientific methods, while the great enduring beliefs which have achieved the status of myths usually contain some important—if partial—truth.

Both systematic authentication and consensual approval can be further broken down. Systematic authentication involves a testing of the logical structure of a theory for internal consistency and a testing of the theory's results for external consistency with the observable facts of the real world.

Consensual approval may mean the approval of the general public as of a given time, or the approval of some special reference group—a social class, a religious sect, an ideological movement, etc.—in the past, present, or future. Ideas which lack logical, empirical, or general consensual support may still sustain themselves as acceptable to a consensus of those who regard themselves as special guardians of a particular truth—i.e., as the consensual reference group that really matters. Sometimes the elitism implicit in such a position can be tempered by depicting the idea in question (religious salvation, political reconstitution, etc.) as beneficial to a broad sweep of mankind outside the group, so that the group is only a temporary surrogate for a larger constituency which will ultimately approve the idea. But, of course, this proposition is itself still another idea lacking either empirical verification or general consensual approval.

There are many variations on the two basic ways of verifying ideas, and many combinations of these variations are used—often involving combinations from both systematic and consensual methods of verification in the same argument. For example, a scientific presentation may avoid—indeed, *must* avoid—unlimited verification of every incidental aspect of its arguments by saying, in effect, "everybody knows" this or that, and getting on with proving the things that need proving.[1] Similarly, beliefs resting essentially on consensual approval—religious beliefs, for example—may also employ logical and empirical techniques, such as the scientific "proofs" of the existence of God, which were common in the eighteenth century and in the early nineteenth century, before Darwin. These more or less open combinations present no special problems. A problem does arise, however, when one method masquerades as another—for example, when the results of essentially consensual processes choose to present themselves as scientific, as in the case of much so-called "social science."

This brief and general sketch of the production of authenticated knowledge from raw, unsubstantiated ideas must be elaborated more specifically in later discussions of economic, legal, and political organizations. At this point, it is necessary to consider—in equally brief and general terms—the amount and kinds of knowledge produced, and the manner in which it is used.

THE QUANTITY OF KNOWLEDGE

It is widely believed that modern society has a larger quantity of knowledge than more primitive societies, that this quantity of knowledge is growing, and that the knowledge "required" for the average citizen to live in a modern society is also growing. Certainly the complex apparatus of modern life is beyond the grasp of most non-modern peoples, past or present. What is not so obvious, but true nonetheless, is that most modern peoples would find it equally—or more—difficult to survive individually in a "primitive" or non-modern world. In short, it is not clear or demonstrable that the total quantity of knowledge differs as between "savage" and "civilized" man. What is more readily established is that the *kinds* of knowledge possessed by the average inhabitant of the primitive and the modern world are very different, and that each would be at considerable hazard in the world of the other.

Consider a modern civilized man suddenly stranded in a primitive jungle, cut off from modern technology, and unaided by such primitive peoples as might exist in that environment. Although the civilized man might be a well educated individual, working in a complex profession such as accounting or electronics, it is doubtful whether his knowledge would be sufficient to merely sustain his life in an environment where primitive peoples have lived for untold generations. The civilized man might often have a choice of going hungry or eating wild vegetation which could prove either nutritious or poisonous. Finding a safe place to sleep at night would require more knowledge of the habits and capabilities of wild animals than he possessed. Avoiding snake bites, infected water, and predatory beasts would be among his other problems, and ordinary illnesses easily cured in a civilized community could be far more dangerous away from scientific medical knowledge and without the herbal and other folk remedies available to primitive man. In the same environment, the savage could not merely survive, but thrive, producing housing, clothing, and other amenities. But of course the primitive man's chances of survival if suddenly dropped down in the midst of New York or Los Angeles might also be bleak.

What then is the intellectual advantage of civilization over primitive savagery? It is not necessarily that each civilized man has more knowledge but that he *requires* far *less*. A primitive savage must be able to produce a wide variety of goods and services for himself, and a primitive community must repeatedly duplicate his knowledge and experience in innumerable contemporaries. By contrast, the civilized accountant or electronics expert, etc., need know little beyond his accounting or electronics. Food reaches his local supermarket through processes of which he is probably ignorant, if not misinformed. He lives in a home constructed by an involved process whose technical, economic, and political intricacies are barely suspected, much less known to him. His home is likely to be stocked with many devices working on mechanical and electrical principles which he neither understands theoretically nor can cope with as a practical matter. The chronic complaints and scandals about appliance, automobile, and other repair services testify to the civilized man's utter lack of knowledge of the everyday apparatus on which he depends. A primitive savage could never survive knowing so little about the production and use of spears, grass huts, or with such utter naiveté about which berries are poisonous, which snakes dangerous, or the ways and means of coexistence in the same jungle with lions, tigers, and gorillas.

Civilization is an enormous device for economizing on knowledge. The time and effort (including costly mistakes) necessary to acquire knowledge are minimized through specialization, which is to say through drastic limitations on the amount of duplication of knowledge among the members of society. A relative handful of civilized people know how to produce food, a different handful how to produce clothing, medicine, electronics, houses, etc. The huge costs saved by not having to duplicate given knowledge and experience widely through the population makes possible the higher development of that knowledge among the various subsets of people in the respective specialties.

THE MEANING OF "KNOWING"

Although the phrase "ignorant savage" may be virtually self-contradictory, it is a common conception, and one with a certain basis. The savage is wholly lacking in a narrowly specific kind of knowledge: abstract, systematized, knowledge of the sort generally taught in schools. Considering the enormous range of human knowledge, from intimate personal knowledge of specific individuals to the complexities of organizations and the subtleties of feelings, it is remarkable that one speck in this firmament should be the sole determinant of whether someone is considered knowledgeable or ignorant *in general*. Yet it is a fact of life that an unlettered peasant is considered ignorant, however much he may know about nature and man, and a Ph.D. is never considered ignorant, however barren his mind might be outside his narrow specialty and however little he grasps about human feelings or social complexities. We do sometimes refer to a "learned fool," but the notion of a "fool" implies deficiencies in the *reasoning* process (so that one is easily deceived or fooled), whereas it may actually be *knowledge* that is lacking, so that the "learned" person has simply not learned enough outside a certain sliver of human experience.

The point here is not simply to deplore the use of certain words. The point is to avoid having our own discussion of knowledge drastically shrunk, arbitrarily, and virtually without our realizing what is happening. We need to consider the full breadth of knowledge and its depth as well. That is, we need to consider not only how much we know, but how well we know it.

We start with an idea. It may be a sense impression of some sort—something that happened to catch our eye and intrigue our curiosity. Or it may be a speculation in our mind—a daydream or a theory, for example. As the idea or theory passes through the authentication process, it may be verified, refuted, or transformed to accommodate additional and discordant evidence. But if the authentication process is doing its job, whatever conclusion it is reaching about the idea is becoming progressively more certain (even if that means that the original idea itself is becoming progressively more dubious). Therefore, at some point in the authentication process, the probability of a mistaken conclusion is reduced to the point where we can say that we "know" this or that. Where that point is varies from person to person, so that what is "knowledge" to one is merely a plausible belief to another and only a theory to someone else. Each of us has some point—some probability level— beyond which we will say that we "know" something. But all things fall short of absolute certainty: life itself might be a dream and logic a delusion. Still, because we act, we must decide, and how decisively we can act depends on how well we know the consequences.

How much knowledge there is depends on where we draw the line on the spectrum of probabilities. Within a given probability requirement for "knowing," how much is known varies enormously from one area of human life to another, and from one historical era to another, and of course from one person to another. Because the arena of decision making almost always exceeds the arena of knowledge, there must be belief—or at least hope—to fill in the gaps where there is no knowledge. This means that the ratio of knowledge to belief may also vary enormously from one aspect of life to another. The specific nature of the respective authentication processes available in various aspects of human life then become crucial.

To say that a farm boy knows how to milk a cow is to say that we can send him out to the barn with an empty pail and expect him to return with milk. To say that a criminologist understands crime is not to say that we can send him out with a grant or a law and expect him to return with a lower crime rate. He is more likely to return with a report on why he has not succeeded *yet*, and including the inevitable need for more money, a larger staff, more sweeping powers, etc. In short, the degree of authentication of knowledge may be *lower* in the "higher" intellectual levels and much higher in those areas which intellectuals choose to regard as "lower." A business which produces a product that the public will not buy in a sufficient quantity, or at a high enough price to cover production costs, will have its ideas validated—in this case invalidated—in a swift and painful process which must be heeded quickly before bankruptcy sets in. The results cannot be talked away. But in many intellectual areas, notably so-called "social science," there is neither a swift nor a certain authentication process for ideas, and the only ultimate validation is whether the ideas sound plausible to enough people, or to the right people. The stricter standards and independent, often conclusive, evidence in the physical sciences cannot be generalized to intellectual activity as a whole, even though the aura of scientific processes and results is often appropriated by other intellectuals.

Because what is meant by "knowing" varies enormously, according to the respective authentication processes available, it is by no means clear that there is more knowledge in civilized countries than in primitive countries or among intellectuals as compared to the less educated members of the same society. It is very possible that, as more people cease being farmers with little or no education, and increasingly acquire more schooling, that their standards for "knowing" *decline* while the area of their secondhand and tenuous knowledge expands. As a poet said, "we knew a million things we could hardly understand."[2] There may be not only a qualitative decline in knowledge, but—more important—an erosion of the very meaning of "knowing": for example, a young man might be said to know how to milk a cow if he could write an essay on that subject, and we would no longer demand that he take the pail out to the barn and come back with milk.

It is not necessary, at this point, to insist that the average amount of personal knowledge has declined over time. It is sufficient that we realize that conflicting trends are at work, and that the net result is an open question, rather than the foregone conclusion often assumed by those who depict an ever more knowledgeable society needing ever more years of schooling for its citizens. The march of science and technology does not imply growing intellectual complexity in the lives of most people. It often means the opposite. Matthew Brady required far more knowledge of photoghraphic processes to take pictures with his cumbersome equipment during the Civil War than a modern photographer requires to operate his automated cameras. Science and technology lead to far more complexity in *producing* cameras and film today, but that growing complexity among a handful of technicians permits far more simplicity (and ignorance) in the acutal *use* of modern photographic equipment and materials by a mass of people. Similar trends are discernible in a wide variety of fields. Automobiles are much more complex to build, but far simpler to operate, than in the days before automatic ignition, automatic transmissions, automatic chokes, self-sealing tires, etc. The technology available in the modern home reduces not only the time but the knowledge required by a modern homemaker. Even a mere man can now perform some chores for which girls and young women were once trained for years.

The growing complexity of science, technology, and organization does not imply either a growing knowledge or a growing need for knowledge in the general population. On the contrary, the increasingly complex *processes* tend to lead to increasingly simple and easily understood products. The genius of mass production is precisely in its making more products more accessible, both economically *and* intellectually to more people. Electronic calculators enable mathematical illiterates to perform operations which only highly trained people could perform with ease in earlier times. The printing press performs daily communications miracles beyond the ability of an army of the most highly trained and dedicated scribes of the Middle Ages. Organizational progress parallels that in science and technology, permitting ultimate simplicity through intermediate complexity. An ordinary individual can easily arrange travel across thousands of miles through cities he has never seen by tapping the knowledge of travel agents and/or the American Automobile Association. Or he can weigh the relative merits of commercial products whose individual mechanisms are wholly unknown to him, by reading the (simple) results of highly complex tests conducted by general consumer magazines or by publications specializing in particular items such as audio equipment or motorcycles.

DECISION-MAKING UNITS

Knowledge may be enjoyed as a speculative diversion, but it is needed for decision making. The genesis of ideas and the authentication of knowledge are part of a continuous process which ultimately brings knowledge to bear on decisions—when the system is working ideally. In real life, the process may, of course, *fail* to bring knowledge to bear, when accurate knowledge is available somewhere in the system. What matters, then, is the knowledge actually used at the decision-making point, not the knowledge in process of development or authentication, nor even the knowledge clearly apparent to particular individuals or organizations somewhere in the society. And while decisions may be thought of as made by specific individuals at specific points in space and time, the decision-making process is more usually structured so that various combinations of individuals repeatedly and habitually make certain classes of decisions, so that they form continuously functioning decision-making *units*, which may range from a married couple to a police department to a national government. A single individual may also form a decision-making unit for some purposes, or—more likely—he may be part of several decision-making units simultaneously, and the set of such institutions may change over time.

The emphasis on specific decision-making units is especially necessary in an era given to metaphors about an amorphous "society" deciding to do this or that: "Society" doesn't keep its air or water clean; "society" is punitive, permissive, frivolous, uptight, generous, uncaring, etc. While metaphors may sometimes be useful shortcuts, like other shortcuts they can also take us further away from our destination and delay or even prevent our arrival there.

11

SOCIAL INSTITUTIONS

Metaphors which suggest that "society" is a decision-making unit can be very misleading, by ignoring situations in which decisions are what they are precisely because the actual decision-making units face a particular kind of incentive structure. To ignore the specific nature of the decision-making units is to expect improvement by trying to substitute "the good guys" for "the bad guys," or by waiting for the Messiah or for the general triumph of human reason, whichever seems less improbable or less remote in time. Sometimes the metaphor of "society" is used more tendentiously, to quietly shift the locus of decision making from smaller and more numerous units to a single nationwide decision-making unit. The merits or demerits of such a change in any specific case are simply bypassed by metaphors which proceed as if "society" is doing *this* now and ought to do *that* instead—when in fact one set of decision-making units is operating under one structure of incentives now and the advantages and disadvantages of an alternative decision-making unit and the alternative set of incentives is precisely what needs to be explicitly analyzed, not covered up by metaphors about "society."

There is no one named "society" who decides anything. Even in the most democratic nations few issues are ever decided by a specific nationwide referendum. And even if they were, who could say that a bare majority as of a given instant constitutes the judgment of an organic society subsisting over the generations? Unless national laws are to vary literally from moment to moment, some decision-making units must make decisions which are binding on other units which either disagree or were not consulted. Posterity is of course never consulted.

One of the peculiarities of the American Revolution was that its leaders pinned their hopes on the organization of decision-making units, the structuring of their incentives, and the counterbalancing of the units against one another, rather than on the more usual (and more exciting) principle of substituting "the good guys" for "the bad guys"—i.e., substituting "the people" for "the oppressors," the faithful for the heathens, the Jews for the gentiles, the gentiles for the Jews, and other such substitutions based on differences of history, physiognomy, or mannerisms.

The domain of decision-making units need not be discrete or mutually exclusive. Indeed they cannot be either, or there would be no such social phenomenon as would cause us to refer even metaphorically to "society." Decision-making units seldom have complete control, even of a given segment of a society, and no decision-making unit controls the whole society, except very approximately under a totalitarian regime. Decision-making units overlap one another to some degree, and even where such units are subordinated to others in a hierarchy, the subordination is never perfect in practice. Even in the extreme case of slavery, the subordinate units took actions contrary to the general desires or specific orders of the higher units—ranging from passive or active sabotage to murdering overseers and slave owners.[3] The practical limitations of sheer subordination was repeatedly demonstrated by the various economic incentives which had to be resorted to under slavery, especially for getting higher quality work performed.[4]

In general, the ability of subordinate decision-making units to act independently of, and contrary to, the policies and orders of the higher units is based on differences in knowledge. The powers of the higher units may encompass all the powers of the subordinate units, but they almost never encompass all the knowledge. Because the powers of the higher decision-making units include the power to require transmission of knowledge, the persistence of knowledge advantages by the subordinate units implies either an impossibility or a prohibitive cost to the higher unit of independently acquiring the same knowledge as a check against the accuracy of the knowledge transmitted by the subordinate unit. In short, there are *differences* in their respective costs of acquiring knowledge. More specifically, there are cost differences between higher and lower decision-making units which vary according to the *kind* of knowledge in question.

General knowledge—expertise, statistics, etc.—is usually more economically used by the higher decision-making units. For example, a decision-making unit which encompasses five subordinate units can acquire a given expertise and statistical data which it applies to all five units, whereas if each unit had independently acquired the same expertise or statistical data it would have cost five times as much altogether. For this kind of knowledge, the cost advantage tends to be on the side of the larger and higher decision-making unit. But for highly *specific* knowledge—the local life style, the reliability of particular suppliers, the level of skill of a given executive, etc.—the subordinate units immediately in daily contact with the relevant facts can much more easily and more cheaply synthesize the knowledge and draw inferences.

It is unnecessary to attempt any general rule as to where the overall balance lies in comparing the respective costs of knowledge in larger and smaller decision-making units. What is important is to understand that (1) the respective cost advantages of the large and small units differ according to the *kind* of knowledge involved (general versus specific), that (2) most decisions involve *mixtures* of the two kinds of knowledge, so that the net advantages of the larger and smaller units vary with the kind of decision, and (3) the effectiveness of hierarchical subordination varies with the extent to which the subordinate unit has knowledge advantages over the higher unit. In those cases where the subordinate unit has better information, then in terms of the whole decision-making process the knowledge is one place and the power is another; the quality of decisions suffers as a result. Moreover, subordination itself becomes illusory to the extent that the lower level unit can use its knowledge advantages to evade, counteract, or redirect the thrust of orders from its nominal superiors.

Some examples from various institutions and various societies may illustrate these crucial points. Agriculture has its general principles and statistics, but agricultural production involves much highly specific knowledge about the characteristics and contours of particular plots of land, and about the freshness, flavor and keeping qualities of specific batches of fruits, vegetables and dairy products—all of which are changing by the hour. No expert can say from 100 miles away, and sight unseen, that this year's grape crop is good, or even that last week's good grapes are still good this week. By contrast, an expert on the manufacture of steel can specify the exact quality of steel that will be produced by given combinations of iron ore and coal at given temperatures. For these reasons, steel production has been successfully centrally planned and controlled in various countries, whereas agricultural production has had such chronic problems and periodic disasters in centrally planned economic systems that even the most centralized communist governments have had to make major exceptions in agriculture, allowing decentralized decision-making of various sorts.

For similar reasons, in capitalist countries it is common to have chains of grocery and department stores selling standardized items, but there are no large chains of high quality restaurants of a sort which depend upon atmosphere and finely prepared food. Such restaurants require constant attention to the demeanor of the staff and the delicacy of the chef, and those cannot be effectively controlled by distant experts. Usually the owner and manager of a successful restaurant of this sort is right on the premises, often from the moment it opens each day to the moment it closes at night. By contrast, the top executives of Sears or Safeway cannot and need not be present at their hundreds of stores across the country, for much of the knowledge they need can be gained from statistics, experts, and accounting data.

THE STRUCTURE OF INCENTIVES

While decisions are *constrained* by the kinds of organizations and the kinds of knowledge involved, the *impetus* for decisions comes from the internal preferences and external incentives facing those who actually make the decisions. The incentives may be positive or negative—that is, rewards or penalties. Typically, these incentives are structured in some way, so that there are gradations of rewards (or penalties) corresponding to different kinds of results. It is not just a question of being rewarded or not, but of how *much* reward or penalty is likely to follow from various decisions. Simple as this seems, it is a radical departure from the practice of explaining decisions in terms of "society's" choices or in terms of the official or ostensible "purpose" of an organization. An organization may make decisions which fail to achieve its assigned purpose or fail to serve society's interest, without any "failure" of understanding or ability, simply because it is responding to the actual structure of incentives confronting it rather than to the rhetoric or hopes of others.

Much criticism of "incompetent bureaucrats" implicitly assumes that those in the bureaucracy are pursuing the assigned goal but failing to achieve it due to lack of ability. In fact, they may be responding very rationally and ably to the set of incentives facing them. For example, government regulatory agencies are often very ineffective in controlling the industry or sector which they have a legal mandate to regulate. But it is a common pattern in such agencies for those in decision-making positions to (1) earn far less money than comparable individuals earn in the regulated sector, and (2) after a few years' experience to move on to jobs in the regulated sector. In short, they are regulating their future employers. Under such a set of incentives, it is hardly surprising that decision makers in regulatory agencies approach those whom they are assigned to regulate with an attitude that is sympathetic, cooperative, and even protective. The only protection of the public interest built into the incentive structure are the penalties for blatantly illegal conduct, such as taking bribes to make a particular decision for a particular company. But explicit bribes are seldom necessary in order to get the regulatory agency to adopt the general viewpoint of the regulated sector, in which many regulatory officials expect to make a more lasting and more lucrative career than is open to them in government. Morally, it is possible to deplore individual weakness or selfishness, but rationally there is little reason to expect a different outcome from a normal sample of people facing the same structure of incentives. Reform by "throwing the rascals out" seems less promising than reform by changing the structure of incentives facing whoever occupies decision-making positions.

The regulatory agency example is a case where the institutional incentive structure has to compete with an outside incentive structure that is more attractive financially. Incentive structures can have problems in themselves, aside from outside competition. The mere process of formalizing what is to be rewarded presents many complexities and pitfalls. Most problems, decisions, and performances are multidimensional, but somehow the results have to be reduced to a few key indicators which are to be institutionally reward-ed or penalized: attendance records, test scores, output per unit of time, se-niority, etc. The need to reduce the indicators to a manageable few is based not only on the need to conserve the time (and sanity) of those who assign re-wards and penalties, but also to provide those subject to these incentives with some objective indication of what their performance is expected to be and how it will be judged. But, almost by definition, key indicators can never tell the whole story. This affects not merely the justice or injustice of the reward, but also the very nature of the behavior that occurs within the given struc-ture of incentives. For example, one index of military success is the number of enemy killed. Clearly, it is not the *only* indicator, for if a major military objective can be taken while capturing the enemy, or confronting him with sufficient force to make him retreat, or bluffing him into withdrawal or sur-render, this is even better than having to actually take the objective by storm, with a large loss of life on both sides. However, once the incentive structure clearly rewards the "body count" of enemy dead, it provides an in-centive to more carnage than is absolutely necessary, and since enemy casu-alties can seldom be increased without increasing one's own casualties, it pro-vides an incentive to needless bloodshed and loss of life among one's own troops. Again, moral condemnation without reform of the incentive structure means little. For example, continual criticism of the "search and destroy" missions of the American army in Vietnam did little to change this approach in a war where "body count" was a key indicator, used by the military high command in rewarding and publicizing its units' efforts.

TIME

Key indicators require some specified time span during which they are to be tabulated for purposes of reward or penalty. The time span can vary enor-mously according to the process and the indicator. It can be output per hour, the annual rate of inflation, weekly television program ratings, or a bicenten-nial assessment of a nation. But whatever the span chosen, it must involve some simplification, or even oversimplification, of reality. Time is continu-ous, and breaking it up into discrete units for purposes of assessment and re-ward opens the possibility that behavior will be tailored to the time period in question, without regard to its longer range implications. Desperate efforts just before a deadline may be an inefficient expedient which reduces the longer run effectiveness of men, machines and organizations. The Soviets coined the term "storming" to describe such behavior, which has long been common in Soviet factories trying to achieve their monthly quotas. Similar behavior occurred on an annual basis in Soviet farms trying to maximize the current year's harvest, even at the cost of neglecting the maintenance of equipment and structures, and at the cost of depleting soil by not allowing it to lie fallow to recover its long run fertility. Slave overseers in the antebellum South similarly overworked both men and the soil in the interest of current crops at the expense of reduced production years later—when the overseer would probably be working somewhere else. In short, similar structures of incentives produced similar results, even in socioeconomic systems with widely differing histories, ideologies, and rhetoric.

IMPLICATIONS

The broad sweep of knowledge needed for decision making is brought to bear through various systems of coordination of the scattered fragmentary information possessed by individuals in organizations. This very general sketch of the principles, mechanisms, and pitfalls involved is a prelude to a fuller consideration of the use of knowledge in decision-making processes in the economic, legal, and political spheres, each having its own authentication processes and its own feedback mechanisms to modify decisions already made. Much discussion of the pros and cons of various "issues" overlooks the crucial fact that the most basic decision is *who* makes the decision, under what constraints, and subject to what feedback mechanisms. This is fundamentally different from the approach which seeks better decisions by replacing "the bad guys" with "the good guys"—that is, by relying on differential rectitude and differential ingenuity rather than on a structure of incentives geared to the normal range of human propensities.

The discussion thus far has emphasized premeditatedly-formed and hierarchically-structured decision-making units. These are not the only, nor necessarily the best, decision-making units, nor even the most pervasive kind of decision-making units at a given time and place. Some alternative decision-making units and processes include (1) trial by combat, which is seldom sanctioned today for individual decision making, but is still the ultimate decision-making mechanism between sovereign nations, (2) various arrangements spontaneously evolved by the participants, such as competitive bidding in economic markets or mutual benevolence in groups bound together by religious, artistic, tribal, or other affinities, and (3) premeditated arrangements in which those subordinated to the power of others in one sense are, in another sense, the ultimate arbiters of the fate of their hierarchical superiors—as with democratically elected governments, or with governments operating in the shadows of their own military forces which are both willing and able to depose them. None of these decision-making processes are mutually exclusive. A typical American, for example, lives in a family unit whose internal decisions are based on personal feelings, works in a hierarchically-structured organization whose use of inputs and volume of output are determined in a spontaneously evolved market, is subject to laws established by a government whose members are chosen and removable by the electorate and which conducts its relations with other governments in an atmosphere dominated by their respective capacities for armed combat or mutual annihilation.

The interaction of various decision-making processes makes it all the more necessary to understand the respective principles of the different individual processes. The continual evolution of decision-making units and decision-making processes likewise makes it all the more necessary to understand the effects of different kinds of processes, so as to know where we are headed if current trends continue.

Just as decision-making units and processes vary enormously, so too do the various kinds of decisions. For example, some decisions are *binary* decisions—yes or no, war or peace, guilty or innocent—while other decisions are *continuously variable* incremental decisions: using more or less gasoline, paying higher or lower wages, living a more relaxed or more hectic life. Some decisions are once-and-for-all decisions—suicide, loss of virginity, burning a Rembrandt painting—while others are readily reversible decisions: turning off a television program that is not interesting, cancelling a subscription, ceasing to purchase a given brand of consumer goods or ceasing to use certain clichés, etc. Decisions may also be made individually or as "package deals." One can buy onions, bread, and canned goods in the same store or in different stores, but in choosing between political candidates, one must choose one candidate's whole package—his fiscal policy, environmental position, foreign policy, civil liberties views, etc.—as against the whole package of his opponent's positions on the same subjects.

The kind of decision is not tied to the particular subject matter (i.e., shoes, food, or education) so much as to the particular decision-making process: economic processes, legal processes, political processes, etc. What this means is that as certain kinds of decisions are moved from one kind of decision-making unit to another, it is not merely a case of a different group of people or processes making the decision; the nature of the decision itself can change. That is, what was once a continuously variable decision may become a binary decision. Prior to public schooling and compulsory attendance laws, for example, the decision a family made was how much schooling to purchase for their children; afterwards, the only decision was whether or not to obey the compulsory attendance laws. Before it became a federal crime to carry a letter in competition with the post office, the individual letter-writer could choose among various possible carriers, but afterwards the only decision was whether to communicate in the form of a letter or in some other form.

Decisions also differ with respect to whether they are instantaneous or sequential. An instantaneous decision occurs completely at a given point in time, even if a long period of consideration preceded it, while a sequential decision occurs at various points in time as reactions to previous parts of the decision entail additional adjustments, improvisations, or reinforcements. The basic difference between them is that one decision is made completely on one occasion, while the other decision occurs piecemeal over a period of time. With sequential decision making, all the knowledge which is finally available to the decision maker is not initially available when the sequence of decisions begins, and the course of action followed may be wholly different from what it would have been if all the knowledge had been available at the outset, or if any decision could have been postponed until after all the facts were in.

Many early supporters of the Vietnam war came ultimately to the position that it was not worth the cost, *after* the full cost had been revealed by time, and that early official estimates of prospective casualties and prospective outcomes were either grossly mistaken or deliberately misleading. Another contemporary example of sequential decision making in a very different area is the progression from the Supreme Court's *Brown* decision in 1954 that the state cannot classify students by race for differential treatment to its controversial "busing" position in which that is what it *requires* states to do. Years of opposition to desegregation of the public schools led to progressively tighter judicial control, designed to overcome the various strategies of opposition, delay, and evasion—ultimately arriving at a point the opposite of the court's original premise or intention. In an earlier era, British Prime Minister Neville Chamberlain conducted a foreign policy designed to avoid war with Hitler through relatively small concessions, but the ultimate result of an unanticipated *series* of crises and concessions was to so shift the balance of power in Hitler's favor as to make war inevitable.

None of these sequential decisions was the result of a "society" that was stupid in the light of information now available in retrospect, but rather of piecemeal decisions which acquired a momentum of their own, and of the individual decision makers who were unequal to the unfolding complexities inherent in sequential decision making. Praise or blame is not the point. What is important is to understand (1) when a situation facing us is part of a sequential decision making process, and what that implies, and (2) to understand when our own institutions set up sequential decision-making processes when there is an alternative decision-making process available. For example, Chapter 9 will analyze the criminal justice system as a series of sequential decisions presented to the young criminal in such a way as to lead more people to persist in a life of crime than would do so if all the knowledge of prospects and penalties were made fully available to them at the outset.

In addition to considering decision-making processes, we need to consider decision-making *costs*. These costs are *not* simply the salaries of decision-making officials during the time when they are pondering what to do. Clearly the cost of evaluating intelligence reports on Japanese intentions to bomb Pearl Harbor was not simply the pay of the military functionaries who handled these reports. The cost of those processes included one of the largest military catastrophes in American history, and the loss of life and material not only at Pearl Harbor but in a series of major military defeats in the months that followed, in the wake of the crippling and near-annihilation of the American Pacific Fleet on December 7, 1941. The point here is not to condemn, or even to evaluate, the decision-making process as it existed in the military at that time. The point here is to emphasize that the *cost* of any decision-making process must be assessed in terms of the full consequences entailed by alternative decision-making processes. Such processes cannot be judged by narrowly conceived economic or financial criteria. As we shall see in Chapter 3, even economic decision making cannot be evaluated narrowly in money terms alone.

The chapters that follow will consider the use of knowledge in economic, legal, and political institutions, the nature of the intellectual process and the role of intellectuals as a social class in influencing trends in modern society. Some disturbing implications of those trends will then be weighed.

Chapter 2

Decision-Making Processes

Despite the fashionable practice of personifying "society" as a decider and actor, decision making in the real world can be understood only in the context of the actual decision-making units that exist, and the specific, respective sets of constraints and incentives within which each operates. These various decision-making units and processes are highly diverse, and have equally diverse implications. The persistence through the centuries of very different decision-making relationships, institutionally coexisting within even the most monolithic societies, suggests that there may be substantial advantages and disadvantages to each form of human organization, and that these vary with respect to different activities and decisions. Constitutionalism and pluralism in effect acknowledge and underscore this conclusion.

One of the basic distinctions among human relationships is between informal voluntary relationships, terminable at no cost beyond the loss of the relationship itself, and relationships enforced by designated institutions which can impose substantial penalties, which may range from breach-of-contract suits by a private business to execution for military desertion in wartime. The difference here is not in the seriousness or severity of the loss due to termination of a relationship. The distinction is in whether the loss is a contrived penalty to enforce the terms of the relationship, rather than a loss inherent in the loss of the relationship itself. Lovers are perhaps a classic example of an informal voluntary relationship—the loss of which may be far more devastating than, say, breaking a landlord-tenant lease agreement. Yet the landlord-tenant lease agreement is no longer a voluntary arrangement after it has been signed, just as the relationship between lovers is no longer wholly voluntary once they are married.

Informal relationships need not be so direct as that between lovers. Language is a whole set of intricate relationships, evolved rather than designed, and its "rules" are obeyed without the necessity of any organizational entity capable of imposing penalties for disobedience. For students there may be grade penalties for improper use of the language, and social disapproval might be another penalty for others, but these are mild, incidental, and perhaps ineffective deterrents—certainly as compared to the staggering costs of substantially disregarding the rules of language. Anyone who was either incapable of understanding those rules, or perversely oblivious to them, would find himself in a two-way incomprehensibility with virtually everyone. Again, what is involved is a voluntary relationship, terminable at no cost beyond the loss of the benefits of the relationship itself, though that loss may be very large.

By contrast, organized institutional relationships carry contrived rewards and penalties as compensations for following or not following the terms of the relationship and the desires of the people involved in it. Economic organizations provide goods or services in exchange for money, political organizations provide their services in exchange for votes, and administrative organizations (government bureaucracies, private "non-profit" organizations, etc.) carry out their functions in exchange for such organizational rewards as prestige and such individual rewards as pay, power, and perquisites. It is not that these incentive mechanisms define what is economic, political, or administrative. Rather, they define what is organizational rather than informal or spontaneous. Within the category of organizations, there are then economic, political, and other subdivisions. Moreover, there are also informal (non-organizational economic, political, etc.) activities, though these will not be a major focus here.

None of these categories is hermetically sealed or represents a mutually exclusive entity in any rigorous sense. All that is necessary here is to recognize a spectrum of human relationships, ranging from the most voluntary and informal (lovers) to the most organizationally structured and determined (a military draftee in combat). Different regions of this spectrum can then be discussed under different names, implicitly recognizing that these discontinuous designations apply in the real world to continuously varying complexes of characteristics. For example, a family may be regarded as an informal, voluntary relationship, because its cohesion and functioning are due primarily to incentives intrinsic to the relationship itself rather than organizational-

22

ly contrived, though these contrived incentives also enter, as in family law. The family also underscores the point that "informal" or "voluntary" does not necessarily imply *weaker* incentives. Family incentives are in fact so powerful as to cause defiance of severe legal penalties, and the law itself tacitly recognizes this—as, for example, in not attempting to force spouses to testify against one another. Other organizational entities likewise recognize that their formal incentives are weaker than informal family incentives. Anti-nepotism hiring rules are a common form of this recognition.

Comparisons of different kinds of human decision-making relationships and processes are to some extent comparisons of different kinds of decisions as well. If this *ex post* fact implied an *ex ante* unique relationship between kinds of decisions and kinds of decision-making processes, it would be both logically impossible and socially pointless to try to compare various relationships or institutions as decision-making mechanisms. The discussion that follows not only postulates in a theoretical sense, but assumes as a matter of fact, that given decisions can be made by any of a number of institutions. In this context, the empirical fact that families do not usually make decisions about fighting a war, and bureaucratic organizations typically do not decide matters of love, are merely things to be explained in terms of institutions' respective decision-making advantages. Under some circumstances, families have in fact made decisions about wars (vendettas, dynastic wars) and computer organizations have at least claimed to be able to make love matches. In short, the discussion proceeds on the premise that the institutional locus of particular decisions is not a constant but a variable, and concludes that it is a crucial variable from the standpoint of the well-being of society.

INFORMAL RELATIONSHIPS

Among the advantages of informal relationships as decision-making entities is their low cost of decision making in terms of the time required for deciding, the cost of the requisite knowledge, and the ability to "fine tune" the decision to the problem or prospect at hand.

By the cost of a decision is meant the cost of the *process* of deciding, rather than the costs entailed by the decision itself. For inter-institutional cost comparisons of decision making to be meaningful, such comparisons must be made holding constant the "quality" (however defined) of the decision. This neither postulates as a matter of theory nor assumes as a matter of fact that institutions are equally good at deciding the same things. It merely says that inter-institutional *differences* in decision-making effectiveness may be equally well expressed as cost differences in producing given quality decisions or as quality differences at given costs. By expressing inter-institutional differences in terms of the cost of a given quality of decisions, the discussion avoids getting bogged down in the complexities of weighing the respective advantages and disadvantages of different decisions themselves, and can focus on the cost of the *process* of achieving a given probability of satisfying a given set of values to a given extent.

Because informal decision making is not subject to such organizational requirements as written justifications, varying protocol observances vis-à-vis superiors, peers, and subordinates or the more stringent "due process" requirements found in legal organizations, the process of deciding tends to be less costly. A distinguished economist once observed that Lindbergh's flying across the Atlantic alone was less of a feat than if he had flown across the Atlantic with a committee.[1] Much of the cost of formal decision making is *not* a current outlay (in either financial or psychic terms) for the current decision, but rather an investment (again, in either financial or psychic terms) in "insurance" to protect oneself from future costs in terms of personal or business relationships with the other parties to the decision. Avoiding abrasiveness of manner, verbal misunderstandings, misperceptions of intentions, status threats, and the like, are costly. They are obviously costly in time and tension to the individual. They are costly in more directly tangible financial terms to an organization, which must screen its potential decision makers for their ability to meet these requirements, in addition to the intellectual qualifications for achieving a given quality of decisions. Obviously, as the list of requirements lengthens, the suitably qualified supply of people declines, and the pay required to hire them in competition with other organizations increases. These financial phenomena of institutions are essentially outward manifestations of the underlying psychic costs to individuals.

Informal decision making avoids much (though not all) of these "insurance" costs because less "insurance" is needed. In the extreme case, an individual makes a wholly private decision recognized by all to be legitimately within his arbitrary discretion (an individual watching television alone, a bachelor buying food for himself, etc.), and so he need not take any additional action to insure against adverse reactions from others. More commonly, the other parties to the informal decision-making process are already sufficiently familiar with one another, and have formed sufficiently settled opinions of one another, that "insurance" actions and processes are both less necessary and less effective.

In a sense, this conclusion merely pushes the question back in time rather than answers it. It says that informal relationships may involve lower *current* costs because of *past* investments in mutual familiarization. This in itself says nothing about total costs over the relevant time span. These total costs tend to be lower in informal relationships because the voluntary interactions that lead to familiarity are often pleasurable on net balance, or the interaction would not be chosen and sustained. For friends, kin, or lovers to acquire a given level of familiarity, sufficient to reduce mutual "insurance" costs by a given amount, is likely to cost less than for a detective agency, a credit bureau or an investigative reporter to acquire an equal amount of personal information. The simple fact that the latter groups must be paid salaries to ferret out information suggests that the pleasure of familiarizing themselves with the subject is insufficient to compensate the effort.

The lower information cost of informal relationships can be illustrated by the financing of small, single-proprietor businesses. Here, the crucial variable in determining the prospects of success of a given business of this sort is the character, ability, perseverance, and other personal attributes of the would-be owner-operator. Banks seldom finance the establishment of such businesses, which are typically financed by the individual himself, and/or his friends, family or neighbors—i.e., all people with lower costs of acquiring the necessary information. It is not literally impossible for a bank or other organization to acquire equivalent information, but the cost of doing so would be far higher. A financial institution could not simply *ask* those familiar with the prospective owner-operator for an assessment of him, for they would have insufficient personal stake in the accuracy of the assessment to make it reliable, and their probable bias in his favor would not be offset by a bias in favor of safeguarding their own money. More effective methods of acquiring retrospective personal information about investment applicants—or information in advance about the pool of people from whom prospective investment applicants are likely to come—would involve methods (such as electronic listening devices) whose illegality would greatly increase their cost. The acquisition of the same information through informal relationships is of course not illegal, and is therefore less costly for this reason as well as because of the lower psychic costs of interaction among self-selected people.

Some organizations are able to tap information produced by informal relationships. Employers who hire new employees by word-of-mouth referrals from existing employees get around the problem confronting banks—namely, that those with the most relevant information have insufficient stake in the accurate communication of that knowledge. Employees who value their own future relationship with the employer will not want to recommend someone else who is likely to be a substandard employee. Reliance on such information, even by employers with personnel departments and the supposedly "scientific" selection procedures at their disposal, implies at least some areas in which the organization implicitly recognizes its cost disadvantages vis-à-vis informal relationships.

"Old boy" networks among professional colleagues with stakes in good future relationships with one another are likewise informal sources of knowledge that would be prohibitively expensive for an organization to acquire through purely organizational methods, especially in professions where the relevant characteristics are highly personal—temperament, drive, imagination, intellectual discipline—and therefore cannot be objectively specified or definitively measured by such formal devices as university degrees. Recurrent complaints of "chaotic" referral and hiring methods in such professions ignore this cost advantage of informal relationships. That this advantage can be of major proportions is attested to by (1) the persistence of such referral methods despite repeated attempts at internal reform[2] or even externally imposed legal requirements, as under "affirmative action,"[3] (2) the *dissatisfaction* reported by both employers and employees using alternative and more "objective" or "rational" procedures,[4] and (3) the willingness of employing organizations to pay the price of constricting their own options by limiting their employee choices to those other organizations in which they have sufficiently good informal information sources, thereby balkanizing a market that might easily be many times larger.[5]

Observers' intellectual disdain and/or moral condemnation for practices which utilize the cost advantages of informal relationships often proceed on the implicit assumption that knowledge is either economically free or theoretically "given" in some cohesive block equally accessible to all. In reality, knowledge can be enormously costly, and is often widely scattered in uneven fragments, too small to be individually usable in decision making. The communication and coordination of these scattered fragments of knowledge is one of the basic problems—perhaps *the* basic problem—of any society, as well as of its constituent institutions and relationships.[6]

Informal relationships are not only able to acquire much knowledge at lower cost than formal organizations in some cases, but are generally able to apply it in a more specific or "fine tuned" fashion in making decisions. Among the reasons are that informal decision making is more likely than formal procedures to be incremental rather than categorical, individualized rather than "package deals," and episodic rather than precedential.

Because informal relationships are, by definition, relatively freer of rules than are formal organizations, the former can more readily determine *to what extent* to do something—whether consumption of a good, work at an occupation, or involvement with another person—rather than simply *wheth-er* to do it or not. Thus, for example, personal relationships have many subtle gradations from formality to intimacy, as compared to official relationships among members of an organizational hierarchy—relationships which tend to have fewer gradations and fewer nuances in the relationships between any two official positions (except insofar as these are modified by *informal* relationships among incumbents). A "foolish consistency" is less often necessary in informal relationships. The youngest child in a family may be a privileged character with respect to one set of rules (decorum, errors) and yet more strongly controlled than his older siblings with respect to others (safety, money). Even in cultures normally thought of as male-dominated, there are substantial areas of family decision making where a husband would seldom dream of questioning his wife's decisions, even though such decisions may include budgeting the bulk of his income.[7] The specialization benefits of such reciprocal or interchangeable subordination are sacrificed in a neatly hierarchical organization, where a vice-president outranks a janitor for all purposes—again, except insofar as incumbents may choose to behave otherwise so as to appropriate some of the advantages of informal relationships in a formal organization.

The lengths to which this can be carried in practice may be illustrated by the fact that even under the extreme hierarchic subordination of slavery, there were often skilled, experienced or trusted slaves whose judgments on major economic decisions were relied on by slaveowners to a greater extent than the judgments of the white overseer[8]—so much so that a disaffected coalition of such slaves could cost on overseer his job.[9] The slaveowner's overriding interest in the economic efficiency of his enterprise was thus sufficient to cause him to violate both the principle of hierarchical subordination and the prevailing racial ideology, in order to appropriate the gains arising from the advantages of informal relationships.

Decisions made through informal relationships can be more readily individualized than in an organization bound by its own rules. A child who is ill, grieving or otherwise temporarily impaired in whatever way, can be given special attention and exemptions from normal requirements incrementally—to precisely the extent, for just so long, and for only those activities to which his special needs require, in the judgments of his parents or siblings. He can be "special" for some purposes but not for others, for to be *too* special would impair his own personal relationships with others, as well as the general life of the family. Formal organizations have parallel attempts to allow for illness or injury, for example, but its benefits are generally available to people who fall within categories verbally described in advance, rather than according to an *ex post* judgment of the overall nature and severity of their individual disability. Thus, for example, a worker suffering a minor injury of a sort described in the rules may receive a windfall gain, while another worker psychologically devastated by the ending of a love affair is expected to continue carrying out all duties as if nothing had happened. Here it is not a question of a misjudgment by management—which would be paralleled by similar parental misjudgments—but of the inherent anomalies of hierarchical organizations. Again, in some instances incumbent officials may choose to somehow modify organizational rules in order to obtain the gains of informal relationships but this modification is not inherent in hierarchical organization, is in fact in conflict with it, and consequently its scope is likely to be more severely limited the more hierarchical the organization. Soldiers in combat are not given time off after receiving "Dear John" letters.

Informal decision making thus allows a fungibility of highly disparate factors in terms of their net effects, viewed retrospectively. The proverbial "advantage of hindsight" can be utilized by informal processes. But formal organizational decision making tends toward a prospective categorical specification of factors to be taken into account in specific, programmed ways. Each has its advantages and disadvantages. The advantages of informal relationships tend to be greatest in decisions which turn on individual personal or circumstantial differences of a sort which cannot be explicitly or exhaustively specified in advance, which may result from too wide and varied an assortment of influences to list in advance, or even to convey in any logically compelling way after the fact, and which require a large amount of highly individual information at low cost.

Informal relationships permit decisions to be individualized in another sense as well. Each decision can be considered in relative isolation rather than as part of a take-it-or-leave-it "package deal." A series of love affairs can be varied as to personality types, duration, intimacy, or intensity, but at the other end of this spectrum—marriage in a no-divorce system with powerful sanctions against extra marital affairs—it is a "package deal" with respect to time and with respect to the whole set of personal characteristics of the partner. If one has had enough—temporarily or permanently—of the sensitive introspective type, or the flighty madcap type, one can look for other qualities in subsequent partners, but if one relationship is going to be permanent, an entirely different set of characteristics may be preferable within that constraint. The same principle applies to less personal decisions. Driving a car between two cities is a continuously reviewable, variable or even cancellable decision. Taking an airplane between the same two cities is a "package deal." Once the plane is airborne, the passenger's second thoughts about

alternative destinations, side trips, companions who would add to the pleasure of the journey, optimal arrival time, or whether the trip was a bad idea
in the first place, have no effect on the flight, unless he is prepared to incur
the cost of hijacking the aircraft. No small part of the appeal of the automobile, which social critics are quick to attribute to irrational drives, derives
from its incremental and continuously reviewable decision-making potential—which is curtailed to varying degrees by alternative transportation
modes.

In economic transactions, package deals are often vulnerable. The Ford
Motor Company's loss of its early supremacy in the automobile industry to
General Motors turned on its insistence on offering the famous Model T as a
"package deal," involving not only a given mechanism but also an unchanging body style and a single color (black), whereas General Motors supplied
cars in a variety of annually changing models and in virtually every color of
the rainbow. For a producer to offer a package deal is to gamble that he is
correct simultaneously in his assessment of the acceptability to the consumer
of all of the elements in the package. Even a small "package" presents serious problems in this regard. If the producer's chances of being right on each
of three variables is 75 percent for each variable, his chances of being right
on the whole package are less than half (27 out of 64).[10] The variety of models of many products is one response to the hazards of trying to guess what
specific combination of characteristics will appeal to the consumer. The inability of the producer to know precisely what the consumer wants is a basic
fact of life under any economic system. Different varieties of the same basic
product are one way of dealing with this inescapable fact, and not an arbitrarily imposed "waste" as sometimes claimed. The consumer can be presented with a single take-it-or-leave-it "package" only under some form of
monopoly, private or governmental.

Informal decision-making processes permit individualized decisions in another sense as well. Decisions are not as likely to become precedents constraining future decisions. Choosing cereal for breakfast today does not prejudice one's option to choose eggs tomorrow or to skip breakfast entirely the
next day. The variability and reversibility of informal decisions not only allows corrections of past judgments and adaptations to current desire for variety; it allows future planning to take place at lower cost. The more adapt-
ability exists for a given kind of decision, the less risky it is to make plans for
the future, and therefore the more likely it is that more people will make
more plans in such areas. Dates are more likely to be made in cultures where
this implies little beyond a short-run commitment to be at a certain place at
a certain time, than in cultures where overt expressions of interest in an indi-

vidual of the opposite sex, or subsequent displays of affection toward such individuals imply matrimonial intentions—and where failure to follow through brings social ostracism or even risk to life and limb. Foreign investments are more likely to be made in a country where the proceeds can be withdrawn at will in convertible currency than in a country where legal barriers make this impossible or political barriers make it costly. Similarly, the existence of such instruments of future decision variability and reversibility (i.e., nonprecedence) as brakes and steering wheels is all that makes most people willing to ride in automobiles at highway speeds. Liquidity of assets and the existence of options markets serve similar functions in the economic sphere.

The prices paid for things which modify or nullify the precedential element of decision making is a tangible indicator of the value of nonprecedential processes. The extra costs involved in options markets, and the foregone earnings on more liquid assets are fairly obvious costs. In the case of an automobile, the unwillingness to be bound by past decisions as to direction and velocity is reflected in the cost of brake systems and steering systems. A less tangible but no less real cost is paid by those who forego or curtail social interaction with the opposite sex in cultures where this becomes precedential. Another way of looking at all these things is that the huge costs paid to get out of precedents implies an even higher cost of being bound by these precedents.

Informal relationships are not mere minor interstitial supplements to the major institutions of society. These informal relationships not only include important decision-making processes, such as the family, but also produce much of the background social capital without which the other major institutions of society could not function nearly as effectively as they do. Language has already been mentioned as an informally produced system. Morality is another major item of background social capital, without which the cost of operating everything from credit cards to courts of law would be far more expensive—perhaps prohibitively so. The same could be said for hygiene, civility, and other informally transmitted characteristics without which many (or all) formal organizations would incur huge costs of operation, if they could operate at all.

Informal relationships or decision-making processes are not categorically superior to more formal relationships or processes. Lovers do get married. People not only rent, but lease and buy. Astronauts go up in rockets with neither brakes nor steering wheels. Clearly there must be some offsetting benefits in more structured relationships and precedential decisions—or rather, benefits peculiar to such relationships, which may in any given instance be greater than, equal to, or less than, the benefits of informal decision-making processes.

STRUCTURED ORGANIZATIONS

Among the many variables impinging on one's happiness and well-being, some require relatively frequent adjustments while others do not, and some derive much of their value precisely from their constancy. Obviously, formal organizations would not exist if informal relationships met all human needs.

The apportionment of decision making as between informal and formal processes involves a trade-off of flexibility for security. A's flexibility is B's uncertainty as to what A will do. The cost to B of this uncertainty cannot be measured in terms of A's most likely prospective action nor in terms of A's retrospectively observed action. The cost of uncertainty to B is the cost of preparing for a *range* of possibilities of A's behavior. Depending upon the cost of these precautions to B and the value of flexibility to A, it may be possible for both sides to become better off by signing a contract awarding money to A for agreeing in advance to follow a given course (or restricted range of courses) of conduct. In short, a more rigidified process may be made preferable to both sides. Total risk can be reduced in some cases by rigidity, just as it is reduced in other cases by flexibility.

In many cases a much broader kind of rigid agreement may be in order. Society itself may need to guarantee that certain relationships will remain rigid and inviolate in all but the most extraordinary circumstances. Much socially beneficial prospective action will not take place, or will not take place to the same extent, without rigid guarantees. The heavy investment of emotion, time, and resources necessary to raise a child would be less likely in a society where the child might at any moment, for any capricious reason, be taken away and never seen again. Such behavior is rejected not only for its retrospective injustice but also for its *prospective* effect on parental behavior. Not only will the state forebear from such behavior; it will use severe sanctions against private individuals who do such things (kidnappers). This rigid legal framework of parent-child relationships provides the protective setting within which the most flexible kinds of parent-child social relationships may develop. Formal and informal processes are not mutually exclusive but mutually supporting.

Similar considerations apply across a spectrum of other social arrangements, particularly those involving long and large individual investments of efforts for prospective personal and social benefits. Property rights introduce rigidities into the use of vast amounts of many resources—by excluding all but the legal owner(s) from a serious voice in most of the decisions made about the disposition of the resources—on the assumption that such losses as are occasioned by this rigidity are more than offset by the gains in prospective behavior by people acting under these guarantees.

SOCIAL INSTITUTIONS

Someone who is going to work for many years to have his own home wants some fairly rigid assurance that the house will in fact belong to him—that he cannot be dispossessed by someone who is physically stronger, better armed, or more ruthless, or who is deemed more "worthy" by political authorities. Rigid assurances are needed that changing fashions, mores, and power relationships will not suddenly deprive him of his property, his children, or his life. Informal relationships which flourish in a society do so within the protection of formal laws on property ownership, kidnapping, murder, and other basic matters on which people want rigidity rather than continuously negotiable or modifiable relationships.

Formalized and rigidified decision-making processes (or frameworks for processes) are not only social investments in certain behavior patterns; they are direct consumer goods as well. Peace of mind and a sense of independence and dignity are immediate psychic dividends from operating under known rules, applicable to all, rather than being personally assessed and controlled by other individuals. Informal decision-making processes flourish only where such assessment and control are in the hands of those biased in favor of the individual concerned—e.g., family, friends, and lovers. Similar informal processes in the hands of strangers might be intolerable. In short, the comparison is not solely between two different kinds of institutional processes—formal vs. informal—but between two different kinds of processes engaged in by two different kinds of people.

ECONOMIC INSTITUTIONS

Economic decisions may be made through informal processes or through structured organizations. If the lawn needs mowing, the homeowner may do it himself, tell his son to do it, pay his son to do it, pay another individual to do it, or contract with a lawn-care firm to do it. Similarly he may grow his own vegetables, buy them from a local farmer, or from a store, or buy them already prepared at a restaurant. The theoretical spectrum, ranging from the most informal to the most formal decision-making processes, is far greater than is likely to be encountered in the real world. Why this is so is worth analyzing in order to understand the peculiar advantages and disadvantages of more formal and less formal economic processes.

Theoretically, the various components which typically make up a product could all be bought separately and assembled either by the consumer or by other persons hired by him to perform that service on a one-time basis as needed—the way he hires a plumber or electrician when he needs their services. There is no inherent need for a firm to exist to sell him a finished product. By the same token, there is no need for workers to be employed by such a firm. Theoretically, they could sell their services directly to those who want them, as plumbers, doctors, and shoe shine boys ordinarily do.

For some products and to some extent, there is much consumer assembly of finished products. Stereo systems often contain amplifiers, speakers, turntables and tape decks, each made by a different manufacturer and assembled with knowledge purchased from the publisher of a do-it-yourself book. A whole pre-assembled stereo system may also be purchased at most department stores. A similar range exists among cameras. The view camera used by professional photographers is usually sold as a camera body with no lens or shutter, and with nothing to hold the film. All these essential components are typically available in a wide variety of types and brands, all of which are to be assembled by the photographer into a functioning camera. At the other end of the spectrum is the "Instamatic" camera with all these components preselected, preassembled, and preset for a specific focusing distance, lens opening and shutter speed selected by the manufacturer, who is in effect selling a "package" that includes not only physical items but also the application of elementary knowledge of picture taking settings.

From this it is clear that one reason for the existence of a business firm is to economize on the production or application of knowledge. Any user of an "Instamatic" camera could acquire as much knowledge as is used in presetting the lens and shutter by purchasing an elementary book on photography and investing a few hours in reading it. Since the consumer sees people all around him with adjustable cameras, he knows that it is neither impossible nor probably very difficult to acquire such knowledge. His is therefore an informed choice to purchase the knowledge from the camera manufacturer, rather than produce this knowledge himself from a book. This is a perfectly rational choice where the camera firm can produce the quantity of knowledge needed (for casual snapshots) at a lower cost than the consumer. From the point of view of society at large, fewer resources are used to produce a given product or to achieve a given end result.

One of the reasons the firm has lower costs than the consumer would have is that it engages in fewer transactions in proportion to its volume of output. A consumer who wished to hire a photographic expert to tell him at what distance to focus his lens would have to determine the likely sources of such experts and the means of determining their expertise, as well as not buying more expertise than he needed, and other such problems. The cost of hiring the expert, spread over one or two cameras would be much higher per camera (or per picture) than when a camera manufacturer hires experts to guide its decisions on thousands of cameras. Similar considerations apply to the hiring of many kinds of workers (including management) and to the hire or purchase of specialized equipment.

SOCIAL INSTITUTIONS

In the theoretical extreme, each worker could hire various fractions of his time to various employers, as some workers do in practice to some extent. But *theoretically* the worker would be ready to sell the tiniest fraction of his time to different employers or to change employers at any given instant of the working day when the fluctuations of the labor market might offer a marginally higher wage rate somewhere else. Such behavior would, of course, involve very high transactions costs to the worker—and to the employer, who would have to be constantly prepared to fill vacancies at a moment's notice. Contractual and semicontractual arrangements, including "adequate notice" customs, reduce these transactions costs, at the cost of reduced institutional flexibility in the quantity and quality of labor employed, and in the quantity and quality of work obtainable from given workers in a situation where "instant firing" is often not a feasible option. That many firms voluntarily chose to accept such costs of institutional rigidity implied in having "regular employees"—even before union or legal pressures for job security—suggests that transactions costs would be substantial otherwise. That other firms had to wait for such outside pressures suggests that the relative weights of those costs and benefits vary from situation to situation.

As in the general question of the relative advantages of formal versus informal procedures, the point here is not to determine which is better categorically. On the contrary, the point is to suggest why there is a trade-off. The particular terms of that trade-off, and *the way those terms vary incrementally*, is likely to be far better known to those directly involved than to others operating on general principles.

Even after acquiring the formal institutional structures implied where firms sell to consumers, economic processes still retain substantial elements of incremental rather than categorical decision making. The consumer, by choosing among firms to patronize, implicitly weighs the effectiveness of different sets of workers and managers, rewarding some with fuller, more sustained employment, and forcing others to work less or not at all—despite any institutional guarantees—for lack of consumer demand can force the institution itself out of business. Even where the consumer chooses to buy prepackaged products, his range of choice among such products and retailers of products usually prevents his being forced into the kind of take-it-or-leave-it "package deal" choices common in such fields as politics, where he must vote for one candidate's whole "package" of positions on foreign policy, civil liberties, ecology, race relations, monetary policy, etc. The almost continuous revision of most economic decisions adds a temporal flexibility not found in political systems with fixed terms of office, where recall and impeachment are costly options.

Because economic transactions often involve repeated satisfaction of the same desires, there is continual feedback from those most knowledgeable about the extent to which a given product or service is satisfactory—namely, the consumers. Moreover, this is not merely abstract knowledge but knowledge conveyed in a monetary form, conveying persuasion as well as information.

Economic transactions, whether through formal or informal processes, have as a serious disadvantage the possible disregard of affected interests not party to the transactions. A sale of coal to an electric generating plant may represent a mutually advantageous transaction from the point of view of the coal company and the electric company, and yet create millions of dollars worth of costs in dirt and lung disease which are not represented in the decisions as to the kind of coal to use, the location of the plant, or the presence or absence of devices to reduce harmful emissions. Theoretically, with a perfectly functioning and costless legal system, all these costs would be felt in the form of damage liabilities, which would be foreseen at the time of the economic transaction—leading to the same kinds of decisions as if the excluded third parties had in fact been included.[11] The external costs in some economic processes, and the high transactions costs of organizing thousands of scattered individuals, create special problems for affected third parties. Viewed as a social process, the problem with such economic processes is that the *transacting* parties are not coextensive with the *affected* parties.

Another problem with an economic system is that different people have varying amounts of money with which to convey their consumer preferences to producers. For many social critics, this invalidates any hope of an optimal use of resources via market processes. However, this may be a more formidable problem in theory than in practice. When groups of consumers compete for the same products, each of the competing groups usually includes a wide range of income levels, so that a rich-versus-poor competition need not be involved. Moreover, even where such a competition is involved, lower income consumers often bid goods and resources away from the affluent, through sheer numbers, even if not to the theoretically optimal extent. Much of the outcry against middlemen ("developers," "commercial interests," etc.) who would redirect resources from a "higher" to a "lower" use is implicitly a protest against large numbers of lower-income people whose collective wealth is bidding shoreline, forest, and lakeside property away from a use favored by higher-income people to uses more consonant with the tastes and individual resources of lower-income people: typically higher density use, substituting apartment buildings for individual houses, hotels for rustic cabins, automobile access roads for backpack trails, etc. The middlemen, as such, typically have no bias toward any particular use, but only toward making money—a charge bitterly made by critics, despite the inconsistency of that charge with blaming the middlemen for a *particular* end result.

POLITICAL INSTITUTIONS

Political and legal institutions provide the rigidities—"rights"—people want in some vital areas of their life, where they reject both the transactions costs and the indignity of having to submit to, or negotiate with, those who might challenge or threaten their possession of their home, their children, or their life. Constitutional systems attempt to sharply demarcate these areas of basic rights from other areas in which the discretion and flexibility of individual choice and interpersonal negotiation may achieve whatever arrangements are deemed mutually satisfactory by the individuals concerned. In short, Constitutional political and legal systems attempt to limit their own scope to areas in which they have a relative advantage as decision-making processes, leaving other areas to other decision-making processes, whose advantages may be either in the quality of the decisions or in the personal dignity implied by free choice.

Political systems provide some feedback via the electoral process, so that laws can be amended, repealed, or given varying amounts of financial support. This feedback is neither as fast nor as universal, nor as immediately coercive as in economic market processes. The growing area of administrative decision making is even more insulated from electoral feedback, and legal institutions at the higher, appellate court levels have been made virtually election-proof, except for the confirmation process. As compared to economic institutions, the virtues of political, administrative, and judicial institutions are not so much responsiveness as reliability. Their decisions are not separate and episodic but precedential: political, legislative, and administrative rulings are in effect until explicitly repealed or declared unconstitutional, and changes in court rulings are self-restricted by deliberate reluctance to needlessly upset precedents. The basic framework of political, administrative, and judicial rulings is categorical—legal or illegal, guilty or innocent—though much ingenuity may go into introducing elements of flexibility and incremental decision making into these institutional processes. Still, these flexible and incremental features are not as integral to such processes as to economic institutions.

Political systems allow affected third parties to influence economic transactions from which their interests are excluded. Political decision making can lower transactions costs by allowing a relatively few surrogates to make and implement decisions reflecting the will of millions who have insufficient individual stake (or resources) to incur the huge costs of devising and transacting some of the decisions they believe in.

Social transactions may generate not only costs external to the transacting parties but also benefits external to those parties. Economic institutions do not bring such benefits to bear on the decision makers. Theoretically, the beneficiaries might bring such considerations to bear through offers of reward to the transacting parties to shape their decisions so as to optimize third party benefits, but in practice the number and dispersion of the beneficiaries, and the corresponding cost of identifying and welding these diffuse interests into a coherent bargaining agent typically prevent this.[12]

A special case of external benefits is "social overhead capital"—investments whose benefits accrue to a wide variety of individuals and institutions which do not themselves incur the cost of making the investment. For example, a sewage system reduces the incidence of disease and debilitation, enabling workers to work more days and earn more pay, and enabling employers to have a more reliable workforce and correspondingly higher profits. Raising children to be honest is an investment made by parents, but among the beneficiaries are credit card companies, self-service stores, and the Internal Revenue Service. The fact that those who incur the costs of the investment are not the same as those who reap the dividends makes it more difficult for economic institutions to achieve the level of investment justified by the returns, and thereby creates a role for political surrogates.

The time horizon of the constituent may be his lifetime, and perhaps that of his children, or even the longer range interest of the whole society as an on-going enterprise. The inherent incentive structure facing a political surrogate emphasizes the time remaining between a given decision and the next election. The opportunity for policies with immediate benefits and longer run negative consequences are obvious, not only in theory but in practice. Similarly, differences in information and transactions costs per unit of benefit between the citizen and organized interest groups, as well as between the citizen and his political surrogate, create inherent incentives for policies with concentrated benefits and diffused costs—even though the costs may be several times the benefits, whether measured financially or otherwise.

Another problem inherent in political processes is that the degree of reliability or rigidity desired in a governmental framework, within which individual planning and action can take place, is jeopardized by political incentives to continually *adjust* this framework for the real or alleged benefit of particular groups of constituents. This is a special case of the concentration of benefits and the diffusion of costs. Everyone with an objective interest in a known and predictable set of laws and policies pays the cost of innovative political activities. This means virtually everyone in the society, including those who benefit from particular subsets of changes. It is not merely so-called "liberals" who innovate; so-called "conservatives" may be equally creative with "tax breaks" or monopolistic concessions for a variety of constituent groups as their political opponents are with expenditure programs and government controls for a variety of their constituents. The point is that political surrogates, for whatever constituent coalition they serve, have an incentive to continually adjust the legal framework—*whatever* it may be at a given moment and regardless of its merits or demerits—because of specific concentrated benefits and the diffused general costs of reduced predictability.

This is neither a moral comment on individuals nor an exhortation for more citizen knowledge of specific governmental policy. On the contrary, it is an attempt to explain the causes of these phenomena in terms of differentials in the cost of information, differentials in transactions costs, and inherent conflicts of interest built into political decision-making processes. To exhort the individual citizen to make investments in knowledge comparable to those of lobbyists and political crusaders (both of whom have much lower costs per unit of personal benefit) is to urge him to behavior that is irrational, if not physically impossible in a twenty-four hour day. What might be possible, at lower cost, is an awareness of this problem inherent in political decision making, when choosing among modes of decision making.

The competition of political opponents tends to mitigate these problems somewhat, but the terms of this competition are quite different from the terms of economic competition. Political knowledge is conveyed by articulation, and its accurate transmission through political competition depends upon the preexisting stock of knowledge and understanding of the receiving citizen. Economic knowledge need not be articulated to the consumer, but is conveyed—summarized—in the prices and qualities of goods. The consumer may have no idea at all—or even a wrong idea—as to why one product costs less and serves his purposes better; all he needs is that end-result itself. *Someone* must of course have the specific knowledge of how to achieve that result. What is crucial to economic competition is that better and more accurate knowledge on the part of the producer is a decisive competitive advantage, *regardless* of whether the consumer shares any part of that knowledge. In political competition, accurate knowledge has no such decisive competitive advantage, because what is being "sold" is not an end-result but a plausible belief about a complex process.

Because of differences in the cost of judging processes versus the cost of judging end results, it is even more important in political than in economic processes to have feedback from the diffused individuals who receive the consequences to the few who made the decisions that produced the consequences.

Where political decision making is broadly defined to include judicial decision making, feedback from those affected is even less effective. Moreover, the cost of a court's monitoring the consequences of its own decisions could easily be prohibitive, and especially where the consequences include effects on people not party to the legal action, but whose whole constellation of expectations have been changed. However difficult it may be to directly know what is going on in someone else's mind—such as changing expectations—it has concrete consequences which take place long before the future events contemplated. Restrictions on the future use of property is a reduction in its *present* value, since one component of its present value is its future saleability. In short, a reduction in property rights is a partial confiscation of property; to take away 10 percent of the value of land is economically no different from taking away 10 percent of the land itself.

Similar reasoning applies to other restrictions on other values not expressed in money terms. Changing expectations of future social relationships of school children bring forth varying present reactions of parents. In some cases, these present actions may be more vehement than after the future event actually arrives—as claimed by some supporters of "busing," for example—but this merely illustrates the correspondence between economic and noneconomic translation (or inherent equivalence) of future expectations into present costs or benefits.

JUDICIAL PROCESSES

Judicial decision making is made necessary by the insufficiencies of language, even if everyone were willing to obey the law as he understood it. Political leaders cannot exhaustively specify the application of the principles they legislate. Moreover, the people may choose to bind themselves and their political surrogates in advance, during presumably more sober periods, against actions they might take in rash moments. This simply means that, beyond some point, flexibility of decision making is deemed harmful and the rigidities of Constitutional limitations are preferred within that range of decisions. This parallels the economic law of diminishing returns, under which a given input has varying effects on output over different ranges, including—beyond some point—a negative effect. If flexibility is considered as an input in decision-making processes, then it too, clearly, has a range within which it is enormously valuable, another range within which it is more moderately valuable, and another range within which it is positively harmful.

Otherwise we would leave ourselves unlimited flexibility to take the most sweeping and drastic actions on the basis of the most transient 51 percent majority. Instead special rigidities—"rights"—are deliberately built into the system to apply to such things as life, liberty, and property, where our primary interest is in security rather than in fine tuning the social mechanism to capture fleeting advantages.

Even as compared to formal economic or political processes, judicial decision making tends to be more categorical, rather than incremental. Not only do criminal cases tend to be dichotomized into guilty or innocent, and appellate decisions into constitutional or unconstitutional, the legal precedents apply to all similarly circumstanced individuals—where the similarity is in those *articulated characteristics documentable to third parties,* whether or not these are the characteristics most behaviorally determinative or philosophically crucial. By contrast, informal social processes can adjust the time, scope, and degree of specialness of treatment of the salient characteristics of each individual person and each episode, as determined by closer knowledge, unrestricted by the inherent limitations of articulation or of secondhand data filtered through legal rules of evidence.

No such close weighing of incremental costs and incremental benefits can be expected in judicial processes whose social benefits take the rigid form of "rights" applicable to categories, and costs take the form of correspondingly rigid obligations. In short, judicial decision making especially at the appellate level, consists of "package deals," in which the package is quite extensive in time as well as space, and has contents which are homogeneous only with respect to articulated, documentable variables—and may be quite heterogeneous with respect to all other behavioral or philosophical considerations.

DECISIONS AND KNOWLEDGE

The most basic of all decisions is *who* shall decide. This is easily lost sight of in discussions that proceed directly to the merits of particular issues, as if they could be judged from a unitary, or God's eye, viewpoint. A more human perspective must recognize the respective advantages and disadvantages of different decision-making processes, including their widely varying costs of knowledge, which is a central consideration often overlooked in analyses which proceed as if knowledge were either complete, costless, or of a "given" quantity. Decision-making processes differ not only in the quantity, quality, and cost of knowledge brought to bear initially, but also and perhaps still more so, in the *feedback* of knowledge and its effectiveness in modifying the initial decision. This feedback is not only additional knowledge, but knowledge of a different kind. It is direct knowledge of particulars of time and place, as distinguished from the secondhand generalities known as "expertise." The high personal cost of acquiring expertise, and the opportunities it presents for displaying individual talent or genius, make it a more *dramatic* form of knowledge, but not necessarily a more *important* form of knowledge from a decision-making point of view. Certainly expertise is not sufficient in itself without the additional direct knowledge of results obtainable closer at hand, and at lower cost, by great numbers of individuals who acquire no personal distinction from possession of that kind of knowledge.

"Society" is not the only figure of speech that confuses the actual decision-making units and conceals the determining incentives and constraints. "The market" is another such misleading figure of speech. Both the friends and foes of economic decision-making processes refer to "the market" as if it were an institution parallel with, and alternative to, the government as an institution. The government is indeed an institution, but "the market" is nothing more than an *option* for each individual to chose among numerous existing institutions, or to fashion new arrangements suited to his own situation and taste.

The government establishes an army or a post office as *the* answer to a given problem. "The market" is simply the freedom to choose among many existing or still-to-be-created possibilities. The need for housing can be met through "the market" in a thousand different ways chosen by each person—anything from living in a commune to buying a house, renting rooms, moving in with relatives, living in quarters provided by an employer, etc., etc. The need for food can be met by buying groceries, eating at a restaurant, growing a garden, or letting someone else provide meals in exchange for work, property, or sex. *"The market" is no particular set of institutions.* Its advantages and disadvantages are due precisely to this fact. Any comparison of market processes and governmental processes for making a particular set of decisions is a comparison between given institutions, prescribed in advance, and an option to select or create institutions *ad hoc*. There are of course particular institutions existing in the market as of a given time. But there can be no definitive comparison of market institutions—such as the corporation—and a governmental institution, such as a federal bureaucracy. The corporation may be the predominant institutional way of doing certain things during a particular era, but it will never be the only market mechanism even during that given era, and certainly not for all eras. Partnerships, cooperatives, episodic individual transactions, and long-run contractual agreements all exist as alternatives. The advantages of market institutions over government institutions are not so much in their particular characteristics as institutions but in the fact that people can usually make a better choice out of numerous options than by following a single prescribed process.

The diversity of personal tastes insures that no given institution will become *the* answer to a human problem in the market. The need for food, housing, or other desiderata can be met in a sweeping range of ways. Some of the methods most preferred by some will be the most abhorred by others. Responsiveness to individual diversity means that market processes necessarily produce "chaotic" results from the point of view of any single given scale of values. No matter which particular way you think people should be housed or fed (or their other needs met) the market will *not* do it just that way, because the market is not a particular set of institutions. People who are convinced that their values are best—not only for themselves but for others—must necessarily be offended by many things that happen in a market economy, whether those people's values are religious, communistic, white supremacist, or racially integrationist. The diversity of tastes satisfied by a market may be its greatest economic achievement, but it is also its greatest political vulnerability.

Decision making through any kind of process involves costs created by the decision-making process itself, quite aside from those costs created by the particular decisions reached. Achieving agreement or resolution of opposing views is never free. Nor should these "transactions costs," as economists call them, be thought of as minor incidental expenses. The transactions costs of choosing a new emperor of the Roman Empire often included tens of thousands of lives and the destruction of whole cities and surrounding countrysides in battles among contenders. The devotion of many rational and public-spirited men of later times to the principle of royal succession, which might seem at first to be only an irrational special privilege, is more easily understood against an historical background of astronomical transactions costs in choosing national leaders. Even one who felt that a given king (or kings in general) had only average intelligence, or even somewhat below average intelligence, might still reasonably choose to bear with royal succession if he felt that the likely differences in leadership were not worth the carnage involved in alternative political processes available at the time.

The rise of modern conditions—notably literacy and mass communications—made democratic and constitutional methods of changing national leadership possible. It does not make agreement on issues a free good, however. Again, the tendency to proceed directly to the "solution" of "problems" from some given viewpoint or given set of values overlooks the crucial point that the diversity of viewpoints and values means that costs of concurrence and the amount of concurrence made necessary by different policies can vary enormously. The net difference between policy x and policy y may be far less than the cost of choosing, or one policy may require far more consensus than the other. The Godlike approach to social policy ignores both the diversity of values and the cost of agreement among human beings. The political and/or economic systems which involve less control from higher authorities reduce the costs of concurrence—which can range all the way up to concentration camps and genocide. To those who feel that their values are *the* values, the less controlled systems necessarily present a spectacle of "chaos," simply because such systems respond to a diversity of values. The more successfully such systems respond to diversity, the more "chaos" there will be, by definition, according to the standards of *any* specific set of values—other than diversity or freedom as values. Looked at another way, the more self-righteous observers there are, the more chaos (and "waste") will be seen.

Ringing calls for a national consensus on this or that are often preposterous in the literal sense of putting in front what comes behind. It is true that—viewed in retrospect—those national consensuses that have in fact been achieved have often been both practically fruitful and emotionally satisfying. This is because, given the enormous cost of consensus, it is unlikely to be achieved, except on something of overwhelming urgency to an overwhelming majority of people. Unity in wartime, when national survival is threatened, is an obvious example. In short, it is the high *value* involved in the result—survival, in this case—that makes us willing to pay the high *cost* of consensus. It is not the cost that creates the value, however. Nor can we make other things valuable by incurring large costs for them, such as by trying for a national consensus about them. On the contrary, we satisfy our desires at least cost—which is to say, we can satisfy more of our desires—by minimizing the amount of consensus that is necessary. We easily provide ourselves with food and clothing precisely because there is no consensus needed as to what is the best food or the best clothing. If we had to reach a consensus first, we might destroy ourselves in the process of trying to meet simple basic needs. Man's equally pervasive spiritual needs—whether met in religious or ideological ways—have often led to such mutual destruction, ranging from persecution to wholesale slaughter, when particular religious or political creeds required consensus as part of their tenets. Individualism and pluralism in social, political and economic processes reduce the need for consensus—at the cost of presenting an untidy spectacle of "chaos" to those eager for a consensus in support of their own particular subjective values. The Constitution of the United States implicitly recognizes the very high cost of consensus in some areas by flatly forbidding the government from even attempting to reach a consensus in religious matters. Yet the cost of consensus is implicitly treated as negligible in naive complaints that "the American system seems less well adapted to the mobilization of a positive energetic will."[13] That failing is sometimes known as freedom.

One of the problems involved in understanding decision making through any kind of institutional process is that the *cause* of a decision must be distinguished from the *mechanism* that transmits it. The ancient practice of killing the messenger who brought bad news suggests that this separation of causal factors from transmitting mechanisms is especially difficult in emotion-laden areas. Institutions frequently transmit unwelcome news—such as the unacceptability of one's performance in school or on the job, or the reduced availability of a desired commodity or the unlikelihood of one's political ideals being realized. The question then is whether the institution was itself responsible for this outcome, or was simply a messenger bringing bad news. Attempts to prevent institutions from conveying bad news—e.g., no-fail grading, "job security," price controls, etc.—raise the cost of transmitting knowledge and retard the adjustment to that knowledge.

Before attempting to determine the effect of institutions, it is necessary to consider the inherent circumstances, constraints, and impelling forces at work in the environment within which the institutional mechanisms function. The analysis of these impulsions and constraints—i.e., social "theory"—must at least supplement the consideration of institutional mechanics. Decision making depends not only on the kinds of processes through which decisions are made, but on the nature of the trade-offs involved. Perhaps the easiest kinds of trade-offs to visualize are economic trade-offs, which can be quantified in money terms, but broader social trade-offs may be even more important, even if expressed in less tangible terms. Economic, social, and political trade-offs will be considered in the next three chapters.

Chapter 3

Economic Trade-Offs

An economic system is a system for the production and distribution of goods and services. But what is crucial for understanding the way it functions is that it is a system for *rationing* goods and services that are *inadequate* to supply all that people want. This is true of any economic system, whether it is called capitalism, socialism, feudalism, or by any other name. The Garden of Eden was not an economic system, even though it produced and distributed goods and services, because it produced them in such abundance that rationing was unnecessary. A utopia would not be an economic system, for the same reason. In short, while economic systems of various sorts boast of their achievements in bringing goods and services to people, what makes them all economic systems is that they have systematic procedures for *preventing* people from getting goods and services, denying them access to natural resources, tools or equipment for production, and limiting their ability to work at the tasks they would prefer. Capitalist systems use capitalist methods of denial, socialist systems use socialist methods of denial, but all economic systems must use some method of denial.

Looked at another way, there are *inherent* constraints, given the limitations of nature and the unlimited desires of man, and economic systems are simply artificial schemes for administering the inherent scarcities. The scarcities themselves exist independently of the particular economic systems, and would exist if there were no economic system at all and people simply fought over everything they wanted. Economic institutions exist to introduce elements of rationality or effeciency into the use of inputs and outputs.

The classic definition of economics is that it is the study of the allocation of scarce resources which have alternative uses. If resources—the ingredients of production—were not scarce, there would be no economics. We would be in an Eden or a utopia. Similarly, if each resource had only one possible use, we would simply use as much of each resource as was available to produce as much of its unique output as we could, and the only economic problem would be deciding which particular individual should produce it or consume it. But economics is much more complicated than that because, in the real world, the same resource can be used to produce a wide variety of products. Coal, for example, can produce dyes, electric power, heat, nylon, or liquid automotive fuel, and milk can produce ice cream, yogurt, and innumerable kinds of cheeses, as well as providing an ingredient in a virtually limitless variety of cooked foods. An economic system must determine how much of each resource shall go to each of its various uses, under the inherent constraint that all of the desires for all of the users cannot possibly be satisfied simultaneously.

While economic systems may become very complex, the economic situation or predicament is quite simple: there just is not enough to go around. Like so many simple and important realities, it often gets lost sight of, or is completely ignored, in the midst of complicated reasoning or emotionally powerful rhetoric. For example, some social commentators point to the existence of "unmet needs" in society as evidence of the "failure" of the economic system. But, in fact, because economic systems are essentially systems of rationing, any successfully functioning economic system would have "unmet needs" *everywhere*. The alternative would be to completely satisfy all of some category of needs—the most urgent, the moderately important, and the trivially marginal—thereby leaving still more unsatisfied (and more urgent) needs unmet elsewhere in the economy. We could, for example, completely solve the downtown parking problem in every city in the country, so that anyone could easily find a convenient parking space at any hour of the day or night—but the resources needed to do this would mean severe cutbacks in municipal hospitals, schools, and water supply. The mundane fact of insufficiency must be insisted upon and reiterated because so many discussions of "unmet needs" proceed as if "better" policies, practices, or attitudes would "solve" the problem at hand without creating deficiencies elsewhere. Typical of this attitude is the comment that, "If we can send a man to the moon, why can't we—" followed by whatever project the speaker favors. The fact that we sent a man to the moon is part of the reason why many other things could not be done.

KNOWLEDGE IN THE ECONOMY

When economics is mentioned, many people think of money, and in fact the word "resources" is often used simply as a genteel synonym for money. But in reality, a nation's economic success is far more likely to depend upon its real resources—land, machinery, work skills, etc.—rather than on the number or denomination of the pieces of green paper printed by the government. For an individual, the amount of money at his disposal determines his wealth, but for a nation as a whole, its wealth is its food, housing, transportation, medical care, etc.—not the green paper used to transfer this wealth around within its population. A nation is wealthier, its standard of living is higher, when it has more of these real things, not when bigger numbers are printed on its currency.

Since an economy functions with scarce resources which have alternative uses, there must be some method of coordinating the rationing process and getting the most output from the available input. There are as many different ways of doing this as there are different economic systems. All of these involve the use of knowledge, and how effectively that knowledge is used is crucial. After all, the cavemen had the same natural resources at their disposal as we have today, and the difference between their standard of living and ours is a difference between the knowledge they could bring to bear on those resources and the knowledge used today. Although we speak loosely of "production," man neither creates nor destroys matter, but only transforms it— and the knowledge of how to make these transformations is a key economic factor. Even among contemporary nations, differences in their economic conditions are often far more related to differences in their technological and organizational knowledge than to their respective endowments in natural resources. Japan, for example, has achieved a relatively high level of prosperity while importing many of its inputs and exporting much of its output. What they are essentially doing is selling their knowledge and skills to the rest of the world. Although it is physical material that consumers are buying, this material could have been shipped directly from the supplying country to the consuming country, without passing through Japan—except that the Japanese can transform it from inputs to outputs more efficiently than the consuming nation could.

More pervasively than is generally appreciated, economic transactions are purchases and sales of knowledge. Even the hiring of an "unskilled" worker to pump gas involves the purchase of a knowledge of the importance of dependability, punctuality, and an ability to get along with customers and co-workers, quite aside from the modest technological knowledge required to operate the gasoline pump. This is sometimes dramatically brought home when American corporations attempt to set up businesses in less developed countries, and find that they cannot adequately fill their "unskilled" jobs, even though the country may be full of people who are both poor and unemployed.

Even within an economically advanced nation, where certain skills are so taken for granted that those with them are labeled "unskilled," there are still such differences in the degree of mastery of these forms of knowledge that some employees are preferred to others, and some have to be fired for failure to apply the necessary knowledge. For example, a gas station attendant who does not show up promptly and dependably to help with rush hour business can cause some drivers to take their cars to another gas station, where they can get filled up without waiting in such a long line. By the same token, another gas station attendant who is especially efficient, attentive or pleasant to the customers can add to the volume of business. The gas station owner is therefore in a position to make significant distinctions among employees who are lumped together as "unskilled" workers by distant "experts."

Of course, everyone "knows" the importance of punctuality, dependability, etc., in the abstract or intellectual sense of knowing—just as we "know" in a general sense how to milk a cow, though most of us could not actually go out to the barn with an empty pail and come back with milk. But in an economy, it is not the superficial possession of knowledge in the abstract that counts, but the *effective* application of it. As in the case of Pearl Harbor, the abstract existence of knowledge means nothing unless it is applied at the point of decision and action.

More complex operations obviously involve more complex knowledge—often far more complex than any given individual can master. The person who can successfully man a gas pump or even manage a filling station probably knows little or nothing about the molecular chemistry of petroleum, and a molecular chemist is probably equally uninformed or misinformed as to the problems of finance, product mix, location, and other factors which determine the success or failure of a filling station, and both the manager and the chemist probably know virtually nothing about the geological principles which determine the best way and best places to explore for oil—or about the financial complexities of the speculative investments which pay for this costly and uncertain process. It has been said that no one knows how to make even a simple lead pencil. That is, there is no single person who knows how to mine the graphite, grow the wood, produce the rubber, process the metal, and handle all the financial complications of running a successful business. In short, we are all in the business of selling and buying knowledge from one another, because we are each so profoundly ignorant of what it takes to complete the whole process of which we are a part.

COSTS AND INCREMENTAL SUBSTITUTION

Given the inherent factor of scarcity, any kind of economy tries to maximize the output from its given inputs—or, in other words, to get the most value for its costs. Because resources have alternative uses, and because alternative products produce consumer satisfaction, *substitution* is a crucial factor of economic life, both in production and in consumption. We have already noted how the same ingredient can go into many different products. It should also be recognized that many different products can be ingredients in a consumer's sense of well-being. We normally think of physically similar things as substitutes: Plymouths and Chevrolets, rye bread and whole wheat, vodka and gin, etc. But in fact people may choose between spending their disposable cash on adding another room to the house or on taking a vacation abroad, between stocking their wine cellar and buying a season's pass to the baseball games, or between retiring early and sending a child to college. The particular nature of the satisfactions need not be the same.

Substitution does not imply perfect substitutions. There are all degrees of substitutability: most people would consider two pints of milk as a perfect substitute for a quart of milk, but would consider a cold shower a very poor substitute for sex. How well one thing substitutes for another cannot be determined by how similar they are in physical characteristics, or indeed, by any purely objective criteria. Economists find substitutability in terms of people's subjective preferences as revealed by their overt behavior. If a rise in the price of coffee causes people to buy more tea, then economically speaking, we can say that they are substitutes without having to investigate the chemical or physical characteristics of either. Similarly, if an increase in the price of stereo equipment causes people to buy more clothes instead, then economically these two goods are substitutes, without regard to their material disparities or even the implausibility of the connection.

Substitution takes place in production as well as consumption. Electric wires can be made of copper, steel, or aluminum, and the proportions of the three vary according to the relationship of their respective costs. Again, substitutes need not be *perfect* substitutes; the weight advantage of aluminum is more important for some purposes, while for other purposes any price differential will cause the immediate substitution of steel or copper. Through substitution, an ecomony can—in effect—transform one product into another by shifting some of their common inputs. For example, the economy can easily accomplish the old alchemists' dream of transforming lead into gold by simply shifting the labor, machinery, and managerial skills used to make lead into the production of gold instead. From an economic point of view, it does not matter that this is not "really" transforming one metal physically into another. What matters is that a reduction in the output of one leads to an increase in the output of the other. In World War II, we transformed our automobiles and refrigerators into tanks and airplanes by this very process of redirecting resource inputs into other product outputs.

Neither in production nor consumption does substitution imply total substitution. More likely, it means an incremental substitution, accepting somewhat less of one thing in order to get somewhat more of another. We almost never have to accept anything as difficult as deciding categorical priorities—whether vegetables are more important than shoes, or vacations more important than music. Moreover, because we usually decide to have some of each option, even the relative importance of each possible choice changes as the respective quantities that we already have change. For example, if we had a dozen oranges and a bushel of apples, we would probably be less interested in another bag of apples than in another bag of oranges, and we might give up either for one pineapple or a pound of grapes, even though we might have the opposite preferences if we started from a position in which we had no fruit at all, or in which we had a bushel of oranges and ten pounds of grapes. In other words, substitution ratios are incrementally variable rather than categorically fixed.

Simple as all this is, it goes completely counter to rhetoric that is often heard, and sometimes heeded, about the urgent need to "establish priorities" either nationally or in a business or other organization. At the instant that such rhetoric is uttered, there may indeed be an urgent need for more of one thing at the expense of something else, but it is only a matter of time before the changing proportions of the two things change the relative urgency of adding more of each. Categorical priorities ignore this fact, unless they are very flexible and reversible—in which case they are not really "priorities." But because sober analysis seldom has the appeal of ringing rhetoric, priorities often do get established, and outlive the necessities that gave rise to them. One of the major problems of public policy is to determine what kinds of social institutions lead to flexible and reversible transformations, which permit continuous adjustment to changing circumstances, and which kinds of institutions lead to enduring categorical priorities, which can become as counterproductive under new circumstances as they may have been necessary under the old.

COSTS AND VALUES

Once it is clear that an economy—any kind of economy—is basically a system of rationing inadequate supplies, and a system of incremental substitutions, the concept of "cost" assumes a new significance. The cost of any good is the cost of its ingredients, and their cost, in turn, is *whatever alternative good had to be foregone* in order to use them where they are used. For example, the real cost of a piece of cheese is the ice cream or powdered milk that could have been produced with the same original resource. Indeed, if more cows had been slaughtered instead of being kept alive for their milk, there would have been more steaks, baseball gloves, and other cowhide products, so that the real cost of yogurt includes catchers' mitts.

This is not merely a philosophical way of looking at things. It is the way economies operate in the real world. If the demand for yogurt increased many times, yogurt production would absorb milk that would otherwise have gone into ice cream, cheese, and other dairy products. This would cause more cows to be used to increase total milk production and fewer to be slaughtered—and this in turn would mean less cowhide and higher prices for catchers' mitts. In an economy not coordinated by prices but by government directives, the same end result could occur through an issuing of orders by a central economic planning board, and the more stringent rationing of catchers' mitts would be accomplished by waiting lines or waiting lists instead of by higher prices. The physical dissimilarities between dairy products and cowhide products has nothing to do with their substitutability in the production process. How much, and in which direction, the incremental substitution takes place depends upon their respective values. These values are wholly subjective. To say that people want more yogurt is to say that yogurt has become more valuable to them. Either statement conveys exactly the same information. There is no "objective" value of yogurt which could be determined in a chemical laboratory or under a microscope, nor would any political or philosophical process determine what it is "really" worth.

Value being ultimately subjective, it varies not only from person to person but from time to time with the same person, and varies also according to how much of the given good he already has. Obviously a man in the desert dying of thirst would sacrifice much more for a glass of water than he would in his home, with water available from his faucet. In short, even for the same individual, the value of water can vary from virtually everything he has down to zero—or even below zero, since he would pay to have water taken away if his basement were flooded.

The cost of a given good can be determined in purely physical terms. If so many gallons of milk are required to produce ten pounds of yogurt, and if we know how much ice cream could have been produced with that same amount of milk, then we know the physical rate at which ice cream can be "transformed" into yogurt through incremental substitutions in the production process. However, this statement of physical possibilities says nothing about how much yogurt will in fact be produced relative to ice cream. That depends also on the relative values of these goods to their respective consumers. The knowledge of these changing values may be transmitted by price fluctuations in a market economy, or by voting changes in a politically-controlled ("planned") economy, or by direct orders in a nondemocratic, politically-controlled economy (communism, fascism, etc.).

In other words, while an individual or an economy may appear at first to be weighing the subjective value of a good against its objective cost, ultimately what is being weighed is the subjective value of one good against the subjective value of another good. Faced with identical technology and resources setting the limits of what is possible at a given time, different combinations of goods may be produced, according to the subjective preferences of the decision makers, whether those decision makers are consumers, central planners, or royalty. None of these differing assortments of goods—and therefore different resource uses—need be more "efficient" than any other. Efficiency in turning inputs into outputs can be measured only after specifying the subjective values involved. Even in the apparently objective physical sciences this is also the case. The objective "efficiency" of an automobile engine can be determined only after specifying the subjectively determined goal as the forward movement of the automobile. Otherwise, every engine is 100 percent efficient in the sense that all the energy input is used, either in the forward motion of the car, overcoming the internal friction of engine parts, or in random shaking of the automobile.

Although neither value nor efficiency is wholly objective, the idea that they are dies hard. Denunciations of "inefficiency" and "waste" are often nothing more than statements of a different set of preferences. Schemes to turn particular decisions or processes over to "experts" who will promote scientifically neutral "efficiency" are often simply ways of allowing one group of people to impose their subjective preferences on others. For example, proposals for a city-manager form of government to take municipal decisions "out of politics" are in reality proposals to make local decision making responsive to a different set of interests other than the general electorate. The merits of such a change can be debated from various viewpoints in particular cases, but the point here is the inaccuracy of the usual description of what is going on, and the misconceptions (or dishonesty) behind such descriptions. As a mechanism for the utilization of knowledge in society the city manager arrangement screens out some of the knowledge (from the electorate), allowing more weight to the knowledge of others who have greater access to, or implicit control over, the administration.[1]

AVERAGE VERSUS INCREMENTAL COSTS

When people casually speak of "the" cost of producing something, they usually mean the average cost—that is, the total cost of running the enterprise divided by the number of units of output it produces. But for actual decision-making purposes at any given time, the *incremental* cost is more crucial. The total cost of running an airline obviously includes the cost of airplanes, but in deciding whether or not to make a particular flight, what matters at that point is whether the incremental cost of that flight will be covered by its incremental value to the passengers, as revealed by what they are willing to pay for it. This question has to be faced whether the airline is a private company in an unregulated economy, a government-owned enterprise in a socialist state, or any other combination of economic and political institutions. The mechanisms by which the decision is made will be different, and of course the actual decision may be influenced or even determined by the nature of the institutional mechanism, but the point here is that the problem itself is independent of institutions, and institutions can be assessed in terms of how well they resolve the problem.

An airplane which would otherwise remain idle on the ground during a particular time has a very low cost in the economic sense of cost as a *foregone alternative*. If a plane that would otherwise remain in a hangar overnight is instead brought out at midnight to fly a party of vacationers to a nearby resort, the cost of this short flight that does not interfere with its other schedule of flights is much less than the "average" cost of an airplane flight. In this case, the incremental cost of the flight is little more than the cost of fuel and a flight crew, since the plane itself is there for another purpose anyway. In a price-coordinated economy, the amount of payment by the passengers required to induce the airline to fly under these conditions will tend to be much lower than the amount required to induce the same airline to set aside planes to fly the same distance on a regular schedule. For the latter decision, the passengers would have to pay an amount sufficient to cover not only the fuel and flight crew but to cover also the cost of the plane itself and the airline's various "overhead" expenses. In an economy coordinated by government decisions, the same economic resolution would be efficient, though it would have to be reached institutionally through a political or administrative process. Whether the same resolution would be reached in fact would depend upon the extent to which the particular institutional arrangements convey the same knowledge of consumer preferences (incremental trade-offs) and production costs (incremental trade-offs), and whether that knowledge was conveyed in a form that was "effective" in the sense of constituting a personal incentive to the decision maker.

SOCIAL INSTITUTIONS

It often costs much more to make a commitment in advance to produce a given good or service than it does to produce the same good or service with equipment already provided for other purposes. In some substitutions incremental costs are less than average costs—sometimes only a tiny fraction of average costs. By the same token, if the existing equipment is already being used at its normal capacity, the additional use may cost even more than the normal use, as in the case of additional demand for electricity at a time when the generators are already straining. The difference between average cost and incremental cost is crucial not only in economic institutions in various economic systems but it is also crucial in political, legal, and other systems as well. The incremental cost of a telephone's ringing may be quite low to a resting and slightly bored housewife, but may be maddeningly high to a housewife who is already simultaneously coping with a crying baby, a pot boiling over on the stove, and a fight among her other children. The incremental cost of making certain precedent-setting judicial decisions is not simply the cost in that individual case but the cost of committing legal institutions to settling similar future cases on a similar basis. This cost may be hundreds or thousands of times as large as the individual decision in itself. Looked at another way, where certain decisions may be made in any of a number of different institutions within a given social system, the institutional location of that decision-making process may raise or lower the costs entailed by large multiples of what is involved in the individual decision as such.

DIMINISHING RETURNS

Instead of looking at the efficiency of an economy in terms of how much input is required per unit of output—that is, the cost of production—we can look at how much output can be obtained from a given input. In both ways we can see that there is no fixed relationship between input and output but some general patterns that need to be kept in mind in discussions of economic systems—or even legal, political, and social systems. Generally, the pattern has been that increasing one input while other inputs remain constant, usually increases output—at first faster than the one input is increased, then in proportion, then slower, and finally there is an absolute reduction of output when the one input is added in unlimited quantities. The question is, why this pattern exists.

A lone man farming a vast expanse of land has a limited number of options as to how he will work this land. He may spread his labor thinly all over the whole land area, spending a substantial part of his workday walking over this area instead of actually tilling the soil, or he may decide that he will get more total output by cultivating only half of the land, putting more intensive labor there and cutting back on the amount of his walking from place to place, letting more of his energy go into the actual cultivation. Which of the two approaches he will use will depend on how the various considerations balance out in the individual case. The point here is merely to illustrate the kinds of options he has as a lone farmer (input), which can be compared to the options when there are two units of the same input—that is, two farmers on the same land.

While one farmer could either cultivate the whole land area as one unit or cultivate half the area and leave the other half uncultivated, two farmers have the option of cultivating all the area as a unit or cultivating both halves as separate units. That is, two farmers can either do what one farmer would have done or can, *in addition*, do things which one farmer could not have done. This is true also in the details of the work. For example, in transporting small objects into an area out in the field, two farmers may choose either to carry them or to throw them to one another. A single farmer has only the first option. In carrying heavy and/or awkward loads, one farmer is limited to getting grips in two places no further apart than the span of his arms; two farmers working together can get two sets of grips with each set being much further away than one person's arm span. In short, within a range of work activities, two farmers have all the options available to one farmer, plus some other options as well. How often they will choose to work separately and how often as a team depends upon what the advantages are in practice. The crucial point however is that *more options generally mean better results, where the larger number of options includes all the smaller number of options.* This principle has wide applications within economics and beyond economics, as will be seen in later discussions.

In the case of two farmers on a large tract of land, they can each do whatever one farmer could do and together they can do things that neither could do alone. In the absence of offsetting problems, we would therefore expect two farmers to produce more than twice the output of one farmer on the same ample expanse of land. In short, we may expect a rising output per unit of the input. For similar reasons, we might expect three farmers to also increase output more than in proportion to the increased input, since more elaborate organization of the inputs is now possible. How long the output would increase more than in proportion to the input would depend upon many specific facts, but what is important here is why it could not continue increasing this way forever. Beyond some point, the land would become crowded with people, and their getting into each other's way and distracting one another's attention would begin to offset the organizational advantages.

If the two farmers had been sharing the output as partners, they would—automatically, and perhaps even without thinking about it—have been monitoring each other's work, reducing the prospects of one's taking it easy at the expense of the other. The ease of monitoring and the certainty of being monitored would guard against the level of effort falling below the two farmer's own best judgments of the balance between ease and output. But when the number of farmers reached a hundred, no single farmer could equally easily watch the other ninety-nine, nor would each farmer be equally sure that his relaxations of effort would be detected by the others.

Even if all one hundred farmers had identical notions of how much output was worth how much effort, each farmer individually would have an incentive to put forth *less* than this effort, since his own individual shortcomings would have very little relationship to his own individual share of the output. They might all "know" in an abstract sort of way that the total effort was related to the total output, and so all might desire to keep everyone's performance up to par, but there is a great difference between this desire—even if universally shared—and an organizational way of achieving it. At the very least, devising and maintaining an organized system of monitoring cannot be free, and whether it would repay its cost is an empirical question. Monitoring costs (either the costs of monitoring or the loss of output if not monitored) are an additional factor offsetting the possibilities of rising output per unit of input.

The original assumption that larger numbers of people meant additional options without an offsetting loss of other options is only approximately true for small numbers of people. Crowding, distraction, and monitoring costs offset the gains made possible by cooperative organizational work. As more and more inputs are added, beyond some point, the negative factors outweigh the positive advantages, and there is a falling ratio of output to input. This is the law of diminishing returns—a basic economic principle, with implications that go far beyond economics.

The law of diminishing returns applies to inanimate inputs as well. Although some amount of fertilizer on the land may have a small incremental effect on the size of the crop, and twice as much may cause the increment to be more than twice as great, beyond some point more fertilizer no longer increases the crop in equal proportions, and it is even possible to reduce the crop with excess fertilizer.

Economic decision making within the constraints of a price system with profits and losses seldom leads to production in the region where more input leads to absolutely diminishing output. There is obviously no point spending hard cash for inputs whose incremental effect will be negative. However, this is not to say that such results do not happen, when the incentives in the particular decision-making process make it rational for the individual decision maker, however detrimental it may be to "society," which is not a decision-making unit.

Internal communication systems in large organizations are often open to many individuals who may wish to send memoranda, announcements, official documents, paychecks, survey questions, or plain gossip. The number and frequency of such internal communications influences how much attention the average recipient pays to each item. Infrequent arrivals of internal mail are likely to receive more attention per unit than a flood of material arriving every few hours. In other words, the law of diminishing returns operates, so that beyond some point there are diminishing increments of attention as the quantity of mail increases. With a sufficient inundation, there will be less total attention paid—less information effectively received—than if fewer communications had been sent. The situation can reach this level of absolutely diminishing returns only because there are virtually no costs to the numerous individual decision makers who decide whether to add more material to the internal communications system. They may all know that the recipients' attention and patience are already strained, but each individual sender also knows that his action alone will have very little effect on that. As long as it is worth the bother of typing or mimeographing, the sender has every incentive to send, because part of the costs created by his decision will be externalized to others, in the form of generally diminished attention. When they all do it, they all lose—but this happens only because "all" is not the decision-making unit.[2] A more serious social problem arises when whole institutions have incentives to push their activities well past the point of incrementally diminishing returns, into the region of absolutely diminished returns.

TIME

Among the constraints affecting economic trade-offs are those which depend on time. The choice between spending money on entertainment today and using that money to buy seeds to plant apple trees is not only a choice between two different sets of benefits; it is a choice among benefits to be received at two very different times. Other things being equal, the present is always preferred to the future, if only because life itself is uncertain and the future may never come, for the individual decision maker. Looked at another way, future benefits must be greater than present benefits to make it worthwhile to wait.[3] There is some level of difference that will make present and future benefits equally valuable to a particular individual at a particular time. How much difference and how much time are matters that vary from person to person and vary incrementally with the same person. To someone dying of thirst a gallon of water right now might be more valuable than a swimming pool two years from now, even though the same person under normal conditions would prefer to wait for the pool. In short, with intertemporal substitutions, as with substitutions at a given time, there is no such thing as "the" rate of substitution, either in production or consumption. There is also no such thing as "the" value of a given object, for the time when that object is to be received changes its value. A swimming pool *right now* would be more valuable than a gallon of water even to a man dying of thirst. Clearly, then, it is more valuable than a swimming pool two years from now. More generally, any given asset is of greater value, the sooner it is to be received. The legal right to that asset can be sold for more in the market, the sooner it will become available. Apple trees that are half grown will sell for more than apple trees that were just planted, and apple trees that are fully grown will sell for the highest price of all, even if the only differences among these trees are the times when they were planted—which is to say, the time left before they produce apples.

Like so many important economic principles, the discount for time is so simple that it is readily forgotten in the rush of practical decisions or at the sound of heady rhetoric. For example, state and municipal governments in financial distress may unilaterally postpone payment on their bonds, with the assurance that those bonds will later be paid off "in full." But even if this promise is carried out to the letter in money terms, the very fact that the bonds are paid off later means that they are *not* paid off "in full." A hundred dollars three years from now is worth nearly twenty-six dollars less than a hundred dollars today, when the interest rate is 8 percent—and this does not even allow for inflation. In other words, a three-year postponement is economically the same as a confiscation of about one-fourth the value of the asset, even if there is no inflation. With even mild inflation, it can easily amount to a confiscation of, or default on, a third or more of the total amount entrusted to the government by those who bought its bonds.

Merely moving any asset backward and forward in time changes its value substantially. This is demonstrable with economic assets measured in money, but the principle applies far more broadly in social institutions in general: "Justice delayed is justice denied" is an old legal axiom—and "the law's delay" is an expression that goes back at least as far as Shakespeare.[4] The dispatch or delay inherent in various institutional processes can be equally (or more) important than the end result conventionally expressed as if it were a constant value. The popular habit of referring to a fixed dollar amount, or a given physical thing, or a particular social outcome, as if these were also fixed values, without regard to the time involved, means more than intellectual confusion. It means opportunities for rule changes affecting "only" time to make major arbitrary changes in people's fate. Merely by such apparently innocuous decisions as changing the effective date of a law, modifying the retirement age, or lengthening a waiting period, the government can transfer billions of dollars around the economy, including directing some of it towards itself. Merely by lending to enterprises (including government-run enterprises) at an artificially low interest rate, the cost of their whole operation can be grossly misstated and a venture made to appear to be "paying its own way"—on paper. The movement of assets through time is a two-way movement. Not only may present benefits be postponed; future benefits may be moved forward into the present—at a discount corresponding to the interest premium paid (in market transactions) for postponement. An agricultural society can eat up the seeds needed for the next crop, increasing current food consumption at the expense of future food consumption. A nation may reduce its ability to defend itself militarily, thereby gaining additional consumer or governmental spending power in the present, at the expense of either higher military expenditures or forced capitulations in the future. The individual may gain in various ways by betraying his pledges and obligations, at the expense of lower future benefits from activities requiring credibility.

INVESTMENT AND DISINVESTMENT

Moving assets from the future to the present is never costless to the recipient, just as moving assets from the present to the future is never costless to the donor. The process of transforming current assets into future assets is known in economics as "investment." However, the process itself extends far beyond financial activities. When someone carefully puts his things away, at home or at work, he is deliberately sacrificing present time that could be used for other activities in order to require less time to find his things again in the future. When someone takes the trouble (and sometimes pain and embarrassment) to make his feelings clear to someone else, it is a deliberate loss of present psychic well-being in order to forestall a greater loss of future psychic well-being through misunderstandings. The purpose is to have a greater net psychic well-being over the relevant time span, just as the purpose of financial investments is to have a greater net worth over some relevant time span. The essential similarity between financial and nonfinancial "investment" processes has been noted by such economists as John Stuart Mill in the nineteenth century and Adam Smith in the eighteenth century, but it has been only the past generation of economists who have elaborated theories of "human capital" in its various forms of education, health care, migration, and other activities designed to enhance future well-being of either a financial or a psychic nature, so the term "disinvestment" can also apply to moving assets from the future into the present, without regard to whether financial or psychic assets are involved. Such phrases as "burning the candle at both ends," "a short life and a merry one," "eating up your capital," or "living off future generations" all refer to similar processes although measured in different units. Most expressions describing disinvestment have pejorative connotations, but there is nothing intrinsically wrong with a ninety-year-old man's selling some of his half-grown apple trees to pay for current expenditures on things to promote his present health, comfort, and happiness. To try to hold the trees until maturity might make less sense.

Disinvestments made by a given decision maker for himself must be distinguished from disinvestments made for him by others. The legal system provides safeguards against private individuals' disinvesting someone else's assets. However, there is no legal protection against the government itself doing the same thing. For example, governments' inflationary policies may disinvest part of any financial assets set aside for one's old age, leaving less future real assets in the hands of the individual who saved them and putting more present real assets in the hands of the government that issues the inflated currency. The transfer is no less real for having been implicit and therefore not subject to constitutional limitations on confiscation of property "without due process of law." Probably more assets have been confiscated this way than by the exercise of government's right of "eminent domain" under constitutional guarantees. Nor are those who have lost their savings predominantly wealthy people with large bank accounts or stocks and bonds. Much saving takes place in forms not usually thought of as savings—life insurance and employee pension funds, for example. Through pension funds, American workers own a higher percentage of the total industrial assets of the United States than do workers in an avowedly communist nation like Yugoslavia.[5] The confiscation of employee pension fund assets through inflation is not so much a redistribution from one income class to another as it is a redistribution from the pensioners' future assets to the government's present assets.

RISK

The element of time introduces the element of risk. Perhaps the most fundamental risk is that we may not live through the time required to see a given economic activity concluded and remunerated. Many other risks exist, of partial or total loss of whatever is invested, or even losses extending beyond the initial investment to reach other personal assets to cover damages or other liabilities incurred in the process of unsuccessfully seeking gain.

Although risks may be calculated mathematically, as in the actuarial tables of life insurance companies, the *cost* of a given risk is no more objective than any other cost. Some people can sleep soundly with their rent unpaid, and creditors threatening to repossess their car or attach their salary. Other people worry about their money in a government-insured bank account. In between are numerous gradations of individual concern for a given risk, and therefore a different psychic cost paid in carrying that risk, or different financial costs paid to reduce the risk. For example, bondholders may accept a lower rate of return than stockholders as the price they pay to reduce the risk of losing their investment.

The godlike approach to analyzing "society" and its (metaphorical) behavior often overlooks risk, the subjective nature of risk, and/or the wide variation of its cost among individuals. In the area of risk, as in some other areas, the diversity of individuals invalidates reasoning based on figures of speech about a society acting as if it were a single decision maker. With a given objective likelihood of various undesirable events, the costs of these risks to society at large can vary enormously, according to which particular members of the society are carrying how much of these various risks. If risky activities like drilling for oil wells (most wells have no oil) were financed by nervous people, the cost would be much higher than if such activities were financed by devil-may-care types who are happy to be able to dream of striking it rich some day. For an optimal distribution of risks, knowledge must somehow be communicated through the system as to who is more willing and who is more reluctant to bear the various levels of risk which are inherent in undertaking different economic (or other) activities. This kind of knowledge is far too specific and changing to be reduced to a science or to be mastered by "experts."

Each individual is of course an expert on his own degree of aversion to risk, and knows how much he wants to put aside for a rainy day, and roughly how he wants to distribute those savings as between cash in his pockets, deposits in an insured bank account, payments into a pension plan, investments in low-risk bonds, or speculation in oil or commodity futures. (For most people, zero is the amount that they are willing to risk on the last two activities.) On the other side of the market are numerous people who are knowledgeable about the specific techniques of producing specific things— that is, people who have the most accurate knowledge of just how risky particular ventures happen to be and what payoffs could be reasonably expected. In other words they know how much they can afford to pay in return for the use of resources needed to carry out their economic activities. They will try to pay as little as possible, just as creditors or investors will try to get as much as possible, but each knows how far he is prepared to go in a given direction. Each is an expert in his own situation, however little he may know about the other's situation, and the process of haggling for a deal—either directly or through such intermediary institutions as banks, insurance companies or mutual funds—is essentially a communication of social knowledge, each fragment of which originates with the individual who is in a position to know the most that is known on his tiny part of the subject.

This knowledge is never perfect, nor can it be, regardless of the kind of political or economic institutions in a particular country. From this process emerges a sorting out of those activities involving the least risk, being financed (at lowest costs) by those least willing to bear risks and most willing to leave the big payoffs to those ready to take big gambles. This need not involve direct individual investment in specific economic enterprises, and usually does not. Incoming funds (savings deposits, insurance premiums, etc.) are pooled by intermediary institutions and the overall risks reduced further by spreading the investments around in numerous, relatively safe, ventures which pay modest amounts for the use of the money to buy the resources they need. Although the transactions are usually between impersonal organizations, the very personal aversion to risk of those supplying the money is the controlling factor. A bank cannot bounce a depositor's check for his rent because the bank itself has "insufficient funds," due to risky investments that did not work out. An insurance company cannot refuse to pay for a policyholder's operation or funeral because the oil drilling it financed did not turn up any gushers. Any such result in these kinds of institutions—patronized by people averse to risk—would bring on the immediate destruction of the financial institution itself, and probably criminal investigation of its officials. On the other hand, nothing nearly as dire happens when a corporation reduces (or skips) a dividend payment to its stockholders, whose risk taking is understood by all to be part of the reason why they receive dividends at all. And for people investing in wildcat oil drilling operations, there may not be much likelihood of their getting anything at all on any predictable date, and with only the hope of a magnificent payoff now and then. In short, though these various financial organizations have no feelings, their behavior is constrained by the different feelings of those who supply their respective investment funds.

No single individual, nor any collection of individuals, could have in their heads all the complex technical information on production processes and the nuances of personal feeling involved in matching millions of investment sources and users. The most efficient and imposing bank, corporation, or government bureau has only scratched the surface. The astronomical amount of knowledge in the whole system is sorted and coordinated in fragments by the simple process of each transactor seeking the best deal from his own subjective viewpoint and not necessarily (or even usually) by knowing *why* the deal that suits him best emerged as it did from the millions of other possibilities in the market.

While risk may be easy to understand by considering formal organizations and transactions designed primarily to deal with risk, its effects are pervasive far beyond such situations. Anyone who buys an automobile knows (or discovers) that he is not really buying transportation, but is in fact buying a given *probability* of transportation on given occasions. If he keeps the car long enough, there will be occasions when he has to walk or take the bus or get a ride with a friend. He may do this voluntarily, as an investment, by leaving his car in the shop for regular maintenance, or he may forego that investment for the present benefits of constant use of the automobile, and involuntarily walk, take a bus, etc., at a later time when the car breaks down as a result of lack of maintenance. Cars which are very similar in the quality of ride, convenience of operation, or aesthetic considerations, may sell for very different prices if they differ substantially in their respective probabilities of continuous service—that is, if they differ in the frequency of breakdowns or the amount of maintenance required. These may be differences in brands of cars or differences in the same car purchased new and used. In either case, cars' price differences need not reflect transportation differences, but may reflect simply risk differences. As in the case of other kinds of risks, however objective the probabilities may be, the costs of risk are highly diverse with respect to individual situations and subjective preferences. An auto mechanic or someone else who is handy with tools may find the cheapness of a particular car more than compensates its special troubles, while a heart surgeon with no understanding of engines may find a car that won't start an intolerable problem when he has to rush to treat someone in the intensive care ward.

The fact that costs differ vastly with respect to individual knowledge and preferences creates an opportunity for people who specialize in bearing particular kinds of risks. A farmer may have considerable knowledge of how to grow a particular crop, but little knowledge of the economic data or complex principles which cause the prospective price that he can expect for his harvest to vary by large amounts as of planting time. Someone else who has specialized in studying the economic facts and principles may have a much narrower range of expectations of future prices for that crop, even if he could not actually grow the crop himself if his life depended on it. Either individual could directly acquire the knowledge that the other possesses by investing the time needed for both the theoretical understanding and the practical experience to apply it. A less costly alternative may be to transact with one another on the basis of their existing knowledge. The farmer can reduce his risk at the cost of selling his crop during the planting season for somewhat less than the average of his range of expectations of prices at harvest time. If he thinks the price of his produce is going to range somewhere between sixty cents apiece and a dollar apiece, he might consider eighty cents apiece as his best guess, but accept seventy-eight cents apiece as a guaranteed price in advance—in effect paying someone else two cents apiece to take the risk off his hands. The buyer may accept this if he has either a more optimistic estimate, or reason to have much more confidence than the farmer in the same estimate of eighty cents apiece, or merely stronger nerves.

Buying for a guaranteed price and selling at whatever price later emerges in the market is a way of earning a residual claim to the difference. This residual claim may be a positive amount or a negative amount, as many a bankrupt speculator has learned. People who are not pure speculators may nevertheless engage in economic speculation as a part of their normal activities. A farmer who plants in the spring without any guaranteed price for his harvest the following fall is working as a speculator as well as a farmer, whether he thinks of it in those terms or not. A student who chooses to study for a particular profession is also speculating on the state of that profession in future years, as well as on what his own values will be in future years, since changing values may make him dissatisfied even if the profession itself is exactly as he foresaw it. Perhaps the greatest speculation of all is bringing a child into the world, where he may become the pride and joy of your life or cloud or destroy whatever happiness you may find from other sources.

RESIDUAL CLAIMS

The typical business enterprise buys or rents its inputs for a fixed price, and sells the resulting output for whatever price emerges in the market, earning a residual claim loosely referred to as "profit," though often discovered to be a loss. Strict economists point out that much of what is conventionally called "profit," especially in a small, owner-operated business, is nothing more than wages received in a variable form. Even a successful owner-operated business—and the bankruptcy rate is high—often pays no more under the name "profits" than the proprietor would have earned for the same amount of work for someone else who paid him under the name of "wages." To determine what the enterprise itself is earning, it would be necessary to deduct the wages for the proprietor's work and the interest he could have earned elsewhere on the money he has invested in the business. By this economists' standard, many successful small businesses are making no profit at all. In many cases the residual claim after such deductions would be negative, so that the owner operator is in effect paying for the privilege of being his own boss.

In a large corporate business, the executives are in fact paid salaries under the name of salaries, and the residual claimants are the stockholders. If the residual claim is positive, the tax collectors also share in it, though if it is negative, they do not. ("Win and the government wins with you; lose and you lose alone.") Both the friends and critics of private business tend to refer to them as "profit-making" enterprises. But this is the fallacy of defining a process by its hoped-for results, rather than by its actual characteristics. A similar fallacy occurs in discussions of the "cooling off" period under a labor injunction, "public interest" law firms, "sensitivity training," and "quality, integrated education." What the actual business process involves is the payment of some people at fixed rates (employees, executives, bondholders) and others in residual claims (stockholders and sometimes tax collectors). Viewed in retrospect, the particular method of payment means little. A given fixed amount can always be made equivalent to some given variable amount, with appropriate discount or premium for time and/or risk. Indeed, different methods of payment can be mixed, as when employees have profit-sharing plans and executives are paid partly in stocks, or when investors have some mixture of stocks and bonds. It is only when viewed *prospectively* that the method of payment has socially significant effects.

Residual claims set in motion different behavior patterns from fixed claims. Whoever has the legal title to the residual claim has an incentive to make that residual—the difference between production costs and consumer value—as great as possible. The same thing, from a social point of view, is that the residual claimant has an incentive to supply what is desired by consumers at the least sacrifice of inputs used for things desired by other consumers. To the residual claimant, these social consequences of his behavior are secondary at best. But from the point of view of the economy at large, this behavior pattern that grows out of the *attempt* to maximize residual claims is crucial, and whether the residual claim turns out in fact to be large or small, or even positive or negative, is secondary.

The role of the residual claims method of payment is especially important in situations where multiple inputs and numerous persons are used, raising the cost of monitoring individual performances. It is always possible to hire people to watch other people, but how conscientiously they will watch and report is as problematical as the original behavior that requires watching. Hiring more monitors to monitor the first set of monitors merely raises the same question on a new level rather than providing an answer. While the residual claimants cannot monitor the *process*, they can easily monitor the *results*. They know whether the residual claims of one organization are greater or less than another—and this provides incentives for each organization to monitor its own performances so as to keep costs low and therefore the residual claims high. How they achieve this result is of little interest to the residual claimant. In a broader social point of view, it means that the need for knowledge in the system is minimized, because the ultimate monitors can effectively monitor results without needing to know the specific techniques or conscientiousness of those who directly produce the results. The residual claims method of payment creates a set of monitors *who do not need to be monitored themselves*, because they have the incentive of self-interest to see that residual claims are maximized.

If the management is doing well, but could do better, it is not even necessary for the residual claimants to know that in order for something to happen. If some alternative management knows it, the prospective residual claims under that alternative management are greater than existing claims under existing management. The alternative management can afford to pay existing residual claimants more than their claims are worth under existing conditions in order to buy control of the corporation, improve its efficiency, and make larger residual claims in the future. In other words, one corporation "takes over" another by buying up the less efficient corporation's stock at prices that represent more than its current value to stockholders, because the more efficient management can earn more with the same plant, equipment, and employees. Through competitive bidding for a controlling share of stocks, knowledge is effectively applied by those who have it—other managements—even though the initial owners might have been insufficiently knowledgeable to realize that the executives initially in charge were not getting the most out of the resources of the firm. Looking at this from the point of view of the efficiency of the economy as a whole, corporations are monitored not only by existing residual claimants but by prospective residual claimants as well—each with the incentive of self-interest, eliminating the need for additional (and endless) layers of monitors.

Viewed in retrospect, residual claims are not very significant as a percentage of national income (about 10 percent) or as a return on investment (about 10 percent per annum). As a percentage of the selling price of goods, residual claims can be quite trivial. Supermarkets average about a penny profit on a dollar's worth of groceries, and only the huge volume of business they do every day makes this add up to a profitable operation. It is not as a retrospective sum that residual claims have a major impact on the economy. It is as a prospective incentive that it profoundly affects behavior and the efficiency of production. If residual claimants were guaranteed in advance the very same sums which they end up earning, the whole economic system would function differently. With everyone in the economic system essentially on guaranteed salaries, the monitoring problems would be massive.

THE PHYSICAL FALLACY

From the discussion so far, it may be apparent that a given physical object has a value that varies greatly according to the location of that object in time and space, and according to the risks associated with it. Otherwise people would not go to the trouble and expense of transporting things, or insuring them, or buying them on credit with interest charges. Indeed, no exchanges of goods (for other goods or for money) would ever take place, unless the same physical things had different values to different people. Yet the opposite view—that a given physical object is always a given value—has had a profound effect on human history. Over the centuries, highly diverse consequences have followed from a belief in the invariable value of a physical object—a belief that can be characterized as "the physical fallacy."

In medieval times, the physical fallacy led to the doctrine that an object had a "just price" based upon objective costs incurred by the producer and not upon the subjective valuation of the consumer. Any other price was considered morally sinful and as something that should be legally prohibited.[6] A special case of the "just price" was the medieval prohibition on usury, which has not wholly disappeared, even in the modern world. Because the "same" sum of money was returned as borrowed, it was considered cheating to require additional payments (interest). But the whole transaction was made precisely because the same sum of money did not have the same value at different times. A borrower who could save enough to repay a loan by a given time could instead have waited until that same time and used those same savings for whatever purpose for which the loan was used. That he preferred having the loan immediately—that is, preferred money at one time over the same sum at another time—was the whole point of borrowing. Both the "just price" doctrine and the usury prohibition refused to recognize differences in value due solely to location in time or space. Both were among the earliest and most persistent forms of the physical fallacy.

An economist who was a prisoner of war during World War II found many of the characteristics of a market economy spontaneously arising in the prisoner-of-war camp, despite the absence of the established institutions on which they are supposed to depend.[7] A large volume of trade arose among prisoners who received identical rations and identical Red Cross packages, indicating that (1) the same things had different values to different people at a given time, and that (2) the same things had different values when moved back and forth through time, since those prisoners who saved various items to the end of a ration period could lend them to others who had run out, collecting a larger quantity of the same items in return after the new rations or Red Cross packages were received. What is of wider social significance is that those prisoners who performed these services were both widely utilized and deeply resented. The physical fallacy arose as spontaneously as the transactions which demonstrated its falsity.

Whether in medieval society, a prisoner-of-war camp, or a modern market economy, the "middleman" essentially changes the location of things in space and time. If the same physical thing is assumed to have the same value without regard to space or time, then the middleman is simply cheating people. How this situation could persist over time, through repeated transactions, is unexplained. If A sells to B who sells to C, and B is simply cheating, then both A and C can benefit by direct transactions with each other—A charging somewhat more than he normally charges B, and C paying somewhat less than he normally pays B. Why would both then *continue* to deal with each other through a middleman? Obviously they would not.

In reality, they deal through the middleman because he is changing the value of things by relocating them, holding them to times that are more convenient, assuming various risks by stocking inventories—and doing so at *less cost* than either the producer or the consumer could. Otherwise either the producer would sell at retail or the consumer would buy wholesale, and either could perform these middleman services for himself. But given the highly fragmented nature of knowledge, those who have mastered the complexities of the production process have seldom also mastered the very different complexities of inventory management and numerous other services performed by middlemen in the process of relocating things in time and space. Consumers typically lack both the knowledge and the economies of scale needed for low cost inventory storage. Storing wholesale quantities of various goods in the home means having a bigger home, and the higher cost of a bigger home will seldom be covered by the "savings" from buying wholesale. In other words, purchasing storage space in a residential neighborhood is almost always more expensive than purchasing storage space in a warehouse district. In short, middlemen can continue to exist only insofar as they can perform certain functions more cheaply than either the producer or the consumer. But no matter how varied and complex these functions may be, they amount ultimately to relocating things in time and space, and the physical fallacy which denies value to that operation necessarily indicts middlemen as mere cheaters.

No small part of the historic anti-Semitism of Europe (and corresponding anti-Chinese feeling in many Asian countries) is due to the Jews' role as middlemen. Legally—that is, forcibly—denied access to many occupations in the production of goods, Jews could survive in Europe only by finding interstitial services not covered by the sweeping discriminatory bans against them. They became middlemen in the movement of goods and money over time and space—the latter because the Catholic Church's moral prohibitions against charging interest did not apply to them. The virtually universal dislike and suspicion of middlemen focused on an ethnically-identifiable group of people, separated by religion and customs from the rest of the population, and therefore a perfect target. The economic success and political vulnerability of the Jews over the centuries has been paralleled by that of the Chinese middleman minority throughout Asia. In both cases, general discrimination has been punctuated by sporadic confiscations, mass expulsions and mob violence. The history of both groups (and of other middlemen minorities in other parts of the world) has wider implications for the political vulnerability of market economies in general.

Perhaps the greatest achievement of market economies is in economizing on the amount of knowledge needed to produce a given economic result. That is also their greatest political vulnerability. The public can get the economic benefits of such systems by judging results without understanding processes. But in their political behavior, the public must judge processes—including economic processes of which they may be ignorant or misinformed. Public misunderstandings can lead not only to misinterpretations of economic benefits as harm, but to actual harm resulting from policies designed to "correct" perceived problems. Once the process is underway, every perceived problem—whatever its reality or origin—calls for political solution, and these "solutions" tend to create a never-ending supply of new problems to be "solved."

Lenin said that "Anti-Semitism is the socialism of fools." In other words, Jews were being singled out for criticism on the basis of arguments which would more logically apply as a general indictment of the whole capitalist economy. That is the argument here as well—that both have been criticized on the basis of the physical fallacy. Not only Marxism or socialism in general, but a wide variety of other revolutionary or reform movements incorporate a belief that those who directly handle physical objects are "really" the producers of economic benefits. Even Adam Smith said such things at times,[8] though it was inconsistent with the rest of his message. The physical fallacy has a long and varied pedigree.

Since man does not create physical matter, those who handle material objects in the production process are not producers in that sense. Economic benefits result from the transformation of matter in form, location, or availability (intellectually or temporally). It is these transformations that create economic benefits valued by consumers, and whoever arranges such transformations contributes to the value of things, whether his hands actually come into contact with physical objects or not.

The physical fallacy typically has temporal blinders as well. The production process is arbitrarily conceived to begin at a point after many prerequisites have already been assembled, and only those people actively involved beyond that arbitrary point are conceived to be involved *at all* (or "really") in causing the result desired by the consumer. Those involved earlier, before the arbitrary point at which the story was begun to be depicted, then appear at the end—as if for the first time—as recipients of unearned proceeds. Aside from ethical questions about using such a depiction, intellectually it is essentially a linear picture of a circular process.

In the full circle, the consumers' desires as to physical characteristics and location in time and space must be ascertained by someone who is able to assemble the human and other resources necessary to produce that combination of material and temporal results. Only after the subjective intangibles of consumer evaluation and producers' costs in risks and time preferences have been balanced and resolved prospectively can the mechanical portions of the physical process proceed. Once the process has gone full circle, it can continue and repeat only insofar as the actual valuations of the end results by the consumers prove sufficient, in retrospect, to cover costs incurred on the basis of prospective estimates. It is a knowledge process, based on estimation and feedback. The physical process is only an intermediary consequence of these intangible estimates, and can continue only insofar as the estimates of some are subsequently validated by the subjective evaluations of others. The risky nature of this process is evidenced not only by the vast numbers of business bankruptcies each year, but by the fact that even such successful giant businesses as the Chrysler Corporation or U.S. Steel have operated at millions of dollars' losses in some years. But these risks are inherent in a situation where some produce for others, rather than being artifacts of a particular set of institutions. Other kinds of economic systems may resolve or conceal these risks in various ways, but the risks and the costs they entail will not go away.

Much of the Marxian *tableau* (and related social visions) depend, in a crucial way, on analyzing in retrospect only surviving and successful businesses. In this approach, the whole market process—risks, estimates, consumer validation, etc.—all evaporates, while the analysis concentrates on selected results in terms of theoretical examples of survivors. Because firms can survive only insofar as prices cover costs, this vision of survivors-only can proceed as if it is axiomatic that prices are somehow automatically suspended above costs, with the gap between them containing a profit to be siphoned off by those who happen to hold the legal title to the means of production—this arbitrary title being the economic cause as well as the institutional mechanism behind their proceeds. To generalize about any group from the experience of its successful survivors alone is often to miss the whole point of the process in which the group as a whole is involved. Using such an approach, one could, for example, prove that no one was killed in World War II.

Where such a vision of the market economy proceeds empirically rather than theoretically, it can appear plausible only for relatively brief historical periods. The great successes of one era tend to disappear into oblivion in subsequent eras—witness *Life* magazine, the Graflex Corporation, and W. T. Grant, all of whom were once giants dominating their respective fields. The disappearance of these once dominant enterprises within the past generation is part of a longer history of such disappearances. Virtually none of the top industrial giants of a hundred years ago are still with us today. Such disappearances are perfectly understandable in a vision of a risky process of estimation and subsequent validation. They are hard to explain in a vision of prices mysteriously suspended above costs for the convenience of "capitalists."

A revealing episode in the early career of Walt Disney may illustrate the physical fallacy on a smaller and more human scale. Back in the 1920s, when Disney first emerged as a cartoonist, his early successes led him to found a studio and to employ other artists to draw the thousands of pictures required for animated cartoon movies. Disney Studios was particularly successful with an early cartoon character called Oswald Rabbit, whose copyright was held by a movie distributor rather than by Disney. This distributor decided to eliminate the need to pay Disney by hiring away his cartoonists and both producing and marketing the product. From the standpoint of the physical fallacy, Disney was superfluous. He neither drew the cartoons nor transported the films to theaters nor showed them to the public. The distributor, with the Disney staff and the copyright on Disney's character, expected to profit from his *coup*—but without Disney's ideas the previously valuable character suddenly became worthless as a money-maker at the box office. What had really been sold all along were Disney's ideas and fantasies. The physical things—the drawings, the film, and the theaters—were merely vehicles. It was only a matter of time before another set of vehicles could be arranged and the ideas incorporated in a new character—Mickey Mouse—which Disney copyrighted in his own name.[9]

Many of the products which create a modern standard of living are only the physical incorporations of ideas—not only the ideas of an Edison or Ford but the ideas of innumerable anonymous people who figure out the design of supermarkets, the location of gasoline stations, and the million mundane things on which our material well-being depends. It is those ideas that are crucial, not the physical act of carrying them out. Societies which have more people carrying out physical acts and fewer people supplying ideas do not have higher standards of living. Quite the contrary. Yet the physical fallacy continues on, undaunted by this or any other evidence.

OPTIMALITY

Because each individual has his own set of preferences, there is no single standard of values by which one economic system might be said to be better or worse than another absolutely, or even to be better or worse compared to its own performance at some other time. How could an observer say whether more pineapples and less beer was better than the reverse, or whether more growth was enough to balance a reduction in employment? But because there is no *absolute* standard, that does not mean that there is no standard at all. Although we cannot reduce all the different sets of individual preferences to one set, we can conceive of an optimal performance by an economy as representing the satisfaction of the diverse sets of preferences to such an extent that no one could be made any better off (by his own standards) without making someone else worse off (by his own different standards). Economists call this "Pareto optimality," after the Italian economist who conceived it and analyzed its implications.

A theoretically perfect economy, operating with unlimited knowledge, no external costs or benefits paid for outside the units that created them, and no monopoly or government intervention, would achieve an optimal allocation of resources under existing technological constraints. With higher technological levels, there would be more output and more satisfaction of tastes, but there is some optimum level and mixture of output for each level of technological possibilities. The existence of a market—that is, the possibility of uncontrolled exchange at the option of the transactors—means that if A could be made better off by changing his mixture of goods, services, leisure, assets, etc., without making B, C, or D, etc., any worse off, he and the other parties who have what he wants could swap to their mutual advantage. If A can be made better off by $2.00 worth, without making B any worse off, then he can make it worth B's while to swap by offering him a dollar extra and keeping a dollar for himself.

There has, of course, never been any such ideal economy under capitalism, socialism, feudalism, or any other system. The concept does, however, serve as a benchmark by which to (1) measure the performance of one economy against another, and against its own performance at other times, and (2) to pinpoint the reasons why particular activities, institutions or policies do or do not lead toward the theoretical optimum.

Government constraints on the terms which individual transactors can choose among for themselves tend to reduce the number of transactions desired and carried out. If there are various possible sets of transactions terms which would be mutually acceptable to A and B, there is likely to be a smaller set of terms simultaneously acceptable to A, B, and C—where C is the government. As the government adds its own set of prerequisites to those of the negotiating parties, the number of negotiations that result in mutual agreement is almost certain to decline. Various forms of government price control, minimum wage laws, interest ceilings, etc., reduce the number of mutually desired transactions—which are the only kinds of transactions actually carried out in a voluntary, market economy. The government may determine and decree a "living wage" under a minimum wage law, but unless the worker actually finds an employer willing to pay him that much, he will remain unemployed with a hypothetical right.

Similarly, either an individual monopoly or a collusion of buyers and sellers acting in concert may set prices that are not mutually acceptable to as large a number of potential transactors as under competition. The real harm done by such monopolistic combinations is not so much in setting their *own* terms for transacting, but in being able to forcibly preclude *other* potential transactors from entering the competition to offer more advantageous terms. Without the power to exclude others, monopolistic negotiators would soon find themselves with competitors and without the transactions they need for their own economic well-being. Business must be able to keep out imports, restrict the entry of competing firms, or make price-cutting illegal. Labor unions must be able to blockade "scabs," boycott nonunion output, or keep teenage potential competitors out of the labor market with child labor regulations and compulsory school attendance laws. It is not in setting their own transactions terms—which they could never persist in, in the face of unlimited competition—but in forcibly precluding others that monopolistic organizations (business or labor) lead the economy away from its optimal performance.

Forcibly precluding competitors means either threatening violence one's self (as in some labor disputes) or having the government threaten violence by passing a law or issuing regulations. Government edicts without a threat of violence are mere suggestions, and suggestions by themselves ("jawboning") have a notorious record of ineffectiveness in the economy. The fact that actual violence does not usually occur in no way undermines the crucial importance of violence in the outcome. Most armed robberies also do not lead to actual violence: common sense usually causes the victim to turn over his money without a fight and causes the robber to take the money and go. Yet no one would deny that the prospect of violence is central to armed robbery, even if in retrospect it turns out that there is seldom actual violence in the commission of that crime. The government's threatened violence is not direct corporal punishment for violating laws and regulations. Rather it is a threat to take assets by force—either in money ("fines" or "damages") or in kind (legal rulings restricting the behavior, including the continued existence, of the firm in question). It is violence in the same sense in which armed robbery is violence. The power of the government is so overwhelming to the private individual or institution that it is seldom necessary to add that defiance of the government rulings will cause policemen or soldiers to forcibly drag the offender away to jail.

The role of prices as transmitters of knowledge is more readily seen in a changing economy than in a static one. If the economy maintained the same technological capabilities at all times, and tastes were unchanging and population size stationary, one way or another most of the essential knowledge about how things ought to be produced would eventually percolate through the system. When all these (and other) variables are changing constantly, however, the knowledge problems become staggering—if viewed from the standpoint of a given individual trying to understand it all. But if, for example, new deposits of iron ore are discovered at a time when there is a growing demand for office furniture and a declining supply of trees, all that the stores that sell office furniture need to know is that the wholesale price of steel desks, tables, and cabinets is falling relative to the wholesale price of the same items made of wood. They may do no more than reflect these relative price relationships in the retail prices they charge for steel and wooden office furniture. Those consumers who absolutely swear by either steel or wooden office furniture may just continue their respective preferences, but others, who are either more flexible or more pressed for cash, will tend to substitute the material that is getting cheaper for the material that is growing more expensive. The net result is that the economy as a whole incrementally substitutes the material that is becoming more abundant for the material that is becoming more scarce, without either the consumers, the retailers, or even

74

the wholesalers necessarily understanding *why* prices are changing the way they are.

In short, nobody needs to know the whole story in order for the economy to convey the relevant information through prices and secure the same adjustments as if everyone had known. Someone somewhere far back in the production process undoubtedly knows why iron ore is becoming more abundant, but he may or may not know the relative scarcity of wood, and it is doubtful if he has concerned himself with anything as remote or as specialized as the market for office furniture. Yet his knowledge is transmitted through prices to people with whom he has no direct contact.

Economic optimality is not moral justification. This is especially so in a changing economy, where rewarding "merit" may be incompatible with re-allocating resources in accordance with changing technology and changing tastes. In a totally unchanging economy, it is conceivable that the hardest working, most foresighted, imaginative, or skilled individuals would end up with earnings reflecting these valuable characteristics, so that economic efficiency and morally justified rewards would both result. In an economy constantly changing in technology and taste, however, rewarding "merit" and efficiently re-allocating resources are often contradictory goals.

When the automobile began to replace the horse and buggy, a conscientious, hard-working and intelligent buggy-manufacturer could not earn what someone with the same characteristics was earning in the automobile industry. That is precisely why and how people and capital were transferred out of the horse-and-buggy industry. It is why and how they (or others) were transferred into the automobile industry. The disparities in rewards for equal effort, risk, ability, etc., are precisely the systemic means of voluntarily transferring human and non-human resource inputs from one place to another in a changing economy. If they are to be equally rewarded for "merit"—that is, for their input—regardless of how this affects output, or the desirability of that output to consumers, then either transfers must be involuntary (based on orders from authorities) or else the transfers are unlikely to take place at all, leaving the economy stagnant.

While some losses and gains from changing economic conditions may reflect differences in foresight, many are windfall losses and gains, based on things which neither the gainers nor the losers were able to predict on the basis of their knowledge or understanding beforehand. At one time, before uses were discovered for petroleum, the presence of oil in a piece of land lowered its value, since this unaesthetic ooze could find its way to the water supply or make a nuisance of itself elsewhere. It was the kind of land that unscrupulous operators would unload on the unsuspecting. Some people found themselves owning land with oil on it through gullibility—but when such land later became valuable, the owners became just as rich as if they had wisely foreseen it all.

Since the total income from residual claims is only about 10 percent of national income, the purely windfall portion of this 10 percent can hardly be a major element of national income. In view of the very large windfall gains and losses involved in life in general (economically and otherwise), it is hard to explain, on purely rational grounds, the enormous concern over this particular deviation from strict "merit" reward. The country or the period of history of one's birth can easily halve or double one's life expectancy and change one's income by factors of ten or a hundred times, and the difference between being born malformed, or mentally retarded, or to abusive parents—rather than merely being "normal"—has consequences that dwarf other unmerited inequalities that happen to be quantifiable.

The role of inherent risks, growing out of high costs of knowledge, is ignored in analyses which proceed as if an omniscient observer is describing predetermined events in an economic or social system. It is precisely the lack of omniscience which is responsible for many institutional features and many social and economic results. Windfall gains and losses—whether in the sale price of land or in the difference between wages in a growing versus a declining industry—are part of these phenomena. Alternative institutions must be judged not by how they would operate with implicitly given knowledge but how they function in the face of uncertainty and risk. It is always possible to institutionally prevent or confiscate "unmerited" gains or losses, at a sufficiently high cost in enforcement efforts, reduction of freedom of choice, or losses in allocational efficiency. But eliminating the social phenomena growing out of uncertainty or risk in no way reduces the uncertainty or risk themselves, but merely changes the way the system as a whole can adjust to them.

To reward "merit" is to reward some subjective estimate of input as judged by some unitary scale of values applied by some observer(s). To reward output is to reward tangible results as assessed by those actually using the output, in the light of their own respective, diverse preferences. Only by the rarest coincidence would these different procedures lead to the same result. The question, then, is what is to be gained by substituting one set of surrogate preferences for diverse individual preferences, and adding the costs of consensus about values?

The issue of "merit" and reward is part of a more general set of issues revolving around so-called "income distribution." The familiar metaphor of "income distribution" conceals the crucial fact that most income is *not* distributed, either in capitalist, socialist, feudal, or most other economic systems. People are paid for services rendered, either by themselves or by their property. Some varying amount of income is also distributed from some central governmental funds, usually without regard to services rendered. It is confusing at best and disingenuous at worst to talk as if we simply have distribution A now, and it is merely a question of having distribution B instead. We currently do *not* distribute most income in any kind of modern economy—and the case for a particular distribution is a case not only for a changed result but for a revolutionary change in institutional processes from what now exist *either in socialist economies or capitalist economies.*

The moral question of how does one "justify" the existing "distribution" also misstates the issue. What is called the existing distribution of income is simply a set of retrospective data at a given point in time. These data are generated by an ongoing process in which buyers choose among alternative products available at varying prices, and the sum total of those prices paid during some time span become various people's incomes. The question is not what to decide, as to whether specific retrospective data are justified, but rather who shall decide which prospective transactions are justified on what terms in an on-going process. More to the point, shall observers who experience neither the benefits nor the cost use force (the government) to supersede the judgments of those who do? The issue is not between one particular set of statistical results and another. The issue is between one kind of social process and another, and between one set of decision-makers and another.

When large incomes growing out of residual claims are involved, no one has decided that the *total* was either justified or unjustified, nor is it clear who would possess the knowledge to do so. What each buyer has decided, however, is whether what he himself received was worth it to him—a subject on which he is much better informed. To call for a justification of the overall totals is to call in fact for a *re*-justification by nontransacting observers to supersede the individual decisions of the transactors. Sometimes the moral issue is posed in more apparently neutral terms as claiming that optimality is meaningful only if one "accepts" the initial distribution of income. Pareto optimality is meaningful only if one accepts the criterion of individual satisfaction by varying individual preference standards. Once such a conception of optimality is used, it is difficult to see how another unitary set of preference standards can supersede this in the interest of "correcting" the "income distribution."

The timeless nature of "income distribution" data misstates issues in another way. Individuals typically have varying incomes over a lifetime—usually smaller incomes at the beginning and larger after more experience, skill, etc., have been accumulated. Any set of data as of any given point in time freezes millions of people at many different phases of their respective life cycle. Those in the lowest fourth at any given time include many young people who will be in the top fourth at some later point in time. It is misleading to say that an intern is "poor" while a doctor is rich, when in fact intern is simply a stage on the way to becoming a doctor. By "rich" and "poor" we think of people who are, in some long-run sense, in high or low income brackets. But an instantaneous statistical picture counts the genuinely poor and those with transiently low income the same. Concern for genuine poverty is a reasonable concern, but it is something else to be exercised over the fact that young adults do not yet earn as much as their parents or grandparents. The average income of families headed by someone in the forty-five to fifty-four year old bracket is nearly double the average income of families headed by someone twenty-four years old or younger.[10] This is greater than the ratio of white income to black income. Of the top wealth-holders in the country (with assets of $60,000 in 1974), almost twice as many were over fifty as under fifty.[11] These age phenomena permeate income statistics which are commonly interpreted as if they were social class phenomena.

SUMMARY AND IMPLICATIONS

Economic trade-offs involve trying to produce the most value at the least cost. An individual or an organization may think of costs in money terms. But from the point of view of the economy as a whole, costs are ultimately *foregone opportunities* to use the same resource inputs for producing something else. In short, weighing prices against costs is ultimately weighing one resource use against another.

The terms on which one use can be traded off for another use vary incrementally. There are subjective differences in the values of goods to a consumer, partly according to how much of each he already has. There are objective differences in production costs, according to how much of each is being produced. There are objective differences in production costs, according to whether production takes place when equipment is underutilized or when it is already straining at its capacity. The law of diminishing returns applies in both production and consumption, and insures that tradeoffs are incrementally variable rather than categorically fixed in some rigid "priority" ranking. Price fluctuations are one evidence of this incremental variability and a means of transmitting knowledge of current trade-off rates through the economy.

Trade-offs take place not only at a given time, but between one time and another. The value of the same physical good (or sum of money) varies with the time at which it becomes available. "Investment" is the process of postponing the availability of benefits, and the terms of the trade-off of present for future benefits are shown by the incremental difference in value between the two times—the so-called "return on investment." This is most easily visualized in a money economy, but the principle is the same in an economy run by orders rather than prices. The same principle can also be seen in noneconomic activities, such as putting things away properly to facilitate finding them later, or explaining oneself to others to avoid future misunderstandings.

Price changes convey the changing relative scarcities of different resources, even to persons with no direct knowledge of any of the resources. The *results* can and must be compared by people unacquainted with the respective *processes* that produced these results. Price movements economize on the knowledge needed for given decisions. Where such prices are artificially maintained by force, rather than through voluntary transactions, they convey misinformation as to relative scarcities, and therefore lead the economy away from the optimal use of resources. Accurate prices resulting from voluntary exchange permit the economy to achieve optimal performance in terms of satisfying each individual as much as he can be satisfied, by his own standards, without sacrificing others by their own respective standards. The results must, however, appear "chaotic" to any observer judging by any given set of standards applied to all. Third-party assessments of the individual terms of the transactions—or of the "income distribution" totals arising from these transactions—are equally unlikely to coincide with the varying individual assessments of the trade-offs made. Neither in economic nor in moral terms is it the question whether a given set of statistical income results for a given time span is justified. The most basic question is not what is best but *who shall decide* what is best. The general case for third-party overriding of individual transactors' preferences is seldom made explicit, and so cannot itself be assessed. Its many oblique versions rely heavily on insinuation, metaphor, and the physical fallacy. Figures of speech about "society" as decision maker ignore the diversity of individual preferences which are responsible for many of the very phenomena in question—whether economic, social, or political.

Perhaps the most widespread misunderstanding of economics is that it applies solely to financial transactions. Frequently this leads to statements that "there are noneconomic values" to consider. There are, of course, noneconomic values. Indeed, there are *only* noneconomic values. Economics is not a value itself but merely a method of trading off one value against another. If statements about "noneconomic values" (or, more specifically, "social values" or "human values") are meant to deny the inherent results of trade-offs, or to exempt some particular value from the trade-off process, then such propositions need to be made explicit and confronted. Dedication to high and selfless ideals can be no more effectively demonstrated than by trading off financial gains in the interest of such ideals. This is an economic trade-off.

Prices are important not because money is considered paramount but because prices are a fast and effective conveyor of information through a vast society in which fragmented knowledge must be coordinated. To say that we "cannot put a price" on this or that is to misconceive the economic process. Things cost because other things could have been produced with the same time, effort, and material. Everything necessarily has a price in this sense, whether or not social institutions cause money to be collected from individual consumers. Prices under capitalism are not simply a mechanism for transferring wealth among persons; they are a way of carrying out the rationing function inherent in all economic systems. Someone must *recognize* a price on everything, and the only real question is who, and under what institutional incentives and constraints.

Chapter 4

Social Trade-Offs

Trade-offs may be easier to visualize in economic terms, but they are no less pervasive and no less important in social processes. Political and judicial institutions, the family, and voluntary associations of various sorts must also balance opposing effects under inherent constraints—must seek an optimum rather than a maximum. The most basic inherent constraint is that neither time nor wisdom are free goods available in unlimited quantity. This means that in social processes, as in economic processes, it is not only impossible to attain perfection but irrational to seek perfection—or even to seek the "best possible" result in each separate instance.

Courts which devote the time and effort required to reach the highest possible standard of judicial decisions in minor cases can develop a backlog of cases that means dangerous criminals are walking the streets while awaiting trial. Lofty intellectual standards, rigidly adhered to, may mean rejection of evidence and methods of analysis which would give us valuable clues to complex social phenomena—leaving us instead to make policy decisions in ignorance or by guess or emotion. Unbending moral standards may dichotomize the human race in such a way that virtually everyone is lumped together as sinners, losing all moral distinction between honorable, imperfect people and unprincipled perpetrators of moral horrors. In the early days of the Civil War, some leading abolitionists condemned Abraham Lincoln as being no better than a slaveholder, and no more a defender of the Union than Jefferson Davis.[1] Their twentieth-century counterparts have morally lumped together the wrongs in democratic countries with mass murder and terror under totalitarianism.

Rejection of a social optimum cannot mean that something *better* than this optimum will be achieved. It may mean that something far worse will result from a failure to recognize the inherent limitations of the situation—limitations of knowledge, resources, and human beings. Had the whole society adopted the position of a few perfectionist abolitionists and refused to support Lincoln and the war effort against the Confederacy, the abolition of slavery would not have come sooner but much later, if at all. Similar perfectionism among people of diverse political persuasions led to concerted efforts to bring down the troubled Weimar Republic. However morally satisfying it may have been to believe that "nothing could be worse" than the Weimar Republic, many of those who contributed to its downfall learned too late in Nazi concentration camps just how much worse things could be.

Social trade-offs involve not simply an incremental substitution of one consideration for another in specific decisions. These trade-offs apply to the decision-making mechanisms themselves. Legal procedures which do *not* meet the highest standards available may deliberately be established to deal with jaywalking and parking violations, precisely so that the system can devote more of its time and talents to reducing the likelihood of a mistake in judging a murder case.

A certain amount of foolish decision making and thoughtless inefficiency may be tolerated—*must* be tolerated—in any large organization, because there are only a limited number of wise, experienced and thorough people available, and they need to be put in a few key positions and their efforts concentrated on a few crucial decisions. Anyone at the bottom of an organization can spot some mistakes by his hierarchic superiors, and so can outsiders. The real choice for the organization as a whole, however, is between existing decision makers and their potential replacements for the *whole range* of decisions each must take. Some improvements may be possible in specific instances by having subordinates correct superiors' mistakes, but this is not costless in terms of organizational discipline or in terms of the time spent by subordinates and superiors discussing what is and is not a mistake. In some cases—an extreme example being a combat unit under enemy fire—the time spent discussing alternatives may be more costly than either alternative itself. The closer decisions are to that end of the spectrum, the more rational it is to have unquestioning obedience, even if the superior makes no better decisions than the subordinate.

At the other end of the spectrum—an appellate court reviewing a murder conviction—full and free discussion may be appropriate, without regard to which members of the reviewing court are hierarchically senior. Whatever honorific or administrative prerogatives belong to the Chief Justice of the U.S. Supreme Court, his is just one vote out of nine in determining the substance of the law. It is not that one process is necessarily more important than the other. Human life is at stake in both cases. The difference is that the passage of a small amount of time radically increases the risks to life in one decision-making situation, while executions are automatically postponed for whatever time it takes for an appellate court to make up its mind.

The trade-offs involved in social decision-making processes parallel those in economic decision-making processes. Present costs and benefits must be traded off against future costs and benefits in interpersonal relationships ranging from child rearing to love affairs. External costs are involved wherever people living near each other have different values as regards noise or the appearance of the neighborhood. In short, the principle of diminishing returns applies at least as much to emotions as to economic processes. A mother who would be devastated by the loss of her baby may nevertheless welcome a few hours away from the infant at times, to renew her spirits. Indeed, in virtually all personal relationships—even between the most ardent lovers—there are times (however brief) when each feels the need to be alone or at least to be with others.

It is not a mere coincidence that the trade-offs of economic processes parallel those of other social processes. The economic process is only a special case of human decision making in general, so it is hardly surprising to find similar principles at work, even on very different subject matter. However, the large difference in subject matter not only obscures the underlying principles, but modifies their application as well.

Some of the social trade-offs worth special attention include (1) the sorting and labeling of people, activities, and things, (2) the role of time, and (3) trade-offs involving safety of one sort or another.

SORTING AND LABELING

One of the most basic and pervasive social processes is the sorting and labeling of things, activities, and people. This includes everything from the sex separation of bathrooms to municipal zoning ordinances, air traffic control, and racial segregation. Even the changing moods and circumstances of a given individual are sorted and labeled by those who deal with him, in order not to talk to or interact with him in particular ways "at the wrong time." Sorting and labeling processes involve a trade-off of costs and benefits. In general, the more finely the sorting is done, the greater the benefits—and the costs. Beyond some point, making the sorting categories finer would not be worth the additional cost—for the particular decision-making purpose.

For example, if we find boxes of explosives stored in an area where we were planning to hold a picnic, that may be sufficient reason to locate the picnic elsewhere, without inquiring further as to whether the explosives are dynamite or nitroglycerin, though that distinction might be important for other purposes at other times.

The general benefits of sorting and labeling must be distinguished from the special benefits of qualitative selectivity. A basketball coach can select a taller sample of boys from a given population, but the average height of the whole population is unaffected by whether or not they are sorted and labeled. From a social point of view, what matters most are the benefits of sorting and labeling *given* things, activities, and people in society as a whole.

There can be a substantial difference in value between a sorted and an unsorted collection containing the same quantities of identical items. If a flood sweeps through a supermarket, washing all labels off the canned goods, the cans will have to be sold at a fraction of their original prices, if not thrown away. No customer will pay anywhere near the full price for an unlabeled can which could turn out to contain vegetables, fish, or coffee. The supermarket will then have to buy more canned goods from wholesalers to restock their shelves, paying large sums of money to replace the unlabeled canned goods with new canned goods with the same identical contents as the old, but more valuable solely because of having been sorted and labeled. In a similar way, there may be a net social gain when people who like a quiet contemplative life sort themselves out from those who enjoy rousing parties and/or motorcycles—even though there are the same numbers of each kind of person after the sorting as there were before. The demand for retirement communities, for apartment developments catering to young singles, and other specialized communities is one indication of gains merely from sorting and labeling a given population.

Among the costs of sorting and labeling is a loss of diversity. That cost differs from person to person, according to tastes and preferences. It also varies incrementally with how much diversity an individual already has. An elderly person who works among younger people and has frequent visits with offspring and grandchildren may prefer the day-to-day tranquility of living among contemporaries, without fear of becoming wholly isolated in an unnaturally homogeneous environment. More generally, the need for diversity is itself not homogeneous, but varies from person to person and varies incrementally with the circumstances of the same person. There is a sorting and labeling of people by the extent to which they wish to be sorted and labeled. The coexistence of both specialized and general communities is one indication of this.

Sorting and labeling, whether of people or of things, is a sorting and labeling of probabilities rather than certainties. We *believe*, with varying degrees of confidence, that a certain person would like a certain Christmas gift, or would be amused by a certain remark, or be pleased with a certain action. We never really *know* and the very fact that there are such words in the language as disappointment, regret, etc., is testimony to the pervasiveness and persistence of this feature of the human condition.

ORGANIZATIONS

Despite the elusiveness of certainty, the remarkable success of such things as franchise operations is evidence of the value of merely *reducing* the range of uncertainty. A "Holiday Inn" is not necessarily better or worse than any other hotel. There are undoubtedly many independent hotels that are better and worse (by whatever standard) than the average Holiday Inn, or even better or worse than any Holiday Inn. Moreover, Holiday Inns vary among themselves. Yet the fact that thousands of hotel owners are willing to pay in various ways for the privilege of using this franchise designation means that the economic value of a given physical structure is greater with a Holiday Inn sign in front of it than without it—and that in turn means that millions of travelers are more likely to stop there *for some reason*. These travelers are also aware that there are better and worse hotels; all that the sign does is reduce the range of uncertainty as to quality and price. The value of the franchise, and its spread internationally, is evidence that this is no small consideration. The growth and prosperity of many other franchising corporations in various fields suggests that this form of sorting and labeling is of great value to customers, especially in a highly mobile society where individual knowledge of individual establishments is rare or more costly.

Many people are uneasy with the thought of making decisions on the basis of merely probabilistic indications like franchise names, and especially with the idea of sorting and labeling *people* by one or a few characteristics. The only reason for doing so in either case is the cost of alternative procedures, with finer categories, which might produce incrementally more accurate predictions. Yet the large number of people murdered by spouses each year suggests that even the most intimate knowledge of other people will not produce certainty as to their future behavior. The only question is—how much more knowledge (risk reduction) is worth how much more cost? Obviously this varies with the decision. No one wants to select a spouse on the basis of crude rules of thumb, but then neither does anyone want to put the same amount of thought into selecting a television program that he or she puts into selecting a mate. The argument here is not in favor of crude decision-making processes. The argument is simply that the fineness of the sorting and labeling process is incrementally variable with respect to both costs and benefits, so that it must stop somewhere short of the quality of decision-making that is *possible,* and so must—and should—make "avoidable" mistakes.

Looked at another way, "avoidable" mistakes are not necessarily a condemnation of a decision-making process—if alternative processes which would have avoided these particular mistakes in these instances would also have cost so much in so many other instances (either in money or in other mistakes) as to outweigh the costs of the "avoidable" mistakes. Decision-making processes are often judged by standards which ignore this simple fact. This is done not only by naive people but even by experts. For example, an experienced traveler who has been through a given area many times may be able to select local hotels, restaurants, and auto rental agencies much more advantageously than by relying on franchise names, and may be able to factually demonstrate the superiority of his choices to the other choices which he disdains. Yet if his disdain extends to the *method* of choice (franchise names in this case) he is very mistaken. Experts who loftily dismiss the public's method of choice in many areas often fail to consider the cost of knowledge. By definition, the expert has already paid these costs in the past, and the incremental cost to him of making individual choices after that is virtually zero. Nothing is easier for an expert than to show instances where things, activities, and people were misjudged. What is misleading is to imply that therefore wrong methods of sorting and labeling were used.

PEOPLE

There is a fatal charm about the idea of "judging each person as an individual." Our sympathies immediately go out to the person who has been "wrongly" denied a job, credit, college admission, or an opportunity to participate in some activity because that person fails to meet certain "arbitrary" requirements, but demonstrably should have been acceptable because of other considerations. An onlooker may find it silly that a department store clerk will not accept a personal check from a Rockefeller but will accept a credit card from an unemployed laborer. But the real question is whether credit policies shall be made by specialists higher up in the organization and passed down as rules restricting the discretion of lower level employees, or whether the financial future of the organization shall be put in the hands of store clerks and rest on their personal assessments of customer credit worthiness.

The variation in the fineness of sorting categories, from one organization to another in the same field, is sometimes cited as proof of the irrationality or arbitrariness of the rules of the organization with the coarser sorting procedure. But acceptance of a Rockefeller's personal check by the owner-operator of a small retail shop is no reason why a department store clerk should accept it—given that there are very different knowledge costs when the immediate salesperson and the financially responsible official are one and the same person, compared to the situation where the two functions are performed by different individuals widely separated in a large organization. Similarly, a student with modest S.A.T. scores may be rejected by a large and mediocre state university and yet be accepted by a higher-quality small college which takes into account other evidences of his intellectual ability. Neither institution's admissions procedure may be defective. A state university admissions committee with over 100,000 applications to go through in a few weeks may have to immediately reject all those below some cutoff score, in order to give any personal attention at all to choosing among those remaining. However, a college with a total enrollment of 500 students may be able to give all applicants individual consideration from start to finish, at relatively little cost. Neither process is inherently more efficient. What would be more efficient would be for Rockefellers without credit cards to shop in places where officials empowered to approve checks are near at hand, and for talented youths with low scores to apply to colleges where applications from such persons can be accurately assessed more cheaply.

Most objections to sorting and labeling in general—and particularly to the sorting and labeling of people—are based on *ignoring the costs of knowledge,* or ignoring *differences* in the cost of knowledge between one decision-making process and another. Even objections on purely moral grounds to "discrimination" against various groups often turn out to involve ignoring knowledge costs. When an individual from a group with a certain behavior pattern has a very different behavior pattern himself, judging him according to the group pattern, and making decisions accordingly, may impose serious costs on that individual. It also imposes costs (foregone opportunities) on the other person who made the incorrect assessment—and therefore provides an incentive for seeking alternative methods of assessment, if such are available at a cost commensurate with the benefit. However, insofar as the factual basis of the group assessment is accurate, the only cost paid by the group *as a whole* are costs created by its own behavior.

Those group members who do not in fact create such costs may pay a high price for being in the same category with others who do—and the cost-creators in turn pay correspondingly less than the costs created by their own behavior. It might be desirable from a moral or political point of view that public policy diffuse those costs over the general population rather than leave them concentrated on blameless individuals in the same category. That is a question of policy which depends on more variables than those being considered here. For the present analysis, the point is that *group* discrimination—costs imposed by group A as a whole on group B as a whole—is not proved by showing (in retrospect) that individuals of identical relevant characteristics are treated differently (in prospect) when they come from group A rather than group B. The two individuals may have identical probabilities of repaying credit, abstaining from violence, being a considerate neighbor, and contributing intelligent ideas. But only God can know that in advance free of charge. The cost of knowledge of these individuals' characteristics may be very different when the individual comes from Group A than from group B, if these two groups as a whole differ in any of these characteristics.

Psychological and political "realities" often lead to rhetoric which camouflages, or even boldly misstates, the causes of cost burdens, as well as the nature of proposed remedies. For more than a century, individuals fleeing ethnic ghettos have bitterly complained of resistance to their movement into other neighborhoods as an imposition of costs on the whole group from which they were fleeing by those groups toward whom they were fleeing. This pattern has occurred repeatedly, from the time of the Irish immigrants in the middle of the nineteenth century to blacks, Hispanics, and others today.

But no amount of impersonal phrasing about wanting to escape "slums" or the "conditions" there can change the basic fact that what is being attempted is to move away from *people* whose *behavior* is regarded as offensive. For exactly the same reason, there is resistance or flight by those in surrounding neighborhoods. Painful as this situation is for all concerned, it is made even more difficult to resolve when the rhetorical misstatement of it becomes a basis for insisting that not only the cost-bearing victims among the excluded group but also the cost-creating members of the same group be relocated. Sometimes this goes beyond the "fair housing" approach of creating a legal right to relocate anywhere on one's own initiative, to a government policy of creating financial incentives to undo sorting and labeling by deliberately locating subsidized housing in neighborhoods different from those normally inhabited by the tenants—or even more directly, forcing excluded groups to relocate by demolition of their dwellings by "urban renewal."

At some point in these political developments, those who believe the rhetoric literally may be puzzled to find themselves opposed by those excluded people who were initially their allies. Cost-bearing members of excluded groups are often much clearer as to what they are doing in trying to sort themselves out from cost-creating members of the same group. The last thing they want to do is to import into their new environment the same cost-creating people whom they have fled. When the building of low-income housing projects in middle-class neighborhoods has been bitterly opposed by blacks already living in such neighborhoods, many white liberals have been shocked by the apparent inconsistency of such behavior with the rhetoric which they and middle-class blacks have shared in earlier struggles for "fair housing" laws. The middle-class blacks are, however, *behaviorally* consistent in continuing to sort and label by social characteristics (other than race) even if this means opposing former white allies to whom rhetorical consistency is more important.

In short, even the principal victims of that form of social sorting and labeling known as racial segregation do not object to sorting and labeling, as such, but object instead to racial segregation for preventing *them* from sorting and labeling on other (nonracial) bases. Students of black social history have long noted the difficulties of the small black middle class in attempting to preserve and perpetuate its values and behavior patterns while surrounded by people with very different values and behavior patterns, whom they were forced to live among because the larger society's sorting and labeling categories were coarse enough not to go beyond race. Objection to sorting and labeling, as such, is an entirely different phenomenon, supported by an entirely different group of people, and taking many forms: objections to school grades, occupational hierarchies, institutional authority, I.Q. tests, and all forms of address, attire, residence or work place differentiation of status or function. Even among individuals, organizations, and whole societies which have cast away particular forms of sorting and labeling, substitute forms reappear, even amidst the most ostentatious egalitarianism. Everyone may be called "comrade," but some comrades have the power of life and death over other comrades.

The advantages of sorting and labeling may sometimes be mistakenly ascribed to other factors. For example, one of the important things an education system does is to sort and label people, and they may be more valuable to an employer because they have been sorted and labeled, rather than simply because of the education as such. The difference between a "dropout" and a graduate is not merely that one has somewhat more information than the other, as a result of staying in an educational institution longer. Dropouts as a group tend to differ from graduates as a group in perseverance, regularity, and discipline—qualities of value even in jobs where the difference in information between the two groups is of little or no significance. Statistics on income differences between dropouts and graduates often arbitrarily attribute the higher income of the graduate to the value of the education, especially when the statistics are quoted by educational institutions seeking larger appropriations, grants, and public donations.

One of the functions of the "publish or perish" policy of many universities is that it forces faculty members to sort and label themselves by exhibiting their professional abilities before their peers. It is not necessarily publication, as such, that is rewarded but rather that the sorting and labeling of scholarly ability is facilitated by publication. A string of mediocre publications may in fact be damaging to the individual, though valuable to the profession in sorting and labeling its members. Those who cannot meet even the minimum standards to be published in any scholarly journal obviously fall at the bottom of the sorting categories. In addition, there is a hierarchy of standards among the many academic journals in any given field, and some articles and books are judged more impressive than others by their scholarly audience.

Those academics with substantial ability and little desire to publish may be "underrated" by this system, but this reflects in part the high cost which their reticence imposes on institutions which must sort and label faculty members by some system for the apportionment of rewards. If those with such reluctance to publish are willing to forego the reward in order to avoid the bother, it may be a perfectly rational result for both the institution and the individual. The question of the relative weight of publication and other factors—teaching, administrative responsibilities, etc.—is a different question. The "publish or perish" policy implies only that scholarly ability is one essential characteristic that must be sorted and labeled.

The general social benefits of sorting and labeling must be sharply distinguished from the *differential gains* of those judged favorably or those who interact with favorably judged individuals. Sorting and labeling does not in itself change the characteristics of the people, activities, or things that are sorted and labeled. The differential gains of the "winners" are offset by the correspondng disadvantages of the "losers." General social gains come from the greater ease of matching individuals and circumstances, so as to maximize benefits and minimize costs. Just as there is a greater demand for canned goods *as a whole* when they are individually labeled than when the labels have been washed off, so there is a greater demand for a labor force whose individual characteristics are known to some degree than when every employment decision has a wide penumbra of uncertainty about it. Even the "losers" in a sorting process may end up better off than they would have been without sorting. It is not a zero-sum process. Those social classes or ethnic groups whose behavior patterns are offensive to others may find a more sympathetic reception among neighbors who share their values and priorities. For purposes of understanding the value of sorting and labeling, it is unnecessary to agree with any particular set of values as to what is a "better" or "higher" standard. It is enough that there are *different* values, so that sorting people out can improve everyone's position by their own respective values.

THE FINENESS OF SORTING

Finer sorting categories are not always preferable, even in those cases where they are available at no additional cost. Contrast the situation of "group punishment" for individual misconduct, as in small military units, with group punishment in countries where family honor is a paramount consideration. When a misdeed is committed by some unknown member of a given platoon or squad, the military authorities may choose to punish the whole platoon or squad, merely as a result of the high cost of acquiring knowledge of the individual culprit—especially in cases where the other members of the unit know who the culprit is, and will punish or control him socially or otherwise, even though they might not be willing to tell on him to the authorities. However, in countries where family honor is sacred, the whole family may be punished by shame, even though everyone knows the identity of the particular individual who was guilty of the misdeed. In the latter case, larger sorting categories (the family) are used even though finer categories (the individual) are available at no additional cost. The social purpose is not so much retrospective justice as prospective control. Individuals' conduct can be controlled more effectively by those most intimately familiar with them than by public institutions. The cost of knowledge is far cheaper to family members than to either policemen or to courts, who must filter documentable allegations through rules of evidence, losing much knowledge in the process. Moreover, the range of sanctions are far more finely graduated in the family, and can be invoked *in advance* of any wrongdoing by raising the child to feel guilt or pride in behavior that would reflect shame or honor on the family.

Clearly, there is a loss of retrospective justice when individual B is shamed (punished) for conduct by individual A, especially if B is a contemporary rather than a parent, and still more so if B is a member of a subsequent generation, and therefore lacked any control over the past acts for which he is sharing the punishment. Offsetting this is the gain in social control, which apparently is considerable. One indication of the effectiveness of sorting and labeling by family rather than by individual is the vast difference in juvenile delinquency between American teenagers in general and teenagers of Oriental ancestry living in the same society, subject to the same temptations and public constraints. The virtually nonexistent delinquency among Japanese-American and Chinese-American youngsters has long been noted by those studying these groups, despite high and rising delinquency rates among American teenagers all around them.

Recent outbreaks of delinquency and violence among Chinatown youth gangs only highlight the factor of family honor as a control. These youth gangs have arisen since the arrival of large numbers of Chinese refugees from Hong Kong, where they were "Westernized" (i.e., atomized) before arriving in the United States. Neither Chinese genes nor Chinese culture in general seem to be related to control of delinquency, which seems to depend upon a whole social fabric building on family honor—a fabric destroyed as refugees tore themselves loose from their environments in China and converged on Hong Kong, where they arrived as individuals or as isolated families, and lived in a Westernized culture further undermining whatever remained of their original social values. Chinese-American delinquents and youth criminals are overwhelmingly of recent Hong Kong origin. Similarly, among Japanese-Americans, studies indicate that the rare young delinquents among them tend to come from outside the Japanese-American community. The virtual nonexistence of juvenile delinquency among those raised in the traditional Oriental community in the United States is striking evidence of the social effectiveness of sorting and labeling by larger units which are able to exert internal control over the individual better than public institutions can.

Similar principles have been involved in the Americanization of nineteenth century Jewish immigrants. When the massive immigration of Eastern European Jews to America began in the 1880s, there was already a small German-Jewish community in the United States, and they were alarmed at being categorized with their co-religionists from a wholly different cultural and socioeconomic background. Yet despite their initial efforts to disassociate themselves from the Eastern European Jews, the public at large tended to lump all Jews together, and to become more anti-Semitic as a result of the new unassimilated arrivals. Again, despite the retrospective injustice of such gross sorting and labeling categories, this provided an incentive for the more Americanized, cultured, and economically successful German Jews to assume some responsibility for helping the Eastern European Jews toward similar success and acceptability in their new culture. Similar things have happened in other ethnic groups: the Urban League played an acculturating role among blacks and the Catholic Church among the Irish, for example. Partly this was philanthropic, but partly also it was enlightened self-interest on the part of more fortunate members of a group who realized that they were inevitably being categorized with the rest of a group that was unacceptable to the larger society. Judging each person "as an individual" would have removed this incentive. The position here is not to claim that sorting and labeling categories should be larger than the individual. The point is simply to bring out the social trade-off that is involved between retrospective individual justice and prospective social control.

Similar principles apply in the very different world of organized crime. From the point of view of career criminals, there is some optimal quantity of violence associated with economic crimes, such as robbery. With zero violence and zero threat of violence, no one would turn over his economic assets to the criminal. But beyond some point, violence causes public outcries which bring more police power to bear in a given sector, reducing crime opportunity for other criminals as well as for the one who committed some "senseless" violence against an economic crime victim. Where each criminal is a separate decision-making unit, these external costs of his crime have no deterrent effect on his conduct. When crime is organized into larger units, however, these larger units have an incentive to minimize public outcry per unit of economic crime, which usually means reducing the amount of "senseless" violence against the victims. In short, with organized crime as with Oriental families, internalizing the external costs created by individuals means greater social control and greater responsiveness to public reactions which might safely be ignored by an individual malefactor whose identity was unknown to authorities or whose guilt would be difficult to establish through formal legal processes. In both cases, the source of this greater control is the lower cost of knowledge by those with whom he is closely associated. The relative abandon with which organized crime figures kill each other only reinforces the point; there is little or no public outcry at the death of a mobster.

TIME

Time is perhaps the ultimate constraint. Few things can be done instantaneously, and with unlimited billions of years virtually anything is possible. Even complex human beings may evolve from an initially lifeless planet. On a more mundane level, the cost of constructing a house literally overnight would be many times the cost of constructing the same house in the normal time or constructing it in whatever "free time" was available sporadically over the next decade.

Time is, of course, never free. Its value is whatever alternative opportunities must be foregone in order to use it for a particular purpose. The value or cost of time is often overlooked, as among bargain hunters who ignore the time spent searching for "bargains" (not simply the time spent finding the things actually purchased, but the time spent looking at the whole array of possibilities from which the purchased items were selected), or waiting for service in low-priced stores, or seeking frequent repairs for low-priced items with less durability. The "same" merchandise generally sells for a higher price in stores with a more varied stock (of brands or sizes), more (or better) salespeople, and more numerous cash registers, with correspondingly shorter lines at each—all of which save time. It is not really the same merchandise because what is being purchased is not simply the physical item but also the associated services required for its discovery and use.

Another way of looking at this is that every item has both a money price and a time price, and it is the combination of the two that is its full cost. Since the value of time varies from person to person, in terms of his foregone opportunities (whether earnings or other activities), this invisible combined price may be equalized by competition while the visible money price components remain disparate. Flea markets, for example, incur virtually no costs of stocking a standard selection or wide variety of given items, nor for various after-sales services, and the consumer pays low money costs and high search costs to get what he wants, or pays other intangible costs by not getting exactly what he wants in the condition that he wants. At the other end of the spectrum is the more elaborate kind of department store, with personnel trained to explain and demonstrate the intricacies and nuances of the specific kind of merchandise in their respective departments, a wide range of brands, qualities, and sizes of each commodity stocked, and with defective items sorted out for return to the manufacturer, whether discovered by the store before display or returned by the customer for a refund after the sale. Where on the spectrum between these two kinds of sellers a particular buyer will go depends on his own incremental trade-off between time and money, determined largely by his income and impatience. In this context, persistent money price differences for the "same" merchandise sold at different kinds of stores do not prove the consumers "irrational," nor the merchants dishonest, nor the economy noncompetitive.

In social as in economic processes, the value of anything varies with the time at which it becomes available. This applies both to benefits and to costs. Swift punishment for criminals has long been recognized as a more effective deterrent than the same punishment applied after much delay. By implication, a lesser punishment applied immediately—the old fashioned "curbstone justice" once applied by the policeman on the spot—may be as effective as a harsher punishment applied after years of "due process." Due process may be preferred for its greater accuracy, objectivity, or dignity, but the point here is that there is a trade-off, based on the varying cost of punishment to the recipient according to its location in time.

In economics, a financial increment or decrement accompanies transfers of given physical or money units back and forth through time. The absence of explicit interest payments in social trade-offs does not mean that the same principle is not at work. Because imprisonment is costly to the taxpayers as well as to the criminal, a shorter sentence begun soon that is as effective as a longer sentence begun later means money savings for a given deterrent. Alternatively, the law could retain the same length of sentence and achieve more deterrence for a given amount of money, if that was preferred. In other words, the implicit "interest" received by the public for moving imprisonment forward in time can be either in money or in kind. Conversely, losses incurred by moving imprisonment backward in time by lengthening legal "due process" may also be costly both in money and in kind, including crimes committed by criminals free on bail, awaiting trial or appeal.

TIME HORIZONS

In social trade-offs in general, the diminishing value of deferred benefits or costs is often referred to in terms of the time required for such benefits or costs to reach the vanishing point as influences on present decision making. This period is the individual's "time horizon." Time horizons are subjective. They vary not only from individual to individual, but from one socioeconomic class to another, among ethnic groups, or among age brackets. Ironically, older individuals may have longer time horizons than younger, more impetuous, individuals, even though, objectively, younger people generally have more years of life ahead of them. But older people's plans often extend well beyond their own life span, as in decisions made for their children's well-being—the preservation of an estate, or in extreme cases, suicide by parents who consider themselves "burdens" to their children (once generalized among Eskimos)—or the older person's time horizon often includes concern for their own good name after death which serves as motivation for decisions involving philanthropy, religious conversion, or a place in history. For younger people the end of their own life is often beyond their time horizon, and these post-death concerns still more so. It may well be that the time horizon lengthens with the birth of children and the assumption of a parental outlook, not only as regards one's own children in particular but posterity in general. Whatever the cause, a time horizon extending beyond the lifetime of the individual becomes a spontaneous moral control on individual action, analogous to moral constraints extending in space at a given time.

Differences in time horizons among social groups change the effectiveness of social policies involving either benefits or penalties, especially when one social group, with a given time horizon, predominates among the policy makers and another social group, with a different time horizon, predominates among those to whom the policy applies. For example, "job training" programs which require present efforts to increase prospective employment and earnings sometime in the future may prove relatively ineffective with age, ethnic, or socioeconomic groups with short time horizons. Participation in such programs may be based on such *current* opportunities as these programs present, and maximizing benefits at least cost may mean maximizing in the short run sense of doing as little as possible to receive the financial or other immediate benefits from the program—which is to say, preparing for future employment as little as possible. The attempt to use such future-oriented programs as means of luring present-oriented youngsters away from crime runs up against the fact that "most crimes are committed opportunistically by youths who want small amounts of money right away."[2] A job training program may well increase the youth's earnings ability by many times what he can successfully steal, provided that both calculations are made over a long enough time span, but if his time horizon is shorter than the program, none of its future benefits may enter his calculation—which may nevertheless be as rational within his time horizon as the opposite result is for those with a longer time horizon. No one has an unlimited time horizon, and there is no logically compelling objective reason for preferring one time horizon to another.

Jobs are a meaningful alternative to crime when the jobs have similarly short time dimensions. The availability of casual, day-to-day jobs is apparently inversely correlated with petty crime rates. Where the opportunity for such pickup jobs is reduced—as by bad weather—petty crimes tend to increase, since people who live from day to day "have to eat" when the jobs stop and seldom have much money saved.[3]

One of the reasons why relatively simple precautions reduce the incidence of crime is the short time horizon of many criminals. Almost no feasible precaution can make it impossible to steal, break-in, or victimize by violence. But merely by raising the immediate cost—in time, effort, or risk—it discourages many whose aversion to perseverance and postponed benefits is part of the reason for their being criminals. Few homes are burglar-proof and few people mugger-proof, but the incidence of burglary is much lower in New York than in Los Angeles while the incidence of mugging is just the reverse, because access to New York apartments is usually a little more difficult than in Los Angeles (due to architectural style differences) and access to people to mug is somewhat more difficult in Los Angeles (due to fewer pedestrians in residential neighborhoods). Apparently criminals are rational within their framework. One of the reasons for the absence of simple precautions is the subsidization of losses: insurance policies spread and thus minimize the impact of the cost of theft; police property recovery costs paid for by the taxpayers likewise reduce the connection between carelessness and consequences; "victim compensation" policies by government extends this externalization of costs still further. Insofar as individual precautions merely cause the criminal to turn to someone else as an easier victim, the private benefits exceed the social benefits. An argument might be made for legal compulsion to reduce vulnerability in general—antitheft devices in cars, better locks required by building codes, brighter lighted streets, etc.—but since such requirements would be categorical rather than incremental, they could easily go past the point where the benefits balanced the costs.

THE ANIMISTIC FALLACY

From the point of view of the social utilization of knowledge, time permits entirely different methods for the production and distribution of knowledge from those usually conceived of, and does not depend upon articulation, rationality, cognition, or any of the other formal processes taught in academic institutions. With unlimited time, either the processes of nature or the competition among men may lead to an intricate pattern of results unplanned by anybody. The fitness or accuracy of these systemic adaptations may be revealed primarily—or even exclusively—in results rather than in articulated rationality. But because man insists on *some* articulated explanation after the fact, an explanation which overlooks the crucial role of time may emerge as a wholly different—and wholly fallacious—depiction of what has happened.

Perhaps the simplest and most psychologically satisfying explanation of any observed phenomenon is that it happened that way because someone wanted it to happen that way. This applies not only to social phenomena but to natural phenomena as well. Primitive peoples explained the movement of leaves on a tree by some spirit or god who wanted the leaf to move, had the power to make it move, and so it moved. The analogy of this to purposeful and deliberate human activity is obvious. It is only at a much more developed state of reasoning that the movement of leaves is explained by wind currents of a nonpurposeful (but also nonrandom) nature, based on differences in air pressure. The more primitive kind of explanation remains a more spontaneous or "natural" kind of explanation—one that arises first in a wide variety of areas, and is later abandoned only when forcibly displaced by a demonstrable alternative. Some events are in fact the result of purposeful activity toward the goal achieved, but the general presumption that this *must* be the case can be classified as "the animistic fallacy."

The animistic fallacy has had many great, historic forms—in religion, in biology, and in economics, for example. Time is a crucial ingredient in the alternative, systemic or evolutionary, explanations of the same phenomena. The religious "argument from design" for the existence of God asserted that the observed nonrandom pairings of environments and creatures, the male and female sexes, the cooperating organs of the body, etc., all proved that a purposeful intelligence had designed the universe to fit together. Even such philosophic skeptics as David Hume and John Stuart Mill found these arguments weighty. After Darwin's theory of evolution provided an alternative explanation of the same natural phenomena, even religious believers no longer rested their beliefs on the animistic "proof" of the existence of God. Darwin was a landmark, not only in the history of biology, but in the history of intellectual development in general. He showed how—*with sufficient time*—nonpurposeful activity could lead to nonrandom results: he divorced *order* from "design." Yet the animistic fallacy would say that the absence of "planning" must lead to chaos—and the economic and political consequences of that belief are still powerful today.

Animistic explanations require little or no *time* for the events they postulate to take place—only six days for the creation of the world, in one religious version, and in principle omnipotence could have made it happen in an instant. Evolutionary explanations, on the other hand, necessarily imply sufficient time for initially random events, behavior, or individuals to be sorted out by environmental forces in such a way as to leave a surviving population with nonrandom characteristics adapted to the environment. Initial mutations may happen to range from beneficial to fatal, but *surviving* mutations tend to represent improved adaptations to the environment. After millions of years of natural selection, what will be observed will be primarily surviving mutations. One may choose to regard the process as a whole as Providential without committing the animistic fallacy of asserting that the observed order could *only* be a result of deliberate design.

SYSTEMIC ANALYSIS

Social phenomena may also be explained either animistically, from the intentions of the individuals involved, or in terms of the mutually constraining complex of relationships whose results form a pattern not necessarily similar to the intentions of any of the individuals involved. The animistic fallacy is not the exclusive property of either the political left or right. Conservative economists of an animistic bent explain rational behavior in a timeless context, sometimes with the moral conclusion that the wise are rewarded for their foresight and the unwise penalized for their lack of it—that "supernormal brains" explain large profits for example. On the left, social planners eager to save the world from "chaos" engage in another form of the animistic fallacy. Both approaches ignore time, for there is no selective adaptation process to take place. However, the animistic fallacy is rejected decisively by such ideologically disparate figures as Adam Smith and Karl Marx, both of whom analyzed in systemic terms.

Smith had no faith whatever in the intentions of businessmen, whom he characterized as mean and rapacious,[4] but argued that the characteristics of a market economic system would lead to beneficial results which were no part of the intention of those acting within the system.[5] Karl Marx, of course, had a far less benign view of the results of a capitalist system, but he—like Smith—analyzed the results in terms of the presumed characteristics of the system, not the apparent intentions of individual capitalists. In the preface to the first volume of *Capital*, Marx dismissed any idea of explaining the capitalist system by capitalists' intentions.[6] Engels sweepingly rejected that approach with respect to social phenomena in general, "for what each individual wills is obstructed by everyone else, and what emerges is something that no one willed."[7]

Attempts to explain striking differences among social groups (class, ethnic, regional) at a given point in time often lead to the animistic fallacy. The relative success or failure of these groups—whether measured in money or such social variables as family stability or crime rates—is often attributed to some merit or demerit on their part or on the part of some other group (including "society") in dealing with them. "Ability" or "discrimination" are thus among the first explanations seized upon, much as primitive man explained the rustling of leaves by someone's deliberate moving of them. But once it is clear that results observable at a given point in time may be part of a process that stretches far back in time, it is no longer automatically necessary that their current situations be a result of either meritorious or unworthy actions by contemporaries—either group members or others. Differences in cultural values, for example, have deep roots in centuries past and profound impact on current behavior.

Groups from an agricultural background have classic patterns of problems when transplanted to an urban, industrial and commercial environment. A social history of the Irish peasants who immigrated to American cities in the nineteenth century reads remarkably like a preview of the history of blacks from the rural South in those same cities in the twentieth century.[8] The many historical, genetic, and other differences between the two groups only makes their parallel patterns all the more remarkable. Conversely, it is virtually impossible to explain the profound differences between contemporary Italian and Jewish immigrants in their responses to schools, libraries, and settlement houses[9] in terms of any contemporary differences in their socioeconomic conditions in the nineteenth century immigrant neighborhoods where they lived side by side. But even the most casual acquaintance with the histories of Jews and southern Italian peasants in earlier centuries shows how far back these cultural patterns go.[10]

Many of the attitudes, beliefs, and emphases of agrarian peoples are quite reasonable as adaptations to an agrarian environment, however counterproductive these approaches may turn out to be in an urban commercial setting. A fatalistic view of the future, for example, is fully understandable in a culture where people's whole lives hinge on the random variability of the weather. It is a challenge to try to find any group which emerged from centuries of agrarian life and became a success in an urban environment in one or two generations. Conversely, the long-urbanized Jews, who became the most successful of all American ethnic groups in the cities in which they concentrated, had an almost unbroken record of failure in agrarian undertakings in various parts of the United States.[11] Generalized "ability" or "discrimination" seem to offer little explanation of such social phenomena, as compared to the explanation of evolutionary adaptation. For other social phenomena, the results may be different.

The point here is not to deny any effect of intentional actions, or even to claim that these are necessarily less than the effects of evolutionary social processes. The point is to challenge the presumptive priority of timeless, intentional explanations—i.e., the animistic fallacy. It is *plausible but false* to say that "decisions made at random, or without any relation to each other do not fall into any pattern."[12] Darwin demonstrated that falsity in biology, and such disparate thinkers as Adam Smith and Karl Marx have rejected the same fallacy in analyzing social processes.

CULTURE AND INDIVIDUALISM

Highly rational intellectual "models" of human behavior suffer from an air of unreality whenever these hypothetical, computer-like incremental adjustments by coolly calculating decision makers are compared to the flesh-and-blood reality of decision by inertia, whim, panic, or rule of thumb. In reality, rational principles themselves suggest a limit to how much rational calculation to engage in. Deliberate decision making is not a free good; that is why there are thermostats and payroll deductions. Decision making has costs, including time, stress, fatigue, insomnia, and heart attacks. Clearly, it is something that must be economized.

Culture is one way of economizing on deliberate decision making and on the explicit marshalling of data and principles which it entails. Culture provides a wide range of beliefs, attitudes, preferences, and customs whose authentication has been historical (Darwinian) and consensual rather than scientific. Culture offers low cost inputs into the decision-making process, and—when there is freedom—leaves to the individual the choice whether prospective incremental improvements in the quality of the particular decisions are worth the additional costs of more rational calculation. For a wide range of decisions, many people find it optimal to rely heavily on cultural values, and therefore end up dressing, talking, eating, or housing themselves within a general pattern that can be recognized as characteristic of the particular culture. Thorstein Veblen argued that if decision making were in fact as rationally individualistic as sometimes depicted, "the institutional fabric would not last overnight,"[13] for there would be no set of shared values which we call a culture. Edmund Burke observed: "We are afraid to put men to live and trade each on his own private stock of reason; because we suspect that this stock in each man is small, and that the individuals would do better to avail themselves of the general bank and capital of nations and of ages."[14] The cost advantages of cultural norms are particularly great when time is short. The cultural norm "is of ready application in the emergency"[15] when the cost of a "better" decision is likely to far exceed any gain from individually recalculating the experience of centuries in dealing with the human condition. A mother who sees her child about to fall springs instantly into action without any Hamlet-like deliberation, just as soldiers in battle obey the orders of a pre-appointed individual among them, rather than pay the high cost of stopping to deliberately select either a meritorious leader or a rational course of action. Conversely, the cultural norms themselves recognize the relative advantages of deliberation when time is ample—for example, in such sayings as "haste makes waste" or "marry in haste and repent at leisure."

The relative advantages of cultural and rationalistic inputs into decision making vary not only with the particular kind of decision and the time available to make it, but also with each individual's subjective evaluation of his own ability to distill more from his own particular experience than the culture has distilled from the general or "average" experience of generations. Partly this is a question of how closely the general or average situation fits his own situation. There are, after all, few "average" people—these being statistical constructs with fractional children and other doubtful attributes. But, even aside from questions of appropriateness or relevance to the individual case, cultural norms may be rejected simply because of the confidence of some individuals in the superiority of their own thinking, as buttressed by the consensual approval of like-minded peers:

We entirely repudiated a personal liability on us to obey general rules. We claimed the right to judge every individual case on its merits, and the wisdom, experience, and self-control to do so successfully . . . we recognized no moral obligation, no inner sanction, to conform or obey. Before heaven we claimed to be our own judges in our own case.[16]

This was the economist John Maynard Keynes describing himself and the clique to which he belonged. This viewpoint is, however, both older and more widespread. Of the eighteenth-century rationalists in France it was said: "They have no respect for the wisdom of others but . . . a very full measure of confidence in their own."[17] A somewhat more modest version reposes faith in contemporary opinion among "enlightened" (i.e., like-minded) people.

The trade-off between culturally determined decisions and individually determined decisions involves a prior sorting and labeling of decisions by their degree of importance and uniqueness. Within some range neither cultural norms nor rational calculation will be applied, but fancy and caprice will be allowed to choose—as between blue or green bedspreads or automobile colors, however much rational thought may have gone into the selection of furniture or of an automobile.

Sometimes the choice between cultural and individual decision making is a choice between "feelings" and articulated rationality. Given the imperfections of language and the limitations of specific evidence, it is by no means a foregone conclusion that the mere formally logical articulation is in fact more rational, much less empirically correct. When the choice between the two processes is not within one individual but between one individual and another (or between one group and another), it is even less likely that the more articulate position is the more valid position. This is not an argument for mysticism rather than logic. It is simply a recognition that the weight of generalized but unrecorded experience—of the individual or of the culture—may be greater than the weight of other experience which happens to have been written down and spelled out. While specificity and articulation are important, they are not categorically preemptive: every small-sample study cannot overturn the common sense of mankind or the experience of the ages.

Obvious as this may seem, it contradicts the philosophy of rationalism, which accepts only what can "justify" itself to "reason"—with reason being narrowly conceived to mean articulated specifics. If rationalism had remained within the bounds of philosophy, where it originated, it might be merely an intellectual curiosity. It is, however, a powerful component in contemporary attitudes, and affects—or even determines—much political and social policy. At its most extreme, it exalts the most trivial or tendentious "study" by "experts"[18] into policy, forcibly overriding the preferences and convictions of millions of people. While rationalism at the individual level is a plea for more personal autonomy from cultural norms, at the social level it is often a claim—or arrogation—of power to stifle the autonomy of others, on the basis of superior virtuosity with words.

Rationalism is at one end of a spectrum with evolutionism at the other. The evolutionary process sees the determining rationality in a *process*—unarticulated in whole (animals) or in part (humans)—not in the individuals involved in the process. From this viewpoint, the evolutionary process is no less powerful in its effects for being undiscovered or unplanned. This applies not only to biological evolution but to social processes as well. People have articulated intentions, but history is not a record of those intentions being realized so much as it is a record of entirely different things happening as a net result of innumerable strivings toward mutually incompatible goals. Hegel and Marx called this "the irony of history" and Adam Smith called it "an invisible hand" determining the social result of an individual's action—"a result which was no part of his intention."[19] Darwin's biological generalization of the same principle made the point even more vivid, since his evolutionary theory applied to animals whose intentions (or "instincts") hardly included the evolution of their species, and even to inanimate life such as trees and grasses with no apparent intentions at all, but which develop elaborate ecological patterns nevertheless. In short, intentions must, at the very least, compete with powerful nonintentional forces.

When culture is conceived of as an evolutionary product—an ecology of human relations—it is by no means clear that any and all well-articulated reasons for changing particular parts of this social ecology must be valid. Even if plausible in the specific case, a policy's unintended consequences throughout a complex system is a weighty consideration. Articulated rationality can seldom predict very far or very specifically, and much depends on the speed and accuracy of social feedback mechanisms—and on whether the feedback includes incentives to adjust or abandon counterproductive policies.

Given the virtually limitless complexity of evolutionary or ecological processes—whether social or biological—and the limited scope of even the most rational and well-informed mind, it is by no means inevitable that the wisest, hardest working, or otherwise "best" individuals will be the most rewarded at any given point in time. Evolutionary processes may select the best *results* without selecting the most meritorious *individuals*. Even in nature, the "best" fish (by whatever standard) will die in a lake that dries up in a drought, while weaker, less intelligent, poorer swimming fish will thrive in a body of water with abundant nutrients and few dangers. In a price coordinated economy, those individuals who happen to be holding resources which suddenly acquire great value to others (oil lands when uses were discovered for petroleum) grow rich in spite of themselves. The relevant question is not whether the "best" individuals are selected in this kind of process, but whether the best social result is obtained by such processes for moving resources, or whether alternative schemes would get what is wanted where it is wanted faster or better in some other sense. The shortages, waiting lines, and production bottlenecks which accompany more apparently "rational" methods of allocating resources suggest that knowledge costs are a handicap that is more readily overcome when each holder of a valuable resource has an incentive to spread knowledge of its availability as quickly and widely as possible in order to get the maximum rewards, however individually undeserved. A similar principle is involved when an informer receives a reward for revealing the location of a wanted criminal. The question is not so much whether the person deserves the reward as whether it is worth it to the rest of the people to have the criminal out of circulation. In short, the Darwinian "natural selection" principle may mean a natural selection of the "fittest" situation or process, not necessarily individuals. The degree of rationality in the process is by no means limited to the degree of rationality of the individuals, as is often erroneously claimed.[20] Rather, "mankind has achieved things which have not been designed or understood by any individual,"[21] though their value has been retrospectively authenticated by millions who could judge the results without being able to judge—much less design—the process.

Cultures reward with honor as well as with money. Often honors impute morality and/or wisdom to the recipient, but honorific titles and forms of address may be awarded immediately upon taking certain offices (judge, legislator, etc.)—that is, before any such qualities could manifest themselves in the incumbent. But this is consistent with the general social use of rewards as prospective incentives for desired conduct, whether or not they are in keeping with retrospective justice.

Cultures give patterns to human behavior not only by the options they offer of predigested inputs into the decision-making process, and of rewards for socially desired behavior, but also by their penalties for behavior that is not desired. Although less quantifiable than either economic or legal penalties, social penalties are not necessarily less severe or less effective. One of their greatest advantages over formal penalties is the extent to which they economize on the need for knowledge. In extreme cases, no matter how well concealed the transgression, the transgressor himself knows and inflicts punishments of conscience on himself, reflecting the cultural values planted in him. Such self-inflicted punishments have even led to suicide—a death penalty chosen as preferable to continuing to suffer the internal punishments for crimes successfully concealed from everyone else. For the law, by contrast, a crime must not only be discovered but also proven "beyond a reasonable doubt" under stringent legal technicalities; the costs of *effective* knowledge (sufficient for legal penalties) are far higher than with informal social penalties. Moreover, informal controls can impose prior restraints which the criminal law cannot. Many students of crime and punishment regard the formal, legal penalties as only occasional backup to the informal controls that suffice for keeping most people law abiding.

One measure of purely social or moral sanctions is that they have effects even in circumstances where there is no formal power at all. Among slaves, for example, the mores of the group affected individual behavior. In the antebellum South, when a male and female slave were caught out in violation of curfew, the mores of the slave community called for him to volunteer to take her lashes in addition to his own.[22] More generally, there was group solidarity which forbade betrayal to slave owners,[23] and encouraged actions to aid and shield one another,[24] and kept alive family ties,[25] despite a total absence of legal sanctions for the slave families and in the face of hostility toward slave family ties by the white community.

Purely social controls are effective only to the extent that personal emotional ties give value to the goodwill of others and credence to their norms. If social possibilities, like economic possibilites, are *inherently* constrained, then the question is only which particular institutional mechanisms or processes best convey these constraints to individuals. Even if the prospect of total individual freedom under anarchy were institutionally permitted, it could not be substantively *realized*, since the free acts of one would constrain the free acts of another, leading to *less* freedom in general—in the same way that an uncontrolled crowd pushing toward a fire exit has less chance of achieving its goal than if they were evacuated in some orderly manner.

Given that some social processes must convey inherent constraints, the choice is among various mixtures of persuasion, force, and cultural inducements. The less of one, the more of the others. The degree of freedom that is possible is therefore tied to the extent to which people respond to persuasion or inducement. The "conformity" so lamented among Britons and Americans may be related to the freedom which has survived for centuries in both societies, while much of the world has gone from one form of despotism to another. In any event, the harder it is to persuade or induce, the more it is necessary to force, given that people must mutually accommodate in some way if life is to go on in an interdependent society. The celebration of unbounded individualism means, beyond some point, the acceptance of force—either private (crime, riot, vigilanteism) or public (authoritarianism). Terrorists or rioters who say that they want to force a democratic government to "reveal" its "true" authoritarian or "fascist" nature are in fact simply revealing one of the fundamental trade-offs in all forms of society, however democratic or humane. It may even have been a toleration or a romanticizing of runaway individualism that created the terrorist mentality and environment in which it could flourish—up to some inherent limit of toleration. Fascism, in fact, began in Italy in response to unchecked public disorders.

Cultures contain many cues and inducements to dissuade the individual from approaching ultimate limits, in much the same way that a special warning strip of land around the edge of a baseball field lets a player know that he is about to run into a concrete wall when he is preoccupied with catching the ball. The wider that strip and the more sensitive the player is to the changing composition of the ground under his feet as he pursues the ball, the more effective the warning. Romanticizing or lionizing as "individualistic" those people who disregard social cues and inducements increases the danger of head-on collisions with inherent social limits. Decrying various forms of social disapproval is in effect narrowing the warning strip.

Cultural cues are more effective, either as warnings or as guides to more positive relationships, when the individuals involved are part of the same culture. While rationalism tends to investigate cultural characteristics in terms of their specific minutiae—which may be quaint or "irrational"—the real function of these cultural cues is to convey information in a code readily understood by those using it, so that consistency and dependability are more important than the particular devices themselves. Someone who approaches a woman in a deferential manner or addresses a man with, "Excuse me, sir . . ." is setting a particular framework of intentions as a sort of implicit contract as to the relationship sought—a contract which can then be monitored by the other party to determine how much of what follows in fact fits within the framework of the implied declaration of intentions. A breezy "Hi ya, babe" or "Hey, Mac" implies a different set of intentions, and is also subject to subsequent monitoring within a different framework, or to rejection at the outset. The specific meaning or merits of the explicit words themselves are not at issue. It is the given cultural context that conveys a particular constellation of intentions, regardless of the explicit, grammatical meanings of the words. Where different cultures or subcultures coexist side by side or in an overlapping pattern, the same words or other cultural cues carry different meanings to different people. This means both more misunderstandings and higher levels of defenses or "insurance" behavior to minimize the dangers of misunderstandings. Moreover, the least careful or most bigoted members of the different cultures acquire a disproportionate ability to create intergroup conflict, since one of the cultural interpretation problems is determining to what extent a given individual or set of individuals represent the general sentiments (especially hostility) of another group.

The values of individualism are recognized not only in laws and the Constitutional rights regarding privacy, freedom of conscience etc., but in social doctrines of toleration, pluralism, and a general live-and-let-live attitude. The limits of individualism cannot be sharply defined and set in concrete for posterity. The nature and implications of the trade-off need to be recognized, however. In particular, the demands of unbounded individualism need to be weighed in the light of inherent social constraints which can only change their form but cannot be eliminated without eliminating civilization. Moreover, the claim for individual toleration cannot extend to cancelling other people's right to judge as they will what a given individual does. Much of the modern demand for individualism—including John Stuart Mill's *On Liberty*—is a plea for exemption from social feedback from those negatively judging individual behavior. Such an exemption is especially inconsistent when it emanates from those actively criticizing the rest of society. However democratic the language in which it is phrased, it is not a demand for equal rights or a general freedom, but for a nonreciprocal special privilege.

Morality as an input into the social process is subject to diminishing returns, and ultimately to negative returns. With no morality at all, force would be more prevelant—a loss both to those subject to it and to the efficiency of the social processes. A modicum of honesty and decency greatly reduces the incessant and desperate efforts otherwise necessary to protect life and belongings from every other human being. Beyond some point, social morality becomes irksome to individual autonomy. Finally, if each individual were to become absolutely committed to moral behavior as he saw it, no society would be possible among diverse individuals or groups. Both Karl Marx and Adam Smith recognized that there were levels of morality whose incompatabilities would destroy a society. Marx in fact looked for these incompatabilities of morality—ideologies—to destroy capitalism. For Marx, those ideologies were ultimately based on class self-interest, but direct self-interest could be compromised and accommodated to avoid mutual destruction, while ideologically reified self-interests become moral imperatives which both sides follow to a fatal showdown. This showdown is, of course, what Marx wanted for capitalism, assuming that it would lead to a socialist victory and the end of the conditions which gave rise to class-based rival ideologies. Obviously, if he had thought that similar ideological confrontations would survive under socialism, leading to the same self-destruction of that—and subsequent—systems, then life would become one interminable turmoil, and the relative merits of any given system would mean little. For Marx, destructive morality was justified only by the prospect of a rational and enduring order at the end of it all. He was merciless in his criticism of those who simply pushed moral principles, without regard to their destructive social costs.[26]

Smith recognized the same principle of destructive levels of morality, but opposed those who "insist upon establishing, and upon establishing all at once, and in spite of all opposition"[27] whatever their moral position requires. He contrasted moral or ideological principles in the abstract—what he called "a certain spirit of system"—with "the love of humanity" and "real fellow feeling," which should moderate "fanaticism" in which people become "dupes of their own sophistry."[28] In contrast to "the man of system," the man of "public spirit" will "accommodate" others' aversions and even prejudices:

When he cannot establish the right, he will not disdain to ameliorate the wrong; but, like Solon, when he cannot establish the best system of laws, he will endeavor to establish the best that the people can bear.[29]

In very different ways, Smith and Marx both recognized that morality, like other inputs into the social process, follows the law of diminishing returns—meaning, ultimately, negative returns. People can be too moral.

Morality can be incrementally counterproductive even where it has not yet reached levels that are categorically destructive of the whole society. Policies for "social justice" are often retrospective, while their effects create current and prospective costs. Beyond some point, those costs can exceed the costs of the initial inequity being corrected. If some group suffers a given loss of X—whether measured in financial or other terms—as a result of social events beyond their control or foresight, they might be regarded as victims of a social injustice, which should be corrected. But if the cost of correcting it (again, in either financial or other terms) is some procedure costing 2X to the taxpayers or to other third parties, then those who would have to bear these costs are likewise victims of events beyond their control or foresight—and to a greater extent. The injustice has merely been relocated in space or time—and increased. For example, in order to prevent retrospective injustice to people in the horse and buggy industry (who entered a centuries-old occupation in good faith and with no way of knowing that a Henry Ford was coming along), the government could have somehow inhibited the introduction of the automobile, but millions of other people living in isolated locations would have lost an opportunity to expand their horizons in many ways—and that could amount to a larger loss than the cost of changing occupations from the horse-and-buggy industry to some other part of the economy.

A people sensitized to act against virtually any injustice is a people engaged in a never-ending creation of costs, including artificially escalating levels of new injustices. To confiscate a family fortune that originated unjustly in times past is to create uncertainty among millions of home owners to-day who sacrificed for years to give their families a place to live. The government may have no intention whatsoever of confiscating the latter kind of private property, but once the common guarantee of property rights has been violated, uncertainty about all property rights increases—an *immediate* cost, measurable in tangible money terms in declining market values, regardless of whether the feared eventuality ever actually occurs. In short, an immediate confiscation—or rather destruction—of part of the value of other property would automatically take place as the result of a retrospectively just act of confiscating an ill-gotten fortune—which might well be only a tiny fraction of the value of all the losses suffered by millions of other people, such as homeowners. Moreover, in addition to the immediate costs arbitrarily imposed on third parties in this way, retrospective justice causes prospective changes of behavior—for example, in this case, a general shifting of assets from visible and immobile forms like homes and factories to more concealable and portable forms like gold. The incentives to work or to plan ahead would be affected, as time horizons shrink with increased uncertainty, reducing the level of job-creating investments in the country. Unemployed workers with neither homes nor fortunes could be among the chief current and future victims of this act of retrospective justice.

The point here is not to claim, as a categorical principle, that every act of justice or every consideration of morality must be counterproductive. Rather the point is to recognize, as an incremental principle, that *unbounded* morality ultimately becomes counterproductive even in terms of the same moral principles being sought. The law of diminishing returns applies to morality, as to other valuable social inputs.

In addition to the situation in which morality becomes counterproductive with respect to its own set of values, it may also become counterproductive by its effects on other values. For example, preoccupation with the morality of individual privilege may lead to ignoring important social considerations that are also involved. The question may be asked, what has a particular individual ever done to deserve the wealth, privilege, and power of being king—the answer usually being "nothing"—when the more weighty social question may be the costs and benefits of monarchy as compared to whatever realistic political alternatives exist at a given time and place. In less extreme cases, where the individual has made some contribution to his own good fortune, the question may still be asked whether it was enough to justify his advantages, when again the larger question may be whether there are institutional alternatives which would produce as good social results for others. The fortunate individual himself may tend to answer within the same moral framework as the critic, and depict himself as deserving—perhaps even regarding himself as a "self-made man," to use an incredibly naive and arrogant expression. But the social issue may be systemic rather than individual, and preoccupation with morality can be a distraction from considering that larger issue.

SUMMARY AND IMPLICATIONS

Social decision-making processes, whether formal or informal, face the same basic problem of seeking to maximize well-being subject to some inherent constraint—whether of time, wisdom, or economic resources. Both the constraints and the maximization process are easier to quantify or visualize in economic processes, but the principles applied in economic processes are general social principles. Social values in general are incrementally variable: neither safety, diversity, rational articulation, nor morality is categorically a "good thing" to have more of, without limits. All are subject to diminishing returns, and ultimately negative returns.

While the crucial question for social decision-making processes is the impact of those processes on society as a whole, attempts to answer that question cannot automatically proceed as if society as a whole is the decision-making unit. Rather, what must be considered are the incentives and constraints facing the actual decision makers, in order to determine if their decisions are likely to produce socially optimal results. It is in large part a question of how effectively knowledge is transmitted—not simply how well-informed the initial decision was, but how effectively feedback controls subsequent modifications, *regardless* of whether or not the decision makers want to change. Effective social knowledge is knowledge of social impact that *forces* decision makers to adjust accordingly, both initially and subsequently, just as effective economic knowledge forces a business to adjust to consumer preferences under threat of bankruptcy. Insofar as institutions are insulated from this forcibly effective knowledge, it is purely optional on the part of the decision makers to what extent even to acquire information about social consequences, much less act upon it. Since such information has costs, and stifling one's own predilections and self-interest, or admitting errors, involves perhaps even higher costs, there is every institutional incentive to resist the transmission of socially effective knowledge. The question of the effectiveness of institutions for their social purposes (as distinguished from the purposes of those who run them) is largely a question of the conductivity of the incentive structure with respect to external knowledge.

Money is obviously a sensitive conductor of knowledge where individual or institutional solvency is at stake. The fungibility of money facilitates incremental rather than categorical decisions and permits the incremental weighing of highly disparate effects in one medium of accounting. This is not creating an artificial equivalence but recognizing an inherent trade-off. The options weighed are not limited to simultaneous alternatives but extend across time as well as space, since they involve savings and investments of varying degrees of maturity, as well as current consumption and production decisions. Despite the common contrast between financial considerations and personal emotions, both share these characteristics as conductors of social knowledge to individual decision makers across space and time. A family decision on moving to a new home involves weighing such disparate emotional considerations as the future need of a growing infant for his own room, the disruption of the older children's current neighborhood friendships, the effect of the new school on their future college (and therefore career) prospects, the emotional strains on the breadwinner(s) caused by the cost of the new home—and many more such concerns, all weighed in the emotional currency of the family's well-being. Even if one individual makes the decision, the emotional ties between that individual and the other family members conduct their needs to him as incentives and constraints which typically force a decision quite different from what would be optimal from that individual's own standpoint alone. A father may, for example, locate his family far out in the suburbs for the sake of the children, giving himself an exhausting daily commute to work, even though there are apartments available within walking distance of his office and closer to the entertainment centers that he and his wife enjoy. All these considerations are fungible and incrementally variable where high emotional conductivity transmits the present and future needs of others to the decision maker as personally felt incentives and constraints. In this way, there is created the social equivalent of the economic agent who is a residual claimant and therefore can function with social effectiveness as an "unmonitored monitor." By contrast, the rules of an organization are often categorical, as when a municipal ordinance requires that all city employees live within the city limits or postal regulations require packages to be prepared to certain specifications.

The concept of an "unmonitored monitor" with a broad mandate may seem dubious as a way of getting a job done. Articulated specifics (job descriptions, organizational rules, etc.) enforced by tiers of monitors are much more rationalistic. However, the ultimate question is not plausibility but results. Unmonitored monitors are among the most hard-working and dedicated people in the society. Mothers and businessmen are classic examples. In their very different ways, these two unmonitored monitors have become notorious for the intensity and duration of their efforts, and are often admonished to "take it easy" by those closest to them, even though the latter are often the beneficiaries of their efforts. Similar levels of dedication are much rarer among rank and file business employees or rank-and-file civil servants—though both of the latter groups are under layers of supervisors and controlled by numerous articulated rules. Admonitions to rank and file civil servants to "take it easy" would raise suspicions of sarcasm. Nor is it a matter of different groups of people performing differently because of disparate values or psychology. The very same individuals who perform in lackluster fashion as employees of business or government may, as parents, drive themselves to do all that they can for their children.

No one is a *wholly* unmonitored monitor. There are legal restrictions on business management and laws on child neglect and abuse. However, these laws seldom reach either the areas or the intensity of efforts achieved in parental or business activities. The businessman who works nights and weekends is usually going far beyond what is necessary to avoid being fired or to prevent the business from being sued or going bankrupt. Similarly, most parents could probably reduce their efforts and expenditures on their children by half without becoming legally liable for neglect or abuse. Indeed, some of the largest expenditures on children arise when putting them through college, at an age when there is no legal liability to do anything for them. In short, even where there are formalized rules, the articulated rationality of these rules does not begin to explain the efforts and sacrifices of unmonitored monitors. It is the high conductivity of both money and emotional ties which transmits knowledge of other's needs with such dramatic effect.

High conductivity is an economizer of costly knowledge, in much the same way as the transmission of electricity through copper wire economizes on generating costs, even though it is physically possible to transmit electricity through less conductive material. The conductivity of the human nervous system also economizes on knowledge. A baby pulls his hand back from a hot object without having to know how heat destroys his tissues. The rare medical phenomenon of people whose nervous systems do not transmit pain also demonstrates how conductivity is an economizer of knowledge. Such people must have very frequent complete medical checkups, for they feel none of the painful symptoms which either alert the rest of us to trouble intellectually or else incapacitate us from continuing the harmful activity. As a substitute, they must seek vastly larger amounts of costly, explicit, articulated medical knowledge. Some such people have been rushed from a routine medical checkup to an emergency operation for such conditions as acute appendicitis, from which they had felt no pain. To the extent that social institutions are insulated from the pain of feedback, they may either neglect dangerous conditions or else require inordinate costs of knowledge to preserve themselves or the larger society. Sometimes the institutions deliberately seek to insulate or anesthetize themselves to painful feedback, but sometimes that happens as an unintended consequence of the way decision-making units are set up—for example, a special subway authority oblivious to the injuries and deaths its safety policies are causing among bus or automobile passengers.

Effective social decision making need not depend on the transmission of explicit feedback to decision makers, nor on the degree of their rationality and insight in reaction to it. Where individuals, institutions, or processes are competing for survival, the best adapted survive, whether their adaption is due to brainpower or luck, and the social benefits are maximized either way. Individual merit is neither necessary nor sufficient for optimal social decision making.

Chapter 5

Political Trade-Offs

The government as a decision maker is often regarded as simply the institutional personification of "society." But the diversities, conflicts, and disparate incentives and constraints which make "society" a meaningless abstraction as a decision-making unit also make government a fragmentary aggregation of decision makers. An experienced Washington insider refers to "the warring principalities that are sometimes known as the Federal government."[1] This is not the classic "separation of powers" into legislative, judicial, and executive branches. These "warring principalities" are all part of the same executive branch. Executive agencies of the U.S. government have not only followed policies at cross purposes with one another; they have even sued each other in court. Theoretically, they are all under the control and the direction of the President, but the fact that these internecine disputes can persist and be publicly aired not only in the press but in the courts suggests that Presidents often find it politically prudent to stay out of these power struggles. Moreover, the areas of autonomous decision making within government can be even smaller than a given agency or bureau. Supervisors may "have little control over their nominal subordinates, who enjoy de facto tenure,"[2] even when they are not civil servants, because of those subordinates' links to particular Congressmen and their staffs or to the press or to outside constituencies.[3]

Governmental decision-making units must be analyzed like other social or economic units which choose courses of action designed to maximize their own well-being, under the particular incentives and constraints of their respective situations. This obvious point must be emphasized because of a large literature which recognizes *non*governmental activities as self-interested but arbitrarily treats any governmental activity as axiomatic proof of an objective social need for such activity.[4] Despite the existense of some self-sacrificing public officials, to postulate that such officials generally control governmental decision making seems less realistic than the opposite view that "parties formulate policy in order to win elections, rather than win elections in order to formulate policy."[5] For nonelected governments, the postulate that government activity is solely a response to social needs seems even less reasonable as a basis for analysis.

As noted earlier (Chapter 2), political surrogates are a way of economizing on knowledge in government decision making, since each citizen cannot become fully informed on every issue. However, this arrangement also means a built-in advantage for political surrogates over their constituents in the use of knowledge. No small part of the political art consists of the exploitation of that advantage—whether by misstating the costs and benefits of particular programs, by ominously referring to the weighty considerations "known only to the President" in his conduct of foreign policy, or the intricate rules of "the bureaucratic maze," known only to insiders and therefore insulating much governmental activity from outside scrutiny. All kinds of political systems (democracy, monarchy, feudalism, etc.) put enormous emphasis on the personal "loyalty" of subordinates—not loyalty to the public, or even to the government, but to their immediate superiors—thereby sealing off a source of leaks of knowledge to outsiders.

Although "society" is far from being a decision-making unit, even in governmental decisions, it is of course the most important unit on whom the *impact* of political decisions is to be considered. Therefore the trade-offs to be considered here are those political trade-offs of enduring social significance, rather than the "horse trading" that goes on among politicians. Among the major political trade-offs to be considered here for any political system are those involving (1) freedom, (2) rights, and (3) time.

FREEDOM AND FORCE

One of the most important political trade-offs is between the amount of freedom and the amount of other characteristics desired in a society. The problem is made more difficult by intellectual ambiguities and philosophical disagreements that have long surrounded the very meaning of freedom: "We all declare for liberty; but in using the same word, we do not mean the same thing."[6] This is at least as true today as when Abraham Lincoln said it.

Freedom here will refer to a social relationship among people—namely, the absence of force as a prospective instrument of decision making. Freedom is reduced whenever a decision is made under threat of force, whether or not force actually materializes or is evident in retrospect. This prospective definition of force is essential to avoid such absurdities as concluding that armed robbery does not usually involve force. Force here is not used metaphorically, however, to refer to benefits so enticing as to make the decision a foregone conclusion. A special wariness is necessary in discussions of freedom, not only because of the inherent problems of the concept, but also because an Orwellian Newspeak has made it fashionable to describe the trade-off of freedom for other things as an expansion of "new freedoms" or of freedom in some "larger" sense. The incremental trade-off of freedom for other things is accepted by everyone except a pure anarchist. But the extent of this historic trade-off is too momentous an issue to be concealed or confused by pretty words.

Force is the antithesis of freedom, but force must be used, if only to defend against other force. Force used against murder, for example, includes not only such force as may be used by police intervening to prevent a murder, or to capture a murderer, but also force applied to innocent third parties who may be detained or subpoenaed as witnesses or forced by law to serve as jurors. It is not an absolute sacrifice of freedom nor an absolute prevention of murder. But it is simply an incremental trade-off at varying rates, and the question at any given point is how much more freedom are we prepared to sacrifice for how much prospect of reducing the murder rate—or how much more freedom are we going to demand at the cost of how many more lives of murder victims? Trade-offs involving freedom are often painful, if only because only other urgent needs are considered worthy of weighing and balancing with it.

The government is the general repository of force—whether that government be democratic, totalitarian, feudal, etc. Totalitarian governments, by definition, have no significant trade-offs of freedom left to consider, since freedom has already been sacrificed for some alternative consideration, whether rhetorical or material. Democratic governments are constantly weighing incremental trade-offs toward or away from freedom. Indeed, democracy itself is a consideration that is traded against freedom, and at one time this trade-off was both recognized and feared.[7] Contemporary opinion often simply incorporates freedom into the very definition of democracy, so that a government that eliminates freedom is not "really" democratic. This trade-off, too, is much too important to be dealt with by verbal sleight of hand. To include freedom in the very definition of democracy is to define a process not by its actual characteristics as a process but by its hoped for results. This is not only intellectually invalid, it is, in practical terms, blinding oneself in advance to some of the unwanted consequences of the process.

A lynch mob may be a more accurate expression of the majority will than a court of law—especially an appellate court of appointed judges—and yet lynch mobs are condemned and "law and order" upheld because certain freedoms are deemed more important than democracy. Democratic institutions will be defined here to mean institutions which carry out the popular will in its decisions—whether those decisions be wise or foolish, generous or oppressive. When the undemocratic governments of the Reconstruction era in the South were replaced by governments more responsive to the majority, the minority suffered oppression and terror on a scale seldom seen in modern civilization. Such residual protection as the black minority retained came largely from sources having little to do with political democracy—notably markets,[8] morality,[9] and appellate courts.[10]

When freedom is conceived of as a relationship among people, trade-offs of freedom for material goods, scientific progress or military power, for example, become quite explicit, instead of being subsumed under a general expansion of "freedom" as sweepingly redefined. The growth of the decision making powers of government may facilitate various specific forms of material progress—even if at the expense of material progress in general—while reducing freedom. That trade-off needs to be made explicit. It is instead muddied over by those who define freedom as options (freedom to)[11]—and who have many options to promise in exchange for our freedom. The options approach asks, "What freedom does a starving man have?" The answer is that starvation is a tragic human condition—perhaps more tragic than loss of freedom. That does not prevent these from being *two different things*. No matter what ranking may be given to such disagreeable things as indebtedness and constipation, a laxative will not get you out of debt and a pay raise will not insure "regularity." Conversely on a list of desirable things, gold may rank much higher than peanut butter, but you cannot spread gold on a sandwich and eat it for nourishment. The false issue of *ranking* things cannot be allowed to confuse questions of *distinguishing* things.

The mere fact that something may outrank freedom does not make that something *become* freedom. Moreover, in social trade-offs as in economic trade-offs, all rankings or preferences are incremental at a given point and changeable at other points. Nothing desirable at all is categorically less desirable than something else. Food may be incrementally preferable to any amount of freedom to a starving man, but that does not mean that dessert after a banquet is incrementally preferable to the freedom to go home at the end of the evening. The great social desiderata are so frequently discussed in categorical language that it is easy to forget their incremental nature—and to talk nonsense with seeming profundity as a result. Both Adam Smith and John Rawls made justice the primary virtue of a society,[12] but their meanings were not only different but nearly opposite, because one was speaking incrementally and the other was speaking categorically. To Smith some amount of justice was a prerequisite for any of the other features of society to exist,[13] but he was far from believing that all increments of justice invariably outranked increments of other things, and in fact he regarded such a belief as counterproductive and doctrinaire.[14] To Rawls, justice is categorically paramount in the sense of not being incrementally inferior to any other consideration, so that one consideration of justice may be sacrificed only to another consideration of justice, but not to any other desired goal.[15] According to Rawls, a policy that benefitted all of the human race except one person should not be adopted, no matter how much they were benefitted, nor even if the one person were completely unharmed, because that would be an "unjust" distribution of the benefits of the policy. Perhaps not many people are likely to agree with Rawls' conclusion, but many use the same arbitrarily categorical approach to social analysis which led logically to such conclusions.

When two things have to be traded off against one another, it is necessary to understand clearly (1) that they are in fact two different things, and to consider (2) explicitly on what terms we are prepared to incrementally trade the one for the other. Nothing is gained by claiming—or insinuating—that both are the same thing, or that one is just more of that thing than the other. At least nothing is gained from the standpoint of rational decision making. In political reality, *much* is gained by those who wish to take the decision making power of others into their own hands. Much verbal sleight of hand is practiced with such statements as "security is merely an aspect of freedom."[16] Freedom has cost too much blood and agony to be relinquished at the cheap price of rhetoric.

NONGOVERNMENTAL "POWER"

Not only is freedom confused with other things, so too is its opposite, force. The widespread recognition of the need to use force to counter other force is used to justify expanding governmental force to counter things that are not force at all, but are called force metaphorically for the sake of justifying coercive action against them. Attacks on economic "power" are a common form of justification for expanded government force.

Often the rhetoric is preserved by such devices as referring to a firm's retrospective percentage of sales during a given period as a share of the market they "control," as if in some prospective sense. Metaphors and vague definitions are used to justify an expansion of government power which is neither vague nor metaphorical but very concrete. But with power as with freedom, a sufficiently wide or vague definition brings in many examples. What is crucial in judging such an example is distinguishing between (1) situations in which an individual's options for dealing with alternative transactors are forcibly reduced or eliminated, and (2) situations in which a given transactor adds so much more to his options than anyone else that acceptance is a foregone conclusion. A monopoly or cartel reduces the consumers' options, while a successful competitor adds to those options. Reducing consumers' options requires not simply raising one's own price—anyone can do that—but forcibly keeping others from entering the competition and undercutting that price. This usually requires either an exclusive franchise from the government, or some law or regulation limiting competition. These government created monopolies or cartels are the beneficiaries of governmental force, not its target. The situation of the transactor who offers better terms than others may seem to be a strange candidate for a "power" menace to be combated by government, though in reality many regulatory and antitrust activities do just that, as will be seen in Chapter 8. The point here is simply that a trade-off involving more use of force in economic decision-making is denied by depicting governmental force as merely an offset to existing private force, with no net increase.

DEMOCRACY

Democracy has been defined here by its characteristics as a process, not by its hoped for results, such as freedom, the dignity of the individual, or other benefits expected or alleged. Whatever the merits of democracy, it has its institutional limitations and operates within an area of circumstantial constraints—like all other political, economic, and other systems. The open endedness of hopes has sometimes led to the view that a majority can or should have whatever it wants—a view defined here as "the democratic fallacy." The democratic fallacy implicitly presupposes unconstrained circumstantial options, so that if a majority does not get what it wants, it can only be a result of some denial of their democratic rights in some intentional sense. Choice through the ballot box has often been equated with choice through the market. But inherent constraints mean that democratic governments have no wider array of options to offer than anyone else—regardless of what options many may believe to exist—and that one crucial difference between ballots and prices is that prices convey effective knowledge of inherent constraints, while ballots do not. If I desire a Rolls Royce and simultaneously a normal standard of living, the price tag on the automobile immediately informs, convinces, and virtually coerces me to the conclusion that these two things are inconsistent. But if I believe simultaneously in a large military arsenal, low taxes, a balanced budget, and massive social programs, there are no constraints on my voting that way. Some time after a voting decision, it may become apparent that what was asked or promised did not in fact materialize, but this can easily be blamed on the dishonesty of political candidates, with no greater public awareness that the set of options simultaneously desired was inherently unrealizable from the onset. Instead of feedback to the voters to reduce their desired set of options to what is simultaneously realizable, the message may be to choose different persons as leaders, or different ideologies, movements, etc., in order to continue pursuing that same set of options. Indeed, when social progress is viewed retrospectively, it is often regarded as axiomatically attributable to such insistence on better things, rather than to technological and organizational advances over time which created wider arrays of options from which to choose. It is as if the historic increase in the Gross National Product was incidental to a rising living standard caused by political activity.

The question here is not whether voters have a right to choose whatever they want. Voters can only *choose* process characteristics and *hope* for results. Consumers buy results and leave the process to those with specialized knowledge of such things. There is no argument here for denying voters their democratic choices. The point is merely to claim that the terms of the choice are readily misstated politically. The prevalence of inflation among the most diverse kinds of governments and across thousands of years of history, suggest that no small part of the political art consists in misstating options and in trying to give the appearance of simultaneously satisfying competing claims when they cannot be satisfied in reality.

A more extreme version of the democratic fallacy goes beyond the idea that a majority can or should have whatever it votes for, to claim the same right for particular minority subsets of the population. It is regarded as a "failure" of a democratic system—or as showing that the system is not "really" democratic—when determined, conscientious people cannot get what they want through legitimate channels. Justifications for law breaking (extending in principle all the way to terrorism) by frustrated insurgents are based on this premise. In this version of the democratic fallacy, the ignoring of inherent constraints within which all decision-making processes function is simply extended to ignoring all other people's desires as an obvious (and valid) reason why a particular subset's desires were not achieved.

Sometimes the subset is presumed to know the majority's "real" interests better than the majority itself, and so is acting democratically in some "larger" sense. This confuses the characteristics of a hoped-for result with the characteristics of a decision-making process. *Numerous* subsets' hoped-for results are preferable to the majority's perception of things, in the view of those subsets. Democracy is simply one decision-making process for resolving such conflicts among disparate perceptions. To resolve the conflicts by other processes—including violence—is to trade off democracy for something else. To conceal that trade-off by calling that something else "democracy" too is to ignore the fact that virtually all political systems or movements are ostensibly for the benefit of the people. The hoped for results of kings, emperors, military juntas, and various dictators would thus all have to be called "democratic" in some "larger" sense.

Like other trade-offs, the trade-offs involving democracy are frequently denied or misstated by including other things in a wider ranging and more vague definition of democracy. "Participatory" democracy has arisen in this way, as another concept defined by hoped for results rather than by characteristics of the process itself. In principle, participatory democracy is distinguished from, and complementary with, representative democracy. In a representative democracy when the voters choose surrogates who actually make the decisions, the surrogates may either be or become part of a small set of people with interests and perspectives different from those of the public at large. The theory behind "participatory" democracy, is that more decisions should be made by the public itself directly rather than through representatives. To this end, numerous local boards, commissions, councils, or advisory participants of one sort or another are to have "input" into the decision-making process. The implicit assumption of the theory is that there will be not merely more numerous decision makers but more representative ones. But, turning from hopes to institutional mechanics, there is usually nothing to lead institutionally toward that result, and much to lead in the opposite direction. Those individuals who have the leisure, the education, and the inclination to "participate" may be very unrepresentative of the public. In practice, participatory democracy means that broadly elected representatives are to share power with self-selected representatives of narrow vocal constituencies. From the standpoint of the institutional transmission and authentication of knowledge, it means that instead of having insiders judge processes and outsiders judge results, some outsiders are to judge and change processes on the basis of their part-time experience on the inside and their unrepresentative interests on the outside. It is essentially an incremental trade-off of the public's right to decide by elected representatives for a self-selected constituencies' opportunity to be insiders.

Whatever the substantive merits or demerits of particular trade-offs involving freedom, force, or participation, the crucial point is to see the trade-offs as trade-offs, rather than as they are sometimes depicted, as simply "more" freedom or democracy as conveniently redefined.

RIGHTS

Rights have already been noticed as rigidities (Chapter 2). They are also boundaries limiting the exercise of governmental power and carving out areas within which individual discretion is free to shape decisions. In addition to these Constitutional rights of citizens in general, there are special rights, such as the right of exclusive use of specific things (property rights) or rights arising from specific reciprocal commitments (contracts) and rights created by specific legislation (employment rights, housing rights, etc.). By "rights" here is meant legal entitlements, regardless of their moral merits. Rights in this sense are simply factual statements about the availability of state power to back up individual claims. They are simply options to use governmental force at less than its cost of production—ideally at zero cost. In reality, some cost of time and effort are required even to phone the police, and to vindicate many rights a long and costly legal battle up through the appellate courts may be necessary. Where a right worth X (in money or otherwise) would cost 2X to vindicate, then for all practical purposes such a right does not exist for the individual. Where most of the cost falls on the government, the trade-off is between the social costs involved in a particular violation of individual rights—i.e., the effect on other people of letting such violations go unpunished—compared to the costs of enforcement.

Social trade-offs are involved in the creation of rights, the defining of rights, and the assigning of rights to individuals. When a given kind of activity is dealt with by the creation of rights rather than by alternative decision-making processes, there is a loss of flexibility (incremental adjustment) and reversibility. Something that is incrementally preferable at a given point becomes categorically imposed at all points by the force at the disposal of the government. Insofar as the law of diminishing returns applies to social as well as economic processes, this means that many benefits are pushed to the point where they cease to be benefits and may even become counterproductive.

PROPERTY RIGHTS

The creation of rights involves questions not only of whether to create rights as a mode of dealing with a particular trade-off, but to whom to assign such rights as are created. Property rights involve both kinds of decisions. Many things are left unowned—wild animals or birds, fish in the sea, human beings, air and sunshine—because the enforcement of property rights is deemed either impracticable or undesirable. Ideas cannot be copyrighted for both reasons, whereas a given permutation of words can be copyrighted, both because it is feasible to determine authorship and because it is deemed more important to provide a prospective reward as an incentive for future writing than to incrementally increase the circulation of existing writings by eliminating royalty charges.

Property rights in general must be distinguished from the particular form of property rights in so-called "capitalist" countries. A socialist government also owns property. If socialism meant literally an *abolition* of property rights, rather than their reassignment, then any individual citizen would be free to build a house, ride a horse, or play baseball on land that the government had set aside for growing food, and life would become impossible in such a society. But, in reality, whether under capitalism or socialism, property rights are basically rights to exclude—meaning in operational terms, the availability of governmental force to eject and/or punish others for using the same property without permission. However, the *right* to exclude does not mean that exclusion will result. Rights to exclude are negotiable in market economies, and may be sold or rented, in whole or in part. Property rights are also divisible among decision-making units. One person or organization may own the right to farm a given field while another decision-making unit owns the right to the minerals underneath and still another owns the right to string electric wires overhead. Almost never does one property owner own every conceivable use of a given property. An owner of a mountain does not own the right to fly over the mountain, nor does he own the right to every stream that originates in his mountain, in the sense of being able to dump anything that he wishes into those streams.

Whether in a socialist or a capitalist context, a property right is a differential privilege[17] of some to exclude others from decisions or activities involving some physical or intangible object of value. This differential privilege is not personal; the current owner can have last week's owner jailed for trespassing. In a socialist or communist society, a deposed official dare not presume to continue directing enterprises formerly under his control. The basis for a property right is therefore not an individual attribute or merit but social expediency. The social question then is—what is to be gained or lost by defining a property right, and on what basis should the right be assigned, and shall it be transferable? The defining and assigning of property rights goes on in all kinds of societies—in socialist societies the assignments are based on political election or appointment, until further notice—while transferability at the discretion of individual transactors is the defining characteristic of capitalist processes.[18]

To define a property right is to carve out and tie into a package various possible activities associated with a given object of value. It is essentially a judgement that certain decisions go together, in the sense that different decisions about each of the activities separately are unlikely to be as socially beneficial as decisions about the set of activities collectively. If separate property rights to a living hog's head are defined independently of property rights to his heart, stomach, or hind legs, so that these rights can be held by different decision-making units, it is unlikely that the hog will live an optimal length of time from the viewpoint of the production of pork chops, ham, and chitterlings. If the owner of the hog's heart removed his property, the value of all the other property would be reduced. If these separate property rights are transferable, it obviously would be to someone's self-interest to acquire these separate, risk-ridden rights at values greater than they have to the separate owners, and combine them into one, far less risky right to the whole hog. In other words, the right to the whole hog is more valuable than the sum of the rights to all his parts. The *definition* of a property right is therefore an important step, especially in systems which forbid subsequent transfer of these rights.

In feudalistic systems, where land is inherited as an indivisible property required to remain with a given family (entails), the whole society loses if those lands are in parcels so small or so situated that they are far less productive than if they could be combined into larger units or traded off to get contiguous parcels, or if land served by a given stream were under the same decision-making unit. Conversely, a property may be too large to be effectively managed by one decision-making unit, so that it would produce more output for the society at large if it were under several decision-making units. These problems are not unique to feudalism. Wherever the initial definition of property rights is imperfect—which is to say, wherever it is done by human beings—and subsequent transfers are prohibited or restricted, similar problems arise. A socialist government may, for example, "entail" a whole industry to one planning commission, leading to avoidable "mistakes" in the industry which are not the result of stupidity or perversity but merely due to the high cost of monitoring the property as defined. Were the property transferable, it would be more valuable in smaller units—more valuable not only to the buyers but to society at large.

Leaving property rights wholly undefined is even more disastrous than imperfectly defining them. Wild animals are often hunted to extinction precisely because they do not belong to anyone. They can by fiat or metaphor be said to belong to "the people," but unless it is feasible to apply force to exclude poachers, there is no property right in reality. It is precisely those things which belong to "the people" which have historically been despoiled—wild creatures, the air, and waterways being notable examples. This goes to the heart of why property rights are socially important in the first place. *Property rights mean self-interested monitors.* No *owned* creatures are in danger of extinction. No owned forests are in danger of being leveled. No one kills the goose that lays the golden eggs when it is his goose. Even chickens who lay ordinary eggs are in no danger of being killed before their replacements have been provided. No logging company is going to let its own forest become a mass of stumps, though it may do that on "public" land.[19]

By creating monitors with a vested interest in the maximization of a given set of values, property rights reduce the social cost of monitoring efficiency. In systems of nontransferable property, the monitor's incentives are to maximize those values realizable during his own tenure, whether as inheritor of an entailed estate or as a member of a modern planning commission with a fixed term. Where the property is transferable at will, the present value of a property at any given time includes future values realizable long after the time horizon (or even lifetime) of the existing property holder, who therefore has no incentive to restrict his maximization to the short run. In socialist systems, property transfers take place through political decisions to replace members of the planning bodies or to reorganize the planning structure itself. The property itself never belongs to those individuals, but they benefit both financially and psychically from managing it, and visibly successful management may create a capital gain in the form of increased likelihood of promotion to higher levels of pay or power. All of this provides short-run incentives for short-run maximization of politically visible values. Morality, ideology, or a sense of history must then be relied upon as incentives for longer-run maximization policies. That such incentives apply to only a limited number of individuals, or to individuals in only a limited number of positions of historic visibility, may be indicated by the fact that long-run investments in the Soviet economy are directed by only a few people at a time. Under short-run incentive structures, individual decision-making units tend to avoid technological innovations with short-run costs and long-run benefits "as the devil shies away from incense," to quote Soviet Premier Brezhnev in a complaint about Soviet managers.[20]

Because property rights are essentially rights to exclude, with the aid of force supplied by the government, the costs to be weighed in this social trade-off are the costs paid not only by those excluded but by the society at large. Indeed, when an economy is recognized as a rationing scheme that must deny most things to most people (few individuals could afford to buy one of every item produced in the whole economy), this question reduces to the losses sustained by society at large. Patent rights exclude alternative producers from supplying the patented goods, reducing competition and the efficiency which depends on it. Copyrights reduce the dissemination of knowledge and entertainment, by pricing some potential users out of the market with royalty requirements. With both patents and copyrights, it is not the royalties actually paid that constitute the social loss; these are only internal transfers. It is the transactions that do *not* take place because of prospective royalty charges that constitute the net social loss. The cost of policing property rights is also a social consideration involved in a trade-off against the benefits. The whole costly apparatus of title records, title search, civil court systems, marshals for evictions, etc., are part of the cost of property rights in general, and of highly fragmented property ownership in particular. The costs may also include losses to those individuals intended to be benefitted.

Rights in general may be conferred for individual as well as social benefit. Property rights are intended to secure gains to society at large, including numerous persons who own no significant property. This point is insisted upon in socialist ideology, where the government holds property rights "for the benefit of the people," but it is also implicit in capitalist private property right law as well, where it is the social expediency rather than the individual gain that is the controlling rationale.[21] However, there are many rights intended to benefit primarily or exclusively those to whom the rights directly apply. Civil rights laws, for example, are generally intended to benefit racial or ethnic minorities, and minimum wage laws are generally intended to benefit low-wage employees. The appropriate question here is the trade-off of costs and benefits for those subsets of the population, as well as for the population at large.

EQUAL RIGHTS VERSUS SPECIAL RIGHTS

While all forms of society require some set of dependable expectations enforcable by group pressure or force, in many nations it is not enough that rights exist; they must, in principle, also be *equal* rights. Equality as a legal or political principle does not depend upon a belief in empirical equality of any sort. Quite the contrary. If it were literally true that "all men are created equal," there would be no case for equal protection of the law, or perhaps even for laws at all. If every person had exactly the same intelligence, strength, aggressiveness, organizing ability, etc., there would be no need for the law to protect one from another, because one would never be in a position to successfully take advantage of the other. Even though a coalition of such equal individuals could overwhelm any isolated individual, they would all be equally capable of foreseeing this and organizing counter coalitions to offset that danger. It is precisely the inequalities of people which makes the equal protection of the law so important—that there must be an overwhelming organized force ready to be thrown into the balance, so that a weak little old lady shall have as much right to live as the most stalwart young man or that frauds that deceive the unwary shall not be immune to retribution by officials who are more knowledgeable.

There are, of course, few people who are equal in any empirical sense. Most people who are considered equal are usually regarded as such because they have *offsetting inequalities*—that is, neither of them is superior in every aspect, nor are they equal in every aspect. In this context, "equality" over all depends upon what weights are arbitrarily assigned to the various traits in which one or the other predominates. So too would any general notion of "superiority" or "inferiority." All these attempts to sum up disparate characteristics ignore the diversity of personal values which makes it impossible to have objectively recognized, fungible units in which to add up totals. Most of us would give a heavy weight to the fact that individual A is not a homicidal maniac, while individual B is, and so prefer A even if B were universally recognized to have more charm or beauty. But there are few traits on which there is similar agreement, even as regards rank ordering, much less relative weights.

Where a particular segment of the population has different rights from the general population at large—either explicitly or in practice—the costs of transacting with that segment will tend also to be different. Anyone with a choice of transacting with illegal aliens, ordinary citizens, or persons with diplomatic immunity, would face different risks (costs) of legal liability against himself and different prospects of seeking legal redress for any damages he might suffer from individuals from each of these respective groups. If the individuals in these three categories were otherwise identical, any prospective transactor—whether as a prospective landlord, employer, or spouse—would face the least risk of legal trouble from an illegal alien and the most from someone with diplomatic immunity. The abuses suffered by the former and inflicted on others by the latter are both notorious. What is important here is not this retrospective experience of these two special groups, but what that implies more broadly for prospective behavior in society at large The more special rights are created for any particular groups, the higher the transactions costs of dealing with that group and the fewer transactions that group will be able to consummate. Special health and safety legislation for youths or women make youths or women less desirable employees than others and thereby reduces their employability. This is not a phenomenon of private capitalist employers only. Soviet managers have avoided hiring younger workers whenever possible for the same reason.[22] As rights of legal redress for fired workers have grown, so have hiring requirements, to eliminate many who would otherwise be employable if the employer did not need a higher level of assurance before assuming the increased risks of legal liability for firing.[23] Relatives often have special rights on a job, without any explicit agreement to that effect; antinepotism rules make them less employable to avoid these costs.

Consumer rights raise the price paid for products and services, since higher quality, or greater producer liability, both have costs. The question is whether the amount by which the price is raised is more or less than the increased value created by the rights. If the increased quality or enlarged responsibility of the seller were worth it, there would be profit incentives for the producer to raise his quality, responsibility, and price together without consumer protection laws. It has long been common for stores with easy return, money back policies and free repair services to charge more than stores that sell "as is." Some stores even sell service contracts separately, so that the same physical item can be bought at two different prices from the same dealer with two different levels of dealer responsibility. Those for whom the price differential is sufficient incentive to speculate in consumer appliances can buy without the service contract, and others can substitute money for boldness incrementally. These subjective differences in the costs of risks are ignored when laws in effect prescribe categorically how much liability insurance must be sold with each product. Assurances that the consumer must "really" be better off this way can seldom be checked empirically. One large historical instance of imposed product quality "improvement" occurred when the British Parliament in the nineteenth century imposed higher health and comfort standards on ships carrying Irish emigrants. In view of the foul and disgusting state of the ships at that time, it might seem to be a foregone conclusion that this was a net benefit. Yet the records show that the Irish rushed to get on ships heading out *before* the law became effective—and the outflow of emigrants slackened immediately thereafter.[24] The cost of the higher quality was apparently weighed differently by the Irish themselves than by the British Parliament.

Perhaps the crucial problem involved in creating special "rights" is that they typically involve reducing the set of options available to the transactors, without any offsetting increase in other options. There is no reason to believe that people will generally make a better set of choices out of a smaller set of options, where the larger set includes all the options in the smaller set. If the purpose is in fact to *deny* the ostensible beneficiaries their choice and substitute someone else's choice, that is another matter.

Because the negative impact of special legal rights on the recipients is seldom recognized by the voting public, this cost seldom serves as a restraint on political decision making. Indeed, the creation of rights is less constrained than the creation of other ostensible benefits for special constituencies. While political benefits can usually be expected to increase voter support among the recipients, they lose voter support among those who pay the costs—either the taxpayers in general or others on whom the burdens are placed. Rights, however, cost the taxpayer little more than the paper and ink needed for printing them. From a politicians' viewpoint, rights are therefore a virtually ideal benefit to confer on special constituencies. Where the rights' social costs consist largely of a reduction in would-be transactions affected by the rights, what matters politically is whether those tangibly benefiting from the improved *terms* of the transactions (minimum wage laws, rent control) can perceive their offsetting losses from reductions in the *number* of transactions consummated (unemployment, housing shortages), and whether the other transactor can be publicly discredited ("exploiting" employers or "greedy" landlords). Where the terms are more visible than the number of transactors, and the other transactor is politically vulnerable, there is little constraint on the proliferation of special rights for special groups.

The trade-off between equal rights and special rights is often denied by the same verbal methods used to obscure the trade-off between freedom and other values. The two things being traded off are simply put under one label, so that special rights for special groups are described as simply equal rights in some "larger" or "truer" sense, and instead of a trade-off there is—rhetorically, at least—simply an expansion of the one benefit. This verbal sleight of hand avoids confronting the costs of special rights both to society and to the supposed beneficiaries.

GENERAL RIGHTS

Where certain general rights involve virtually universal desire—such as the desire not to be murdered—incorporating it into specific law eliminates the transactions costs of pointlessly litigating anew each time the net harm of the individual act, in a common-law approach without any explicit law against murder. Making price fixing illegal *per se* similarly spares courts repeated reruns of introductory economics in antitrust cases. It may seem like a strange and weak justification for enacting basic rights into law that this will save a little court time. Such laws, however, transmit virtually unanimous knowledge—not only about the abhorrence of the crime but about the determination to act against its perpetrators. No such information either exists, or would need to be transmitted if it did, in cases involving *voluntary* transactions. If it were somehow impossible to kill anyone except with his own voluntary cooperation, the case for laws against murder would be much weaker than it is, and there might be something to be said for litigating each episode from scratch to determine what harm had been done.

Even laws against murder are subject to diminishing returns, and ultimately negative returns. A terminally ill patient who has permanently lost consciousness may be kept organically "alive" for months or years after his brain is dead, as insurance against a murder or manslaughter charge against the doctor or hospital authorities. Other terminally ill patients whose only consciousness is of overwhelming pain may have their agony artificially prolonged for the same reason, even though drugs are available to relieve this pain—with the side effect of shortening their "life." The economic ruin of a patient's family or the suffering of the patient himself are the implicit "premium" paid for this "insurance" policy against homicide charges. It is an external cost to the decision-making medical authorities, and so does not constrain their behavior. Disproportionate as the costs and benefits might be in any individual case—the costs to the patient and his family being so much more than the benefits to the doctor—the larger social question is how many people would take on the care of terminally ill patients (or patients who might become terminally ill) if it meant facing daily prospects of homicide charges from more humane medical procedures?

The tragedy is implicit in the categorical nature of laws in general, and homicide laws in particular. The legal system is still wrestling with the problem of trying to introduce some incrementalism into this area—for example, with individual court orders to disconnect life saving equipment from terminally comatose patients, essentially dead people whose organs and medical bills are being prolonged. But the psychic and legal costs of obtaining such court orders make them practically unavailable to many people. The point here is not to "blame" anyone. Quite the contrary. This situation is a tragedy in the classic sense of a humanly unavoidable devastation. It may even be that there is no real "solution" that would not open the way to the deliberate sacrifice of other sick people for their estates, their organs, or to simply be rid of an inconvenience.

The law against murder has been used as an illustration of the diminishing returns to laws and policies in general, precisely because it is one of the most universal of all laws, occurring in the most diverse social and legal systems and enduring through the ages. There is no distracting side issue of the desirability of the goal. Diminishing returns and negative returns to such an essential law are a sobering indication of the limits of any law or policy—and of the limits of knowledge, on which decisions depend. Even if, at a given juncture, it is obvious to the patient, his family, and the doctor that suffering should not be artificially and pointlessly prolonged, the transmission of that knowledge in *categorically articulated terms documentable to third parties* is what determines whether the murder laws will apply.[25] In general, diminishing returns and the limits (costs) of knowledge inhibit the application of all laws and policies, however obvious or desirable their goals might seem.

Where the basic general rights involved are rights against the government—as in the Bill of Rights—saving transactions costs is no small consideration, given the gross disproportion between the resources of the government and those of a private individual. Putting the burden of proof on the government likewise saves transactions costs. Without such rights and with no burden of proof difference, each person would have to litigate against general government arguments as to his harmfulness until his money ran out and then plead no contest. Saving transactions costs is saving the rights themselves from meaninglessness.

TIME

Time is important in many ways in political decision making, including the time horizons of decision makers and voters, the time dimension of interest groups, and problems created by arbitrary divisions of the time continuum for political assessment purposes.

Because politicians' own time horizons are so short, the voters' longer time horizons are crucial for transmitting a more farsighted perspective to government decision making. But time increases the cost of political knowledge and the cost of effective feedback to decision-making individuals or institutions. Consequences that take much time to become visible are less likely to be understood by the average voter in retrospect, and given the turnover of elected and appointed officials, the prospect of long run negative consequences may be little or no deterrent to an individual decision maker at the time the political decision is made. Where there is an enduring political party apparatus—a "machine"—concerned about its long-run office-holding prospects, the external costs of individual decision making may be internalized to some extent and enforce a somewhat longer time horizon than otherwise. However, with the growth of "independent" or individualized (perhaps "charismatic") politicians, the political time horizon tends to shrink back to the individual's own office-holding years. It may be significant, for example, that New York City's financial crisis of the 1970s grew out of policies and practices adopted during the administration of one of its most charismatic and independent mayors during the 1960s, and that the contrasting financial solvency of Chicago at the same time was maintained in one of the last bastions of municipal machine politics.

Members of a political machine have a large investment in its future election prospects, which correspond with their own individual prospects of advancing up the seniority ladder to higher office. The more independent the individual politician is, the less is his fate tied to the long run consequences of his decisions in a particular unit of government. Negative consequences after he has departed that unit can even be used as evidence of his superiority to his successors. What matters to the independent political decision maker is how his current decisions in his current position promote his immediate prospects for higher positions elsewhere. If a given set of policies enhance a mayor's presidential prospects, the possible damage of those policies to the city after he is in the White House is hardly a political deterrent.

The effect of a party apparatus, in contrast to a charismatic leader, can be seen in nondemocratic states as well. The incumbent leader of the Soviet Union at any given time could make himself more popular by liberalizing government restrictions or by reducing military spending and allowing the people's standard of living to rise accordingly. The immediate dangers to his own regime during his own term of office could be minimal, and yet the larger dangers to the internal and external goals of the Communist party could well be sufficiently serious to cause that party to depose the leader for even trying to initiate such reforms. A party with a longer time horizon requires more pervasive control than an individual with only his own term of office to consider. Nonparty dictatorships in noncommunist countries may be equally (or more) authoritarian, but they are seldom as pervasively totalitarian, in the sense of intruding as far into private lives, religious beliefs, or the indoctrination of children. Nonparty dictatorships are therefore more subject to change, if only on the death of the individual dictator, as in Spain or Portugal.

TEMPORAL BIAS

We tend to conceive of various interest groups—the steel industry, agriculture, construction workers, doctors, ethnic minorities, etc.—as integrally persisting through time, and of various special interest legislation or policies as being for the benefit of such groups as enduring entities. In reality, however, the constant turnover of individuals and/or organizations in particular sectors makes possible sharp divergences between the interests of the incumbents as of a given time and the enduring interest group of which they are a transient part. For example, laws making it difficult for employers to fire anyone are an obvious benefit to existing employees. But such laws create incentives for such employers to raise hiring standards and to substitute capital for labor incrementally—both actions raising the unemployment rates among workers subsequently entering the labor force. The net result can be a reduction in employment opportunities for "labor" over time, though an immediate gain in employment opportunities for incumbent employees. It may be a perfectly rational goal for incumbent employees to seek such laws protecting jobs and for incumbent politicians to pass such legislation. Many of those whose future job prospects are being traded off for present advantages are too young to vote or have not yet been born. Similarly, state laws often protect incumbent corporate managers from "takeover" efforts by other corporations which might fire them after buying the business. From a social point of view, it may make little sense to protect less efficient executives from more efficient executives. However, it is *incumbent* management which decides where to locate corporate headquarters and installations, and those states which shield incumbent management by obstructing "takeover" efforts have an advantage in attracting taxpaying and job creating businesses. It is a perfectly rational decision for states to do so, even when it is against the national interest. In short, it is perfectly rational for incumbent labor and incumbent business to seek goals which are antithetical to the economic interests of labor and business as long run interest groups. And it is equally rational for incumbent politicians to accommodate them with laws that are in no one's long run interest.

It might seem as though, when the transient representatives of an enduring group are replaced by a new generation, existing legislation adapted to the previous generation would be repealed. But such adjustment to later feedback is inhibited by *differences in the cost of knowledge* to incumbents and nonincumbents. First of all, incumbents know who they are individually, what they have in common, and what they have at stake. People who *might* have become doctors if the A.M.A. did not restrict entrance to medical schools, or who might have created an entirely different kind of railroad if the Interstate Commerce Commission did not control that industry, will never know that with anywhere near the same certainty—that is, with anywhere near as low a cost of knowledge. An incumbent need only be sane to know what his occupation is, and only moderately intelligent to realize what he and his cohorts could lose under alternative institutional arrangements. But someone who finds that dishwashing is the best job he can get cannot know that he could have become a construction foreman if the construction union did not restrict entry. Even if he could know, he could not locate all the *other* individuals who might have been his co-workers or employers in the hypothetical construction industry as it would have existed without union restrictions, so that they might form a counteracting special interest group. Similarly, all the potential executives, investors, employees, and subcontractors of the kind of railroad companies that could have come into existence without I.C.C. regulations face incredible costs of knowledge in trying to locate one another, even if each somehow knew that he was personally one of the losers from I.C.C. policies.

This temporal bias as between existing and prospective members of an interest group is sometimes further accentuated when a new set of interested third parties is created by legislation establishing institutions to regulate, promote, or otherwise interact with the interest group in question—for example, the Civil Aeronautics Board, the Agriculture Department, and similar governmental organizations linked to given industries. They are linked not to the industry or interest group as it might evolve on its own, with an ever changing mix of organizations, people, and power relationships. They are linked to a large extent to *incumbent* organizations and individuals in the industry or interest group. Normal displacement of such organizations and individuals by new competitors as time goes on is therefore often resisted by them through political, governmental actions. Incumbent businesses may be saved from bankruptcy by restricting the entry of rivals, forbidding or inhibiting price reductions by other incumbents with lower costs, or holding back technological innovations that threaten the continued profitability or survival of incumbents with older technologies.

Much political discussion of competing interest groups overlooks the competition among temporally separated segments of the "same" interest group. Temporal bias affects not only the division of costs and benefits within such an interest group, but the effect on the economy or society at large of the later direction taken by such groups under constraints established to benefit the first generation of incumbents sufficiently well organized to achieve their political goals.

The bias of political decision making in favor of incumbent decision makers in nonpolitical institutions is part of a more general temporal bias of political decision making, whose time horizon tends to be bounded by the next election. Insofar as the voters' time horizons extend further, on particular issues, the political decision may reflect long run considerations on those particular issues. However, for the voters' time horizons to effectively control political decision making requires that the voters be able to foresee the long run consequences of current policies. For some policies this is more feasible than for others. For many policies, including economic policies, the long run consequences involve technicalities seldom understood outside the circle of specialists. Moreover, empirical feedback can correct initial understanding only to a limited extent, since individual decision makers have often gone on to other (usually higher) positions on the strength of what was once believed about their decisions, and if it was difficult for voters to understand what was done when it was done, that difficulty may be even greater when trying to recreate the initial situation in voters' minds years later in order to reassess the options chosen. This is not impossible, however, when the initial decision involved corruption that was later exposed (Teapot dome) or a war growing out of previous appeasement (Neville Chamberlain). The point here is simply that the knowledge costs insulate long run decisions from voter feedback to some degree, and that in the absence of voter feedback, there is no institutional incentive for elected officials to take a view that extends beyond the next election. Just how short a time horizon this is may be indicated by the fact that the average time remaining before the next election is one year for an American congressman and three years for a U.S. Senator. Of course, earlier in their terms they have more time remaining before the next election, but later they have correspondingly less. Their term of office—as of the day they take office, two years and six years respectively—gives the maximum time horizon, but the average time horizon is only half of that.

Time is especially important in economic decisions involving "fixed costs"—that is, costs that do not vary in the short run. Bridges, bus lines, and hospitals, for example, have large fixed costs for their basic structure and equipment relative to the other kinds of costs—such as labor costs—which vary with the use of the facility or service. Municipal bus lines can continue to operate without adding to taxpayer's burdens, as long as the fares cover the short run costs, such as the cost of gasoline and the bus drivers' pay. For the longer run, however, the fares would also need to cover the fixed costs of replacing the buses as they wear out. At a given point in time, the need to raise bus fares to cover both kinds of costs can be politically denied without fear of feedback within the elected officials' time horizon. As long as the existing fares continue to cover the cost of gasoline, bus drivers' salaries, and similar short run costs, fare increases can be postponed without any immediate reduction in the quantity or quality of bus service or any increase in taxes—regardless of how inadequate the fare may be for replacing the buses themselves when they wear out. That is a problem for future bus riders, future taxpayers, and future administrations. For the present, there are obvious political gains to be made from a humane stance of protecting the public (or the poor) from higher fares. When the buses age and begin breaking down, leading to more overcrowding in the remaining buses, longer waits between buses, and less comfortable buses, this affects not only the transportation system but the whole social ecology of the city. Those who find the municipal transit sytem intolerable have incentives to use their own automobiles and/or

. move out to the suburbs. Seldom will the voters who elected a champion of the bus riders' cause in a given year connect that event with an accelerating exit to the suburbs and a shrinking municipal tax base a decade later.

INHERENT CONTINUITY AND ARBITRARY DISCRETENESS

Time increases the cost of political knowledge in many other ways. The inherent continuity of time must be arbitrarily broken up into discrete units for political decision making and voter assessment purposes. This means that what happens within those arbitrarily discrete units of time assumes an importance in a given system of incentives and constraints out of all proportion to its importance in the longer, continuous stream of time. Other, nonpolitical institutions suffer similar problems, but often also contain mechanisms for bringing the weight of the excluded future to bear during the arbitrarily selected current period. Corporate stockholders, for example, not only consider the annual dividend but the current price of the stock itself, which reflects future prospects of the company as evaluated in the market. A mother not only considers the current fact that a piece of candy will stop her child's crying; because she is going to be the child's mother for the indefinite future (i.e., socially and emotionally responsible for the same unit over time), she also has to consider the longer run effect of giving him candy on his nutritional, dental, and psychological future.

Among the social costs of an arbitrary discreteness of time in a given system is an ease of misstatement (high costs of voter knowledge) through choice of temporal units. These include not only short-run maximization at long-run costs, but also highly variable interpretation of long-run trends. For example, as of 1960, the growth rate of the American economy could be anywhere from 2.0 percent per annum to 4.7 percent per annum, depending upon one's arbitrary choice of the base year from which to begin counting.[26] The growth rate of the American economy was a major political issue in that year's presidential election campaign, and the high cost of voter knowledge was therefore of major potential political impact. Since the "normal" growth rate had been about 3 percent, economic growth under the incumbent administration was either above or below normal, depending on the year from which the counting began. Nor was this a peculiarity of 1960: for the previous presidential election year (1956) the corresponding range of growth rates would have been from 2.1 percent to 5.1 percent depending on the arbitrary choice of base year, and for the election year before that (1952) the possible range was from 1.3 percent to 5.3 percent.[27] Any of these administrations could have been either a great success or a great failure by this criterion, depending upon the arbitrary choice of temporal units. Internationally, the Soviet government has long impressed many people around the world with Russian economic growth rates based on 1926 as a base year, when the same statistics would have translated into far lower growth rates if 1913 had been chosen instead. Considering the enduring world-wide comparison of Soviet type systems with Western and other alternative systems, the high cost of temporal knowledge can have very weighty consequences for mankind.

CATEGORICAL VERSUS INCREMENTAL DECISIONS

Political, and especially legal, decision making tends toward categorical rather than incremental decisions. Partly this is due to the fears engendered by the overwhelming power of government, which is allowed to function only under numerous safeguards—which is to say, numerous limitations on the discretion of individual decision makers. These fears come not only from the public subject to governmental power in a democratic system, but also from leaders—democratic or nondemocratic—who fear political repercussions from decisions made by anonymous lower level officials too numerous to monitor, as to their exercise of dicretion. Numerous and relatively inflexible rules reduce the cost of monitoring, by reducing the basic question to whether or not established procedures were followed. Individual discretion may not be wholly banished as a consideration, but "a government of laws and not of men" is in part a cost saving device. Looked at another way, in a world of zero cost knowledge (omniscience), there would be no need for any rules to guide either the initial decision maker or any higher officials who might subsequently review his decision. Both the initial decision and any subsequent review of it could be in general terms of how intelligently some issue could be resolved. But initial and reviewing officials and the general public all accept some trade-off of discretionary flexibility for institutional dependability and insurance against discriminatory use of the vast powers of government. "Red tape" is an implicit premium paid for this "insurance."

Governments can and do combine discretionary decision making and dependable rules, but neither can go to its logical extreme without destroying the other, and there are trade-offs at all points in between. Traffic is usually regulated by wholly arbitrary priorities established mechanically by traffic lights at intersections, without any regard to whether the traffic in one direction has more personally or socially justifiable reason to go first. Clearly there will be times when someone who is due at an important meeting (to himself or society) will sit waiting impatiently for the light to change while someone else who is merely out for a joyride proceeds across the intersection. Traffic laws, like all other arbitrary rules, imply such social "inefficiencies"—and imply also a decision that the costs of eliminating the "inefficiencies" too far exceed the benefits to even try. As a safety valve for extreme cases, the traffic laws themselves incorporate exceptions for emergency vehicles whose sirens convey the knowledge that an exception is about to occur. Arbitrary, categorical or "bureaucratic" rules in general cannot be criticized as wrong merely because some individual consequences are sometimes nonsensical as compared to what an intelligent and impartial person would have decided in the light of all the facts of the particular case. Neither the facts, nor intelligence, nor impartiality, are free goods. Categorical rules are a recognition of this and an attempt to economize on the resources available in the light of their costs. The case for incremental or discretionary decision making is a case for accepting the risks of discriminatory, unintelligent, or corrupt decision making. Such a case can be made in specific instances. What is important is to understand the trade-off.

POLITICAL MACHINES

Much of the history of municipal reform politics in the United States is a history of a shifting trade-off between unresponsive, bureaucratic, "good government" and corrupt political machines flexibly attuned to the general priorities and personal urgencies of the citizens. Supporters of reform movements have tended to be upper-class people with the education, experience and influence to penetrate the bureaucratic maze, while corrupt machines stayed in power by adjusting categorical rules to the needs of desparately vulnerable people who could hardly understand the language of official "good government," much less cope with its complexities. Corrupt political machines play much the same role in politics as middlemen in economics. They were corrupt because the law sanctioned no such role, much less the personal enrichment that went with it.

In democratic countries, political machines are, among many other things, mechanisms for economizing on the cost of knowledge, and especially its effective transmission. Just as the least technically knowledgeable consumers rationally sort by brand name (including franchises), rather than attempt finer sorting by detailed product characteristics which they are not qualified to judge before purchasing, so those less politically knowledgeable vote for or against the political machine according to their perception of its performance, rather than rely on their knowledge of specific candidates and issues. This provides an incentive for political "bosses," with greater knowledge of individual office holders and specific issues, to monitor both in such a way as to maximize the long run public acceptance of the machine, just as name brand products manufacturers or franchising organizations have an incentive to engage in quality control as surrogates for consumers who lack their special knowledge.

In none of these cases does quality control imply perfect quality, nor is it clear that it would be socially optimal to seek maximum product quality (or even minimum variation in quality) rather than optimum product quality variation in view of costs. Political machines are particularly liable to financial corruption, to varying degrees—especially when representing constituencies to whom such corruption is less shocking than it is to social critics or to classes who would not be attracted to a machine in any case. Quality control is not according to some abstract ideal, but according to those qualities actually valued by the relevant constituency.

The particular era of machine politics domination, and the social classes and ethnic groups to whom they appealed, all highlight the high knowledge cost of its alternative—"rational" or bureaucratic "good government." Political machines were at their peak from about the middle of the nineteenth century to the middle of the twentieth century—at a time when ethnic (including religious) divisiveness among voters made public trust difficult, when few of the ethnic minorities had the leisure, the education, or sometimes even the knowledge of English to cope with the organs of government that vitally affected their daily lives. Police protection, garbage collection, schooling for their children, and many other governmental responsibilities were in the hands of people and organizations that were incomprehensible, uncontrollable, and often openly contemptuous of the unwashed, polyglot populations of many large cities. The cost of transmitting these latter groups' knowledge of consequences effectively to decision-making points through the formal political and bureaucratic maze was far higher than the cost of centering attention and loyalty on some political "boss" who could override, circumvent, or otherwise "corrupt" the formal processes to get done what had to be done. Very often these political bosses literally spoke their language, and made it their business to understand intimately their constituents' lives, and the things that were important and unimportant to them. By contrast, reform or "good government" political leaders were usually distant, aloof, prosperous Anglo-Saxons who knew little about the cultural mosaic of the big city slums except that it was foreign and therefore "wrong." In short, reform or "good government" politicians were largely ineffective as conduits for the knowledge of governmental impact on the lives of the kind of people who turned to political machines. It was not simply that the masses were "ignorant" and "misled" as the reformists tended to view it. Being ignorant and therefore subject to misleading might imply much *random* political behavior, but not the overwhelming loyalty to one political machine that characterized immigrant ghettos. The value of these political machines to culturally bewildered and economically desparate people is only underscored by the financial corruption of machine politicians, who were re-elected by voters generally well aware of these illegalities.

The social composition of the supporters and opponents of political machines suggests another important trade-off: between the comprehensiveness of the law and its comprehensibility to the public. The more thoroughly and specifically law attempts to cover contingencies, the more complex the law becomes and the less understood it is. Since law is intended not merely to retrospectively judge behavior but to prospectively guide it, it fails in this latter—and larger—function to the extent that the public cannot figure out what the law expects or requires of them.

The optimal mixture of comprehensiveness and comprehensibility for the more affluent and more educated classes obviously involves more complexity than the optimal mixture from the standpoint of those with simpler financial arrangements and less training in verbal complexities of the sort found in laws and legal documents. The trade-off tends to be biased toward complexity, not only by the greater influence of the affluent, but also by the rationalistic assumption that more (or more precise) articulation is "a good thing"— without regard to diminishing and negative returns. But the failure of the law to explicitly cover contingencies does not imply greater uncertainty, chaos, or litigation. Those with more complex affairs can produce their own contractural complexities within the framework of simple general law. There is a social trade-off between legal complexities produced at public expense and those produced at private expense.

BUREAUCRACIES

Political decision making tends toward the categorical in another sense as well. Specific governmental organizations do not simply administer to some generalized well-being of the public, as various social or economic units are free to do. That is, nongovernmental units are usually free to determine their own respective degrees of specialization, and to change these over time as they see fit. Wells Fargo used to run the "pony express," but now they have abandoned this and conduct more or less conventional banking activities instead. A baby food manufacturer may diversify its activities to include life insurance, and a bowling equipment manufacturer can produce motor vehicles as well. A typical mother changes her whole routine and role several times as a child proceeds from infancy to adulthood. By contrast, a governmental agency has a specific set of assigned activities to pursue, rather than a general goal to maximize, such as profit making or family well-being. Governmental agencies are generally authorized to carry on *processes* rather than to achieve *results*. If the postal officials were to become convinced that communications could be vastly improved by a large-scale shift from the use of letters to the use of telephones, telegraph, and various forms of person-to-person radios, it would still have no authority to use the money at its disposal to subsidize these latter activities instead of carrying the mail. If there were a government baby food producing agency, it could not decide on its own that a point had been reached at which some of its money should be incrementally redirected toward life insurance, as Gerbers has done; a government photographic agency could not decide to produce raincoats, as Eastman Kodak has done.

Given categorical mandates and the law of diminishing returns, it is virtually inevitable that governmental agencies would eventually end up doing things which seem irrational as isolated decisions. The aggrandizement familiar in all kinds of human activities—from the dressing of babies to the spread of multinational corporations—applies as well to governmental agencies. But where other expansions are constrained not only by budget limits but also by incremental returns from *other* lines of activity, governmental agencies with mandated activities have every incentive to push those particular activities as far as politically possible—even into regions of negative returns to society. This is especially apparent in preventive activities, designed to contain various evils. As those evils are successively reduced, either by the agency's own activity or by other technological or social developments, the agency must then apply *more* activity per residual unit of evil, just in order to maintain its current employment and appropriations level. If the agency is supposed to fight discrimination against minorities, it must successively expand its concept of what constitutes "discrimination" and what constitutes a "minority." Urgent tasks such a securing basic civil rights for blacks ultimately give way to activities designed to get equal numbers of cheerleaders for girls' high school athletic teams.[28] A nongovernmental organization, such as the March of Dimes, could—as it did, after conquering polio—turn its attention to other serious diseases, but if it had a government mandate strictly limited to polio, it would have little choice but to continue into such activities as writing the history of polio, collecting old polio posters, etc., while children were still dying from birth defects or other maladies. The point here is not that the leaders of the March of Dimes were either more intelligent or morally superior to the leaders of government agencies. The point is that a non-governmental organization subject to feedback from donors or customers has incentives and constraints that lead to institutional decisions more attuned to rational social trade-offs.

More diversified government agencies—such as the Department of Health, Education, and Welfare—have opportunities to change the internal mixture of its activities in response to changing social priorities, but only to the extent that the HEW leadership is in a position to impose agency-wide considerations on the "warring principalities" under its nominal control. By the same token, private organizations supported by a narrow constituency—such as the NAACP Legal Defense Fund supported by affluent white liberals[29]—may pursue certain activities well into the region of diminishing returns from the viewpoint of its ostensible beneficiaries (blacks) or the society at large, however important its historic mission may have been in the past. In short, it is not the political versus the private control of organizations which is crucial. It is the scope of the organization's mandate, and what that implies about its likelihood of pursuing some activity past the point of negative social returns. The safeguards required for the use of massive government power and huge sums of government money often confine the decision makers' discretion to a given line of activity and contain numerous rules within that activity. Moreover, because taxpayers cannot monitor numerous government agencies the way donors, customers, or family members monitor fewer and closer activities, the feedback to nongovernmental organizations is usually faster and more effective in diverting their efforts into new areas as the most urgent needs in the original area are met.

Bureaucracies, by definition, are controlled by administrative or political decisions, not by incentives and constraints communicated through market price fluctuations.[30] While an ordinary business enterprise is constrained to keep its costs of production below the value of the output to the consumer—and has incentives to keep it as far below as possible—such incentives and constraints are not merely absent in a bureaucracy but are replaced by other incentives and constraints tending in the opposite directon. The rank and pay of a bureaucrat is determined by his degree of "responsibility"—in categories documentable to third parties judging a process rather than a result. He is paid by how many people he manages and how much money he administers. Overstaffing, "needless" paperwork, and "unnecessary" delays may be such only relative to social purposes—not relative to the incentives established. Every "needless" employee is a reason for his superior to get a higher salary; so is every "wasted" expenditure, and every "unnecessary" delay preserves someone's job. The more "channels" the citizen has to go through, the more work is generated for the organization. For a bureaucrat assigned a given task (result), the incentive is to require as many people and as much money as possible to achieve that result. What is politically possible depends upon how *visible* his costs are, not their magnitude in relation to the value of the result. Moreover, the bureaucracy can expand the demand for its services by simply pricing them below cost. There is no such thing as an objective quantifiable "need" for anything. When the price is lower, a larger quantity is demanded. Profit-and-loss constraints mean that a private business can expand its sales this way only as long as its price covers its costs of production. A government bureaucracy, which can dispense its goods or services below cost—including at zero price, in some cases—can always demonstrate a large "need" for its output, and therefore a "justification" for a large staff and budget.

It has been claimed that bureaucratization in general cannot proceed to lengths that are counterproductive, either in terms of organizational efficiency or their limitations on individual freedom, in a democratic country. Otherwise, a "bureaucracy-wrecking" party could be elected,[31] with the support of "every citizen who believed he was paying more to support wasteful bureaus than he was receiving from those minorities-serving bureaus that benefitted him directly."[32] This would be true *if knowledge were costless.* But one cannot destroy "bureaucracy" in general, but only specific and highly disparate bureaucracies. If government is not a zero sum game, there may be substantial benefits to avoiding anarchy, and these benefits shield specific inefficiency from a broad axe attack on government bureaus. More narrowly, each bureau's activities may produce some benefit, even if some bureaus as a whole produce no net benefits. For a citizen attack on wasteful bureaus to succeed requires knowledge of the point at which benefit turns to waste or counterproductive activity. Even the most bitter critic of the Food and Drug Administration's policies retarding the introduction of lifesaving drugs may hesitate to destroy the whole agency and allow all kinds of poisons to find their way into our food and water supply. As long as bureaucratic waste or restriction stays within broad limits, and shields itself from specific detection, it may persist indefinitely despite its incremental costs exceeding its incremental benefits—as the voters *would* judge these, if they knew. The contrary view is a special case of the democratic fallacy, which equates market decision making under explicit cost constraints expressed in price tags with vote casting on the basis of plausibility and with high knowledge costs per voter.

INSTITUTIONAL CHANGES

The difference between incremental and categorical decision making has implications not only for the location of given kinds of decisions inside or outside government; it has implications for how and where government decisions can most effectively be located. Periodic campaigns to "reform" or "streamline" the government bureaucracy under some "rational" plan to "end duplication" look very different within this framework. Duplication, for example, means that similar processes or results in a given field are obtainable through different organizations, usually located within larger and more diversified organizations with ostensibly differing purposes. The Veteran's Administration and the Public Health Service both operate hospitals, for example. Often this means that a given citizen has the choice of where to go with the same problem, whether that problem be consumer fraud, antitrust violations, or cases of racial discrimination. When duplication means individual choice, a set of unpaid "unmonitored monitors" has been created, able to effectively constrain the behavior of each agency with the implicit threat of going to some other agency if the same service is not provided as well. The economies of scale that might (or might not) result from consolidating the activity must be weighed against the higher costs or lower quality that are apt to result when monitors become a captive audience for a government monopoly instead. Moreover, the location of similar activities within a variety of conglomerate government organizations means that the phasing out of the activity becomes more feasible within a decision making unit that has other activities which can absorb the people and the appropriations. A more rationalistic plan of gathering all like activities into an agency devoted solely to that activity means in fact creating incentives to keep that activity alive as long as possible and to pursue it as far as possible, with little or no regard for social costs and benefits. The costs of duplication at a given time must be weighed against these longer run costs of consolidation.

Political decision making tends to be categorical rather than incremental in another sense as well. The programs of government officials or political candidates tend to be expressed in categorical rather than incremental terms. The lifeblood of politics is popular emotion, and categorical declarations capture that emotion. No one is going to man the barricades for a little more of A and a little less of B. Nor are they even likely to ring door bells on cold election nights for such incremental considerations. Therefore political activity—whatever its substantive or ideological content—has built-in incentives for categorical presentation of alternatives. The competition among political groups does not therefore bring to bear more accurate knowledge, as in economic competition, but promotes exaggerated hopes and fears—and sometimes deeds. Nor is this a transient pre-election phenomenon. Once such categorical exaggerations have been set in motion, they become incentives and constraints on subsequent policy making, in even the most totalitarian regimes. The press in a free country is to some extent a constraint on the categorical rhetoric of politics in government, but the selling of newspapers to subscribers and news programs to advertisers also depends on maintaining a certain level of public excitement which is also promoted by categorical clashes. There is little incentive for any institution to promote an incremental approach to political decision making.

The government tends to categorical decision making not only because of the incentives it faces but also because of the incentives it creates for those outside government. By conferring a valuable right on some group at the expense of some other group(s), the government provides an incentive for expensive, internecine struggles to be the group that receives rather than gives. Naked group struggles, openly recognized as such, would provide the basis for incremental adjustments of competing claims. But in order to get more public toleration for private interest, the dispute is verbally or ideologically transformed into a clash of principles—which must then be resolved categorically. All-or-nothing decisions raise the stakes, and the resources devoted to being the winner, and lower the probability of a socially optimal result from this socially disruptive process.

There is clearly some optimal level of change and of the divisiveness that accompanies it. With everyone paralyzed by fear of divisiveness, no change would ever have taken place—politically, economically, or socially—and we would all be still living in the caves. But if every change immediately set off new struggles to change that change, the relative merits of each of the successive states might mean less than the incessant turmoil. Whatever the optimal rate of change for a given political entity as a whole, that optimal rate for a given political practitioner or party is likely to be greater, since he can gain as the ostensible champion of whatever group he selects or creates by his divisiveness.

SUMMARY AND IMPLICATIONS

The government has been conceived of as a framework of rules within which other decision making units can make decisions without the high transactions costs of maintaining private force for the purpose of protecting their physical safety or of protecting their belongings or of maintaining threats to enforce the carrying out of agreed upon contracts. As a framework, the government simply delineates the boundaries within which other units determine substantive choices, the government making its own forces available to defend the established boundaries. But while the government sets the basic framework for others—narrowly or broadly, depending upon the degree of freedom in the country—it is also itself subject to incentives and constraints, institutionally and individually. Government is not simply "society" or "the public interest" personified. Indeed, in modern democratic government—especially in the United States—it is often not a consolidated decision making unit but an overlapping montage of autonomous branches, agencies, and power cliques—each of these responsive to different outside coalitions of interest groups or ideologists.

The simple fact that governments are run by human beings with the normal human desire for personal well-being and individual or institutional aggrandisement must be insisted upon only because of a long intellectual tradition of implicitly treating government as a special exception to such incentives and constraints. This tradition stretches from the impartial "philosopher king" of Plato to the exalted "statesman" of the mercantilist literature of two to three centuries ago to the public spirited government as conceived in modern tracts that bill themselves as "empirical social science and not value statements"[33] In this modern literature, as in their historic predecessors, governmental take overs of decisions from other institutions are treated as themselves sufficient evidence—virtually proof—that such actions are needed to "remedy deficiencies"[34] of other decision making processes which are "irrational" in some way.[35] A mere enumeration of government activity is evidence—often the sole evidence offered—of "inadequate" nongovernmental institutions,[36] whose "inability" to cope with problems "obviously"[37] required state intervention. Government is depicted as acting not in response to its own political incentives and constraints but because it is *compelled* to do so by concern for the public interest: it "cannot keep its hands off" when so "much is at stake,"[38] when emergency "compels" it to supersede other decision making processes.[39] Such a tableau simply ignores the possibility that there are political incentives for the production and distribution of "emergencies" to justify expansions of power as well as to use episodic emergencies as a reason for creating enduring government institutions.

This ignoring of political incentive structures extends to the effects of government action as well as its causes, often "pretending that the effect of a law and appropriation will be what their preamble says it should be."[40] Much complaint about bureaucratic "inefficiency" or "stupidity" presupposes that bureaucrats are pursuing the goals stated in the preambles to the legislation authorizing their existence, rather than responding to the incentives created in the "details" of that legislation. Not even physical or engineering efficiency can be calculated without first defining a goal. Where bureaucrats are pursuing their own individual or organizational goals, they are hardly being "inefficient"—much less "stupid"—in terms of other goals that

146

other people wish they were pursuing. This is not merely a matter of verbal fastidiousness but of practical policy: replacing the allegedly "inefficient" or "stupid" people with more intelligent people, or people with a record of efficiency in private industry, could not be relied upon to improve the implementation of the social policy described in preambles, as long as the structure of incentives and constraints remains the same.

The importance of actual institutional characteristics as a guide as to what to expect is obscured by the common practice of defining political institutions by their hoped-for results: the *Environmental Protection* Agency, the *Equal Employment Opportunity* Commission, the *Defense* Department, etc. The change of the latter name from "War Department," which describes what a military organization actually does or prepares to do, to "Defense Department"—presumably incapable of ever launching a military attack—was symptomatic of this pious obfuscation.

Incentive structures are important in explaining political behavior, not only in a static sense but in following dynamic changes of political patterns. Incentives operate not only by guiding the actions of given people, but by changing the mix of people drawn to particular activities. Very different kinds of people may be attracted or "selected"—in an impersonal Darwinian sense—by one set of incentives than by another. Used car dealers tend to differ from Red Cross volunteers. Movements for political change—that is, insurgents in general, whether moderate reformers or violent revolutionaries— are essentially attempts to change incentive structures, however much they may choose to describe themselves in terms of their hoped-for results. But prior to the achievement of any success—whether reform or revolution— people who man insurgent movements are "selected" in a Darwinian sense under an entirely different pattern of incentive structures from the incentive structures that they are advocating. Insofar as the insurgency becomes successful, the new incentives tend to select a different mix of persons. For example, socialists under capitalism may differ from socialists under socialism.

A capitalist system, especially when it is actively defending itself, may offer few direct personal benefits for being a socialist and may impose various costs, ranging from social disapproval to jail, depending upon the condition of civil liberties in the particular country. Narrowly self-interested persons, or persons of weak will or timid disposition, are unlikely to be attracted to socialist movements under these conditions. But when socialism has become established, especially if in the form of a totalitarian orthodoxy, it is being a supporter of capitalism that now carries a high cost and being a supporter of socialism that offers higher reward. The mixture of people attracted to socialism should be expected to change accordingly.

147

SOCIAL INSTITUTIONS

It is not necessary to have the whole society change, as from capitalism to socialism in this illustration, to have different kinds of people emerge as supporters of particular institutions—thereby changing the function of those institutions. Something similar has in fact been observed to happen in a more limited way when regulatory agencies are created and then pass through a familiar institutional metamorphosis. Those who supported the creation of a particular regulatory institution typically had few self-serving goals that justified the costs and risks they incurred. Many were simply zealots for a particular cause. Once the institution has been created, however, it offers careers, power, prosperity, and visibility—attracting a new group of participants and supporters. As time goes on, these latter tend to replace the former, either because the careerists are more ruthless in seeking the best jobs or because the zealots' ardor has cooled with time or with the achievement of a significant portion of their goals, or from the attraction of new crusades elsewhere. This transition of personnel over time often turns the agency's policies completely around, to accommodate the new priorities of a new class of people attracted by the new structure of incentives and constraints. This "life cycle of regulatory agencies" is a common place observation among political scholars.[41] Outcries of pain and anger from the supporters of the institutional change are also common—as is the case after a successful revolution, which is to say, institutional change on a larger scale. The "betrayal" of ideals is a reiterated refrain in a wide variety of insurgent movements, whether moderate or extreme. Seldom is there a recognition that the institutional success of the insurgency has itself created new incentives attracting new kinds of people and sometimes reorienting some members of the original group. Another factor is that a successful insurgency often puts leaders of the insurgents into closer contact with knowledge that was either unavailable or not so vivid when the insurgents were outsiders, and thereby forces correction of plausible beliefs that will not stand authentication.

The alternative, non-systematic or intentional explanation—that people "sold out" to opponents—has the serious difficulty that often the behavior that is characterized as a "sell out" occurs at a time when it would make the least sense to sell out. Bolsheviks who risked imprisonment, torture, and death to oppose the Czars were later discredited and executed by the Soviets for "selling out" the revolution. Analogous things have happened on a smaller scale in American civil rights movements, British Labor Party circles, and various other successful insurgent movements. The systemic explanation has the advantage of explaining not only why the general changes occur in individuals, but why different kinds of individuals selectively rise to the top after a given institutional change, as a rational response to changed incentives, however bitterly disappointing to those who failed to foresee the consequences of their own efforts. In general, it is unlikely that two very different sets of incentive structures will attract two mixes of people who are equally satisfied with any given policy.

Whether incentive structures remain fixed under conservatives or change under insurgents, they are as central to an explanation of political behavior as they are to explanations of behavior in other economic or social processes.

Chapter 6

An Overview

The use of knowledge in decision-making processes affecting social well-being depends not only on the supply of ideas—which are usually abundant—but, on some process of authentication to weed out and reshape those ideas in the light of feedback from actual experience resulting from their application. Whether or not the results are socially rational depends on the proportion between the costs and the benefits, as both change incrementally. Rationality in this sense means nothing more than its basic root notion of making a ratio—weighing one thing against another in a trade-off.[1]

There are various authentication processes, ranging from consensual approval to scientific proof, and a virtually limitless variety of institutional processes for carrying out this authentication, or weeding-out, process. The fragmentary nature of social knowledge means that the authentication and feedback must involve numerous individuals, and that they must be connected by some system of mutual incentives and constraints. Feedback which can be safely ignored by decision makers is not socially *effective* knowledge. Effective feedback does not mean the mere articulation of information, but the implicit transmission of others' knowledge in the explicit form of effective incentives to the recipients. A corporation's profit and loss statement or a baby's whimpers are such transmissions. Both galvanize people into action in response to other people's feelings, even though one is articulated and the other not. It is the effectiveness of the incentive transmission, not the explicit articulation, that is crucial.

The degree of social rationality—how finely costs and benefits are weighed—does not depend upon the degree of individual rationality. What is individually rational within a given set of institutional incentives and con-

150

straints may be socially wasteful in the sense that more desires could be satisfied with the same resources under alternative institutional processes. Conversely, individual rationality is not a precondition for systemic rationality. That is easily seen in biological evolution, where the adaptation of organisms to environment does not presuppose planning for such a result, and certainly not by the organisms themselves. Where intention does exist among the individuals involved in a systemic process, that does not mean that their intentions determine the outcome. The inherent constraints of their situation—the limitations of resources in economics, the diversity of views in a democracy, and the cost of knowledge in social systems in general—as well as the nature of the particular institutional process through which knowledge of these constraints is conveyed to them as individual incentives, also shape the result.

Simple, general, and obvious as all this may seem, its implications contradict much social theory. Implicit denials that the trade-offs exist are commonplace, especially when what is being traded-off is something momentous, such as freedom or human life. The things for which freedom is incrementally (and sometimes categorically) sacrificed are rhetorically included in some "larger" definition of freedom, just as modifications of democracy (such as constitutions and an appointed judiciary) are included in some "larger" definition of democracy. The trade-off of human lives and suffering involved in safety regulations or homicide laws is likewise seldom faced squarely, even though every incremental change in the stringency of such laws sacrifices some people to save some others, as well as trading-off life for other considerations. Historically, the racism that arose with slavery in America was one means of denying the momentous trade-off involved between the high moral and political ideals of the country and the material gains from violating other human beings' rights—a denial made possible by depicting those other human beings as somehow not "really" human beings in the full sense. In short, the rhetorical denial or evasion of trade-offs has occurred across the social or political spectrum, from the pro-slavery denials of U. B. Phillips to the pro-Soviet denials of Sidney and Beatrice Webb.

Sometimes the denial of trade-offs takes the form of claiming that an increase in the use of force in decision-making processes is not "really" a net increase because governmental force is simply nullifying or "countervailing" already existing private force. Thus, just as disparate benefits can be subsumed under the same word to deny trade-offs, so can disparate things regarded as negative. The postulated "power" of private organizations frequently boils down to nothing more than an ability to offer more options, or more preferred options, than their competitors, thereby gaining more voluntary transactions. But the merits or demerits of a particular expansion of government power can be evaded by rhetorically depicting it as not "really" an increase of decisions by force but only a displacement of private force, however metaphorical the latter may turn out to be under scrutiny.

The constrained options which make trade-offs necessary are likewise often implicitly or obliquely denied. This is obvious in political statements to the effect that "if we can afford to do A, why can't we afford to do B?" With constrained options, the very fact that we did A reduces our ability to do B. Sometimes the implicit denial of constrained options takes the form of attacking as undemocratic any failure to achieve majority preferences—or perhaps even the preferences of some minority subset which has earnestly pursued its goals through legitimate channels. But constrained options are as inherent under democratic government as under any other form of government; perhaps more so, since each subset's desires must be balanced against other people's desires. Another symptom of ignoring constrained options is a quickness to condemn official "overreaction" to an emergency in terms which suggest the existence of a wide spectrum of smoothly blending options, when in fact the choices available at the time may have been few, discrete, and all unpleasant.

The effectiveness with which knowledge is transmitted and coordinated through social processes depends upon the actual characteristics of those specific processes. But again, a basically simple, general, and obvious proposition is beclouded by rhetoric—in particular, by the practice of characterizing processes by their hoped-for results rather than by their actual mechanics. Consider, for example, the following proposition: once the legal authorities have defined, combined, and assigned property rights, the subsequent recombination or interchange of those rights at the discretion of individuals shall be illegal. Would great numbers of men and women voluntarily risk their livelihoods and their lives to create this institutional arrangement? History says that they have, for that institutional arrangement is socialism. The *hoped-for results*—variously described as "social justice," "ending the exploitation of man," or more generally, serving "the people"—have largely defined socialism for those attracted to this movement. The same has been true of "civil rights" movements, "public interest" law firms, or even "profit making" businesses. But unless we believe in predestination, the crucial question in all these cases is, what is there about the specific institutional process that necessarily implies the hoped-for results? The rate of bankruptcy among newly formed "profit-making" businesses suggests that the question is as appropriate in narrowly economic enterprises as it is in more idealistic social ventures.

Defining social processes by their characteristics as transmitters of knowledge in incentive form not only reduces the opportunity for rhetoric to evade hard questions; it helps reveal the reason for various apparent social anomalies. For example, the historic disappointments and mutual recriminations among successful insurgents are easier to understand once insurgency itself is defined as attempts to change institutional incentive structures. By definition, the initial insurgents began under a different set of incentives from those which they seek to create. Once they achieve their goal, the new incentive structure tends to attract and select successors with different characteristics, as well as perhaps modifying the characteristics of some of the original insurgents. This has been the history of Christianity, Marxism, the contemporary civil rights movement, regulatory agencies, and numerous other insurgencies highly disparate in terms of hoped-for results and alike only in successfully changing incentive structures for society—thereby changing the social process selectively attracting their own subsequent membership and leadership. People who chose to be Christians under the persecution of the Roman Empire were not the same as people who chose to be Christians after Christianity had become the state religion.

Emphasis on the characteristics of social processes implies a systemic analysis of social causation, in contrast to an individual or intentional analysis of why things happen as they do. At the extreme of the intentional approach is the animistic fallacy which explains the phenomena of society or nature as the fruition of a deliberate plan by leaders, God, conspiracies, or other intentional agents. In the animistic approach, the rationality and morality of the agents involved is crucial to the outcome. But in the systemic approach, the outcome does *not* depend on the individual agents' subjectively pursuing the end result of the system. Much futile controversy in the social sciences has resulted from attempts to show that individual agents do not have either the goal or the degree of rationality necessary to *intentionally* produce the end results claimed by a *systemic* analysis.[2] Where the results are systemically produced, it is no more necessary for the agent to share that goal than it was for prehistoric trees or dinosaurs to know genetics in order for evolution to take place.

The systemic approach is a methodological rather than a philosophic or political position. Both Adam Smith and Karl Marx were systemic social analysts. In Smith's classic, *The Wealth of Nations*, laissez-faire capitalism was advocated—as a system—because of (beneficial) systemic characteristics which were "no part" of the "intention" of capitalists,[3] whom Smith excoriated as dishonest, oppressive, and ruthless,[4] and for whom he had not a single good thing to say in a 900-page book. By the same token, Karl Marx's *Capital* condemned capitalism for (detrimental) systemic characteristics which Marx refused to attribute to the individual moral feelings of the capitalist, who remained objectively the creature of circumstances, "however much he may subjectively raise himself above them."[5] Marx's criticism was of the capitalist system, as such, and an argument based on charges of immorality among capitalists would have been an argument for moral reform rather than institutional revolution. Both Smith and Marx dealt with the systemic logic of capitalism, and neither based his theory on individual intentions, or on a hyper-rational man, which both have been accused of.[6] Smith was not Samuel Smiles and Marx was not Charles A. Beard.[7]

The divergence between individual intention and systemic result affects both causal and moral arguments. The political right and left share a moral version of the animistic fallacy which attributes such systemic results as statistical "income distribution" to personal morality—wealth implying merit (the right) or guilt (the left). Morality is intentional and therefore individual, while purely systemic results are neither just nor unjust, though some results may be preferred to others. War, slavery, or genocide can be morally condemned as deliberately chosen policies, but the repeated ravages of bubonic plague were simply tragic consequences of sociobiological systems in a given state of knowledge. Systemic results can be improved, as by the expansion of technological boundaries, but such social improvement is morally neutral. The desire to judge systemic results morally can be seen in the medieval practice of attributing plagues to sins which had aroused the anger of God, or the modern practice of attributing unhappy systemic results in general to the moral failings of a personified "society."

The treacherous academic analogy of "solving" social "problems" often goes counter to the concept of optimizing subject to inherent constraints. Inherent constraints imply limitations not only to what can be judged morally but also limitations on what can be achieved rationally. There may not be any "solutions" analagous to academic exercises with pre-arranged happy endings and no loose ends left dangling. This has not only intellectual but social implications. Whatever systemic results are possible in any particular economic or social system must leave unsatisfied desires, and simultaneous political and economic equilibrium requires that the political system *accept* those unsatisfied desires rather than assume automatically that it can "solve" such "problems." This point is no brief for any particular system; the principle is general. As was said long ago: "It is no inconsiderable part of wisdom, to know how much of an evil ought to be tolerated . . ."[8]

The systemic approach implies coping incrementally with tragic dilemmas rather than proceeding categorically with moral imperatives. This applies both to categorical defenses of the status quo and to categorical revolutionary opposition to it, and to positions in between. It was the great conservative thinker Edmund Burke who refused to categorically defend the status quo, saying, "A state without the means of some change is without the means of its conservation,"[9] and "he that supports every administration subverts all government."[10] In the British struggle with the American colonies, Burke warned his fellow members of Parliament against categorically raising the question of sovereignty "with too much logic and too little sense."[11] Unlike Hobbes and Locke before him, Burke did not defend existing institutions with categorical deduction. He said: "I do not enter into these metaphysical distinctions; I hate the very sound of them."[12] On the other end of the political scale, even such revolutionaries as Marx and Engels were unsparing in their criticism of other revolutionaries who categorically opposed capitalism without regard to time, conditions, or the inherent constraints of technology. From a Marxian systemic perspective, socialism became preferable to capitalism only *after* capitalism had created the economic prerequisites for socialism and after capitalism had exhausted its own potentialities as a system.[13] Even European colonialism was approached in this way, as "historically justified" during a particular era,[14] much to the embarrassment of later Marxists who tended to treat this as an ethnocentric aberration[15] rather than inherent in the systemic Marxian approach.

Once institutions are seen as implicit transmitters of knowledge in the explicit form of incentives—whether financial or emotional incentives—the question can then be faced as to how accurately and effectively the particular transmission is. To what extent do the desires, caprices, or exigencies of the institution itself cause the incentives presented to the recipients to differ from the desires of the individual sender—that is, the public or the consumer? How quickly, accurately, and effectively does feedback reach the decision makers, whether they want it or not?

If individual incentives are not enough to overcome stubbornness, systemic constraints will. For example, if an individual businessman should happen to be uninterested in money, his suppliers, creditors, and employees are, and it is only as long as he can earn enough money to pay them that he can survive as a businessman. Conversely, those businessmen who most closely supply what consumers want—whether by foresight or sheer luck—will be systemically enabled to expand their share of the total output of the product.

Insulation from feedback takes many forms. Perhaps the most effective insulation is simply force. The pain felt by helpless victims may be information available to the user of force—whether it be a criminal or a government—but such information is not effective feedback as far as behavior is concerned. Totalitarian regimes may in fact have *more* information about their citizens than do governments constitutionally limited in their use of secret police surveillance methods. The Nazis were informed as to the sufferings of inmates in their concentration camps, but this information was not feedback in any effective sense. On the other hand, the mere suffering of embarrassment may be sufficient to modify the behavior of those decision makers causing the embarrassment, when they are dependent on the dollars, the votes, or the personal goodwill of those offended. Panic-stricken censorship, apologies, and/or denials of responsibility by decision makers are evidences of effective feedback mechanisms. Both the transmission of feedback and insulation from it have costs. The effectiveness of social processes in communicating knowledge to decision-making points depends in part on these costs—absolutely and relative to one another. A bureaucracy which can envelope its processes in intricate and unintelligible regulations and bury its performance under mountains of tangential statistics has achieved the security of insulation from feedback. Knowledge costs—whether inherent or contrived—are institutional insulations.

Time also insulates, if only because it raises the cost of intellectually connecting cause and effect, either in prospect or in retrospect. This insulation is more effective in situations or processes where continuous time can be broken up into discrete units and each unit judged separately—as in a political term of office. Where time *effects* are continuous, and are continuously experienced even within discrete decision-making periods, as in economic decisions whose present values reflect future prospects, insulation from feedback is much harder to achieve. If a farm has been made unusually productive during the current year by devoting all efforts to cultivation of the current crops, to the neglect of care of the soil, fences, barns, animals, etc., the future cost of that neglect will be reflected in the *current* sale price of that property. In this situation, effects are quickly and cheaply transmitted back and forth across continuous time. By contrast, an overseer in charge of a farm for a discrete period of time is insulated from time effects that fall beyond his tour of duty, if the owner is absent—whether that absentee owner is private or governmental. This too has been borne out by experience in such disparate settings as the antebellum South and the Soviet Union.[16]

The knowledge-transmitting capacity of social processes and institutions must be judged not only by how much information is conveyed but how effectively it is conveyed. A minimal amount of information—the whimpering of a baby, for example—may be very effective in setting off a parental search for the cause, perhaps involving medical experts before it is over. On the other hand, a lucidly atriculated set of complaints may be ignored by a dictator, and even armed uprisings against his policies crushed without any modification of those policies. The social use of knowledge is not primarily an *intellectual* process, or a baby's whimpers could not be more effective than a well-articulated political statement. Again, simple and obvious as this may seem, it contradicts not only general depictions of "society" as a decision maker but more specific demands for *intellectual* input into specific decisions to make them socially better. The key question is not the intellectual question of what to decide but the institutional question of what social process shall decide, in the light of the characteristics of that process and of the problem at hand.

Some knowledge is so widespread, so widely applicable and so certain that it is not worth the cost of repeatedly verifying it in each specific instance: people do not want to be murdered, to have their children kidnapped, to be defrauded, or to be jailed without trial. Laws can incorporate such desires into enduring social institutions backed up by governmental force. The high degree of consensus makes the benefits large and the costs relatively low, since only those who ignore the moral consensus need be dealt with by force. In areas where the consensus is less certain, the benefits are smaller and the costs of enforcement higher. Beyond some point, for some range of decisions, it is socially more effective to allow each individual to use his own discretion. His own discretion does not mean that he will decide every case ad hoc, for the individual is free to structure new constraints for himself and any agreeable others via contracts, club rules, association bylaws, and rules of games and sports. The boundary of the law merely defines the limits of private discretion—whether it is exercised individually or in concert.

However elaborate, or even rigidified, these private arrangements become, they can resemble governmental institutions only in outward form. The government remains an organ of force while voluntary organizations can achieve compliance only insofar as the benefits they offer exceed the costs they impose on their members—whether in dues, fines, or restrictions on their behavior. But if the government decides to pursue a given policy, no such limitations on its costs apply, because all taxpayers are financially liable, regardless of their individual weighing of costs and benefits. Insofar as there are costs to finding out costs (for a nonmarket activity), these knowledge costs insulate government costs from general comparison with benefits by the voters at large.

Those social processes which rely on emotional ties—the family, friendship, churches, and various voluntary associations—facilitate mutual accommodation among those directly involved and between them and the larger society, without the use of force. The advantages of this lie not only in avoiding the unpleasantness of force, but also avoiding its inefficiencies as a social mechanism. Formal force through government, especially constitutional government, requires explicitly articulated rules (laws or regulations), which necessarily contain loopholes, since language is not perfect. This means that some transgressors against the spirit of the law are exempted from the consequences, and other persons not actually transgressing the real purpose of the law may nevertheless get punished for technical violations of the words. Informal rules are often unarticulated, and so are applied without regard to these rigidities of language. Flirtation with someone's spouse does not have to be in a particular form spelled out in advance in order to be detected and socially (or personally) punished.

Because the scope and effectiveness of informal social controls depends upon the strength of the emotional ties involved, specific laws and policies affecting the emotional strength of these social processes cannot be considered solely in terms of the immediate issues without regard to how they affect the long-run effectiveness of families, churches, philanthropy, etc. The number of decisions taken out of the family by compulsory school attendance laws, child labor laws, and other direct institution-to-child programs all reduce the degree of responsibility of the family for its members, both objectively and—ultimately—subjectively. Whatever the merits of such institutional programs in principle or in practice, the external costs of weakening informal institutions must also be considered for a socially optimal result. However, the tendency is for such programs to be discussed seriatim in terms of their isolated merits. Complex informal social trade-offs do not easily lend themselves to categorical political decisions.

The effectiveness with which knowledge is transmitted and coordinated depends not only on the institutional mechanisms at work but also on the nature of the decisions involved—for example, the extent to which the law of diminishing returns applies, whether the decision is sequential or a once-and-for-all decision, whether its consequences are restricted to one lifetime or spread well beyond the human life span and so have muted feedback. Systems can be compared not only in terms of how well they make current decisions with current impact, but how well they bridge the barrier of time—especially time that exceeds the human life span—through such devices as "present values" reflecting future benefits or emotional ties to a family as an on-going unit over the generations.

The consideration of causation in systemic rather than intentional terms does not wholly exclude the individual factor. However, particular kinds of systems tend to offer certain kinds of individuals more scope. If, for example, certain businesses or occupations (used-car dealers, various repair services) offer unusual opportunities for dishonest dealing, dishonest individuals will have a competitive advantage in such fields. A discovery that this field has more than the usual share of unscrupulous persons does not therefore imply that that is *why* there is more dishonest behavior in that field. On the contrary, especially if this is a long-run phenomenon, persisting through several complete turnovers of people, the more likely explanation is in terms of systemic incentives and constraints.

The general principles sketched here in Part I provide a background for considering the changes under way in social, economic, and political processes in the United States and internationally—and for considering what their future consequences are likely to be.

Part II

TRENDS AND
ISSUES

Chapter 7

Historical Trends

Part I analyzed some more or less enduring features of various social processes, and their implications for the coordination of fragmented individual knowledge. Part II will analyze some of the historic *changes* which have occurred, and are occurring, in such processes—and the long-run implications of such changes. The next three chapters will deal with historic trends in specific economic, legal, and political processes. They will center on the American experience, for purposes of keeping the discussion specific and manageable, but many of these trends have been common in Western civilization and beyond, and some have in fact gone further in various other countries than in the United States. This chapter will briefly sketch a broader background picture of trends in social institutions and processes over the past century.

The twentieth century has brought so many changes across the face of the earth—in science, culture, demography, living standards, devastation—that it is difficult to disentangle purely institutional changes from this tapestry of human events. Indeed, it is impossible to fully do so, for at least one of the great world wars of this century grew out of a particular brand of totalitarian institution and its drive to conquer "today Germany, tomorrow the world." In addition to the carnage of war, the twentieth century has seen the unprecedented horror of deliberate slaughter of millions of unarmed human beings because of their categorical classification: Jews, Kulaks, Ibos, etc. These too have been intertwined with institutional change.

In terms of general trends in the social application of knowledge, there are a number of ways in which decision making has tended to gravitate away from those most immediately affected and toward institutions increasingly remote and insulated from feedback. The variety of institutional changes, even in a given country, presents an intricate, kaleidoscopic picture, which becomes still more complex when extended to international scale and interwoven with the fast changing historical events of the century. Still, on a spectrum stretching from individual decision making at one end to totalitarian dictatorship at the other, the general direction of the drift is discernible. It is fairly obvious in the case of national changes from democratic to nondemocratic governments (as in various Eastern European and South American countries) or—among autocratic governments—from loosely controlling and removable autocrats to enduring and pervasive party totalitarianism (as in Russia and China). Even within democratic nations, the locus of decision making has drifted away from the individual, the family, and voluntary associations of various sorts, and toward government. And within government, it has moved away from elected officials subject to voter feedback, and toward more insulated governmental institutions, such as bureaucracies and the appointed judiciary. These trends have grave implications, not only for individual freedom, but also for the social ways in which knowledge is used, distorted, or made ineffective.

These institutional changes have been accompanied by social changes. Perhaps the most far-reaching social change in the past century—in the United States and elsewhere in the Western world—has been that vast numbers of people have ceased being residual claimant decision makers and become fixed claimant employees. When the bulk of the population consisted of farmers (whether owners, tenants, or sharecroppers), the options and constraints facing the economy as a whole were transmitted more or less directly to those individuals, in the form of varying rewards for their efforts, whether those rewards were in money or in produce. The connection between efforts and outcomes was clear, though not all-determining: the weather, blights, and other menaces to crops and livestock made risk also a very personally felt variable. The transformation of Western economies from agriculture to industry brought with it a reduction in the proportion of the population consisting of autonomous economic decision makers. However much "consumer sovereignty" was retained, as producers their role as fixed claimants to some extent insulated them from the direct consequences of their own decisions, largely by limiting the scope of their decision making itself. This was not necessarily a net increase in security, either objectively or subjectively. They might find their futures varying considerably from prosperity to privation— but largely as a result of decisions made by others. The immediate question here is not whether they were better or worse off on net balance, but rather, what did this mean for their knowledge of what was happening, and for the social consequences of that knowledge?

Parallel with these economic developments, the political expansion of the franchise meant that people with progressively less decision making experience in the economy were acquiring progressively more power to shape the economic sector through the political process. A price-coordinated economy, as such, can function without being understood by anyone. But insofar as it must function in a given legal and ultimately political structure, the extent or manner in which these latter structures allow it to function depends upon how others judge its results—or whether they choose to judge or control its *processes* instead.

Another historic change in the past century has been the rise of intellectuals to prominence, influence, and power. The expansion of mass education has meant an increase in both the supply of intellectuals and in the demand for their products. They have become a new elite and, almost by definition, competitors with existing elites. The very nature of their occupation makes them less inclined to consider opaque "results" than to examine processes, quite aside from such other incentives as may operate when publicly discussing their elite competition. Intellectuals have spearheaded criticisms of price-coordinated decision making under individually transferrable property rights—i.e., "capitalism." As far back as polls, surveys, or detailed voting records have been kept, Western intellectuals have been politically well to the political left of the general population.[1]

Another way of looking at all this is that there has been a political isolation of residual claimants to variable incomes as a small special class operating in response to incentives and constraints no longer generally felt throughout the society. Knowledge of changing economic options and constraints *conveyed* through price, investment, and employment decisions by this class (capitalists) has all the appearance of having *originated* with this class, and thus serving the sole interests of this class. The extent to which this is true or false in particular instances is not the central point here. The point is that this appearance is necessarily pervasive—and politically important—regardless of what the particular facts may be. It is only after the conceptual separation of questions of causation from questions of communication (the slain bearer of bad news problem) that the factual issue can even be addressed.

Finally, no discussion of the trends of the past half century would be complete without one of the great socially traumatic episodes of this era, the Great Depression of the 1930s. Both in magnitude and duration it outstripped all other depressions in history. The unemployment rate reached 25 percent and corporate profits in the United States as a whole were negative two years in a row. This depression was unique not only in the magnitude and duration, but in the degree of government intervention—episodic and enduring—occasioned by it. Although questions might be raised as to whether these three characteristics of the Depression were related, the popular explanation has been that it was a failure of the market economy and demonstrated the need for government economic activity. While this thesis can be, and has been, challenged on the basis of scholarly analysis,[2] the point here is merely that this central economic episode of the past century *reinforced* other trends toward the political isolation of residual claimant decision makers and price-coordinated economic systems. To some extent, the Great Depression undermined political support for traditional Western values in general, including freedom and democracy—as shown by the rise of the Nazis in Germany, fascism in Spain and parts of Latin America, and the post-World War II spread of communism around the world.

The next three chapters deal in detail with specific developments in social institutions, and their consequences—especially as regards the crucial question of how any system coordinates its scattered and fragmented knowledge for optimal social effectiveness, and the even more momentous question of the implications for human freedom.

Chapter 8

Trends in Economics

Economic systems have been seen as institutional processes for weighing costs and benefits. Costs in turn are foregone alternative benefits. Costs and benefits are ultimately subjective, but that does not mean that they vary arbitrarily or that one way of weighing them is as rational as the next. The physical and psychic costs of digging a ditch are subjective to whoever digs one. However, the compensating inducement necessary to get *A* to dig a ditch is objective data to *B*. If *B* simply wants a ditch dug, and does not care who digs it, then the lowest of the various subjective costs of ditch digging—among *A*, *C*, *D*, *E*, etc.—becomes his necessary objective cost. Conversely, how much someone wants a ditch dug is subjective to him, but is objective data to anyone else considering doing such work.

Prices convey the experience and subjective feelings of some as *effective* knowledge to others; it is implicit knowledge in the form of an explicit inducement. Price fluctuations convey knowledge of changing trade-offs among changing options as people weigh costs and benefits differently over time, with changes in tastes or technology. The totality of knowledge conveyed by the innumerable prices and their widely varying rates of change vastly exceeds what any individual can know or needs to know for his own purposes.

How accurately these prices convey knowledge depends on how freely they fluctuate. The use of force to limit those fluctuations or to change the relationship of one price to another means that knowledge is distorted to represent not the terms of cooperation possible between *A* and *B*, but the force exerted by *C*. Looked at another way, the array of options people are willing to offer each other are reduced when force is applied to limit the level or the fluctuation of prices, and the array can shrink all the way to the vanishing point when the price is specified by a third party, if his specification does not happen to coincide with trade-offs mutually acceptable to entities contemplating transactions. Price fixing as a process cannot be defined by its hoped for results—"a decent wage," "reasonable farm prices," "affordable housing." Price fixing does not represent simply windfall gains and losses to particular groups according to whether the price happens to be set higher or lower than it would be otherwise. It represents a net loss to the economy as a whole to the extent that many transactions *do not take place at all,* because the mutually acceptable possibilities have been reduced. The set of options simultaneously acceptable to A and B is almost inevitably greater than the set of options simultaneously acceptable to A, B, and C—where C is the third party observer with force, typically the government.

The form in which force is applied to constrain price communication varies widely, including (1) establishing an upper limit beyond which force will be applied (fines, jail, confiscation, etc.) to anyone charging and/or paying such prices, (2) establishing a lower limit, (3) indirectly raising some prices by taxing particular items moreso than others, and indirectly lowering some prices by subsidizing the product with assets forcibly transferred from the taxpayers rather than having the product paid for only by assets voluntarily transferred by consumers of that product.

Direct price controls are not the only method of superseding the market. Other methods include forcibly controlling the characteristics ("quality") of the product, forcibly restricting competition in the market, forcibly changing the structure of the market through antitrust laws, and comprehensive economic "planning" backed by force. Again, the use of force is emphasized here not simply because of the incidental unpleasantness of force, but because the essential communication of knowledge is distorted when what can be communicated is circumscribed. All these ways of distorting the free communication of knowledge (preferences and technological constraints) have been growing, but each has its own distinct characteristics.

CONTROLLING PRICES

FORCIBLY RAISING PRICES

Minimum wage laws and laws forbidding businesses from selling goods "below cost" are typical of government's forcibly setting a lower limit to price fluctuations. Although minimum wage laws may be more extensive in their coverage, the laws against particular businesses' selling "below cost" are more readily revealing as to the nature and distortions of such processes.

It may seem strange—indeed, incomprehensible—that a business enterprise set up for the explicit purpose of making a profit would have to be forcibly prevented from selling at a loss, quite aside from the larger social question of whether such a prohibition benefits the economy as a whole. Yet much government regulation—of airlines, railroads, various agricultural markets, and of imported goods in general—limits how low prices will be allowed to go, whether in the explicit language of forbidding sales "below cost" or of preventing "ruinous competition," "dumping," "predatory pricing," or more positively of "stabilizing the industry" or creating "orderly markets" or other euphonious synonyms for price fixing.

In addition to these direct prohibitions on lower prices, the administration and judicial interpretation of antitrust laws makes sales "below cost" damning evidence against a business. Moreover, the government's required permission to enter various regulated industries or professions—transportation, broadcasting, medicine, etc.—is often denied or restricted to keep competition from forcing prices "too low" or "ruining" *incumbents*—often erroneously described as "the industry."

The government is not behaving irrationally from a political standpoint. Neither are businesses behaving irrationally from an economic standpoint when they *seem* to be selling "below cost." The costs of an industry are difficult—if not impossible—for third parties to determine. As we saw in Chapter 3, costs are foregone options—and options are always *prospective*. The past is irrevocably fixed, so all options are present or future. The objective data available to third parties refer to past actions taken in response to the prospective options subjectively foreseen as of that time. Those subjective forecasts themselves exist neither in the objective data of the past actions nor in the objective record of subsequent events, which may or may not have conformed to the forecasts. Apparently the foreseen costs were less than the foreseen benefits when Napoleon invaded Russia, or when the the Ford Motor Company produced the Edsel.

Government regulation can never be based on these fleeting and subjective appraisals of alternatives which actually guide business decision makers. Even if businessmen could remember everything exactly and describe it precisely, the government would have no way of verifying it. Government regulations and their estimates of "cost" are based on objective statistical data on actual outlays. Therefore businesses which determine their prices on the basis of options facing them at a given time often price below objective cost as defined by past expenditures on production.

If the hypothetical Zingo Manufacturing Company is launched with the idea that the world will be eager to buy zingoes, it may spend great sums producing that product, only to discover after the fact that consumers are so disinterested that zingoes can be sold only at prices which cover half of the past costs incurred in producing them. The options at that point are to (1) sell the existing zingoes at this price or (2) to incur additional costs by holding zingoes in inventory, in hopes of being able to drum up more consumer demand through advertising or other devices, or (3) declare bankruptcy and let it all become the creditor's problem. Depending upon the capital reserves of the firm, selling "below cost" may allow them to minimize their losses on this product and survive as a firm producing some other product(s) in the future. But, regardless of which future option may be preferred, *past "cost" data are irrelevant*. As economists say, "sunk costs are sunk." They are history but they are not economics.

The general principle applies much more widely than in economic transactions. Once Napoleon realized that he was losing in Russia, it mattered not how many lives had been sacrificed for the goal of conquering the country, or in capturing the Russian territory currently held; if future prospects were not good, he had to pull the army out of Russia, and write off the whole operation as a loss. In retreating, Napoleon may well have been returning territory to the Russian armies "below cost" in terms of the lives originally sacrificed to capture it. In military terms, as in economic terms, a given physical thing does not represent a given value without regard to time or circumstances. Land which was prospectively valuable as a strategic area from which to attack the rest of the country may turn out in retrospect to be just so much impediment on a retreating army's escape route.

Businesses sell "below cost" not only when they have mistakenly forecast the future, but also when their costs for a given decision under specific conditions are less than the usual costs under the usual conditions. As seen in Chapter 3, the use of otherwise idle equipment may involve far lower incremental costs than acquiring equipment to serve the same specific purpose. Pricing according to these incremental costs ("marginal cost pricing" in the jargon of the economists) may be rational for the seller and beneficial to the buyer but is often attacked, penalized, or forbidden by the government. Regulatory agencies have consistently opposed low prices based on low incremental costs, and have insisted that the regulated firms base their prices on *average* costs, including overhead. The extent to which regulatory agencies— the Interstate Commerce Commission, Federal Communications Commission, Civil Aeronautics Board, etc.—keep prices *above* the level preferred by individual firms remains largely unknown to the general public, to whom such agencies are depicted as "protecting" the public from high prices or "exploitation" by "powerful" businesses. However, the government agencies are not being irrational, nor are the businesses altruistic. High volume at low prices has been the source of more than one fortune. Each side is responding to the respective incentives faced.

Low incremental costs are also no defense in antitrust prosecutions alleging sales "below cost" to "unfairly" drive out competitors. The U.S. Supreme Court, in a noted Sherman Antitrust Act case, ruled against a firm whose "price was less than its direct cost plus an allocation for overhead"[1] even though overhead is not part of incremental cost. In this, as in many other antitrust cases, injury to an incumbent competitor was equated with injury to the competitive *process*, which the antitrust laws are supposed to protect.

Consumers are equally well protected against low prices based on low incremental costs in a number of other government-controlled areas, such as various agricultural markets. The government itself has an "almost universal avoidance"[2] of incremental cost pricing for public goods and services, such as the Post Office or toll roads and bridges. Toll charges, in fact, typically are highest for those who create the least cost and lowest for those who create the most. The capacity of a highway or bridge is usually based on the volume of rush-hour traffic, so that the costs of building and expanding the facility are due to rush-hour users. The incremental cost of other people's using it during nonrush hours, when it has idle capacity, are far less and perhaps virtually zero. Yet discount books of toll coupons are likely to be made available on terms which make them attractive only to regular rush-hour users, not to occasional users who are more likely to be nonrush-hour users. However economically perverse, this pricing method makes *political* sense to elected officials, because regular users are more easily organized into political pressure groups. That is, regular users' costs of organization are spread over more units of benefit, so that a rational equation of their individual costs and benefits leads them to more political activity per person, as well as in the aggregate, compared to sporadic users.

The growth of regulatory agencies, the expansion of antitrust laws by legislative enactment and judicial interpretation, and increasing government control of pricing in a variety of ways and areas all put lower limits on price fluctuations, among many other effects that they have. The question is, what effect does this have on the transmission of knowledge? It overstates the actual cost of many goods and services, leading some consumers to do without, even though they are willing and able to pay enough to induce the producers to make more of those goods and services, if the producers were free to accept their offers. Knowledge is distorted in the transmission, due to the use of force by third parties—in this case, various organs of government.

While government actions inhibit or prevent the transmission of knowledge in the summarized form of price fluctuations, the government substitutes its own decisions in the form of more explicitly articulated knowledge, in either words or statistics. Articulation, however, can lose great amounts of knowledge. The continuously adjusting process of decision making through transient subjective estimates of prospects is not recorded or available in verifiable form to third parties. Retrospective data generated by this prospective process are fragmentary artifacts analogous to bits of broken pottery or remnants of clothing, from which an anthropologist tries to reconstruct the life process of prehistoric peoples. The anthropologist has no choice but to infer what he can from whatever he finds, but no one would *prefer* such inferences to the knowledge of someone who actually lived in prehistoric societies, if such people were available. A similar disparity of knowledge is involved when decisions are forcibly transferred from those who are part of an ongoing process to third-party observers of statistical artifacts. Such statistical artifacts are not merely incomplete but often positively misleading, by being cast in terms wholly different from those of the process they seek to depict. For example, we have already seen in Chapter 4 that the subjective "time horizon" is *not* indicated by objective data on remaining life span; babies have notoriously short time horizons. Similarly, the averaging of fixed "overhead" costs over output provides a categorical, retrospective picture of a prospective, incremental process of decision making. The social utilization of idle or only partly utilized resources—electricity generating capacity during off-peak hours, half empty airplanes, factories operating below capacity, etc.—is inhibited when effective knowledge of such low cost opportunities is distorted by forcibly preventing low prices from reflecting low incremental costs.

The element of force is crucial to the distortion. The knowledge transmitted by voluntarily chosen prices conveys the terms on which various forms of mutual cooperation are available. The knowledge transmitted under government price constraints reflects the desire to escape punishment, and the knowledge conveyed by such prices does not reflect the full array of options actually available to the economy. In particular it does not convey the cheapest options. For example, a large, far-flung corporation can communicate among its many plants either by using the already existing telephone network or by building its own telephone system connecting its plants. It may require far fewer of the economy's resources to use the existing telephone network, but if these low incremental costs to the economy are forbidden to be conveyed by low prices, the corporation may find it cheaper (in its own financial terms) to build a socially redundant telephone network for itself rather than pay high prices reflecting the "average cost" of telephone service.

The crucial importance of force as a distorter of knowledge transmission is overlooked in abstract discussions of the merits and demerits of "marginal cost pricing." Such discussions attempt to directly determine *what* should be done rather than decide *who* should make that determination. Such questions as the precision with which incremental ("marginal") costs can be calculated,[3] the cost of such precision,[4] circumstantial variations in incremental costs,[5] and the disparity between actual decision making variables and statistical artifacts,[6] are serious social issues only in the context of forcibly "solving" economic "problems" directly from a unitary or godlike perspective, or as academic exercises. Where force is not involved, then *whatever* methods of coping with these difficulties emerge, the least cost methods among them will have a decisive competitive advantage in voluntary transactions, whether those methods result from intuitive insight, rationalistic expertise, or simply stumbling across something that happens to work. It does not depend upon the intentional *modus operandi* of businessmen,[7] but on the systemic effects of competition.

Minimum wage laws likewise prevent transmission of knowledge of labor available at costs which would induce its employment. By misstating the cost of such labor, it causes some of the labor to be unemployed, even though perfectly willing to work for wages which others are perfectly willing to pay. The term "minimum wage" law defines the process by its hoped-for results. But the law itself does not guarantee that *any* wage will be paid, because employment remains a voluntary transaction. All that the law does is reduce the set of options available to both transactors. Once the law is defined by its characteristics as a process rather than by its hoped-for results, it is hardly surprising that there are fewer transactions (i.e., more unemployment) with reduced options. What is perhaps more surprising is the persistence and scope of the belief that people can be made better off by reducing their options. In the case of the so-called[8] minimum wage Law, the empirical evidence has been growing that it not only increases unemployment, but that it does so most among the most disadvantaged workers.[9] This undermines some of the key assumptions of the price fixing approach.

Some who might not support the general proposition that people are made better off by reducing their options may nevertheless believe that one party to a transaction or negotiation can be made better off by eliminating his "worst" options—that is, low wages for a worker, high rents for a tenant, or sales at a loss for a business firm. But, almost by definition, these are *not* their worst options. They could have no transactions at all (or fewer transactions)—that is, be unemployed, unhoused, or unable to sell. Third parties may be morally uplifted by saying, for example, that they would rather see people unemployed than working at "exploitation" wages, but the mere fact that people are voluntarily transacting as workers, tenants, or businessmen reveals their own very different preferences. Unless price-fixing laws are to be judged as moral consumer goods for observers, the revealed preference of the transactor is empirically decisive. The fact that the worst-off workers tend to be the most adversely affected by minimum wage laws suggests that what is typically involved is not unconscionable "exploitation" but the payment of wages commensurate with their desirability as employees. If the lowest paid workers were simply the most "underpaid" workers relative to their productivity, there would be more than the usual profit to be made by employing them, and a minimum wage law could simply transfer that extra profit to the workers without costing them their jobs.

The "exploitation" explanation of low wages tends to emphasize the intentional morality of the employer ("unconscionable") rather than the systemic effects of competition. Nothing is more common in economics than the attraction of new competitors whenever and wherever there is a profit above the ordinary. If hiring low paid workers presented such an opportunity—that is, if "exploitation" had some substantive economic meaning—the competition attracted would bid their wages up and keep them more fully employed than others. In fact, however, their marginal desirability to employers is indicated by their precarious and intermittent employment patterns, and by their generally higher rates of unemployment. In short, for workers as for business, knowledge transmitted by low prices (wages) is generally accurate knowledge, and forbidding its transmission costs both the economy and the intended beneficiary of such price fixing. Were the facts themselves to be changed—by improving the job qualifications of low paid workers, for example—the effects of that would be quite different from merely forbidding or distorting the transmission of knowledge of existing facts. In a purely informational sense, the employer still knows low productivity or high-risk categories of workers, but that only insures that the lack of *effective* knowledge transmission through prices (wages) will lead to less employment of them.

There is no inherent reason why low-skill or high-risk employees are any less employable than high-skill, low-risk employees. Someone who is five times as valuable to an employer is no more or less employable than someone else who is one-fifth as valuable, when the pay differences reflect their differences in benefits to the employer. This is more than a theoretical point. Historically, lower skill levels did not prevent black males from having labor force participation rates higher than that of white males for every U.S. Census from 1890 through 1930.[10] Since then, the general growth of wage fixing arrangements—minimum wage laws, labor unions, civil service pay scales, etc.—has reversed that and made more and more blacks "unemployable," despite their rising levels of education and skill, absolutely and relative to whites. In short, no one is employable or unemployable absolutely, but only relative to a given pay scale. Increasingly, blacks have been priced out of the market. This is particularly apparent among the least experienced blacks—that is, black teenagers, who have astronomical unemployment rates.

The alternative explanation of high black teenage unemployment by "racism" collides with two very hard facts: (1) black teenage unemployment in the 1940s and early 1950s was only a fraction of what it was in the 1960s and 1970s (and was no different from *white* teenage unemployment during the earlier period), despite the obvious fact that there was certainly no *less* racism in the earlier period, and (2) unemployment rates among blacks in their mid twenties drops sharply to a fraction of what it was in their teens, even though the workers have not changed color as they aged, but only become more experienced. The intentional explanation—"racism"—may be more moralistically satisfying, but the systemic explanation fits the facts. A decade of rapid inflation after the federal minimum wage law of 1938 virtually repealed the law as an economic factor by the late 1940s and early 1950s—before a series of amendments escalated the original minimum. During the late 1940s and early 1950s, when inflation and the exemption of many occupations from wage control made the minimum wage law relatively ineffective, black teenage employment was less than a third of what it was in the later period, after the minimum was raised to keep pace with inflation and the coverage of minimum wage laws extended to virtually the entire economy. To give some idea of the magnitude of this effect, black teenage unemployment in the *recession* year of 1949 was lower than it was to be in any of the most *prosperous* years of the 1960s or 1970s. Moreover, even in countries with all white labor forces, teenage unemployment has been similarly vulnerable to minimum wage laws.[11] This is in keeping with the lesser work experience of teenagers and therefore the greater distortion of knowledge involved when minimum wage laws misstate their value to the employer. Statistical data happen to be kept by age and race, but the more general point is that the negative effect of forcible distortion of knowledge hurts most those for whom the distortion is greatest.

While the government is the central repository of force, it is by no means the sole repository of force. Labor unions often use force, threats, and harassment during strikes to stop or reduce the flow of customers or employees to the work place and/or the shipment of goods in or out from a struck business. Many major employers do not even attempt to operate during a strike, because of the high prospect of violence and the low prospect of effective law enforcement.[12]

This private use of force to prevent the effective transmission of prices reflecting economic options has very similar effects to those of governmental force in the form of minimum wage laws. The systemic effect of pricing the most disadvantaged workers out of a job is sometimes compounded by intentional effects of barring various minorities from unionized occupations, either explicitly or tacitly. Virtually every immigrant minority was the target of such union exclusions at one time or other during the nineteenth century, and "white only" clauses existed in many union contracts or constitutions in both the nineteenth and twentieth centuries, until civil rights legislation in the 1960s barred such words. However, such intentional discrimination is not necessary in order for unions to have adverse systemic effects on the employment opportunities of disadvantaged groups, similar to those of minimum wage laws which usually[13] have no intentional discrimination at all. Whether by intentional or systemic effect, labor unions have historically had a devastating impact on the employment opportunities of blacks. Some occupations once dominated by blacks—railroad and construction occupations in the South, for example—became "white only" after unionization.[14]

The history of blacks in skilled occupations in the South and North graphically illustrates the difference between intentional and systemic variables. From an intentional point of view, the South would seem to be the most averse to the employment of blacks in skilled occupations, but in reality blacks remained in such positions longer in the South than in the North,[15] because the systemic effects of labor unions and "liberal" or "progressive" wage-fixing legislation came much later to the South.

FORCIBLY LOWERING PRICES

Very similar principles are involved when prices are forcibly kept below the level they would reach if allowed to fluctuate freely. Rent control, interest rate ceilings, and general wage and price controls during wartime or under comprehensive "planning" are examples of forcibly limiting how high prices can go.

Since prices are simply knowledge of available terms of trade-off, to limit how high the price of A can go in trade-offs for B is economically the same as limiting how low the price of B can go in trade-offs for A. All that differs is the phrasing. It should not be surprising, therefore, when upper limits on rents lead to housing shortages just as lower limits on wages lead to unemployment. A mere change of phrasing shows that minimum wage laws limit how much labor can be offered for a given job, causing a shortage of jobs at that price, just as rent control limits how much rent can be offered for a given housing unit, causing a shortage of housing units at that price. All "shortages" and "surpluses" are *at some given price*, and *not* absolutely in terms of the scarcity or abundance of the item in quantitative terms. The severe housing shortage during World War II occurred with no significant change in either the amount of housing in the country or in the size of the population. Indeed, more than ten million people left the civilian population, and many left the country, during World War II. More housing was demanded by the remaining civilian population *at rent-control prices*. The effective knowledge conveyed by artificially low prices was of far more abundant housing than actually existed or had ever existed.

There is no fixed relationship between the number of people and the amount of space "needed" to house them. Whether or to what extent children will share rooms or have their own individual rooms, the time at which young adults will move out to form their own households, and the extent to which single kinfolks or roomers live with families are all variable according to the price of housing and the incomes of the people making the decisions. Virtually every American ethnic group, for example, has at some point or other gone through a stage at which taking in roomers was a pervasive social phenomenon.[16]

Artificially low prices under rent control facilitates the disaggregation of existing families or living units into smaller groups of individuals with separate households, and facilitates the use of more space per person in existing households, so that very quickly "no vacancy" signs appear almost everywhere. After that point, people who find themselves having to move for compelling reasons may have to double up or live in garages or other makeshift, overcrowded housing, precisely because of the *general* use of more space per person in the country as a whole. While young couples with growing families may find themselves increasingly overcrowded in housing that was once adequate, older couples whose children have left home have little financial incentive to give up larger housing units that the family once needed, because rent control makes the larger unit affordable and leaves few alternative places to move into. In the absence of rent control, there is an incentive for a continuous interchange of different sized housing units among families at different stages of their life cycle. The growing young family trades off other things for housing incrementally, while the older family with children "leaving the nest" can trade off excess space for other things they want. Prices convey effective knowledge of these ever-changing trade-offs, directing each set of decision makers to where they can get the most satisfaction—from their own respective viewpoints—from their respective assets. Rent control distorts—or virtually eliminates—this flow of information. The same set of people and the same set of physical assets continue to exist, but the simple fact that they cannot redistribute themselves among the assets in accordance with their divergent and changing desires means that there is less satisfaction derived from a given housing stock. Though it is the same physical matter, its value is less.

TRENDS AND ISSUES

The losses resulting from rent control are not losses of physical matter or of money. Both can exist in the same amounts as before—and therefore cannot be measured in "objective" statistical data based on the relevant transactions (renting). The *reduction* or nonexistence of *desired* transactions is precisely the loss and no numbers or expertise can objectively measure thwarted desires. The most that can be objectively documented are waiting lists, illegal payments to landlords, and other scattered artifacts analogous to the broken pottery and remnants of clothing available to anthropologists studying prehistoric peoples. In a longer time perspective, rent control prices convey distorted knowledge not only about the optimal allocation of existing housing but about the trade-offs people would be willing to make to get new housing. Renters are forbidden to convey the full urgency of their desire for new housing, in the form of financial incentives that would reach landlords, financial institutions, and builders. This urgency may be growing as the old housing continually deteriorates and wears out, but the effective signal received by builders may be that there are few resources available to be traded off for more housing. The effective signals received by landlords with old buildings may be that there is little available to be traded off to get the maintenance and repair needed to keep them going—even though the tenants might prefer paying more rent to seeing the building deteriorate or the landlord abandon it entirely, as has happened on a mass scale in New York City, where rent control has persisted long after World War II.

Rent control illustrates not only the ease with which political systems can distort the transmission of knowledge in an economic system. Its history also illustrates how difficult it is for effective feedback to correct a political decision. Political decision making units are defined by geographic boundaries, not by particular subsets of people who experience the consequences of given policies. Rent control laws passed decades ago to benefit "New Yorkers" or tenants in New York were initially judged through the political process by *incumbent* New Yorkers and *incumbent* tenants, on the basis of the prospective plausibility of such laws. A generation later, deaths, births, and normal migration in and out of the city mean that the electorate has turned over considerably, and very few of them have personally experienced the effects of rent control from start to finish. Many of those who actually experienced the deterioration of housing under rent control in New York City are now living *outside* New York City, some as a direct result. Their experience does not feed back through the electoral process in the city. The current New York City electorate includes great numbers of people who arrived in the city—by birth or migration—when it was already experiencing the effects of rent control, so they have no "before" and "after" experience to compare. They do not know, for example, that the city once had a larger population,

178

no housing shortage, and no masses of abandoned buildings. Their personal experience does not go back far enough to enable them to spot the fatal flaw in the argument that rent control cannot be safely repealed while there is still a housing shortage. Lacking this personal experience, they would have to be trained in economics to realize that a "shortage" is itself a price phenomenon, and so will persist as long as the rent control persists.

While time and complexity insulate many political decisions from effective feedback from the general electorate, some offsetting knowledge is furnished by groups with lower knowledge costs because they are more obviously affected adversely—the real estate lobby and landlord associations, in this case. In general, special interests have not only lower costs of knowledge of their own interests, but an incentive to invest in discovering how other groups' interests are similarly affected, so as to acquire political allies. However, to the extent that special interest arguments are automatically discounted, this knowledge is ineffective or even counterproductive. Landlord and real estate interests, for example, provide pro-rent control forces with an enemy to fight, a sense of moral superiority in fighting, and a reassurance that they are acting in the interests of others who need protecting—though this last crucial point rests on an implicit conception of the economy as a zero-sum (or negative-sum) game. Once the economy is seen as a positive-sum game—that voluntary transactions are mutually beneficial or they would not occur—then the losses suffered when such transactions are forcibly restricted can also be mutual. The fact that the complaints issue first or exclusively from one party may reflect only his lower costs of knowledge of the effects on him.

More generally, to totally discount all special interest arguments is to implicitly assume that society is inherently a zero-sum game—which is difficult to reconcile with the fact that societies of some sort of other have existed among all peoples and ages.

The effects of rent control on the quality of housing illustrates a more general characteristic of price control and of the limits of articulation. Whatever price is forcibly set by an observer, he must define the product whose price is being controlled—and his articulation can seldom match the unarticulated experience of actual, voluntary transactors. The result is that prices set below the level that would have prevailed otherwise lead to quality deterioration. In the case of rent controlled apartments, maintenance, repair, painting, cleaning, heat, hot water and general monitoring all decline. This is less damaging to brand new buildings than to older buildings which require more upkeep to avoid becoming slums. Since low income people are more likely to live in older buildings, they are most likely to find their homes become unheated slums with uncorrected building hazards. In the extreme, they may find the building totally abandoned by the landlord, once the cost of maintaining it at minimum legal levels exceeds the rent permitted. In New York City, such abandonments average about twenty-five thousand buildings per year.[17]

Rent control is not unique in affecting the quality of the product. General price controls during World War II brought on a proliferation of inferior off brands, some made by brand-name producers who did not want to damage the long-run reputation of their regular label. Sometimes the quality deterioration took the form of deteriorated service, leading to much contemporary comedy based on arrogant butchers, insolent salespeople, etc. In general, price control involves articulating not only a price—which is easy—but also articulating the characteristics of a product. Although it may *seem* easy to define a product such as an apartment or a can of peas, actual experience demonstrates the crudity of articulation as compared to unarticulated experience. An apartment is not simply a physical thing, but involves a multitude of associated services, changes in the quantity and quality of which affect operating cost, the vacancy rate, and the price that can be charged in an uncontrolled market. When rents are forcibly lowered by the government, costs are voluntarily lowered by the landlords through declines in the quantity and quality of service, so that the "product" itself changes. A perfect legal specification of a product, perfectly monitored, would make this impossible. But the pervasiveness of this deterioration—including total abandonment—indicates the limits of articulation and third party monitoring.

In the absence of rent control, tenants monitor changes themselves and communicate their reactions to the landlord not only verbally but—more convincingly—through changes in the vacancy rate. They can even monitor services of which they are generally unaware, in the sense that they might not list them if asked to articulate what they want in an apartment building. For example, many tenants might not articulate a concern for management's monitoring of people who enter the building—and yet if the building becomes a hangout for loiterers, hoodlums, or addicts, the vacancy rate would rise. Conversely, if the management officiously screened all entering guests, the same negative reaction would occur. In other words, a service which is seldom articulated must not only be performed but performed within limits on either side, if the landlord is to minimize his vacancy rate and maximize his rental income. The multiplicity and importance of these auxiliary services is most dramatically seen, not in uncontrolled markets where they become routine, but by their *absence* in rent-control buildings and in government housing projects. Typically there is far more explicit articulation of housing rules in such places but far less effective monitoring.

Even a simple can of peas cannot be exhaustively defined and completely monitored under price control. The flavor, appearance, texture, and uniformity of peas within a can and from one can to the next, depend on the selection and control of crops and the sorting and processing of the peas. In an uncontrolled market, these are all adjusted according to the incremental cost of each improvement and the incremental value of the improvements as revealed by how high a price the consumer is willing to pay for brands which reliably supply the desired characteristics. If this price is forcibly set below the market level by a third party, the supplier has incentives to supply less of these qualities and thereby reduce his production costs.

Just as a price forcibly set below the market level tends to reduce the quality of the price controlled product, so a price forcibly set *above* the market level tends to increase the quality of the product. Minimum wage laws tend to cause employers to hire fewer but better qualified workers—that is, they make less skillful, less experienced, or otherwise less desirable workers "unemployable." Higher quality workers and more "unemployability" in a given work force are the same things expressed in different words.

Interest rate ceilings—usury laws—tend similarly to reduce a major service performed by the lender (risk taking) by causing him to eliminate more borrowers as insufficiently good risks. When one considers that the risk of losing money considerably exceeds 50 percent when drilling an oil well (that is, a well whose hoped-for result is oil), it is clear that high risk alone will not deter capital suppliers if the rate of return is allowed to vary sufficiently to compensate the risk. But by forcibly restricting the rate of return on personal loans to what is "reasonable" in the experience of good-credit-risk, middle-class people who write such laws, credit is often denied or restricted to low income people who may be only slightly less dependable risks and would be able to get credit at only slightly higher interest rates. Instead, they are left with no other choice but to resort to illegal "loan sharks" whose interest rates are much higher and whose collection methods are much rougher. Like other forms of price controls, usury laws distort the communication of correct facts about credit risks without in any way changing those facts themselves.

One of the more dramatic recent examples of the effect of forcibly keeping prices below the market level has been the so-called "gasoline crisis" of 1979. Because of the complexities in long-standing government regulations controlling the price of gasoline, their full effects began to be felt in the spring of 1979. As in the case of rent control, the effects were *not* primarily on the quantity of the physically defined product—gallons of gasoline in this case—but on the auxiliary services not articulated in the law. Just as rent control tends to reduce such auxiliary services as maintenance, heat, and hot water, so controlling the price of gasoline reduced such auxiliary services as hours of service at filling stations, credit card acceptance, and checking under the hood. Indeed, what was called a "gasoline shortage" was *primarily* a shortage of hours of service at filling stations, and the traumatic effects of this indicate that unarticulated aspects of the physically defined product are by no means incidental. In New York City, for example, the average filling station was open 110 hours a week in September 1978 and only 27 hours a week in June 1979.[18] The actual amount of gasoline pumped declined by only a few percentage points, while the hours of service declined 75 percent. That is, filling stations tried to recoup their losses from price control by reducing the man-hours of labor they paid for, while the motorists' losses of man-hours waiting in gasoline lines went up by many times what the filling stations had saved. Moreover, the motorists suffered from increased risks in planning long distance trips, given the unpredictability of filling station hours en route. This prospective psychic loss to motorists was reflected in dramatically declining business at vacation resorts, for example, but retrospective data on the actual amount of gasoline sold showed only small percentage declines. In short, the real cost of the so-called gasoline shortage was not simply the small statistical change in the quantity of the physical product, but the large prospective change in the ability to get it when and where it was wanted. As in so many other cases, objective retrospective data do not capture the economic reality.

FORCIBLY CHANGING COSTS

Costs to the economy as a whole may be given at a given time under given technology. But, even so, costs as experienced by the decision making unit can be raised by special taxes or lowered by subsidies. Any tax represents force used to influence decisions, and subsidies represent taxes forcibly extracted from others. It is indirect price fixing. A special tax, over and above the normal tax on items of similar value, misstates the cost transmitted through the economic system. The extra money paid by the consumer is not a loss suffered by the economy as a whole. The higher price is just an internal transfer of wealth among individuals in the same system—making the system as a whole no richer or poorer. What makes the system as a whole poorer are the transactions that do *not* take place because of the artificially high price. Where a high price conveys an actual scarcity of material or a reluctance of people to do certain work, then it accurately conveys information about the incremental cost to the economic system. But when the price is simply made higher by government fiat—whether by direct price fixing or by a special tax—then it conveys a false picture of the cost, thereby causing potential consumers to forego the product even though others are perfectly willing to supply it for a price that they are willing to pay.

Information about the availability of goods is distorted in the opposite direction when the government subsidizes goods. Some of the people consuming a subsidized good would be unwilling to pay the cost of it if that cost were accurately conveyed to them in the price. Instead, third parties are forced to pay part of the cost in taxes, regardless of their evaluation of the good and even regardless of whether they ever used it.

Sometimes subsidies are more subtly arranged, without explicit taxation. Where there is a government-run monopoly (such as the Post Office) or a government-regulated industry where competition is kept out by force of law (public utilities), then the prices that are set by government cause some users to subsidize other users. Force is applied, not to those users but to potential competitors, who are not allowed to enter the industry and offer lower prices to those consumers who are subsidizing others. Users of first-class mail pay more postage than is necessary to cover the cost of delivering such mail, while senders of "junk mail" pay less than its cost. The economic system in this case conveys distorted information, making junk mail seem cheaper to deliver than it is, and thereby causing more of it to be sent than if its true cost was conveyed to the senders in prices. Resources that would be more valuable to other people in other uses are used to move junk mail, because its bids for those resources include not only the assets voluntarily sacrificed on the basis of the value of that mail to the sender but also assets which nonsenders of junk mail had to surrender as the price of their own first-class mail—thereby becoming involuntary bidders for resources they neither want nor use.

In an ideally functioning political system with zero costs of knowledge, the extra-payers would have as much ability to end this cross-subsidy as the special interests have to create it. In the real world, however, special interests are—almost by definition—groups with lower costs of knowledge. They know individually what it is that they have in common so that they can contact and organize each other as people or organizations similarly affected by government policy. Their greater political weight then enables them to forcibly take economic resources from others.

As in all systems of price discrimination, cross-subsidy works only as long as competitors can be kept out, and usually only the government has sufficient force to do that effectively. Where price discrimination is attempted in a competitive market, those who are paying more than their own costs can be served more cheaply (and profitably) by firms charging each set of customers according to their own respective costs. Price discrimination under these conditions quickly becomes *attempted* price discrimination, as overcharged customers find other firms to transact with. This has happened, for example, in the railroad industry as it lost its original monopoly with the development of trucking and airlines. Those kinds of freight which had been overcharged to subsidize other kinds of freight simply began being shipped by trucks, planes, or barges.

Given that a monopolistic market is essential for cross-subsidizing (or other forms of price discrimination), it is not surprising that cross-subsidy prices are common in the postal service, public utilities, and other enterprises either run or directly controlled by the government. The cross-subsidization of mail occurs not only as between first-class and junk mail. It also occurs as between users in large cities and those in remote places. The huge volume of mail between New York and Chicago tends to make the cost per letter very low, while the low volume of mail to remote villages makes their cost per letter much higher. In an uncontrolled, competitive market, the respective prices would tend to reflect these large cost differences. In a government market, however, all the costs are lumped together and all the users pay the same postage without regard to how much each contributed to those costs. The knowledge conveyed by the uniform prices is therefore a distortion of the real costs in terms of the resources used up by the economy in directing mail to different places. To the extent that other government controlled prices similarly distort the cost of delivering electricity, water, and other services to rural locations, the whole cost of living in isolated towns or villages is understated to those who are deciding where to locate.

The history of American transportation, from municipal bus and streetcar lines to railroads and airlines, is a history of government-imposed cross-subsidies. Initially, municipal transit was privately owned by a number of firms operating streetcars along various routes. The creation of city-wide franchises—monopolies—was usually accompanied by fixed fares, regardless of distance traveled or transfers required. Short-distance passengers subsidized long-distance passengers. The effects were not only distributional but allocational. More resources were devoted to carrying people long distances than would have been if the true costs had been conveyed to those using the service. Therefore, the creation of suburbs and central business districts was subsidized, at the expense of people living in the city and of neighborhood enterprises. The question is not which of these residential or business arrangements is "better" in some categorical sense. The point is simply that cross-subsidy conveyed false economic information to those making decisions as to where to live or shop, and the fact that the subsidy never appeared in a government budget conveyed no information at all to the electorate.

Like most price discriminators, municipal transit was vulnerable to competitors who chose to serve the overcharged segment of their customers. Around 1914–1915, the mass production of the automobile led to the rise of owner-operated bus or taxi services costing five cents and therefore called "jitneys," the current slang for nickels:

The jitneys were owner-operated vehicles which essentially provided a competitive market in urban transportation with the usual characteristics of rapid entry and exit, quick adaptation to changes in demand, and, in particular, excellent adaptation to peak load demands. Some 60 percent of the jitneymen were part-time operators, many of whom simply carried passengers for a nickel on trips between home and work. Consequently, cities were criss-crossed with an infinity of home-to-work routes every rush hour.

The jitneys were put down in every American city to protect the street railways and, in particular, to perpetuate the cross-subsidization of the street railways' city-wide fare structures. As a result, the public moved to automobiles as private rather than common carriers. . . .[19]

In short, the cross-subsidy scheme not only distorted the location of homes and businesses; it artificially increased the "need" for private automobiles by forcibly preventing or restricting the sharing of cars through the market.

Ironically, years later, some municipalities have tried to encourage car pools to reduce traffic congestion, but car-pooling through nonmarket mechanisms requires far more knowledge than through the market for jitneys, and conveys far less incentive for dependability and cooperation. Because car pools are advance agreements among particular small subsets of persons, rather than a systemic arrangement for all the cars and passengers in the whole set of travelers, enormous sorting and labeling costs are involved in car-pooling—determining specifically who is going where and discovering how dependable and punctual each other person in the subset happens to be. By contrast, the jitney owner made profits by picking up people (usually on his own way to work) and had every incentive to pick them up on time every day, or some other jitney owner would pick them up before he got there. But with nonmarket car pools, a particular set of riders is waiting for a particular car—and it remains illegal for other cars to sell their services to them without a city franchise as taxis. Under these constraints, car pools have done little to relieve traffic congestion, despite much exhortation.

The rush-hour traffic congestion caused by thousands of people going to work separately in individual automobiles has been denounced by social critics as "irrational" and explained by some mysterious psychological attraction of Americans to automobiles. It is, however, a perfectly rational response to the incentives and constraints conveyed. The actual costs and benefits of automobile-sharing are forcibly prevented from being conveyed by prices. As in other areas, claims of public irrationality are a prelude to arguments for a government-imposed rational "solution" to the "problem." Also as in other areas, it is precisely the government's use of force to prevent the accurate transmission of knowledge through prices that leads to the suboptimal systemic results which are articulated as irrational intentional results of a personified "society."

Private force is used to prevent price transmission of knowledge of the availability of drivers. Many unemployed people are perfectly capable of driving, but are prevented from competing for such work, either as employees or as owner-operators of vehicles. Labor unions are the private force. This is not *metaphorical* force, though it may be infrequently exercised force (as in armed robberies), because both sides understand the situation. If any unemployed worker receives X dollars as unemployment compensation but would rather work at 2X, he will be prevented from doing so if the union wage is 3X.

It is not enough that the union have a contract for 3X with a given employer, such as a bus company or taxi fleet. The unemployed individual could work for 2X for himself or for a nonunion firm—if this were not prevented by union threats and/or government force applied directly to make these other options illegal.

Unions do not simply set the wages paid on a predestined number of jobs. The wage rate charged determines how a certain task will be performed— that is, how many "jobs" it will involve. In the case of municipal transit, high wage rates for bus drivers create incentives for large buses—the substitution of capital for labor in transporting a given number of passengers. A leading transportation economist estimates that about eight passengers per vehicle would be optimal in a system where prices were allowed to convey accurate costs of vehicles, drivers, and roads[20]—in contrast to the usual forty- to fifty-passenger buses actually used. If only one fifth as many passengers were carried per bus, there would be five times as many small buses, meaning five times as many jobs for drivers and only one-fifth the waiting time between buses for passengers. It would also be possible to have a far greater variety of bus routes, as the jitneys had, rather than clogging a few main thoroughfares during rush hours and letting passengers off farther from their destinations than necessary, as at present. Under these conditions buses would also be a far more attractive alternative to private automobiles for many people.

Disastrous as the effects of political decision making have been in municipal transportation, it is by no means irrational politically. Indeed, the same set of policies have emerged in so many different cities across the country, and reappeared again and again in national transportation policy regarding passenger railroads and airline routes that it is clearly a consistent effect, reflecting consistent causes rather than anything as random as "irrationality." Central to the decision making in this area has been the maintenance of *incumbent* transportation entities, which often implies the maintenance of incumbent technologies—i.e., subsidized obsolescence[21]—resisting the phasing out of existing modes of operation, as competing modes arise. On the contrary, competing modes with technological or organizational advantages are either penalized or prohibited (as in the case of the jitneys), to preserve incumbent organizations and technology. It is not even a pro-industry position but a pro-incumbent position, since there might well be a far more profitable industry (consisting of new firms), as well as one better serving the public, in the absence of such regulation. To be pro-industry would be an ideological position; to be pro-incumbent is a practical political position, since the incumbents are either organized or easily organizable into effective special interest groups. The same incumbent bias applies to labor—i.e., to unions of existing employees, at the expense of other workers whose job opportunities are sacrificed. For example the federal mass transit subsidy program requires labor union approval of any major expenditure[22] thereby assuring that no changes will be made that adversely affect the incumbent union members.

There is nothing peculiar about transportation that brings about such results. The regulated communications industry shows the same patterns. As in transportation, there was once a plausible case for government intervention, when the alternative of free competition did not seem feasible under existing conditions. In the broadcasting industry, there are inherent technological limits to how many competitors can operate in a given area, because broadcast signals interfere with one another, and beyond some point such interference makes all broadcasts unintelligible. This was a clear case where the government creation of a property right—in this case the right to exclude others from broadcasting on a given station's wavelengths—was a *social* gain, not simply a gain for the property owners. But the government went beyond *defining* a property right to *assigning* a property right. The crucial difference between the two functions is apparent in the case of land, where there are elaborate laws on property rights in general, and elaborate government records on each piece of land, but the actual assignment of ownership occurs almost entirely through market transactions. The defining of a property right in broadcasting over certain wavelengths served the public interest, but the power to *assign* such rights to particular individuals or corporations served the interests of politicians. The regulatory process they created—and continue to influence through appointments and appropriations—had enormously valuable property rights to hand out at their discretion, with little more legal restrictions than vague phrases about "the public interest." In exchange, politicians and their appointees were in a position to receive everything from simple obeisance[23] through campaign contributions, favors to constituents and friends, jobs in the regulated industry, and outright bribes.

In communications, as in transit, new technological developments threatened incumbent organizations and incumbent technology. Cable television made possible an unlimited transmission of stations to any given point, unlike broadcasting through the air. The whole structure of the industry—networks, affiliates, advertising patterns—could have been undermined or destroyed by the new technological possibilities. So too would have been the existing regulatory apparatus, which was no longer needed after the industry was no longer inherently monopolistic. But as in transportation after alternative modes (autos, airplanes) eliminated the railroad monopoly on which the I.C.C. was based, so in communications the response to the elimination of the initial rationale for regulation was to *extend* the regulation to encumber and contain the new threatening technology.

Under this set of institutional incentives and constraints, it is hardly surprising that corruption scandals have plagued broadcasting regulation for decades,[24] and surrounding the outright proven corruption is a large gray area of questionable financial windfalls to politicians, including the fortune of Lyndon B. Johnson.

Sometimes the political gains from regulation are more indirect but no less substantial and no less distorting to the use of resources in the economy. For example, the routes of federally subsidized passenger trains reflect the locations of the constituencies of key politicians, rather than the concentration of people requiring the service:

Because the Chairman of the House Commerce Committee and a prominent member of the ICC come from West Virginia, at various times three passenger trains have been run east and west through the state, which has limited demand for passenger service. Similarly Amtrak has had to provide two routes through Montana on the former Great Northern and Northern Pacific main lines because of the political strength of senators from Montana. Because members of Congress from Ohio have shown no special interest in transportation, that populous state receives a relatively small coverage of passenger trains: Cleveland was not served by Amtrak at all in the initial plan. . . .[25]

Similar political considerations cause the federally financed highway system "to contain a large mileage of lightly utilized freeway, especially in the plains states, whereas the investment would have given society a greater return in the more populous areas of the country."[26] Again, the point is not simply its inconsistency as economic optimizing, but its perfect consistency as political optimizing. A more basic question might be why anyone would expect economic optimizing by people chosen politically, and operating under political incentives and constraints. Vague personifications of "society" and projections of government into that role may be the explanation.

Cross-subsidy is so widespread and so deeply ingrained in government controlled enterprises that a special term of opprobrium is used to describe the disturbance of such schemes by new firms entering to serve the previously overcharged segment of the market: "cream skimming." Thus, when the United Parcel Service began delivering more packages—more cheaply, quickly, and safely than the Post Office—it was charged with skimming the cream of the market by serving urban and suburban areas rather than all the remote areas which are served by the Post Office. A private business has no incentives to subsidize one set of customers at the expense of another. Its individual incentive is to produce the maximum value at the least cost (the difference being its profit), and systemically that means getting the most possible from given resources at the least sacrifices of alternative uses of those resourses.

An uncontrolled, competitive market for package deliveries would not mean that people in remote areas would have *no* packages delivered. It means that the frequency of such delivieries would be less, reflecting the higher cost. Those people in such areas who are able to stop by a post office or parcel service office in town during shopping trips, or when going to or from work, would pick up packages then rather than pay postage reflecting their true cost of delivery.There would also be some incremental substitution of local products for products shipped in. By contrast with market-induced economizing on the use of costly resources, a government enterprise whose residual claimants (taxpayers) are not its decision makers has an incentive to maximize its size and budget by *extending* the "need" for its service as far as possible—even when increasing incremental costs are greater than the incremental value to the customers. Considering the lack of incentives for internal efficiency in a tax supported organization, it is also possible that *all* users of the service—in remote areas as well as large cities—pay more for mail delivered by the government than they would under private management, constrained by profit and loss considerations.

Airports sell monopoly rights to a taxi company, a restaurant, gift shops, and other concessionaires and use the proceeds to subsidize the prices they charge to planes for landing at the airport. Thus, even though economists estimate the cost of a landing at Kennedy Airport during the peak hours at about $2,000, the plane pays only $75.[27] Distorting the knowledge of the true cost of the plane's landing this way means that the airlines make their decisions as if landing at Kennedy Airport is far cheaper to the economy than it really is. A given airline will, for example, fly numerous planes from a given city into Kennedy Airport at various times during the day—these planes sometimes carrying only a fifth or a tenth of the passengers that the seating capacity will hold. In addition, other airlines serving the same city will fly other planes in at similar times, with similarly few passengers per plane. The net result is an inflated "need" for airport facilities—calling (politically) for expansion of given airports and/or the construction of new and expensive airports. Cross-subsidy thus creates a "need" for a larger empire of staff, facilities, and appropriations, whether the particular governmental enterprise is an airport, a postal system, or whatever.

Objective statistics which apparently demonstrate the "need" for more service—the numbers of planes landing and taking off per hour, their waiting time in the air or on the ground, etc.—are completely misleading. *There is no such thing as objective, quantitative "need."* Whether with airports or apartments or a thousand other things, how much is "needed" depends on the price charged. Just as artificially low prices under rent control caused the same population to "need" more apartments, so artificially low landing fees cause far more airplanes to be "needed" to transport a given number of passengers between two cities, in planes with many empty seats. With landing fees increased about twenty-five times, reflecting the true cost of landing a plane at Kennedy Airport, fewer flights per day would be made and a higher percentage of the seats would be filled on each flight. Few private planes with one or two passengers would be using up valuable landing space at major airports if they had to pay thousands of dollars per landing, though a little plane with only the pilot aboard may now choose to land at an enormously expensive airport, delaying thousands of other people circling around in a "stack," because the price he is charged does not convey these alternative uses to him as effective knowledge that he must incorporate into his decision as to where to land.

The average commercial airliner in the United States flies with half its seats empty—which means that only half as many flights would be needed to transport the same number of passengers in existing planes. Actually, less than that would be needed, since (1) planes idled by more effective scheduling would tend to be the smaller planes, (2) future planes would average larger sizes if landing fees rose by the larger amounts reflecting the true economic cost of using major airports. Small private planes would have financial incentives to land at smaller airports, rather than add to the congestion at major airports serving a large volume of commercial air traffic. In short, under prices reflecting cost, the number of flights "needed" in the major urban airports would be less, with less noise to destroy millions of dollars worth of residential property values in the vicinity of airports, and less "need" to confiscate more of such property to expand airport facilities.

The pattern of overuse through underpricing—including zero prices for many government services—is not a case of "irrationality." Its pervasiveness among the most diverse products and services, from airports to stamps, suggests a *reason* for it, not random caprice. It is completely rational from the standpoint of maximizing the well-being of the decision making unit (airport authorities, postal officials, TVA executives, etc.). When discussing under-pricing policy, more "need" can always be demonstrated "objectively" than under market pricing, which would convey knowledge that would cause more economical use of whatever is being sold.

Some idea of the complications insulating regulatory agencies from feed-back from the affected public may be suggested by the fact that specialists studying federal regulatory agencies "cannot even agree on the number" of such agencies, although "it is thought to be over 100."[28] A senator critical of regulatory commissions claims that simple "common sense" is "rare" in many of them, and then characterizes them as "undemocratic, insulated, and mysterious to all but a few bureaucrats and lawyers."[29] Such criticism misses the point that the agencies' own interests could hardly be better served than by being so incomprehensible to outsiders that even a United States senator with a staff at his disposal cannot find out precisely how many such agencies there are, much less exercise effective legislative oversight over their activi-ties. The costs of regulation to the public—that is, its uneconomic effects as well as its administrative costs—have been estimated by the U.S. General Ac-counting Office at about $60 billion per year[30]—about $1000 for every fam-ily in the United States. The regulatory decisions which impose such costs may seem to lack "common sense" as public policy, but such decisions often make perfect sense from the regulatory commission's own viewpoint—espe-cially in favoring such incumbent special interests as have enough at stake to pay the high knowledge costs of continuously monitoring a given agency's activities.

FORCIBLE TRANSFERS OF RESOURCES

In addition to forcibly changing—distorting—the price signals that convey knowledge of scarcities and options, the government has also increasingly used force directly to transfer resources. Massive "urban renewal" programs, for example, have simply ordered people to give up their homes and busi-nesses, in order that land may be cleared and something else built on the site. Similarly, the military draft has forcibly transferred people from one occu-pation to another. Less dramatically, but no less importantly, the government has also forcibly appropriated many property rights over the years, without appropriating the physical things to which these rights are attached. As noted earlier (Chapter 5), to appropriate 10 percent of the value of land is the same thing economically as appropriating 10 percent of the land itself. Politically, however, the two things are quite different. The cost of knowl-edge to the electorate is much higher when part of the value of land is ap-propriated by restricting the options as to its use than when an equivalent appropriation takes the obvious form of expropriating a portion of the land itself. The same principle is involved when the government forcibly changes the terms of contracts already voluntarily negotiated between private parties, as when it changes the so-called "retirement" age—i.e., the age at which one party's obligation to employ the other ceases. Assets set aside for other purposes must legally be expended to retain unwanted services—thereby reducing the real value of given money assets by reducing the options as to their use, just as land that cannot legally be used in as many ways is less valuable than physically identical land unrestricted by entails, zoning, or lost mineral rights.

Much articulation goes into trying to demonstrate to third party observers that the forcible transfers lead to more beneficial results. Yet on general principle, it is not clear that articulation is the best mode for weighing alternative values or that third party observers are the best judges. When a given set of homes and businesses are destroyed to make way for a very different set of homes and businesses, as in "urban renewal," a truly greater value of the second set would have enabled their users (or financial intermediaries) to bid the land away from the original users through voluntary market competition without the use of force by the government (especially since the second set of users almost invariably has higher incomes than the first).[31] Voluntary transfers of land are so commonplace as to cast doubt on the "need" for force, if the second set of uses is in fact more valuable. Actually, force is used twice in urban renewal transfers—once to dispossess the original users and again to transfer assets from taxpayers to subsidize the second set of users. The issue here is not the unpleasantness of force so much as its implications for the claim that the transfer of resources was to a more valuable use.

The particular site of the "urban renewal" may be far more attractive afterwards than it was before, and this adds plausibility to the claim of social benefits. But any site, activity, or person, can be made more attractive by expending resources. Whether the incremental costs experienced by those who pay them outweigh the incremental benefits experienced by those who receive them is the crucial question. When those who pay and those who benefit are the same, as in voluntary market transactions, then it is unnecessary for third parties to incur the costs of deciding on the basis of plausibility, much less pay the still higher costs of obtaining more solid knowledge. Where force must be used to effect the transfer, the incremental costs apparently exceed the incremental benefits of the change as experienced by those directly involved. "Objective" data showing that the people dispossessed moved to "better" housing elsewhere likewise has more plausibility than substance. That "better" housing was always an option before—*at a price*, and the rejection of that option indicates a trade-off of housing for other things more valued by those actually experiencing the options. Forcibly reducing any set of options available can lead to a new collection of results—some part of which is "better" than its counterpart in the old collection, but the real question is which whole collection was preferred by the chooser when he had the choice.

More generally, "urban renewal" has involved visible benefits concentrated on a particular site and costs diffused over a nation of taxpayers, as well as costs borne by dispersed former residents. In other words, the cost of knowledge of benefits is much lower than the cost of knowledge of losses—even when the losses exceed the benefits. Therefore, it is rational for political decision makers to continue such programs, even when irrational economically or socially.

The use of draftees by the army may similarly be rational from the standpoint of the army and irrational from the standpoint of the economy or society. There are no objectively quantifiable "needs" for manpower by the military, any more than by any other organization. At some set of prices, the number of soldiers, civilian employees, and equipment needed to achieve a given military effect will be one thing, and at a very different set of prices for each, the quantitative "needs" for each can be quite different. Even in an all-out war, most soldiers do not fight, but perform a variety of auxiliary services, many of which can be performed by civilian employees, since most of these services take place far from the scenes of battle. From the standpoint of the army as an economic decision making unit, it is rational to draft a chemist to sweep floors as long as his cost as a draftee is lower than the cost of hiring a civilian floor sweeper. From the standpoint of the economy as a whole, it is of course a waste of human resources. Again, the use of force is significant not simply because force is unpleasant, but because it distorts the effective knowledge of options.

The appropriation of physical objects or of human beings is more blatant than the appropriation of intangibles like property rights, but the principles and effects are similar. Neither "property" nor the value of property is a physical thing. Property is a set of defined options, some of which (mineral rights, for example) can be sold separately from others. It is that set of options which has economic value—which is why zoning law changes, for example, can drastically raise or lower the market value of the same physical land or buildings. It is the options, and not the physical things, which are the "property"—economically as well as legally. There are property rights in such intangibles as copyrighted music, trademarked names, stock options, and commodity futures. A contract is a property right in someone else's future behavior, and can be bought and sold in the market, as in the case of contracts with professional athletes or consumer credit contracts. But because the public tends to think of property as tangible, physical things, this opens the way politically for government confiscation of property by forcibly taking away options while leaving the physical objects untouched. This reduction of options can reduce the value of the property to zero or even below zero, as in the case of those rent controlled apartment buildings in New York, which are abandoned by landlords because they can neither sell them nor give them away, because the combination of building codes and rent controls makes their value negative. Had the government confiscated the building itself, the loss would have been less. The landlord in effect gives the building to the government by abandoning it. Indeed, he *pays* to get rid of it, because abandonment has additional costs in the form of legal liability if the landlord is ever located and convicted of abandoning the building, which is illegal.

Property rights which are not attached to any physical object are even more vulnerable politically. Contracts concerning future behavior have been virtually rewritten by legislation and/or court interpretation. These have included both prior restraints on the terms of contracts—interest rate ceilings, minimum wage laws, rent control, etc.—and subsequent nullification of existing contracts, as in laws against so-called "mandatory retirement." Few, if any, contracts require anybody to retire, and about 40 percent of all persons above the so-called retirement age continued to work, even before this legislation was passed. The so-called "retirement" age was simply the age at which the employer's *obligation* to employ individuals ended. The only thing "mandatory" was that contractual obligation—and it has been unilaterally extended by the government. Categorical, speculative articulation by third parties regarding the productive ability of the elderly as a group has superseded incremental judgments of each situation by the person actually employing each worker in question.

As in other cases, moving an asset or obligation backward or forward in time drastically alters its value or cost. Changing the retirement age a few years in either direction is the same as forcibly transferring billions of dollars from one group to another, since the costs of such commitments as life insurance, annuities, etc., depend crucially on time. One of the largest financial commitments arbitrarily changed by changing the retirement age is that of the government's own "Social Security" program—which saves billions of dollars by postponing its own payments to the retired by forcing employers to continue to hire them longer. But because these changes in massive financial obligation (on employers) and defaults (by government) take the outward form of "merely" changing a date, it is politically insulated by the cost of the knowledge required for voters to detect their full economic impact.

CONTROLLING PRODUCERS AND SELLERS

Controlling the terms which individuals may offer each other is only one method of economic control. Other techniques include (1) controlling who can be included or excluded from a particular economic activity, (2) what characteristics will be permitted or not permitted in products, producers, or purchasers, and ultimately (3) comprehensive economic "planning" which controls economic activity in general on a national scale.

FORCIBLE RESTRICTION OF COMPETITION

While prices are crucial as conveyors of knowledge to decision makers, artificial prices which distort this knowledge can persist only insofar as competitors whose prices would convey the true knowledge are forcibly excluded.[32] One reason for forcibly excluding competitors has already been noted—"external" effects, as in broadcast interference, which makes unrestricted competition unfeasible.[33] There are also industries where the production costs are overwhelmingly *fixed* costs—and high fixed costs at that—so that the cost per unit of output is constantly declining over any range of output that is likely to be demanded. In this case, one producer can supply the market more cheaply than two or more, since more output means lower production costs. Examples include industries with huge investments in massive systems of conduits of one sort or another delivering water, gas, electricity, or telephone calls. These are what economists call "natural monopolies," since it would cost more to get the same service through multiple producers than through one producer per given area. Therefore government regulation substitutes for competition as a means of preventing high monopolistic prices from being charged.

This is the idealized economic theory. The reality is something else. Once a rationale for regulation has been created, the actual behavior of regulatory agencies does not follow that rationale or its hoped-for results, but adjusts to the institutional incentives and constraints facing the agencies. For example, the scope of the regulation extends far beyond "natural monopolies," even where it was initially applied only to such firms. The broadcast-interference rationale for the creation of the Federal Communications Commission in no way explains why it extended its control to cable television. The "natural monopoly" that railroads possessed in some nineteenth century markets led to the creation of the Interstate Commerce Commission, but when trucks and buses began to compete in the twentieth century, the regulation was not discarded but extended to them. Airplanes have never been a "natural monopoly," but the Civil Aeronautics Board has followed policies completely parallel with the policies of other regulatory agencies. It has protected incumbents from newcomers, just as the FCC has protected broadcast networks from cable TV, as the ICC has tried to protect railroads from trucking, or municipal regulatory commissions have protected existing transit lines from jitneys or other unrestricted automobile-sharing operations. As a leading authority has summarized CAB policy: "Despite a 4,000 percent increase in demand between 1938 and 1956, not a single new passenger trunk line carrier was allowed to enter the industry."[34]

Regulatory agencies in general have the legal right to exclude firms from entering the industry they regulate. This is a property right worth billions of dollars. The members of the commissions are not allowed to sell this right, but they can dispense it in ways that make their job easier, or their individual fortunes more secure as later employees of the firms they currently regulate. Favoritism to incumbents is a perfectly rational response to such incentives, however inconsistent with the public interest. The only legal guidelines are that entry of firms into the regulated industry must serve the "necessity and convenience" of the public. The regulatory agency determines how many firms are "needed" to serve the public. The idea is that there are quantitative, objective "needs" determinable by third party observers—as distinguished from the economic reality of varying quantities and qualities demanded according to varying costs. But the "need" for railroad service, for example, is "measured in physical rather than economic terms" so that "as long as existing carriers are physically capable of performing a particular service, prospective competitors are to be denied entry—even if their service is cheaper, better, and more efficient."[35] Similar policies are followed by other regulatory commissions.

Because the right to operate in a regulated industry is a valuable property right available at virtually zero cost, the claimants' demand always exceeds the supply, even when only incumbents are allowed to compete. It is to the regulatory agency's political advantage to satisfy, or at least appease, as many incumbents as possible—which is to say, to distribute these operating rights widely, and therefore thinly. Thus legal rights to engage in interstate trucking are spread so thin that they are often rights to operate in only one direction—a "carrier between the Pacific Northwest and Salt Lake City may haul commodities eastbound, but not westbound,"[36] for example—thereby doubling the cost to consumers, who must pay enough freight charges to cover the cost of the truck both ways. Sometimes the right to carry goods between two points does not include the right to pick up and deliver at points in between, so that again the cost of the service is made artificially high by not allowing it to be shared by as many customers as possible. However economically costly this is to the country, it makes perfect political sense as a means of spreading a given amount of patronage as widely as possible to mollify as many constituents as possible.

Since the general public knows little or nothing about such regulatory agencies, their interests are a politically negligible consideration. Whatever the individual morality or intentions of regulatory commissions, the systemic factors leading to such results are (1) the vast disparity in cost of knowledge per unit of benefit as between the public and special interest groups, and (2) the appointment rather than election of commissioners, so that no political competitor has a high personal or organizational stake in informing the public of incumbent commissioners' misdeeds. Political as well as economic competition has been restricted or eliminated. Mollifying as many constituents as possible means not only protecting incumbents from prospective competitors; it means protecting high-cost (inefficient) incumbents from unrestricted competition from low-cost (efficient) incumbents, who could otherwise undercut their prices, taking away their customers, and driving them toward bankruptcy. Rather than quietly enter bankruptcy courts, such higher cost firms are more likely to noisily enter the political arena, probably through the congressional committee controlling the powers and appropriations of the regulatory commission in question. It is politically prudent for the commission to buy "insurance" against such problems—at costs externalized to the public—by maintaining a minimum level of prices designed to insure survival of the highest-cost firms. Lower-cost firms therefore earn more profits per unit of sales but are prevented from completely destroying the high-cost firms. In short, there is something for everybody, which is a politically more viable situation than the "cutthroat" or "ruinous" competition which regulatory agencies constantly guard against.

Insofar as the public is interested in, and able to monitor, the results of the regulatory process, it is usually in terms of product prices or the profit rate of the industry. Almost by definition, they have nothing to compare the prices with—there being no unregulated firm producing the same good or service, in most cases. This leaves the profit rate of a regulated firm as their criterion. The regulatory agency therefore appeases the public by keeping this profit rate "low" in comparison with unregulated firms. That is wholly different from keeping the prices low. A low profit rate on a truck delivery that costs twice as much as necessary, because the truck returns empty for lack of legal authority to do business the other way, may still mean almost double what the price would have been under unregulated competition. Passenger fares may also be double what they would be without regulation when commercial airlines fly half empty—which is the rule. In the latter case, there is some comparison possible, because large states like Texas and California have purely intrastate airlines which thereby escape federal regulation. Pacific Southwest Airlines, for example, flies between Los Angeles and San Francisco at far lower fares—and higher profits—than federally-regulated airlines flying between Washington and Boston, which is the same distance.[37] They simply fly with more of the seats filled,[38] partly because there is no CAB to stop them from charging low fares. In the words of economists studying prices of airlines, the "subtantial traffic gains of the intrastate carriers have more than offset the lower revenue yields per passenger . . ."[39] Indeed low markups and high volume have been the secret of many profitable businesses in many fields.

Although pious words about the "public interest" may abound in regulatory legislation and regulatory rulings, there is no institutional mechanism to compel, induce, or reward commissions for weighing the costs and benefits to the public when they make their decisions. In particular, there are no incentives to keep costs down—and costs make up a far higher percentage of the price of most goods than does profit. A small inefficiency can raise the price of a good by much more than the doubling of the profit rate would. The average profit rate in the United States is about 10 percent, and a 20 percent rate for any firm is considered enormous. Yet if Firm A has only 10 percent higher costs than Firm B, its price would tend to rise as much as if its profit rate had doubled. The political visibility of profit rates results in much regulatory time, energy, and controversy when going into determining whether a "reasonable" rate of return is 6 percent, 7 percent, or 8 percent— differences which may mean very little to the average consumer in dollars and cents. Much less effort goes into determining whether costs of production are higher than they need be, even though production costs may have far more effect on prices. This is partly because of both legal and common sense limits on how far a regulatory agency can go into the actual management of a firm.

Regulated firms whose explicit financial profit rate is restricted have every incentive to allow costs to rise, taking various benefits in nonpecuniary forms, such as fringe benefits (especially for management) more relaxed (inefficient) management, less innovative activity and the headaches it brings, less unpleasantness such as firing people or hiring associates who are offensive in manner, race or sex.[40] In addition, the more costs the regulated firm can accumulate—and get the regulatory agency to accept as valid—the higher its total profits at a given rate of profit.[41] In short, there is little incentive for regulated firms to keep down costs, and much incentive to let them rise, especially in ways that make the management of such firms easier. For example, high wage demands by unions in regulated industries need not be resisted (and strikes risked) as strongly as in unregulated industries, because wage increases become part of the cost on which the regulatory agency sets prices. Some of the highest paid workers in America are railroad workers and municipal transit workers, despite the dire conditions of both industries and the frequent transfusions of taxpayers' money they require.

Many of the most extreme examples of employing unnecessary labor—"featherbedding"—are found in regulated industries. Duplicate crews for handling trains on the road and handling the same trains when they enter the railroad yard, retention of coal-shovellers or "firemen" after locomotives stopped using coal, and elaborate "full crew" laws and practices are among the many financial drains on the American railroad industry, which is financially unable to keep its tracks repaired or maintained in sufficiently safe conditions to prevent numerous derailments per year and the spread of noxious or lethal chemicals which often accompany such accidents. The managements of such financially depleted railroads have likewise enjoyed extraordinary financial benefits, including many of questionable legality. To explain this by individual intentions—"greed"—is to miss the central systemic question: Why can such greed on the part of both labor and management be satisfied so much more in this industry than in others? The incentives and constraints of regulation, compared to those of competition, are a major part of the answer.

Regulation spreads not only because more regulatory agencies are created to regulate more industries, but also because existing regulatory agencies reach out to regulate more firms which have an impact on their existing regulated industry. The FCC's reaching out to include cable TV or the ICC's reaching out to include trucking are classic examples of regulatory extension of the original mandate based on the original rationale to include things neither contemplated nor covered by that rationale. The tenacity with which regulatory agencies hang onto existing regulated activity is indicated by the ICC's reaction to the exemption of agricultural produce from its regulatory scope. It ruled that chickens whose feathers had been plucked were no longer agricultural but "manufactured" products—as were nuts whose shells had been removed or frozen vegetables.[42]

Competition may be restricted not only by direct control of the necessary legal papers required to enter a given industry but also by control of subsidies in an industry whose whole price structure requires subsidy for firms to survive. The American maritime industry, for example, has such high wages and inefficient union rules that its firms cannot survive without massive government subsidy. A firm which is denied such subsidy simply cannot compete with the other firms that have it, because it will have to charge its customers far more than the subsidized firms charge. The Federal Maritime Board determines who gets how much subsidy on which routes, on the basis of its decisions about the "essential" nature ("need") for those routes.[43] Both the maritime industry and the maritime unions are heavy contributors to both political parties, insuring the continuance of such arrangements regardless of the outcome of elections.

Not all governmental restrictions on competition take the form of regulation in the classic public utilities sense. There is much regulation of particular markets such as various agricultural and dairy-product markets, under a variety of rationales having nothing to do with "natural monopoly" or consumer protection. The usual effect of such restrictions is to raise product prices, and in many cases it is rather transparent that that was the intention as well. Sometimes these government interventions go beyond generalized price fixing to, for example, setting a different price for milk for each of its various uses. The terms of the trade-offs of yogurt for cheese or ice cream, etc., are not allowed to be conveyed by prices that fluctuate with consumer demand or technological change, but are fixed politically and therefore distort knowledge of economic alternatives.

Occupational licensing laws are another very different form of economic regulations which nevertheless share many of the political characteristics common in commissions regulating public utilities or common carriers. First there is an enormous *bias towards incumbents*. Escalating qualification standards in the licensed occupation almost invariably exempt existing practitioners, who thereby reap increased earnings from the contrived scarcity, without having to pay the costs they impose on new entrants in the form of longer schooling, tougher qualifying examinations, or more extended apprenticeship.[44] Second, the prices of the services are artificially raised and the undercutting of price either forbidden (taxi rides) or rendered uneconomic by forbidding price advertising (lawyers, doctors, optometrists). Although "the public interest" is a prominent rhetorical feature of occupational licensing laws and pronouncements, historically the impetus for such licensing comes almost invariably from practitioners rather than the public, and it almost invariably reduces the quantity of new practitioners through various restrictive devices, and the net result is higher prices.

Some idea of the magnitude of the effect of occupational licensing may be obtained from the prices of such licenses as are transferrable through market sales. A taxi license in many American cities costs thousands of dollars—up $50,000 in New York City.[45] Where licenses are nontransferrable, as in medicine, the effect of the restrictive practices can be indicated by the income of doctors—which were below those of lawyers in the 1930s but are now more than *double* the income of lawyers as a result of restrictive practices by the American Medical Association, possessing far more control over medical school admissions and hospital staffing than the American Bar Association possesses over corresponding legal institutions.

Another area in which the government restricts competition is in the application of laws on land use—including municipal land use or recreational land policy for wilderness areas. Restrictions on the use of land forcibly prevents bidding for it by certain users—notably middlemen ("developers") selling or renting to working-class people. The political impracticality of openly admitting that government force is being summoned to keep out the poor leads to much vague and lofty discussion in which *people* fade from the picture entirely and such impersonal entities as "valuable open space"[46] and "fragile areas"[47] dominate discussion about the need to "protect the environment"[48] under "rational and comprehensive"[49] allocation of the land through political processes. But the strong class bias is evident in such things as (1) the heavily upper income occupations (executives, doctors, engineers, academics) of members of the Sierra Club, which spearheads much "environmental" political activity,[50] (2) strong working-class voter opposition to zoning and strong upper-class support for it,[51] (3) expensive home building "requirements" having nothing to do with the "environment" or "ecology" but having much to do with pricing the poor out of the market,[52] and (4) the limiting of cheap and fast access to wilderness recreation areas and favoring time-consuming access usable only by those with substantial leisure.[53] A student of the so-called "environmental controversy" finds "an ugly strain of narrow class interests involved in the wilderness issue," an "attempt by the prosperous to bar the rabble" and efforts by those who "already have vacation colonies on secluded lakes" to keep out "developments that cater to the masses."[54]

Defending class privileges in the name of the public interest has required constant alarms and misleading statistics. For example, a picture of spreading and pervasive urbanization is projected by using the Census definition of "urban" as any place with 2,500 inhabitants or more. This technique conjures up a "megalopolis" extending "from southern New Hampshire to northern Virginia and from the Atlantic shore to the Appalachian foothills."[55] In fact, however, the average density of most of that area is about one house per every twelve acres. A few high density areas like New York and other eastern cities contain most of the people (87 percent) in the supposed "megalopolis," most of which is covered with greenery rather than concrete.[56] Zoning law proponents likewise invoke fears of factories and gas stations in residential neighborhoods. But in cities without zoning—notably Houston—no such dire things happen. Middle-class neighborhoods there look like middle-class neighborhoods elsewhere. In lower income neighborhoods, there are sometimes auto repair shops and other such local conveniences—but it is precisely in these neighborhoods with automobile repair shops that zoning is overwhelmingly *rejected* by the voters.[57] Apparently the trade-off between convenience and aesthetics is different for those with less money and older cars. Looked at another way, zoning allows some people to impose their values and life-style on others who may not share the values or be able to afford the life-style.

ANTITRUST

Markets may be controlled by private parties as well as by the government, and the antitrust laws are in general aimed at preventing monopoly and related market distortions. However, the major antitrust laws have been passed at widely varying times and represent varying concepts and conflicting goals. The Sherman Antitrust Act of 1890 is the oldest and most important of the federal statutes, carrying the heaviest penalties, which can range up through millions of dollars in civil damages to dissolution of a firm and/ or jail for its executives. The Sherman Act forbids anyone to "monopolize, or attempt to monopolize," or to engage in "restraint of trade." The Clayton Act of 1914 forbade certain actions incident to monopolistic behavior, such as price discrimination, and the Federal Trade Commission Act of the same year established an organization to monitor and issue orders against a variety of undesired ("unfair") business practices. The most enigmatic and controversial of the antitrust laws is the Robinson-Patman Act of 1936, ostensibly strengthening the Clayton Act's ban on price-discrimination, but in practice creating legal risks and uncertainties for firms engaging in vigorous price competition. The 1950 Celler Amendment to the Clayton Act created new legal obstacles to the merger of firms.

The legal problem of reconciling these overlapping statutes is complicated by the overlapping jurisdiction of the Justice Department and the Federal Trade Commission in antitrust cases, and by the full or partial exemption from antitrust laws of some economic activities, including regulated public utilities and labor unions. Moreover, the vague language of the law leaves ample room for judicial and bureaucratic interpretations which have caused some of the leading economic and legal scholars to claim that the antitrust laws have had the opposite effects from their intentions.[58]

Among the central concerns of the antitrust laws are market structures, price fixing, and price discrimination. A monopoly would not accurately transmit costs through its prices because those prices would be set above a level that could persist with competitors. Competitive businesses set prices reflecting costs of production only because they stand to lose too many sales at prices that exceed what is necessary to compensate others for supplying the same product. It is neither greed nor altruism that explains price differences but rather the systemic differences between competitive and noncompetitive markets. Price discrimination is both a symptom of a noncompetitive market and a further distortion of economic knowledge, as it conveys different information about the relative scarcity of the same product to different users—causing them to economize differently, and thus at least one of them wrongly.

Antitrust laws, like all forms of third party monitoring, depend for their social effectiveness on the articulation of characteristics objectively observable in retrospect, which may or may not capture the decision-making process as it appeared prospectively to the agents involved. There is usually nothing in antitrust cases comparable to finding someone standing over the corpse with a smoking pistol in his hand. Objective statistical data abound, but its interpretation depends crucially on the definitions and theories used to infer the nature of the prospective process which left behind that particular residue of retrospective numbers. For example, merely defining the product often opens a bottomless pit of complexities. Cellophane is either a monopoly—if the product is defined to include the trademarked name, which only Dupont has a legal right to use—or has varying numbers of competing substitutes, depending on how transparent and how flexible some other brand of wrapping material must be in order to be considered the same or comparable. Under some definitions or demarcations of transparency and flexibility, cellophane is monpolistic for lack of sufficient substitutes. But by other definitions it is in a highly competitive market with innumerable substitutes. The controversies following the Supreme Court's decision as to whether cellophane was a "monopoly" (no) suggests that there were other definitions which some (but not all) legal and economic experts found preferable. The point here is that there is no objective and compelling reason to take one definition rather than another, though the whole issue often turns on which definition is chosen. In more complicated products, there are often numerous variations on the same goods, and which of these are lumped together as "the same" product determines what the market is and how much the producer's share of the market is, as variously defined. For example, Smith-Corona has a smaller share of total American typewriter sales than of electric typewriters sold in the United States, or of all portable electric typewriters made by American manufacturers. For many products, so much is imported that a firm's share of American production is economically meaningless: any American producer of single-lens reflex cameras would have a monopoly by definition; all such cameras are currently imported. But the purely definitional monopoly has no effect on economic behavior, in the face of dozens of foreign competitors.

What is involved here is not a technicality of antitrust law but a far broader question about the use of knowledge, and the role of articulation. The basic problem in these definition-of-product issues is that substitutability is ultimately subjective and prospective, while attempts to define it must be objective and retrospective.

Even where a product seems unambiguously definable in some plain sense—a tangerine, for example—a question may still arise as to the economic significance of such a definition. If a worldwide cartel were to gain control of every tangerine on the planet, they could still not double the price of the monopolized product without ending up with millions of unsaleable and spoiling tangerines in their warehouses, while consumers switched to oranges, tangelos, and the like. In short, even where the physical demarcation of a product seems obvious and unambiguous, its economic demarcation may be difficult or impossible. The extent to which the price of one product affects the sales of another product is what is economically important. As a practical matter, sellers can acquire an unarticulated "feel" for this in an ongoing trial-and-error process, but that is very different from third-party observers of retrospective statistics being able to objectively document irrefutable results to courts. For one thing, the discrete time units in which data are collected by observers may be far longer than the almost continuous time dimensions of the actual transactors' ongoing experience, so that the observers' data are more likely to represent an amalgamation of highly disparate price and sales fluctuations during the time interval studied.

Discussions of the systemic effects of monopoly tend to center on the intentions or behavior of monopolists, when what is crucial is the *exclusion* of competitors who would offer different terms to his customers. This exclusion of competitors is of course the defining characteristic of monopoly, so its explicit statement may seem unnecessary. However, a real monopoly is quite rare, where governmental exclusion is not involved, and in practice antitrust suits claiming "monopolizaton" or attempting to prevent mergers or to break up existing large firms usually involve industries where there are not one, but a small number, of firms producing the bulk of a given industry's output. A treacherous analogy or extension is then made to the situation of one seller (monopoly) producing all of an industry's output to the situation of a few sellers producing most of an industry's output—which is implicitly taken to be very similar. But it becomes crucial to recall that the systemic economic effect is not due to what the producer(s) can do but to what the producer(s) can *prevent others* from doing.

204

An industry with four firms producing 80 percent of its output may seem to be a quasi-monopoly, but if there are dozens of other firms producing the other 20 percent, then it has failed to exclude, which is crucial. Any artificial raising of prices above competitive levels by collusion among the four firms risks the fate of the tangerine cartel in our other hypothetical example. Customers can start buying from the dozens of other producers. The retrospective statistic that four firms sold 80 percent of the industry output during a given time span does not mean that there is anything fixed or prospective about that number. Antitrust proponents have scored a verbal *coup* by constantly terming such percentages the "share" of the market "controlled" by certain firms, as if they were discussing prospective behavior rather than retrospective numbers. Such insinuations of exclusionary powers or intimidation require no evidence but instead rely on the time tested principles of repetition. But historically, market shares have changed over time—some drastically—and in some cases the so-called "dominant" firm has disappeared entirely. *Life* magazine and the Graflex Corporation are recent examples. Once the Graflex Corporation sold virtually all the cameras used by newspaper photographers. But they "controlled" nothing; there were always many other domestic and foreign producers of press cameras, and almost all of them disappeared along with Graflex when improvements in smaller-sized cameras made the latter effective substitutes.

The intellectual state of antitrust doctrine may be suggested by the fact that some of the leading authorities in this field refer to these prevailing doctrines in such terms as "a secular religion,"[59] consider them analogous to "evangelical theory,"[60] or simply "wild and woolly."[61] Even a Supreme Court Justice observed that in certain kinds of antitrust cases the "sole consistency" is that "the government always wins."[62] It is therefore especially important to systematically spell out the specifics behind some of the many vague and tendentious terms used in antitrust doctrines ("control," "predatory pricing," "foreclosing" the market, "incipient" monopoly, etc.).

There are two fairly obvious alternative explanations of why one firm or a few firms sell the bulk of the output in a given industry. One is that they in some way exercise "control" over others—either by being able to exclude potential competitors or by intimidating them from competitive pricing by threats to ruin them financially. An opposing explanation is that firms differ in efficiency—whether in production, in the quality of the product, in shipping costs, or in the general quality of their respective managements. Those who argue that concentrated industries represent monopolistic control, in some sense, deny production efficiencies, product quality differences or differences in management. For example, management quality differences are simply *assumed away* in analyses which proceed as if each firm or plant represents the "best current practice" in its production,[63] or that "managerial competence" can be "held equal,"[64] by observers. Economies of scale are sometimes defined narrowly as individual plant economies—ignoring managerial differences among multiplant corporations, as expressed in such things as how wisely each plant is located, so as to minimize shipping costs of raw materials and finished products and the costs of an efficient labor supply, a favorable economic and political climate, etc. Economies are simply *pronounced* to be negligible with such phrases as "only 2.7 percent" of production and transportation costs.[65] But given an average profit rate of 10 percent, a relatively small difference in such costs can translate into the difference between a profit rate that keeps the business viable and one low enough to reduce stockholders' return to less than they could get by depositing their money in an insured savings and loan association—obviously not a situation that can continue in the long-run. Observers are the last people who can declare what is negligible with someone else's money.

The alternative hypothesis is that some industries are concentrated because some firms' products are simply preferred by consumers, either because of their quality, price, convenience or other appeal. If this is true, then the slightly greater profitability of industries with few sellers is not because the whole industry is more profitable (as it would be under collusion), but because some particular firms have a higher profit rate which arithmetically brings up the average, while it economically does *not* make the rest of the industry any more profitable than under competitive conditions. The data in fact show no profit advantage to a firm of a given size in being in a "concentrated" versus a nonconcentrated industry.[66]

The weakness of the case for believing that industries with few sellers have monopolistic practices or results is indicated by (1) the absence of any evidence generally accepted as convincing by either the legal or the economics profession, (2) the arbitrary definitions and sweeping assumptions included in such evidence as is offered, and (3) the policy position of "deconcentration" advocates that the burden of proof must be put on defendants in concentrated industries to show that they are *not* harmful to the economy.[67]

Much of the legal and economic analysis of industries where one or a few firms produce and sell most of the output give great weight to the supposed homogeneity of the product, which should presumably preclude any rational basis for a consumer preference that would lead to such disproportionate market shares. However, on closer scrutiny this supposed homogeneity usually turns out to mean that *brand-new, perfect specimens* of each product as *already located* are identical or similar. The difference between "similar" and "identical" can involve substantial costs of knowledge, as can the process of locating the product. Among the major ways in which apparently similar products differ is in their durability—that is, their performance long after they have ceased to be brand new—and in their respective quality control, which determines what percentage of the specimens will have flaws, as well as in their distributional availability to the consumer in convenient retail outlets.

In such cases, so-called "expert" testimony can be the most misleading kind of testimony. The expert has, by definition, already paid more cost for knowledge than the average consumer, and so has far lower present or prospective incremental knowledge costs than the consumer. The mere fact that he can render a judgment on the product means that he has already located a place from which to obtain a specimen. That he knows how to produce equivalent results from "similar" products means that he has sufficient knowledge of *both* products to make them interchangeable to him, although *not* necessarily to a consumer familiar with only one, and who may perhaps have substantial prospective knowledge costs in changing to the use of the other.

Examples abound. In a famous antitrust case involving Clorox, the Supreme Court said that "all liquid bleach is identical."[68] But the factual finding in the very same case was that "Clorox employed superior quality controls" and that some brands of liquid bleach "varied in strength" from one to another[69]—a fact of no small importance to users considering how much is enough and how much will ruin their clothes. It may well be that there are other brands of liquid bleach absolutely identical to Clorox but the knowledge of which ones they are is not a free good, and whether the uncertainty of a variation is worth the price difference is not a question that must be settled once and for all by third party observers, since consumers find various brands sitting side by side on supermarket shelves. In another well-known antitrust case, competing pies were considered by the Supreme Court as being "of like grade and quality" despite one pie company's "unwillingness to install quality control equipment," to meet the competition of its more successful rival.[70] Undoubtedly a photograph taken with a press camera produced by the Graflex Corporation, which dominated that market, would have been wholly indistinguishable from a photograph taken with any number of other cheaper press cameras, *as of the date both were purchased brand new*. However, since its cameras were usually purchased by professional photographers, and especially by the photographic departments of newspapers, the strong preference for Graflex press cameras could not be attributed to technical ignorance, "irrationality" or the caprice or psychological susceptibilities of uninformed consumers. Experience had simply established the ruggedness of this particular brand of press camera in the rough usage to which it was subjected in crowds, on sports fields, and in war time combat situations.

Sometimes the difference in consumer preference as between products is not due to the characteristics of the products so much as it is due to differences in the *cost of knowing* of other products' characteristics. Photographic experts have determined that a number of films manufactured by Ilford, Inc. produce results virtually indistinguishable from those produced by films manufactured by Eastman Kodak, which dominates that market. That is, a photographic technician equally familiar with the processing of both brands of film, can produce the same end results from either. Nor are the Ilford processing requirements any more difficult than those of Kodak. They are simply not as well known, just as the characteristics of Ilford film are not as well known. Nor are *all* brands comparable to these two. Even the singling out of Ilford as one brand among many others that is comparable to Kodak requires a prior knowledge and sorting of little-known brands. Note that what is involved here is not "taking advantage" of consumers' ignorance. A professional photographer, well aware of the similarity, may nevertheless continue to purchase the one familiar brand rather than exert himself to stock or refer to two different sets of developing data. There is also much to be gained by using one brand to (1) free one's picture taking attention for aesthetic concerns rather than technical considerations, and (2) be able to buy new film identical to the old wherever one happens to be on assignment, which is to say, not having to worry because one company's dealer outlets are not as numerous as another's.

Third-party observers may dismiss product differences as negligible, just as they dismiss production cost differences as negligible. However, there is no "objective" measure of what is negligible. Something is negligible or not negligible *to someone*. In baseball, for example, the difference between a .250 hitter and a .350 hitter is only about one hit out of every three games, which might seem negligible to a casual onlooker, but that can be the difference between being sent back to the minor leagues and ending up in the Hall of Fame. Customers or stockholders may differ greatly from third-party observers as to what is or is not negligible. Products sold to professional photographers and photographic organizations exhibit the same strong customer preference patterns and attendant "market concentration" as products sold to the supposedly "irrational" general public. What is repeatedly ignored in attempts to discount buyer preferences is the cost of knowledge—knowledge of where to buy a product, knowledge of its characteristics and of ways of using it, and knowledge of the way quality varies from specimen to specimen. To approach this from the standpoint of whether the producer "deserves" such a large market share is to dismiss consumers' interests. To say that a firm's reputation gives it an advantage—presumably an unfair advantage—in competition[71] is to say that consumers economize on knowledge by sorting and labeling only to the firm level, in cases where a company's history of product reliability makes finer sorting not incrementally worth the cost. The issue is not so much the retrospective justice of rewarding a firm for establishing a reputation for reliability. What is more important socially is the prospective incentive to all companies to acquire or maintain such a reputation—that is, from a social point of view, to localize monitoring incentives where they can be most effectively carried out.

Preoccupation with the firm's market share has led to adverse antitrust decisions even when there was no adverse economic effects discernible by the courts. In the celebrated antitrust case against the Aluminum Company of America—one of the very few privately created monopolies on record—it was found that the profit rate averaged only about 10 percent,[72] like firms in competitive industries. Nor did the Court find any negative effects on the economy—but Alcoa still lost. Its "exclusion" of competitors consisted solely of building plant capacity in anticipation of the growing demand for aluminum.[73] The chilling effect of the finding could be seen in the later history of cellophane, which was in chronic shortage because Dupont refused to build plant capacity ahead of the growing demand, for fear of antitrust suits.

Most antitrust cases involve legal actions against individual firms having nowhere near monopoly proportions of output or sales. In the celebrated case of *Brown Shoe Company v. United States,* a merger which gave the combined firms a total of 4½ percent of American shoe store sales was found to be in violation of the antitrust laws.[74] Another merger which gave the Pabst Brewing Company 4½ percent of the nation's beer sales was also broken up as a violation of the antitrust laws.[75] In yet another well-known case, the Supreme Court broke up a merger between two local grocery chains in Los Angeles who together had only 7½ percent of the grocery sales in that city.[76] "Secular religion" may not be too strong a characterization for antitrust doctrines which dismember firms that are that far from "monopolistic" control, in industries with sometimes hundreds of competitors. However, the processing of such cases by governmental agencies is by no means irrational as institutional policy. Agencies with a mandate to fight monopoly firms have every incentive to define the term as broadly as they can, to see "incipient" monopoly in as many places as possible—and especially so in an economy where private monopolies are rare. To restrict themselves to fighting real monopolies or significant monopoly threats could mean losing the bulk of their staff, appropriations, and power. A more basic social question is how they find the outside support that is politically necessary to continue such activities into the region of diminishing (or negative) returns. This has to do with the intellectual climate, and so will be discussed in Chapter 10.

Despite the original thrust of antitrust legislation toward preventing high prices from being charged by monopolistic firms, it has increasingly been used to prevent low prices from being charged. A landmark in this development was the passage of the Robinson-Patman Act in 1936. The ostensible purpose of this act was to prevent price discrimination of a kind that would "substantially lessen competition." The immediate political impetus behind the law was the growth of high-volume, low-markup retail chains which bought from wholesalers in huge quantities at discount prices and then undersold the smaller merchants with whom it competed for retail sales to the public. Some cynics called it the anti-Sears, Roebuck law. Price discrimination complaints under the Robinson-Patman Act are usually made in transactions involving wholesalers.

Robinson-Patman Act cases, which depend on how competition is affected by a given action, provide especially dramatic examples of the ambiguity involved, throughout the antitrust laws, between (1) the systemic characteristics which constitute "competition" and (2) the incumbent firms which at any given time constitute the *competitors* of a defendant. Innumerable economists have complained that the administrative agencies and the courts have protected competitors instead of protecting competition. Courts have recognized such distinctions verbally,[77] but in case after case the issue has been whether the defendant's low price adversely affected some competitor(s). Wholesalers' discounts for very large purchases have been declared illegal because smaller retailers "suffered actual financial losses" which were equated with "injury to competition."[78] So were reduced "competitive opportunities of certain merchants who are injured" by having to pay ten cents a case more for table salt when bought in amounts less than a railroad carload.[79] Theoretically, price differences are legally permissible when they can be proved to represent cost differences in serving different customers. However, retrospective cost statistics are subject to highly variable interpretation, so that in practice a seller usually cannot *prove* anything—and the burden of proof is on the defendant, once it is established that he charged different prices to different customers. The Supreme Court itself has acknowledged that "too often no one can ascertain whether a price is cost justified."[80]

The Supreme Court has included fixed overhead costs in claiming that a wholesaler was selling *below cost* ("suffered substantial losses")[81] which changed "market shares"[82]—from 1.8 percent of sales in a local market to 8.3 percent![83] Moreover, the Federal Trade Commission has the power to put a limit on quantity discounts, regardless of cost justifications.[84] In addition the courts have not allowed wholesalers to charge different prices to different *categories* of buyers—such as supermarket chains versus individual "mom and pop" grocery stores—even though the supermarkets are cheaper to serve, unless there is "such self-sameness" among all those in each category as to carry the burden of proof.[85] Even though the Court acknowledged that "a large majority" of independent stores required services that super-markets perform for themselves, "it was not shown that all independents re-ceived these services."[86] In short, sorting-and-labeling costs were ignored by insisting that every store be considered individually and only afterwards clas-sified among those sufficiently similar—as this might be subsequently deter-mined by a court.

The government does not "always win" in Robinson-Patman cases, but the cases where the defendant wins reveal very much the same pattern of eco-nomic (or noneconomic) reasoning. Despite the usual verbal obeisance to the idea of protecting competition as a systemic condition, the defendants who escape legal penalities do so because—in the Court's words—they showed "proper restraint"[87] in their price cutting, evidencing no "predatoriness"[88] toward competititors, whose prices they chose to "exactly meet" instead of undercutting.[89] This is in keeping with the legislative history of the Robin-son-Patman Act, whose philosophy Congressman Patman expressed as one of "live and let live" and "everybody is entitled to a living"[90]—presumably at the consumer's expense.

One of the theories used to justify the Robinson-Patman Act is that big producers would otherwise *temporarily* cut prices, driving out small com-petitors, and later raise prices to monopolistic levels. Concrete examples have been notable by their scarcity (or nonexistence),[91] even though the country existed for 160 years before the Robinson-Patman Act was passed. Even as economic theory, the argument has serious problems, because the only cer-tainty would be the short-run losses sustained to drive out smaller competi-tors, while the longer-run profits needed to recoup these losses are highly problematical, because of innumerable ways that new competition can arise—including buying up the assets of the bankrupted firms at bargain prices and then profitably underselling the would-be monopolists. Actually, neither the empirical nor the theoretical case is made in specific anti-trust prosecutions under the Robinson-Patman Act. It is the defendant who must rebut the *prima facie* case, and the sinister theories merely hover in the background as unarticulated presumptions.

From the standpoint of the social consequences of social knowledge, what restrictions on price competition do is to inhibit or forbid information about the cheapest ways of doing things from being effectively communicated in prices. It is cheaper to deliver 100 boxes of cereal to a supermarket than to deliver ten boxes of cereal to each of ten different "mom and pop" stores. This is effectively communicated when the wholesaler shaves the price of goods sold in large quantity. If he is either forbidden to do so, or is put through costly processes to justify it in finely meshed sorting-and-labeling categories, that knowledge does not guide economic decision making. Burdens of proof on the defendants in areas where irrefutable proof is virtually impossible amount either to a *de facto* prohibition or are economically the same as a large fine (legal costs) for engaging in the activity, without any evidence of its social harmfulness.

As in other areas of law, antitrust decisions have impact far beyond the particular parties involved, and in ways never intended by the law. For example, many grocery wholesalers have their own trucks which deliver to retailers and return empty, while other trucks bring grocery items from factories or processors to those same wholesalers' warehouses and also return empty. From a social point of view, it would obviously make more sense to have the wholesalers' trucks stop by the processors' plants and pick up grocery stock on their way back to the warehouses. The present system is estimated to waste annually 100 million gallons of gasoline—enough to drive 140 thousand automobiles for a year,[92] not to mention the excess inventory of trucks, the wasted labor of the drivers, or the needless air pollution.

As mere information, this is easy to understand, but it is not socially *effective* knowledge because the prices that might transmit it are forcibly constrained by the Federal Trade Commission's interpretations of the Robinson-Patman Act. Ordinarily, food processors would charge lower prices to those buyers who pick up their own shipments than to buyers who require delivery, and this would become an incentive for wholesalers to have their empty trucks stop by on their way back to the warehouse to pick up some more stock. But the FTC has issued advisories that such price differences could be interpreted as violating the Robinson-Patman Act's prohibition against "price discrimination." Therefore the uniform prices that are charged reflect the threat of force rather than the relative costs, and the wholesalers respond to those prices as if it were no cheaper to pick up groceries in empty trucks than to have another truck deliver them—because that is financially true, according to the knowledge conveyed to them by the legally constrained prices. It is, of course, distorted knowledge from a social point of view, but both its transmission and its reception are rational within the legal incentives created by the Robinson-Patman Act. The social rationality of the act itself is another matter.

Large costs are also created by the uncertainties surrounding the interpretations of vague antitrust laws—especially the Robinson-Patman Act, which a leading expert on that act refers to as a "miasma of legal uncertainty,"[93] and which even a Supreme Court Justice has called a "singularly opaque and elusive statute."[94]

Antitrust policy, like utility regulation, exhibits a strong bias towards incumbents—toward protecting competitors rather than competition. This is readily understandable as institutional policy: Competitors bring legal complaints; competition as an abstract process cannot. Competitors supply administrative agencies such as the Federal Trade Commission with a political constituency; competition as an abstraction cannot. It is only when governmental agencies are seen as decision makers controlled by people with their own individual career and institutional goals that many apparently "irrational" antitrust policies make sense. For example, although antitrust laws are ostensibly aimed at monopolistic practices, the actual administration of such laws—and especially the Robinson-Patman Act—has involved prosecuting primarily *small* businesses, most of whom are not even listed in *Moody's Industrials* and very few of whom are among *Fortune's* list of giant corporations.[95] The institutional reason is simple: A case against a small firm is more likely to be successful, because small firms do not have the money or the legal departments that large corporations have. A major antitrust case against a giant corporation can go on for a decade or more. A prosecution against a small business can be concluded—probably successfully—within a period that is within the time horizon of both the governmental agencies and their lawyers' career goals.

The "rebuttable presumption" of guilt after a *prima facie* showing by the government facilitates successful prosecutions, especially on complex matters subject to such different retrospective interpretations that no one can conclusively prove anything. In one well-known case, an employer with only 19 employees, and who had about seventy competitors in his own city alone, had to prove that his actions did not "substantially lessen competition"—and he lost the case.[96] It confirms the wisdom of putting the burden of proof on the government in most other kinds of prosecutions.

In general, the public image of antitrust laws and policy is of a way of keeping giant monopolies from raising prices, but most major antitrust cases are against businesses that *lower* prices—and most of the businesses involved are small businesses.

ECONOMIC "PLANNING"

Economic "planning" is one of many politically misleading expressions. Every economic activity under every conceivable form of society has been planned. What differs are the decision making units that do the planning—which range from children saving their allowances to buy toys to multinational corporations exploring for oil to the central planning commission of a communist state. What is politically defined as economic "planning" is *the forcible superseding of other people's plans* by government officials. The merits and demerits of this mode of economic decision making can be discussed in general or in particular, but the issue is not between literal planning on the one hand versus letting things happen randomly, on the other. This obvious point needs to be emphasized and insisted upon, not only because of the general tendentiousness of the word "planning," but also because of specific laments about how "accident," "chance," or "uncoordinated" institutions[97] lead to "helplessness" as the economy "drifts."[98]

We have already examined particular examples of the government's superseding of other people's plans, as in various forms of price control, control of particular markets, or direct or indirect transfers of resources. What remains to be examined is *comprehensive* economic "planning"—the subordination of nongovernmental economic decisions in general to a design imposed on the whole economy. This can take place while retaining private ownership of physical or financial assets (capitalism), as happened under fascist regimes, or government ownership of the means of production (socialism) may accompany comprehensive "planning," or such government ownership may coexist with market pricing mechanisms instead of "planning," as in so-called "market socialism" (Yugoslavia being an example). There are also welfare states (such as in Sweden) which may call themselves "socialist" but which operate largely through tax transfers of income earned in a private economy, rather than through comprehensive government control of production decisions. The focus of the analysis here will be comprehensive economic "planning" in general, rather than its particular political or ideological accompaniments. That is, the analysis will be in terms of institutional characteristics rather than hoped-for results.

Comprehensive economic "planning" faces many of the same problems already noted in particular kinds of governmental direction of economic activities—essentially, problems of knowledge, articulation, and motivation.

ARTICULATION

In an economy directed by national governmental authorities ("central planners"), the directives that are issued must articulate the characteristics of the products to be produced. Earlier discussions of rent control or price control in general have noted (1) the difficulties of defining even such apparently simple things as an apartment or a can of peas, and (2) the tendency of products—or labor—to change in quality in perverse ways in response to price or wage controls. Both problems are pervasive under comprehensive central direction of an economy.

Examples abound in the Soviet press, where economists and others decry particularly glaring instances and demand "better" specification—rather than raising the more politically dangerous question of whether *any* articulated specification by central planners can substitute for monitoring by actual users, as in price-coordinated economies. For example, when Soviet nail factories had their output measured by weight, they tended to make big, heavy nails, even if many of these big nails sat unsold on the shelves while the country was "crying for small nails."[99] When output is measured in value terms, the individual firm tends to produce fewer and more expensive units—whether clothing or steel,[100] and regardless of the users' preferences. Where the articulated measurements are in units of gross output, the firm tends to buy unnecessarily large amounts of parts from other firms,[101] receiving credit in its final product statistics for things produced by others; where the articulated measurements are in units of *net* output, then the firm tends to make as much as possible itself, even where the cost of parts produced by specialized subcontractors is lower.[102] All of these are perfectly rational decisions from the standpoint of the individual Soviet firm, maximizing its own well-being, however perverse the results may be from the standpoint of the Soviet economy. Even terror under Stalin did not make the individual producer adopt the economy-wide viewpoint. On the contrary, where imprisonment or death were among the penalties for failure to fulfill the task assigned by the central planners in Moscow, the individual firm manager was even more prone to fulfill the letter of the law, without regard to larger economic considerations. In one tragi-comic episode, badly needed mining equipment was produced but not delivered to the mines because the equipment was supposed to be painted with red, oil-resistant paint—and the equipment manufacturer had on hand only oil-resistant *green* paint and non-oil-resistant red paint. The unpainted equipment continued to pile up in the factory despite the desperate need in the mines, because—in the producer's words—"I don't want to get eight years."[103] To the actual users, the color of the paint made no difference, but that incidental characteristic carried as much weight *as articulation* as the most important technical specification.

These are not peculiarities of Russians or of the Soviet economic or political system. They reflect *inherent* limitations of articulation. The American political demand for more high school graduates—in the academic paradigm, a solution to the "dropout" *problem*— led to more of that product being produced, by whatever lowering of standards was necessary. It is easy to articulate what is meant by a high school graduate—someone who receives a certain embossed piece of paper from an authorized agency—but it is much harder to articulate *in operational terms* what education that is supposed to represent.

In price-coordinated decision making, the user can monitor *results* with little or no articulation by either himself or the producers. The kinds of nails that are incrementally preferable will become more saleable or saleable at a higher price, and the producer will automatically emphasize their production, even if he has not the faintest idea why they are more in demand. If a certain color of paint makes mining equipment more saleable, the producer will tend to use that color of paint, but he will hardly forego, or needlessly postpone, sales until he can get the particular color of paint, if the demand for the equipment is such that it sells almost as fast with a different color. Where price-coordinated education (private school) is a feasible individual option, parents who have never sat down and articulated a list of education criteria can nevertheless judge educational results in a given school and compare them with results available from other private schools or public schools and determine whether the differences in results are worth the differences in cost.

Where prices are set by government fiat, they convey no information as to ever-changing economic trade-offs which reflect changing technology, tastes, and diminishing returns in both production and consumption. Price changes are virtually instantaneous, while statistics available to planners necessarily lag behind. As a student of British economic planning has noted: "The ceaseless changes in conditions affecting the daily demand and supply of countless goods and services must render the best statistics out-of-date before they can be collected."[104] Using a relatively few "stale statistics" to "guide a complex and ever-changing economy" means "in practice falling back on ad hoc interventions interspersed with endless exhortation 'in the public interest'...."[105] Nazi Germany had similar economic problems in basing prospective decisions on retrospective statistics.[106] The problem is inherent in the circumstances, and not peculiar to a given ideology, though some ideologies are more insistent on maintaining such circumstances than are others.

Another way of looking at the vicissitudes of articulation is that one cannot articulate what does not exist—namely an objective set of characteristics which determine an objective scale of economic priorities. All values are ultimately subjective and incrementally variable. No single social group, or scale of priorities can define the varying importance of multifaceted characteristics, either to disparate consumers or to equally disparate producers. The millions of users of millions of products can judge incremental trade-offs when confronted with them, but no third party can capture these changing trade-offs in a fixed definition articulated to producers in advance. When user monitoring, conveyed through prices and sales, is replaced by third-party articulation, in words or numbers, vast amounts of knowledge are lost in the process. In the absence of user monitoring of producer output through a

216

market, there must be third-party specification of what the output shall consist of, and this runs into the inherent limitations of articulation.

However many limitations and distortions articulation may have as a means of communicating economic knowledge, its political appeal is as widespread as the belief that order requires design, that the alternative to chaos is explicit intention, and that there are not merely incremental trade-offs but objectively specifiable, quantifiable and categorical "needs." From this perspective, one must "understand the relationship"[107]—which is to say, *articulate* the relationship—among economic sectors in order for them to co-ordinate. Price-coordination simply vanishes as an alternative within the framework of such beliefs. There must be "priorities" and a "time frame" articulated.[108] Indeed, "we need a full presentation of the items we can choose among," which "a completely automatic free market" would not articulate—which is why we "do not accept that approach."[109] Instead we "must be able to see" articulated alternatives in order to "make an intelligent choice."[110] Under the assumption of objectively definable, quantifiable "needs," efficiency is merely an engineering problem rather than a reconciling of conflicting human desires, so that social policy can be analogized to such fixed-objective activities as putting a man on the moon,[111] and even "planning" is simply a matter of "technical coordination" by "experts"[112] using "systematic analysis."[113] In such a framework, even "the public interest"[114] can be confidently discussed as an empirically meaningful notion, along with "objective analysis . . . of what is really desirable."[115] These quoted statements are not the glib remarks of sophomores, but the pronouncements of one of the most famous American senators and one of the most famous American economists—Hubert Humphrey and Wassily Leontief, respectively. They are by no means alone.

KNOWLEDGE TRANSFER

The limitations and distortions of articulation revolve around the simple fact that third-party central planners cannot know what users want, whether those users be consumers or other producers acquiring raw material, component parts or production-line machinery. Complex trade-offs among a given product's characteristics and between one complex product and another, cannot be captured in a fixed definition, however detailed. Indeed, the amount of detail itself involves trade-offs, for beyond some point the detail becomes counterproductive, as in the case of Soviet mining equipment that was supposed to have a particular kind of paint.

It is not merely the enormous amount of data that exceeds the capacity of the human mind. Conceivably, this data might be stored in a computer with sufficient capacity. The real problem is that the knowledge needed is a knowledge of *subjective patterns of trade-off that are nowhere articulated,* not even to the individual himself. I might *think* that, if faced with the stark prospect of bankruptcy, I would rather sell my automobile than my furniture, or sacrifice the refrigerator rather than the stove, but unless and until such a moment comes, I will never *know* even my own trade-offs, much less anybody else's. There is no way for such information to be fed into a computer, when no one has such information in the first place.

Market transactions do not require any such knowledge in advance. When actually faced with either an escalating price for a good which one normally purchases, or a real bargain on something one normally does not purchase, then and only then does a decision between the two goods have to be made—and it is not uncommon for persons in such situations to make decisions that they would not have expected of themselves, even if the results are sufficiently good to cause a permanent change of consumption patterns. Most of us need not think about what our choice would be as between owning a yacht and an airplane, much less an incremental choice between a longer yacht verses a higher-powered airplane. In a market economy, one individual or decision making unit need be concerned with only a minute fraction of the trade-offs in the economy. Under central planning, somebody has to try to reconcile them all simultaneously. In a market economy, even a manufacturer of yachts or a manufacturer of airplanes need not concern himself with the trade-offs between the two products, much less trade-offs between these and numerous other products which compete for the same metal, glass, fuel, storage space, worker skills, etc. Each producer need concern himself only with the trade-off between his own product and money—a fungible medium in which other people measure the trade-offs for their respective products. As a figure of speech, it may be said that the economy trades off one use for another through this medium. This is not only true, but an important truth, for it helps explain why knowledge is economized through price allocation. Another way of saying the same thing is that central planning would require far more knowledge to be actually known by the central planners to achieve the same net result.

Although it may be empirically true that different ideologies generally regard central planning in different ways, it is not ultimately in principle an ideological question. Marx and Engels were unsparing in their criticisms of their fellow socialists and fellow communists who wanted to replace price coordination with central planning. Proudhon's theory that the government should fix prices according to the labor time required to produce each commodity was blasted by Marx in the first chapter of *The Poverty of Philosophy*:

Let M. Proudhon take it upon himself to formulate and lay down such a law, and we shall relieve him of the necessity of giving proofs. If, on the other hand, he insists on justifying his theory, not as a legislator, but as an economist, he will have to prove that the *time* needed to create a commodity indicates exactly the degree of its *utility* and marks its proportional relation to the demand, and in consequence, to the total amount of wealth.[116]

It was clear from the rest of the chapter that he expected Proudhon could do no such thing. Thirty years later, Engels denounced another socialist theoretician who wanted to abolish markets:

Only through the undervaluation or overvaluation of products is it forcibly brought home to the individual commodity producers what things and what quantity of them society requires or does not require. But it is just this sole regulator that the utopia in which Rodbertus also shares would abolish. And if we then ask what guarantee we have that necessary quantity and not more of each product will be produced, that we shall not go hungry in regard to corn and meat while we are choked in beet sugar and drowned in potato spirit, that we shall not lack trousers to cover our nakedness while trouser buttons flood us in millions—Rodbertus triumphantly shows us his famous calculation, according to which the correct certificate has been handed out for every superfluous pound of sugar, for every unsold barrel of spirit, for every unusable trouser button. . . .[117]

Some modern socialist theoreticians have followed up on Marx and Engels' ideas by constructing models of price-coordinated socialist economies.[118] This goes to the heart of the *purpose* of socialism or "planning" in general. If the purpose is to give better economic expression to the desires of the people at large—overcoming the externalities of capitalism, for example—then such market socialism schemes have more appeal than if the purpose is to *supersede* the preferences of the people by the preferences of those who believe that third parties (especially themselves) can define objective "needs" (or its converse, "waste"). The prevalence of central planning over market socialism—both in theory and in practice—suggests something about the purpose or vision being pursued. Even where some elements of market socialism have been introduced, it has usually been after first attempting central planning and finding the results intolerable. Local Soviet agricultural and dairy markets, for example, have been allowed a measure of autonomy and coordination by uncontrolled prices after food shortages and even famines followed earlier attempts at the complete "planning" of agriculture. Private agricultural plots account for about 3 percent of the total arable land of the USSR, and about *one third* of the agricultural output.[119]

The difficulties of understanding other people's complex trade-offs and successfully articulating them to producers are compounded by the difficulties of knowing how to produce what is wanted. It was noted in Chapter 1 that no one really understands completely how to make even a simple lead pencil. The task facing central planners is far more complex than that, involving not only far more complex products, but far more complex trade-offs among the millions of products using the same or substitutable inputs. For example, the Soviet machine tool industry alone produces about 125,000 products, involving an estimated "15,000,000,000 possible relations."[120] Even if the central planners were to assemble all the experts on the production of each of the products in the economy—which would amount to a stadium full of people—the trade-offs between products competing for the same inputs would still remain an unsolved problem. In short, central planners cannot know what the trade-off patterns are in production any more than in consumption. *Others* may know—each for his own minute segment of the economy—but the transfer of that knowledge intact to a central decision making unit is a costly and chancy matter.

Much depends on the incentives and constraints facing the individual on the spot who is supposed to transfer his knowledge to the central planners. A Soviet plant manager knows what his plant can and cannot do better than anyone in Moscow—just as settlers in colonial America knew what was and was not economically feasible under local conditions better than anyone in London, and just as slaves knew what they could and could not do better than any overseer or slave owner. The basic problem is the separation of knowledge and power. Incentives can be contrived by those with power to elicit the knowledge, but such incentives are themselves constrained by the need to preserve the basic relationship—central planning, colonialism, and slavery, in these examples.

Because the central planners' estimates of each plant's capacity will become the basis for subsequently judging each plant manager's success, in transmitting information to the central planners Soviet managers consistently "understate what they can do and overstate what they need."[121] The central planners know that they are being lied to, but cannot know by how much, for that would require them to have the knowledge that is missing. One way of trying to get performance based on true potential rather than articulated transmissions is a system of graduated incentive payments for "overfulfillment" of the assigned tasks. Soviet managers, in turn, are of course well aware that much higher production will lead to upward revisions of their assigned tasks, so that a prudent manager is said to "overfulfill" his assignment by 5 percent, but not by 25 percent.[122] In short, a "mutual attempt at outguessing the other"[123] goes on between Soviet managers and central planners. Knowledge is not transmitted intact.

The distortion of knowledge is far more serious when the whole economy is coordinated on the basis of such articulation, supplemented by central planners' guesses. In a market economy, decisions are made through an entirely different process. The individual enterprise that wants raw material, capital equipment, etc., goes into the market to bid for them on the basis of their own best estimate of what they can achieve with them. Competition with other potential users of the same inputs forces them to bid as high as they can afford to, in the light of their own on-the-spot knowledge of their enterprise and its customers. It is not a question of articulating anything to anybody, but of conveying knowledge implicitly through prices bid. Similarly, there is no point overstating production costs to the customer, when competitors will undercut the price and take customers away. In short, the unarticulated knowledge made implicitly through prices has more reason to be accurate than the explicitly articulated knowledge conveyed to central planners.

The special disadvantages of central planning in agriculture—symbolized by massive importations of American grain by the Soviet Union—are due to special problems of transmitting knowledge. There is great variability in agricultural production and in agricultural output, so that the volume of knowledge that would be needed for central planning on the same scale as in industry would be even more staggering. For example, land varies considerably—even within a few hundred yards—in rockiness, chemical composition, physical contours, and proximity to water (horizontally and vertically), all of which affect what can be grown at what cost. The output varies, often literally from unit to unit, and the freshness, nutritional value and perishability also varies, from day to day and sometimes from hour to hour. All this is in marked contrast to steel production, for example, where a given combination of iron ore and coal in a given furnace produces a given product, whether in Moscow or Vladivostok, and the product can remain in its original condition for years.

The Soviets themselves have long recognized "the very varied conditions which always exist in agriculture."[124] But there is a big gap between such recognition and being able to construct incentives to deal with it, while at the same time not abandoning the political and economic structure of the country. Innumerable "reforms" have swept over Soviet agriculture in succession, trying to cope with that inherent constraint. Many sound agricultural policies originating with the central planners—crop rotation, planting systems, etc.—have been applied *categorically* "regardless of local conditions" and over the opposition of local agronomists, in places where the environment necessary to make them successful was not present.[125] Sometimes this was due to following orders from above, but even when the Soviet Premier warned against "excesses," many local authorities found it safer to follow general official policy rather than risk a personal deviation which might or might not work.[126]

While there is much modern literature on the vicissitudes of Soviet planners, the point here is not that the Soviets are inefficient or that "planning" has difficulties. All human life has difficulties. The point is that a particular kind of institutional incentive structure has a specific set of difficulties, traceable to the articulation and transmission of knowledge. The point is reinforced by the appearance of the same kind of difficulties with the same incentive structures under entirely different historical and ideological conditions.

In colonial America, Georgia was the most elaborately "planned" colony, directed and heavily subsidized from London for twenty years by a nonprofit group of philanthropists, to whom the British government had entrusted the governance of that colony. They issued rations, appropriated funds for teachers and midwives, as well as for cooking utensils and items of clothing—all for people living 3,000 miles away in a land the London trustees had never seen.[127] No other colony had the benefit of so much "planning" or central direction. Yet Georgia ended up "the least prosperous and the least populous of the colonies."[128]

Its problems were the classic problems of planning. Initial miscalculations based upon the inadequate knowledge of the distant planners were not readily correctable by feedback based on the knowledge possessed or acquired by the experience of those actually on the scene. For example, property rights were not freely transferable, so that the London trustees' initial estimates of the amount of Georgia land necessary or optimal for farming became frozen into colonial practice. While their articulated decisions were in terms of "land" as if it were a homogeneous resource, as already noted, land always varies in chemistry, topography, and all the other variables which affect its output potential. Equal rations of land surface were not equal rations of these economically relevant variables, nor was there any way to trade off these characteristics without actual trades between those on the scene and familiar with the nature of the land, and of themselves as farmers, the interaction of which would determine "fertility." In short, the distortions of planning involved not merely inequities, but inefficiencies. Had the initial allotments been freely transferable, the inefficiency at least could have been corrected.[129]

Under the rule that farms must be entailed to a male heir, those settlers with an allotment and no male heir to leave it to had an asset with a shorter time horizon than others—and therefore had less incentive to make long-run improvements, since it could not be sold in the market.[130] The discontents and neglects to which this incentive system led eventually forced the London trustees to relax some of the control over the transfer of land, each concession being made grudgingly "as if it were a sacrifice of principle."[131]

The London planners' lack of knowledge was also reflected in their choice of economic activities to promote. Because Georgia had mulberry trees, it was decided that it would be a good place for silkworms and therefore for a silk industry. As often happens, "expert" testimony (from an expert on the *Italian* silk industry) was enlisted to promote the project, leading to a report "as rich in enthusiasm as it was poor in firsthand knowledge. . . ."[132] A crucial piece of firsthand knowledge that was lacking was that the particular variety of mulberry tree in Georgia was different from the kind of mulberry tree used by silkworms in the Orient. Nor was the climate the same, and half the silkworms in Savannah died as a result.[133] Nor was the labor available in Georgia the same as that in the Orient in skill, diligence, or low pay. Still, there was a favorable "demonstration project"—a gown of silk produced in Georgia for the Queen—though Georgian silk never became commercially successful.[134]

Over a period of twenty years, the British government poured more than £130,000 into Georgia, supplemented by church and private donations, including over £90,000 from one of the trustees. Such massive subsidies made it unnecessary for the settlers in Georgia to pay taxes, and therefore made it unnecessary to have any representative local government to raise taxes— thereby eliminating the need for institutions which could have provided political feedback modifying the distant trustees' plans. The sum spent by the British government was more than it had ever spent on any other nonmilitary project. Meanwhile, the beneficiaries of all this largesse were *leaving* Georgia for other colonies, less well subsidized but also less controlled. Eventually, even massive subsidies were unable to keep the planning project going, and in 1751 the trustees returned the colony to the British government. Like later "planners" they blamed failure not on their own decisions or on the inherent limitations of planning, but on lack of enough additional financial support![135]

NON-ECONOMIC RATIONALES

There are moral and political, as well as economic, reasons for preferring governmental direction of the economy ("planning") to decentralized price coordination ("capitalism"). Perhaps the most common reason for preferring "planning" in general and socialist "planning" in particular is a sense of the moral inadequacy of capitalism—either (1) outright "exploitation" of one group by another, domestically or internationally, or (2) a selfish, every-man-for-himself amorality, or (3) a "meritocracy" which ignores our common cultural inheritance and our common humanity. More narrowly economic reasons for preferring governmental direction to decentralized price coordination include the possibility of internalizing external costs, taking a longer-run view of the consequences of economic decision making and eliminating monopolistic practices which reduce the efficiency of a price-coordinated economy. Politically, one of the major objections to the price-coordination systems of Western society as they have emerged historically is their inequality in wealth and power among people and organizations, and the distortions which this inequality introduces into both political and economic processes.

Capitalist middlemen are often depicted as "mere interceptors and parasites"[136] and profit as simply "overcharge."[137] While episodic interception of goods on their way from producer to consumer might seem plausible, the *repeated and persistent choice* of producers and consumers to route their sales and purchases through a middleman is difficult to explain unless they each find this less costly than dealing directly with one another. Consumers would not have to go to the factories, with all the inconveniences (and sometimes dangers) that might involve. Producers could own their own retail outlets, as some do. However, the rarity of this—even when producers have ample capital available to finance it—suggests that there are different skills necessary for different functions, so that firms which are successful in one stage of the economic process find it cheaper at some point to turn their output over to other firms which have lower costs of carrying out the next phase. If the next firm were *not* cheaper or better at conveying the products to the consumer, the producer would have no incentive to incur the bother and the cost of negotiating with middlemen, shipping his goods to them, and going through the financial problems of collecting payments from them. Perhaps even weightier evidence of the economy's advantages from middleman functions is that even the "planned" Soviet economy—ideologically opposed to middlemen—has found itself driven to setting up similar organizations, not only for consumer goods but also for equipment and supplies used by producers.[138]

In any kind of economic system, inventories are a substitute for knowledge. The two are incrementally traded off for one another according to their respective costs. If a housewife knew exactly what her family was going to eat and in what amounts, neither her refrigerator nor her pantry would have to contain as large or varied an inventory as it does, nor would there be as much "waste" of food as there is. Like so much other retrospective measurement of "waste," this is based on an implicit standard of prospective omniscience or zero knowledge cost. To trace in retrospect the path of a particular unit of a particular product is often to discover "overcharge" or an "exorbitant" markup for that item considered in isolation. But the whole reason for anyone—housewife or multinational corporation—to maintain an inventory is the cost of prospective knowledge, so that a whole aggregation of items is stocked precisely because no one can know in advance which one will be wanted at a given time, and the costs of stocking items which later turn out to be unwanted are covered by (are part of) the cost charged for the particular items which turn out to be in demand. This is most obvious in areas of greatest uncertainty (highest knowledge cost), notably perishable agricultural products. If one-third of all peaches have to be discarded somewhere on the way from producer to consumer, then the cost of *eating* 200 peaches is the cost of *producing* 300 peaches. To trace in retrospect the cost of the particular 200 peaches actually eaten would be to discover a 50 percent "overcharge" even if no one made a cent of profit. Similarly, to ask how much the original farmer was paid per peach compared to how much the consumer paid per peach would be to discover a substantial gap, even if all transportation, storage, and other middleman costs were zero, in addition to a zero profit.

Given that middleman functions serve some economic purpose, and have inherent costs, what is to prevent middlemen from charging *more* for their services than they cost or are worth? Only what inhibits everyone else performing any kind of function anywhere in the economy or society from doing the same thing. Costs, as noted earlier, are ultimately foregone alternatives. It is these alternatives open to competitors which determine how much any given seller can successfully demand. If some existing seller(s) charged more than enough to cover the costs involved—that is, more than the risks and efforts are worth to *alternative* producers, those alternative producers will displace him by underpricing him. Sellers are, after all, more concerned with increasing their *total* profits than with maximizing profits per unit of sale, and whole retail empires have been built on shaving a few cents off the price of various kinds of merchandise. Indeed, the constant efforts to prevent this with "fair trade" laws and the Robinson-Patman Act is some measure of how pervasive the incentives are for price cutting. The desire of businessmen for profits is what drives prices *down* unless forcibly prevented from engaging in price competition, usually by governmental activity. Even Karl Marx recognized that when one capitalist introduces a cost saving, the others have no choice but to follow.[139]

All prices—whether called wages, profits, interest, fees, or whatever—are constrained only by the competition of other suppliers. Profits are no different in principle, except for being residual and variable rather than contractually fixed. Sometimes profits are regarded as special in representing the "exploitation" of other inputs—notably labor—rather than (or in addition to) the consumer. One reason for believing this is simply an emphasis on the physical production process as the source of economic value, and the exclusion of those not taking part in that physical process from any contribution to the economic end result, so that anything that they receive for their nonexistent "contribution" is exploitation.

The most elaborate vision of this sort is the Marxian theory of "surplus value"—or rather, his *definition* of surplus value as the difference between the wages of the working class and total output.[140] Like so many emotionally powerful visions, the Marxian vision is not a testable hypothesis but an axiomatic construction. Output per unit of labor is simply *called* "labor's output," a practice common far beyond the circle of Marxists. Obviously output can be divided by any input, just as any numerator can be divided by any denominator. Instead of output per man-hour we can arbitrarily divide automobiles by ounces of hand lotion. The mere fact that one number is upstairs in a fraction and the other number downstairs does not establish any causal relationship between the two things. The implied connection between automobiles and hand lotions is one we would see through immediately. But once we *begin* with two things which are plausibly connected, we can add the appearance of proof or precision to that plausibility by making fractions out of them. Businessmen often ask for tax reductions on grounds that they need X number of dollars of investment per job, so that increasing employment will result from the tax cut. That investment and employment are connected seems reasonable and plausible in general, but proof or precision by fractions is spurious. Quite aside from the possibility of distributing a business tax cut as dividends or higher executive salaries, even if it all goes into investment, this investment can just as easily go into displacing existing employees with machinery as into hiring new employees. It all depends on the relative prices, the state of the market for the output, and technological developments. None of these prospective variables are captured by retrospective data on total investment divided by total employees.

The Marxian argument is the same game played with a different deck of cards. Output per unit of labor becomes labor's output by definition—indeed by a whole system of subsidiary definitions based on the same arbitrary postulate.[141] The same doctrine expressed as a testable hypothesis would collapse like a house of cards. If labor is the sole—or even main—source of value, then in those economies where there is more labor input and less nonlabor input, output per capita and therefore real income would be higher. The opposite is blatant. In the most desperately poor countries, people work longer and harder for subsistence than in more elaborate and prosperous economies where most people never touch physical goods during the production process. Indeed, it is only in the latter countries that subsistence is sufficiently easy to achieve that it is taken for granted, and that there is time and money to spend on books on the "exploitation" or "alienation" of labor.

Attempts to salvage the exploitation theory sometimes use an international framework to claim that prosperous "capitalist" nations are guilty of "robbery of the rest of the world'" through "imperialism."[142] Sometimes this is based on nothing more than the verbal arbitrariness of referring to a prosperous country's consumption of its own output as its disproportionate consumption of "the world's" output or "the world's" resources. This is a particularly misleading procedure as regards the United States, whose total international economic transactions are an insignificant fraction of its domestic economic activity. Moreover, American international activity is disproportionately concentrated in other industrial nations rather than the Third World which is supposedly the source of American prosperity. The United States has more invested in Canada than in all of Latin America, or in Asia and Africa put together. American investments in Western Europe are even higher than in Canada.[143] Even the data in Lenin's classic, *Imperialism*, shows industrialized nations investing their money in each others' economies more than in any underdeveloped areas,[144] even though the *words* in the text claim that capitalism has escaped its economic self-destruction only by exporting capital to noncapitalist nations. When all else fails, believers in this vision point to specific activities by capitalist nations that have behaved in ways which are regarded as morally wrong. Whatever the merits of their arguments in particular cases, the abuse of power is too universal an historical phenomenon to be made a defining characteristic of capitalism. It seems especially inappropriate as part of an argument for alternative systems with *more* concentration of power.

SUMMARY AND IMPLICATIONS

The twentieth century has seen a definite trend toward third-party economic decision making, under a variety of political or ideological banners, and in many different economic forms. Sometimes it has imposed decision making as regards a given kind of economic transaction, as in rent control or minimum wage laws. Sometimes it has been a more arbitrary attempt to control prices in general, or to regulate particular industries such as transportation or communication. In some countries, it has gone as far as attempting to control the whole economy.

227

The results of modern "planning" have followed a pattern seen centuries ago in different circumstances and with entirely different ideologies and rhetoric. The results of comprehensive "planning" in colonial Georgia parallel the results of Soviet planning, just as various modern schemes of price control have produced results virtually identical to those produced by price control in Hammurabi's Code or in the Roman Empire under the Emperor Diocletian.[145] There is a special irony in this, for much of modern "planning" emphasizes its revolutionary newness—implying, presumably, some exemption from being tested by old-fashioned analytic methods or judged by old-fashioned moral standards. In fact nothing is older than the idea that human wisdom is concentrated in a select few (present party always included), who must impose it on the ignorant many. Repeated attempts to apply this doctrine rigorously, in a wide range of historical settings, suggests that it is less likely to survive as an hypothesis than as an axiom or an ideology.

Chapter 9

Trends in Law

Legal institutions in the United States are anchored in a Constitution that is more than two hundred years old, and which has changed relatively little in its basic philosophy in that time. Most of the later amendments follow the spirit of the original document and its Bill of Rights. Yet despite this, American legal institutions have undergone a revolution within the past generation—a revolution which coincided not only in time, but also in spirit and direction, with changes in economic and political institutions. The centralization of decision making is a pattern that runs through landmark court cases, ranging from antitrust to civil liberties to racial policy to the reapportionment of state legislatures. The net result of these legal developments has been an enlargement of the powers of courts and administrative agencies—institutions least subject to feedback from the public, and therefore most susceptible to continuing on a given course, once captured by an idea or a clique. This represents an historic shift in both the location of decision making and in the mode of decision making. Decisions once weighed in an incremental and fungible medium like emotions or money, with low-cost knowledge readily conducted through informal mechanisms, are increasingly weighed in the medium of articulation, in more categorical terms, and with higher costs of transmitting knowledge through rules of evidence documentable to third parties. The predilections or susceptibilities of those third parties also become more important than was ever contemplated for a constitutional or a democratic society.

Along with historic changes within the law has come an enormous expansion of the sheer numbers of lawyers, judges, and cases. The number of lawyers and judges per capita increased by 50 percent from 1970 to 1977.[1] California alone has a larger judicial system than any *nation* besides the United States.[2]

The quantitative and qualitative aspects of trends in the law are not independent of one another. As courts have expanded the kinds of questions they would adjudicate—including the internal rules of voluntary organizations, and the restructuring of political entities—more and more people have sought to win in court what they could not achieve in other institutions, or have appealed trial results on more and more tenuous grounds. A 1977 survey reported: "Appellate judges estimate that 80 percent of all appeals are frivolous."[3] The cost of all this is not simply the salaries of judges and lawyers. As in other areas, the real costs are the *foregone alternatives*—notably speedy trials to clear the innocent and convict the guilty, so that the public is not prey to criminals walking the streets while legal processes drag on. In civil cases, the costs of delay are obvious in cases with large economic resources idled by legal uncertainties, but they are no less real in cases where child custody or other emotionally-devastating matters drag on. In short, there is a social trade-off between the costs and the benefits of increased litigation or increasingly elaborate litigation. The institutional question is, how are these social costs and benefits conveyed to the individual decision makers: the parties, the lawyers, and the judges?

To some parties the costs of litigation are not conveyed *at all*, but are paid by the taxpayers, as in most criminal cases, where trial lawyers, appeals and prison law libraries in which to prepare appeals are at taxpayer expense. The more deadly costs of having criminals at large while waiting trial or appeal are also paid by the public. All these costs have been increased within recent decades by court decisions. Lawyers, of course, do not pay costs but instead reap benefits as the law becomes more intricate and time-consuming—and lawyers have in fact opposed attempts at simplification, such as "no-fault" automobile insurance. Lawyers' benefits have increased in recent years as payments from clients have been supplemented by payments from others— not only taxpayers but also in institutional arrangements popularly defined by their hoped-for results as "public interest" law firms, supported by donors to "causes." Insofar as the tax money is payable only for particular kinds of cases and the donors have a special focus—as with the "environmentalists" or contributors to the NAACP—then lawyers and legal institutions paid by third parties have every incentive to pursue such cases well past the point of diminishing returns or even negative returns to society at large.

Because the American judicial system of trial courts and appellate courts reaches an apex in the Supreme Court of the United States, the trends there are crucial for the behavior of the whole legal system. Within the past three decades—and especially in the controversial "Warren Court" era—there has been an expansion of the issues which the Supreme Court will adjudicate, and of the extent to which the court will go beyond defining the boundaries of other institutions' discretion to reviewing the specific decisions made. Some degree of this is inherent in any appellate court's functioning—a guilty verdict by a jury in a courtroom surrounded by a raging lynch mob cannot be allowed to stand merely because formal procedure was followed—but neither are appellate courts supposed to re-try issues rather than determine the constitutionality of trials and legislation. Otherwise, in the words of an appellate judge, "Law becomes the subjective preference of the reviewing court."[4]

The U.S. Supreme Court was increasingly surrounded by controversy after Earl Warren became its Chief Justice in 1953. In the early stages of these controversies, those who accused the court of going beyond the legitimate bounds of constitutional interpretation into the dangerous area of judicial policy making tended to be those opposed to the particular social or political substance of the decisions made, while those who defended the court tended to be those in favor of the social and political impacts achieved or expected. It is unnecessary at this point to enter the specifics of these early controversies. As the Supreme Court continued along a path that involved increased judicial activism at all levels and in a variety of issues—lower courts running school systems, ordering prisons to be built, or even ordering a state legislature to pass a tax bill—the nature of the defense of the Court also began to change. Many of those in favor of the social or political results of Supreme Court decisions began to question whether there was any legal or constitutional basis for those decisions. Some argued that a constitutional case *could* be made for the decisions, though the court had not effectively made it.[5] Others lamented that we had simply reached judicial policy making.[6] Still others welcomed the judicial activism and lamented only its concealment—the "masking" of "decisions on the merits" and the court's use of legal formalisms to "hide the reasoning behind its decision."[7] According to this line of thought, the court should not be restricted to the narrow role of interpreting the Constitution as a set of rules but should aspire to the role of applying the Constitution as a set of "values."[8] In short, both friend and foe alike came ultimately to see the Supreme Court as going beyond the previous bounds of constitutional interpretation, and into the realm of judicial policy making.

Trends in American legal institutions will be considered in four broad areas, those dealing with (1) administrative law-making, (2) free speech, (3) race, and (4) crime.

ADMINISTRATIVE AGENCIES

Along with the expansion of traditional legal institutions, operating under traditional constitutional constraints, has come the emergence and proliferation of a new hybrid institution—the administrative commission, combining legislative, judicial, and executive functions, in defiance of the separation-of-powers principle, and constrained in its exercise of power only by sporadic reversals of its decisions by appellate courts or even more rare congressional legislation. These institutions are a development within the past century—the first, the Interstate Commerce Commission, was founded in 1887—but their rapid proliferation began with the New Deal of the 1930s which created many so-called "alphabet agencies": the SEC, NLRB, FPC, etc. These administrative commissions are headed by presidential appointees with fixed and staggered terms which overlap one another and also overlap the term of office of any given administration, in order to promote independent decision making. Members of the commissions or boards heading these agencies are removable only by impeachment, and their regulations, which have the force of law, require neither presidential nor congressional approval, but go into effect automatically after having been published in the *Federal Register*. In addition to making law in this way, the same administrative commissions also act as judge and jury for anyone accused of violating their regulations. They also administer staffs and bureaus which research, advise, and generally patrol their domain. Some of their economic effects have been noted in Chapter 8. Here the concern is with the broader legal and social questions they raise.

The importance of these regulatory commissions is out of all proportion to their public visibility or political accountability. *They create more law than Congress.* Each year federal administrative agencies issue ten thousand or more new regulations.[9] By contrast, it is rare for Congress to pass a thousand bills in one session.[10] Until recent years, administrative agency regulations were directed largely toward limited segments of the economy or society. But while the scope of earlier administrative commissions was generally limited to particular industries such as railroads (ICC), merchant shipping (NMC), or broadcasting (FCC), the newer commissions regulate activities which cut across industry lines and reach directly into virtually every business, school, farm, or other social institution. They prescribe employment procedures and results under "affirmative action" policies, set and administer "environmental" standards, issue occupational health and safety regulations, define the racial distribution of schools' pupil populations, teachers, and administrators—all largely as they see fit, limited only by such attention as appellate courts can give them amid the courts' many other concerns.

232

Sometimes called a "fourth branch of government," the administrative commissions from the outset faced grave challenges to their legality under a constitution that prescribed only three branches of government—and which carefully separated powers at that. The constitutional issue was settled in favor of the agencies, at a time when they were a peripheral factor in government decision making and national life, but that categorial decision remained in effect as the number and scope of such agencies expanded enormously over the decades. This is hardly a criticism of the Supreme Court, for once the incremental growth of regulatory commissions passed a certain point, any reconsideration or reversal of their constitutionality would have undermined a major part of the existing legal system of the country and whole sections of the economy and society dependent upon that set of regulatory "laws." This does, however, once more illustrate the momentous impact of categorical decision making—in this case a stark dichotomy between "constitutional" and "unconstitutional"—and the high costs of subsequently attempting to bring to bear effective knowledge of its consequences.

Administrative agencies enforce their decisions in ways which escape the constraints of the Constitution or of Anglo-Saxon legal traditions in general. American laws are prospective—that is, they describe in advance what the citizen can and cannot do. The citizen cannot simply be punished because his actions prove in retrospect to be displeasing to the government. In addition, the burden of proof is on the government, or on the plaintiff in general. Moreover, the citizen cannot be forced to incriminate himself, under the Fifth Amendment. All these safeguards are readily circumvented by administrative agencies. As noted in Chapter 8, the National Maritime Commission has a financial life-and-death power over merchant shippers by its choice of when and where to grant or withhold the subsidies made necessary by costly, government-prescribed practices which would bankrupt any American shipping company solely dependent on revenue from customers. Legally, these subsidies are not a right, and so the denial of them is not a punishment subject to constitutional constraints. Economically, however, massive government subsidies to one's competitors are the same as a discriminatory fine for having displeased the government, but legally the latter is not a constitutional violation. The maritime *industry* has no constitutionally mandated right to a subsidy, and indeed many economists find the whole scheme ridiculous, but the point here is that once the industry as a whole is being subsidized, to any individual competitor the loss of that subsidy does not restore him to the position of being in an ordinary competitive industry. On the contrary, it is a discriminatory fine for having displeased the National Maritime Commission.

The principle is far more general than the maritime industry, and affects federal revenue sharing, "affirmative action" contract compliance procedures and other administrative activity in which the federal government makes benefits available to other entities on condition that those other entities follow policies which the government has no existing legal power to directly force them to follow otherwise. As a matter of incentives and constraints, it makes no difference whether (1) someone pays X dollars in taxes and is then fined Y dollars for displeasing the government, or (2) pays X + Y dollars in taxes and receives Y dollars back for pleasing the government. Legally, however, it matters crucially. The constitutional safeguards which apply in the first approach are circumvented by using the second approach. There is no prospective law on the books allowing the government to control the racial, sex, or other composition of university faculties, but only such universities as please the government in that regard are eligible for the mass federal subsidies which make up much of the revenue of the leading "private" universities. Universities as a group have no constitutional right to the subsidies, but once most of Harvard's revenue comes from the federal government, Yale cannot survive as a competitor if it displeases administrators who control its eligibility for federal money. Similarly, the federal government can require state and local governments to follow various policies on highways, schools, or welfare, *not* because the federal government has either constitutional or statutory authority to control such things, but because administrators of various funds can unilaterally make those requirements a precondition for receiving the funds. Again, it is the *general* availability of the subsidies which puts the individual competitor to whom they are denied in a worse position than if the subsidy had never existed. The glib doctrine, "to get the government off your back, get your hands out of the government's pocket,"[11] misses the point entirely. To an industry or sector (such as universities or local governments) that doctrine would make sense—*if* whole industries or sectors were decision making units. The real objection, however, is not the vicissitudes of particular claimants but the growth of extralegal powers of the federal government—powers never granted by the Constitution nor by legislation, and never voted on by the public, but as real as any law passed by Congress, and often carrying heavier penalties, including the total destruction of institutions by massive subsidies to their competitors.

Another practice counter to American legal tradition is putting the burden of proof on the defendant. As noted in Chapter 8, the Robinson-Patman Act makes mere price differences to different customers *prima facie* evidence creating a "rebuttable presumption" of illegal price discrimination. In practice, the many possible interpretations of given cost statistics makes such rebuttal virtually impossible and the Supreme Court's conception of classifying customers can make it too costly to attempt. Moreover, the cost justification must first be made to the Federal Trade Commission, which has every incentive *not* to accept it. Like a justice-of-the-peace who is paid out of the fines he imposes, the FTC's judicial decisions affect its own economic well-being, since the size of the appropriations and staff which it can ask of congress in its executive role, and the scope of the power it can exercise in its legislative role depend on how much of a problem it finds its judicial role. In view of these institutional incentives and constraints, it is hardly surprising that the FTC has almost invariably gone further than the courts in the stringency with which it has applied the Robinson-Patman Act.[12] This is, however, neither peculiar to the FTC nor to the area of its jurisdiction.

Very similar principles and results are found in the very different jurisdiction of the Equal Employment Opportunity Commission (EEOC). Here an employer's proportion of minority or female employees must, in retrospect, match the expectations of the EEOC or he faces a rebuttable presumption of discrimination, under guidelines legislated and administered by the EEOC. He must rebut this presumption before the EEOC, acting in its judicial capacity. Again, the EEOC like the FTC, has consistently applied the law more stringently than the courts.[13] It is not the prospective use of law but the retrospective punishment of results displeasing to the EEOC. But because the punishment consists largely of liability to have federal money stopped, it is not *legally* the same as punishment and so escapes constitutional bans on retrospective punishments for acts not specified in advance. Also contrary to the principles behind the Fifth Amendment, employers are forced to confess in advance to "under-utilization" of minority and female employees whenever their employment numbers do not meet EEOC expectations, as a precondition for being eligible for federal money. The Fifth Amendment protects Nazis, Communists, and criminals but not businessmen in this situation, because technically the latter are not being punished or subjected to criminal penalties—even though they may be subject to heavier losses than the fines imposed in criminal cases.

In short, administrative agencies have become a major part of the American legal system, and a part not merely outside the original vision of the Constitution, but also able in practice to enact and enforce laws in ways forbidden to other organs of government by the Constitution. Despite their formal subordination to legislative correction by Congress and judicial review by the appellate courts, regulatory commissions are insulated from effective control by their sheer numbers, by the intricacies and arcane language of their regulations, and by the multitude of other claims on the time of Congress and the courts. Effective feedback comes largely from special interests, each with a sufficient stake to monitor its respective agency, to shoulder the cost of appeals, and to lobby before the appropriate committee of Congress. But a criminal can challenge the verdict of a trial court much more cheaply than an ordinary citizen can challenge the ruling of an administrative agency. Moreover, the kind of personal bias which would disqualify a judge is considered acceptable, or even desirable, in members of a regulatory commission. That advocates of recreational interests ("environmentalists") should dominate commissions concerned with environmental matters is considered as natural as that "minority" activists should dominate the EEOC. This would be a questionable departure from legal tradition, even in cases not dependent upon "rebuttable presumptions," to be rebutted to the satisfaction of such officials.

Costs are a crucial factor in all forms of legal proceedings. A legal right worth X (in money or otherwise) is not in fact a right if it costs 2X to exercise it. This is obvious enough when the rights and the costs can be reduced to money. The principle is no less true in cases where the values are nonfinancial. For example, a woman's right to prosecute a rapist can be drastically reduced—for some women, obliterated—by allowing the defense attorney to put her through an additional trauma on the witness stand with wide-ranging questions and observations, publicly humiliating her but having little or nothing to do with the guilt or innocence of his client. There is some belated recognition of this cost in some places with changed trial rules in rape cases, but this is usually seen as a special problem in a special situation, rather than a general problem of costs in legal procedures. Where a right is so defined, in legislation or by judicial interpretation, that either the plaintiffs or the defendants can impose large costs on the others at little or no cost to themselves, then the law may be so lopsided in its impact that the right can be reduced to meaninglessness or expanded far beyond its original scope or purpose. In the case of rape, it is the defendant who can impose disproportionate costs—reaching prohibitive levels for many women. In other kinds of cases and rights, it is the plaintiff who can create huge costs for the defendant at little or no cost for himself. For example, recreational interests ("environmentalists") can impose large costs on builders of everything from bicycle paths to power dams by demanding that they file "environmental impact" statements, in effect putting the burden of proof on the accused. Although such statements are officially defined by their hoped-for results, they have virtually no demonstrated effectiveness for predicting how any environment will in fact be affected.[14] They are, however, very effective in imposing both direct financial costs and costs associated with delay. For projects requiring large investments, the mere delay can cost millions of dollars and

236

doom the project, since the value of a given physical thing varies with the time at which it becomes available. That is, so-called "environmental impact" requirements impose high costs on one party at low cost to the other party, *regardless of the legal outcome* of the case.

The law and legal critics are both so preoccupied with the ultimate disposition of cases that costs of the process itself tend to fade into the background. Yet these process costs may determine the whole issue at stake. For some, to be totally vindicated after years of filing reports, attending many administrative hearings, trials, and appeals is often meaningless. Under environmental impact laws, the case to be made by the plaintiff to keep a costly legal process going is either nil or may consist solely of speculation. He does not bear the burden of proof.

Although adversary legal systems put much emphasis on litigants, or at most on the categories of people they represent, all legal systems are ultimately social processes serving social purposes, including transmitting knowledge for social decisions based on costs entailed by alternative social behavior. When the legal system causes the trade-offs between opposing private interests, or opposing social concerns, to take place in ways that put more costs on one side than on the other, this affects much more than the justice or logic of the final decision in those cases that are adjudicated. In legal as in economic processes, the transactions that do *not* take place at all may represent the largest cost to the public. The electric generating capacity that is *not* built, and the traumatic blackouts that result from overtaxed electric generating capacity, may far outweigh the annoyance of a handful of lakeside resort owners or the Sierra Club—*if* the costs of the two results could be equally accurately conveyed through either the economic system or the legal system. Where the costs of transmitting one set of knowledge (the demand for electricity, in this case) is artificially made greater than the costs of conveying the other set of knowledge (recreational demands), then the distortion of knowledge can lead to results which neither the economic nor the legal decision makers would have reached had accurate knowledge been equally transmittable from opposing sides at equal cost. In the criminal law as well, the real costs of the legal system are not the financial costs of such transactions as happen to take place, but are primarily the social costs of those transactions that do *not* take place—the cases that are not tried but dropped or plea bargained because of the prohibitive cost of doing otherwise.

FREE SPEECH

It is not merely as an individual benefit but as a systemic requirement that free speech is integral to democratic political processes. The systemic value of free speech depends upon the high individual cost of knowledge—that is, lack of omniscience. "Persecution for the expression of opinions" may be "perfectly logical," according to Justice Oliver Wendell Holmes, when "you have no doubt of your premises." He continued:

But when men have realized that time has upset many fighting faiths, they may come to believe even more than they believe the very foundations of their own conduct that the ultimate good desired is better reached by free trade in ideas—that the best test of truth is the power of the thought to get itself accepted in the competition of the market, and that truth is the only ground upon which their wishes safely can be carried out. That at any rate is the theory of our Constitution. It is an experiment, as all life is an experiment. Every year if not every day we have to wager our salvation upon some prophecy based upon imperfect knowledge. While that experiment is part of our system I think that we should be eternally vigilant against attempts to check the expression of opinions that we loathe and believe to be fraught with death, unless they so imminently threaten immediate interference with the lawful and pressing purposes of the law that an immediate check is required to save the country.[15]

This faith in systemic processes rather than individual intentions or individual wisdom meant that even "a silly leaflet by an unknown man"[16] required constitutional protection, not for its individual merits, nor as an act of benevolence or patronage, nor as recognition of an opaque "sacred" character of an individual's endowment of "rights," but as a matter of *social expediency* in a long-run, systemic sense. For that very reason, it was not a categorical right but one subordinated to that social expediency which justified it in the first place, and therefore revocable whenever it presented a "clear and present danger"[17] to the continuation of that systemic process itself or to the people and government in whom that process is expressed. In short, the right of free speech is not an opaque "sacred" right of an individual, any more than other rights such as property rights are "sacred" individual possessions. All are justified (or not) by the litmus test of their *social* expediency—not in the sense that any individual or group rash enough to imagine themselves capable of following the specific ramifications of each particular statute or privilege in its social impact may centrally control all words or equipment— but in the larger and longer-run sense that we can judge the historic benefits of systemic interplay better than we can determine individual wisdom in word or deed in process. Adam Smith's systemic defense of *laissez faire*, despite his obvious and pervasive disgust with businessmen,[18] paralleled Holmes' systemic justification for freedom for opinions he regarded as harmful or contemptible. Both amount, ultimately, to recognition of different costs of knowledge in judging overall results rather than judging individual parts of a process.

Complications arise with the very meaning of "free" and of "speech." The basic conception of freedom of speech—that the substantive content of individual communication be uncontrolled by government—has been judicially supplemented or extended by considering the economic cost of communication. If the content of speech remains unconstrained by government, but the modalities of its delivery are restricted (e.g., bans on sound trucks at 2:00 a.m.), then beyond some point in such restrictions, the alternative costs of other modes of communication could conceivably price the speaker out of the market. "Freedom" of speech has therefore, in recent decades, come to include concern for the cost of communication—almost as if "free" had an economic rather than a political meaning. "Speech" has also been judicially expanded to include various forms of articulation (picketing, for example) and even inarticulate symbolism (flag burning). Extensions of the concept of "speech" to other activities places other aspects of these activities—harassment and intimidation, for example—under constitutional protection intended only for communication. Similarly, extending the freedom of the press can mean allowing newpapers to be used as protected conduits for threats or ransom demands by individuals or groups who communicate with victims or their families or the authorities via newspaper stories phoned to reporters.

In the 1940 case of *Thornhill v. Alabama* the Supreme Court declared a state ban on picketing unconstitutional as a violation of free speech.[19] The broadness of the ban and the corresponding broadness of the affirmation of the right of free speech as applied to pickets led to subsequent challenges to other picketing restrictions of a more limited sort. Here the court recognized the nonspeech aspects of picketing as subjecting the whole activity to some state control, such as when "the momentum of fear generated by past violence would survive even though future picketing might be wholly peaceful.[20] Moreover, picketing by an organized group "is more than free speech" because the presence of its picket line "may induce action of one kind or another, quite irrespective of the nature of the ideas which are being disseminated.[21] Despite these reservations as to the legal immunization of nonspeech activities by the "freedom of speech" provisions of the Constitution, over the years the courts have generally expanded the scope of activities deemed to be protected by the First Amendment, and extended the constitutional restrictions to organizations *not* part of the governmental apparatus. The First Amendment begins "Congress shall make no law . . . ," but by interpreting the Fourteenth Amendment as bringing the states under federal constitutional restrictions, the Supreme Court applied the rest of the earlier amendments to state governments.[22] Then, in a series of cases, it extended the constitutional restrictions to various private organizations as well.

In the landmark case of *Marsh v. Alabama* (1946) the Supreme Court ruled that the state could not prosecute for trespass a woman who distributed religious leaflets in a privately owned suburb where such distribution was forbidden by the owner. Although the state was not forbidding distribution of leaflets, the state's enforcement of the property owner's rights against trespass was held to be sufficient to transform the property owner's ban into "state action" in violation of a constitutional right. The court said: "When we balance the constitutional rights of owners of property against those of the people to enjoy freedom of press and religion, as we must here, we remain mindful of the fact that the latter occupy a preferred position."[23]

The fact that different costs and benefits must be balanced does not in itself imply *who* must balance them—or even that there must be a single balance for all, or a unitary viewpoint (one "we") from which the issue is categorically resolved. Each individual who chooses whether or not to live, work, or shop in a privately owned development can balance the costs of those rules against the benefits of living, working, or shopping there, just as people individually balance the costs of participating in other activities under privately prescribed rules (e.g., eating in a restaurant that requires a coat and tie, attending a stage performance where cameras are forbidden, living in an apartment building that bans pets). The court here went beyond the function of carving out boundaries, within which *other* institutions could make specific decisions, to making the substance of the decision itself. In doing so, it transformed an individual incremental decision into a categorical decision, confiscated a portion of one party's assets and transferred them to another (a transfer recognized as such by the author of the decision[24]), and substituted its evaluation of the costs and benefits of access to communications for the evaluations of those living, working, and shopping where the leaflets were being distributed.

From a social decision-making point of view, it is a misstatement of the issue to represent the opposing interests as being the property owner and the leaflet dispenser. The owner of a development is a middleman, whose own direct interest is in seeking profit, and whose specific actions in his role as middleman represent transmissions of the perceived preferences of other people—tenants and shoppers—who are the sources of his profits. The real balance is between one individual's desire for an audience and the prospective audience's willingness to play that role. How important another channel of communication is to the audience is *incrementally variable*, according to each individual's already existing access to television, newspapers, magazines, mail advertisements, lectures, rallies—and other places and times where leaflets can be handed out and received.

The prospective audience's incremental preference for tranquility where they live or shop—undisturbed by messages or solicitations to read messages—may be of greater value to them than any losses they suffer from not receiving such messages at this particular time and place, or the value to the soliciting party of reaching them at this time and place, or even the social value of "free speech" as an input into political and other decision-making processes. But no such balancing takes place through legal processes conferring "rights" to uncompensated transfers of benefits.

Both the solicitor and the solicited have alternative channels of communication. To claim that the costs of some alternative channels are "prohibitive" is to miss the whole point of costs—which is precisely to be prohibitive. Costs *transmit* inherent limitations of resources compared to the desires for them, but do not *create* this fundamental disproportionality. All costs are prohibitive to some degree, and virtually no costs are prohibitive absolutely.[25] Clearly, the costs of passing out leaflets would pay for direct mailing instead, or for newspaper ads, telephone solicitation, public gatherings, etc.

"Free speech" in the sense of speech free of governmental control does not imply *inexpensive* message transmission, any more than the right of privacy implies subsidized window shades. It is especially grotesque when the subsidy to message-senders takes the form of forcing others to be an unwilling audience, and where the small number of solicitors are called "the people" while the large number of those solicited are summarized through their intermediary as "the property owner." Even the dissentors in *Marsh v. Alabama* posed the issue in those terms.[26]

More basic than the question of the probable desires of a prospective audience is the question of *who* shall decide what those desires are, either absolutely or relative to the desires of message senders. That is, what decision-making process can best make that assessment—and revise it if necessary? Apparently *some* people were *presumed* to be receptive, or the leaflet distribution would not have been undertaken. By the same token, others were presumed to want to be left alone, or the solicitation ban and the lawsuit to enforce it would not have been undertaken. Therefore, there is a question not only of the estimated numbers and respective social costs of one course of action versus another, but also a fundamental question of how an initially-mistaken perception either way would be corrected by feedback under various institutional processes.

Under informal or noninstitutionalized decision-making processes, with neither the government nor the developer involved, the leaflet distributor would have no incentive to take account of the external costs imposed on people who prefer undisturbed coming and going to receiving his message. Even if a large majority of his potential audience preferred being left alone, as long as this desire was conveyed in civil terms, short of abuse or violence, it may receive little or no weight in the distributor's own balancing of costs and benefits. The distribution would continue, regardless of how little benefit a handful of passers-by felt they received and however much annoyance the others might feel—and regardless of how mistaken the leaflet distributor might be about either of these things.

Formal economic institutions translate the pleasure or displeasure of tenants, shoppers, or other users of a private development into a higher or lower financial value for a given set of physical structures. The property owner, even if he lives elsewhere, or is personally indifferent about leaflets, has an incentive to produce whatever degree of privacy or tranquility is desired, as long as its cost of production to him does not exceed its value to those who want it, as revealed by their willingness to pay for it.[27] More importantly, those property owners who are *mistaken* as to the nature and magnitude of other people's desires for privacy or tranquility find the value of their property less than anticipated, and therefore have an incentive to strengthen, loosen, or otherwise modify their rules of access.

Formal political institutions might reach similar results if constitutionally permitted. Such institutions could, in this case, take the form of a tenants or merchants association or an ordinary municipality. The problem with voting on an issue like this is that the vote of an individual who feels benefited to a minor extent counts the same as the vote of another individual who feels seriously harassed. By contrast, economic "voting" through the market reflects magnitudes of feelings as well as directions. Unfortunately, economic voting may also reflect substantial differences in income, but in general this effect is minimized by the variety of income levels on both sides of a given competition. Wealth distortions seem even less of a practical problem among tenants and shoppers in a given, privately owned development, which would tend to attract its own clientele, less socioeconomically diverse than the whole society. Economic decision-making processes also permit minority representation—in this case by transmitting the desires of whichever side is financially "outvoted" in a given development into a demand for other developments run by opposite rules. Such processes are not bound by the uniformity required of legislation nor by judicial concern for precedent. If a hundred developments adopt rule A, that in no way hinders the 101st development from adopting rule B to attract those economically "outvoted" elsewhere.

Judicial decision making on the substance of such issues loses many of the advantages of either economic or political institutions. Neither the initial court decision nor any subsequent modifications of it are the result of knowing the actual desires of the people involved, as distinguished from the parties in court. Nor, if those desires were known, would they provide any compelling incentive for the court to rule in accordance with them.

The balancing of costs and benefits includes not only tenants and shoppers with varying preferences but the leaflet distributors as well. The property owner's legal right to exclude leaflet distributors as trespassers does not mean that he will in fact do so. They can purchase access, just as individual residential and business tenants do. The solicitors would have to pay enough to counterbalance any net reduction in the value of the property caused by its being less desired by existing and prospective tenants as a result of its reduced privacy or tranquility. Not only would leaflet distributors' interests be weighed through the economic process against other people's interests; there would be automatic incentives for them to modify the place, manner and frequency of their solicitations, so as to minimize the annoyance to others, and so minimize the price they would have to pay for access. Economic processes are not mere zero-sum games involving transfers of money among people. They are positive-sum decision-making processes for mutual accommodation.

The Supreme Court could not, of course, "fine tune" their decision as an economic process would, much less make it automatically adjustable in accordance with the successively revealed (and perhaps continuously changing) preferences of the people affected. Their decision was both categorical and precedential—a "package deal" in space and time. If this is what the Constitution commanded the court to do, discussions of alternatives might be pointless. But even the defenders of the court's decisions in the "state action" cases justify those decisions on *policy* grounds as judicial improvisations—"sound results" without "unifying doctrines,"[28] affirmation of the basic principles of a "free society" with a "poverty of principled articulation" of the legal basis for the conclusions,[29] etc. The court has neither obeyed a constitutional compulsion nor filled an institutional vacuum; it has chosen to supersede other decision-making processes.

The legal basis of the *Marsh* decision was that the privately owned development prohibited activities which "an ordinary town" could not constitutionally prohibit, and that "there is nothing to distinguish" this suburban development from ordinary municipalities "except that the title belongs to a private corporation."[30] Similarly, there is nothing to distinguish the Supreme Court from any nine other men of similar appearance except that they have legally certified titles to act as they do. In neither instance can the elaborate social processes or weighty commitments involved be waved aside by denigrating the pieces of paper on which the end-results are summarized. If par-

allel appearance or parallel function is sufficient to subject a privately purchased asset to constitutional limitations not applicable to the same asset
when in alternative uses, then the economic value of assets in general is reduced as their particular uses approach those of state run organizations in
form or function. Economically, this is an additional (discriminatory) implicit tax on performing functions paralleling those of state agencies. The social
consequences of discouraging alternatives to services provided by government seem especially questionable in a pluralistic society, founded on rejection of over-reaching government.

What distinguishes the economic relationships surrounding private property from the political relationships subject to constitutional state action constraints is nothing as gross as outward appearance or day-to-day functioning.
The administrative routine in the headquarters of the Red Cross might well
resemble the administrative routine in the headquarters of a Nazi death
camp, but that would hardly make the two organizations similar in any socially meaningful way. In the case of economic relationships what is involved
is *voluntary* association, modifiable by mutual agreement and terminable by
either party. In the case of governmental relationships, what is involved is
coercive power, overwhelming to the individual, and pervasive throughout a
given geographic entity, however democratically selected the wielders of
that power might be. The constitutional limitations on governmental power
carve out areas of exemption from it, in order that individuals may voluntarily create their own preferred order within their own boundaries of discretion. The outward form of that voluntarily-created order may in some instances strikingly resemble governmental processes, but its *voluntariness*
makes it fundamentally different in meaning, and in the ultimate control of
its human results. The appellate courts' role as watchdogs patrolling the
boundaries of governmental power is essential in order that others may be secure and free on the other side of those boundaries. But what makes watchdogs valuable is precisely their ability to distinguish those people who are to
be kept at bay and those who are to be left alone. A watchdog who could not
make that distinction would not be a watchdog at all, but simply a general
menace.

The voluntariness of many actions—i.e., personal freedom—is valued by
many simply for its own sake. In addition, however, voluntary decision-making processes have many advantages which are lost when courts attempt to
prescribe results rather than define decision-making boundaries.

The *Marsh* decision set a precedent which was not only followed but extended. If a private development was functionally similar to a municipality,
a shopping center was "the functional equivalent" of part of a municipality.[31] Therefore pickets could not be considered as trespassers in the shopping

center.[32] Again, the issue was posed in terms of the free speech rights of the many against the property rights of the few.[33] The right of the public to be undisturbed, and the intermediary role of the property owners as communicators and defenders of that right, out of financial self-interest, were not allowed to disturb this tableau. In the case of *Food Employees Union v. Logan Valley Plaza* (1968), the few were described in terms of the much larger entities of which they were a part ("workers") and in terms of other large entities, some few of whom might also wish to do similar things ("consumers," "minority groups"), while the contrary interests of the many were described in impersonal terms as property rights or summarized through a handful of intermediaries ("business enterprises").[34] As in the earlier decision, the dissenting opinions accepted much of the same framework and complained primarily of the extent to which the functional analogy to "state action" had been stretched.

In a subsequent case, *Lloyd Corporation v. Tanner* (1972), the Supreme Court pulled back, in a five-to-four decision which emphasized that the leaflets were being distributed in a shopping plaza that was *not* a "functional equivalent" because it was not in a "large private enclave" like Logan Valley Plaza, where "no other reasonable opportunity" to convey a message existed.[35] In short, once more political freedom from governmental prohibitions was confused with economic inexpensiveness in message sending. The dissenting opinion also leaned heavily on the expensiveness of message sending, but simply estimated the costs differently: "If speech is to reach these people, it must reach them in Logan Center."[36] There is, presumably, a right to an audience, regardless of the audience's wishes.

Later Supreme Court rejections of the application of "state action" constraints were similarly based on *how far* "this process of analogy might be spun out to reach . . . a host of functions commonly regarded as nongovernmental though paralleling fields of government activity."[37] But the basic belief that such functional parallelism was the determining factor was not rejected. Again, the majority differed from the dissenters only in how far they were prepared to carry the analogy, not on its validity in principle.

In a still later case of a privately owned public utility that discontinued service without "due process," the failure to invoke "state action" constraints was based on an assessment of insufficient parallelism in function, whereas from the point of view of state *power*, the consumer had no other choice of electric company precisely because the state forbade competition when it licensed this producer.[38] Even if one accepts the "natural monopoly" theory of public utilities,[39] it is not economically inevitable that a particular state-selected firm be that monopoly, regardless of how it treats customers. Natural monopolies exist in some fields because of cost advantages, but cost advantages are never absolute—and sufficiently bad treatment of customers creates opportunities for competitors—except where the state prevents this economic feedback mechanism to act as "checks and balances." To lose the economic checks and balances without any offsetting political checks and balances is to combine the worst features of both institutional processes.

Neither the dissents nor the pullbacks of the whole court in the "state action" area were based on recognition of a different constitutional principle, nor on the recognition of the relative advantages of other decision-making processes for balancing the interests at issue.

RACE

The Constitution, as originally adopted, contained no explicit reference to slavery or to the enslaved race, though "free persons" and "other persons" were distinguished for voting purposes. Slavery entered the Constitution openly for the first time in 1865 when the Thirteenth Amendment banned slavery, and in 1870 when the Fifteenth Amendment asserted the right to vote without regard to "race, color or previous condition of servitude." Sandwiched between them is the momentous Fourteenth Amendment which decrees "equal protection of the laws" to "all persons." It has been estimated that the Fourteenth Amendment is the largest source of the Supreme Court's work. Its ramifications reach beyond the area of race, though it is one of the three amendments transforming race relations in the United States.

Three main strands of legal trends involving race will be considered here: (1) state actions affecting race, struck down by the Supreme Court as unconstitutional, (2) "affirmative action" policies and practices of the 1960s and 1970s, as developed by courts and administrative agencies, and (3) the racial integration of schools as conceived in the landmark case of *Brown v. Board of Education* in 1954 and legally and socially evolved over more than two decades since then.

STATE ACTION

Before the Fourteenth Amendment was passed in 1868, numerous laws in both the North and the South specified different treatment for black and white citizens. More such laws were passed in the South after the Civil War and—particularly in the case of sweeping "vagrancy" laws—virtually reenslaved the emancipated Negro. Other laws had existed even before the Civil

War to control the half million "free persons of color" and to deny them such fundamental rights as the right to testify in court (except against other blacks), to move freely from place to place, or even to educate their own children at their own expense.[40] The sweeping and extreme nature of these denials of the most ordinary and basic rights must be understood as a background to the words of the Fourteenth Amendment. The "equal protection of the laws" had a very plain and simple meaning—and a very *limited* meaning, falling far short of a social revolution. So too did the ban on any state action to deprive anyone of "life, liberty, or property" without "due process." The writers of these words explicitly, repeatedly, and even vehemently denied any interpretations going beyond prohibition of the gross abuses all too evident around them.[41] Even voting rights were not included.[42]

The nineteenth-century Supreme Court decisions under the Fourteenth Amendment followed the limited scope and intentions of its authors. The Court declared that it was only "state action of a particular character that is prohibited"; "Individual invasion of individual rights is not the subject matter of the amendment."[43] Public accommodation laws were therefore held invalid.[44] Even lynchings of prisoners in state custody were ruled beyond the scope of the Amendment.[45]

In the twentieth century, the Supreme Court began to expand the meaning of "state action" in a series of cases (beginning in the 1920s) revolving around white-only primaries in the South, where the Democratic primary was tantamount to election, and where "state delegation" of its power to set voter qualifications to the Democratic party was a transparent subterfuge to prevent blacks from voting.[46] In these cases, governmental bodies took the initiative and made the decisions which denied citizens equal treatment.

A very different series of "state action" cases began in the 1940s. In these new cases, both the initiative and the decisions to treat individuals unequally by race were *private*. The state became involved only subsequently in protecting the legal rights of those private individuals and organizations to make whatever decisions they chose as regards contracts (restrictive covenants) and the use of their own property (trespass laws). In short, the state in these cases simply decided who had the right to decide, as defined in contracts and trespass laws. State *power* was involved in enforcing contracts and laws, but state *decision making* was not.

The Supreme Court conceded that the Fourteenth Amendment "erects no shield against merely private conduct, however discriminatory or wrongful." But state "enforcement" of restrictive covenants was deemed paramount to "participation" by the state.[47] This was called state action "in the full and complete sense of the phrase."[48] Similarly, state enforcement of trespass laws against sit-in demonstrators seeking the desegregation of privately owned businesses serving the public was invalidated as "state action" in violation of the Fourteenth Amendment.[49] Perhaps the furthest extreme of this concept of "state action" was a 5 to 4 Supreme Court decision in *Reitman v. Mulkey* (1967) that repeal of a California "fair housing" law was a violation of the Fourteenth Amendment because the state was thereby guilty of "encouraging" private discrimination.[50]

In other cases, private descriminatory decisions were classified as "state action" because some governmental body was financially, administratively, or otherwise involved with the private party—as in *Burton v. Wilmington Parking Authority* (1961), where a restaurant leased in a government facility was racially discriminatory. The question of *how much* government involvement with a private party was necessary to make private decisions "state action" for legal purposes was never resolved. The Supreme Court deemed the fashioning of a "precise formula" to be "an impossible task" which "this Court has never attempted."[51] In other cases, however, state licensing—even when restrictive[52] or monopolistic[53]—was not sufficient to convert the licensees' decisions into "state action." As the dissenters in *Burton* observed, the lack of clear principle "leaves completely at sea" what was and was not "state action."[54] What was left unresolved was not merely the question of where to draw the line—a "precise formula"—but on what *principle.*

In place of principle, a miscellany of *ad hoc* reasons are sprinkled through "state action" cases: functional parallelism of private to public activity,[55] state receipt of benefits from a private activity,[56] the "publicness" of the activity,[57] or even the fact that the state "could have" acted in an area but chose to "abdicate" instead.[58]

The Civil Rights Act of 1964 made many distinctions between private and state decision making legally unnecessary, since private operators of various public accommodations were statutorily prohibited from racial discrimination, just as the state was constitutionally prohibited. Subsequent cases show the Supreme Court pulling back in the "state action" area—not only on the question of *where* to draw the line, but more fundamentally on the principle involved in drawing it: "Respondent's exercise of the choice allowed by state law where the initiative comes from it and not from the state, does not make its action in doing so 'state action' for purposes of the Fourteenth Amendment."[59] This distinction between state *authorization* of an area of private discretion and direct state *decision making* would annihilate the rationale for most of the prior series of landmark "state action" decisions, beginning with restrictive covenants and ending with repeal of California's "fair housing" law. Although this principle was announced in a nonracial discrimination case, presumably the definition of constitutional principles does not depend on who is involved. Neither in the "free speech" cases like *Marsh* nor in such racial cases as *Burton* did the state initiate the decisions which led to the legal activity. All that the state did was enforce private individuals' general (nonracial) right to exclude. Yet the inconsistencies throughout this series of cases raises disturbing questions about whether this was simply another "results"-oriented area, for which the Supreme Court became known in the Warren era.[60] If so, the underlying consistency of the cases may lie in the social policy preferred by the court in the racial area, and in the greater ease of achieving those results, after the Civil Rights Act of 1964 without strained and shaky reasonings about "state action."

AFFIRMATIVE ACTION

The phrase "affirmative action" is ambiguous. It refers both to a general approach and to highly specific policies. The general approach is that to "cease and desist" from some harmful activity may be insufficient to undo the harm already done, or even to prevent additional harm in the future from a pattern of events set in motion in the past. This idea antedates the civil rights issues of the 1960s. The 1935 Wagner Act prescribed that "affirmative action"[61] be taken by employers found guilty of intimidating unionized employees—for example, posting notices of changed policies and/or reinstating discharged workers with back pay.[62]

Racial discrimination is another area where simply to cease and desist would not prevent future harm from past actions. The widespread practice of hiring new employees by word-of-mouth referrals from existing employees means that a racially discriminatory employer with an all-white labor force is likely to continue having an all-white labor force long after he ceases discriminating, because he will be hiring the relatives and friends of incumbent employees. Opponents of racial discrimination therefore urged that "affirmative action" be taken to break up or supersede hiring patterns and practices which left racial or ethnic minorities largely outside the usual hiring channels. This might include advertising in newspapers or in broadcast media more likely to reach minority workers, or a variety of other ways of creating equalized access to apply for employment, college admissions, etc.

The first official use of the phrase "affirmative action" in a racial or ethnic context was in an Executive Order issued by President Kennedy, requiring that government contractors act affirmatively to recruit workers on a nondiscriminatory basis.[63] Another equally general Executive Order was issued by President Johnson, requiring affirmative action to insure that workers be hired "without regard to their race, creed, color, or national origin."[64] The Civil Rights Act of 1964 likewise repeatedly required in its various sections that hiring and other decisions be made *without regard* to race or ethnicity.[65] In short, special efforts were to be made to include previously excluded racial or ethnic groups in the pools of applicants, though the actual decisions among applicants were then to be made *without regard* to race or ethnicity. This was the initial thrust of "affirmative action."

Both the presidential orders and the congressional legislation required various adminstrative agencies—existing and newly created—to carry out and formulate more specific policy on a day-to-day basis. It was here that "affirmative action" was transformed from a doctrine of prospective equal opportunity to a doctrine of retrospective statistical "representation" or quotas. This transformation was all the more remarkable in the light of the explicit language and legislative history of the Civil Rights Act of 1964, which expressly repudiated the statistical representation approach. While steering this legislation through the Senate, Senator Hubert Humphrey pointed out that it "does not require an employer to achieve any kind of racial balance in his work force by giving any kind of preferential treatment to any individual or group."[66] There was an "express requirement of intent" before an employer could be found to be guilty of discrimination.[67] Ability tests would continue to be legal, even if different proportions of different groups passed them.[68] Another supporter, Senator Joseph Clark, pointed out that the burden of proof would be on the government to show discrimination under the Civil Rights Act.[69] Still another supporter, Senator Williams of Delaware, declared that an employer with an all-white work force could continue to hire "only the best qualified persons even if they were all white."[70] All these assurances are consistent with the language of the Civil Rights Act[71] but not with the actual policies subsequently followed by administrative agencies.

A series of Labor Department "guidelines" for government contractors began in 1968 with requirements for "specific goals and timetables" involving the "utilization of minority group personnel," and by degrees this evolved into "result-oriented" efforts (1970) and finally (1971) it meant that the employer had the burden of proof in cases of "under-utilization" of minorities and women, now explicitly defined as "fewer minorities and women in a particular job classification than would be expected by their availability . . ."[72] These so-called guidelines had the force of law, and given the large role of the federal government in the economy, the affected government contractors and subcontractors included a substantial proportion of all major employers. The "availability" of minorities and women, as judged by administrative agencies, often meant nothing more or less than their percentage in the population.

"Representation" based on population disregards huge differences in age distribution among American ethnic groups, due to differences in the number of children per family. Half of all Hispanics in the United States are either infants, children, or teenagers. Their median age is about a decade younger than that of the U.S. population as a whole, two decades younger than the Irish or Italians, and about a quarter of a century younger than the Jews.[73] Such demographic facts are simply ignored in statistics based on "representation" in the *population*, which includes infants as well as adults. The high-level positions on which "affirmative action" attention is especially focused are positions usually held by persons with many years of experience and/or education—which is to say, persons more likely to be in their forties than in their twenties. The purely demographic disparities among groups in these age brackets can be extreme. Half of all Jewish-Americans are forty-five years old or older, while only 12 percent of Puerto Ricans are that old. Even a totally nondiscriminatory society would have gross "underrepresentation" of Puerto Ricans in the kinds of jobs held by people of that age. More generally, American ethnic groups are not randomly distributed with respect to either age, education, region, or other variables having substantial impact on incomes and occupations.[74]

The qualitative dimensions of "availability" have also been stretched in affirmative action concepts. The *barely* "qualified" are counted as fully as the well qualified or the highly qualified. Indeed, the Equal Employment Opportunity Commission (EEOC) has stretched the concept of a qualified applicant to mean "qualified people to train"[75]—that is, people lacking the necessary qualifications, whose hiring would entail more expense to an employer than if he hired someone already qualified. Applicants or employees cannot be denied a job even for serious crimes. The EEOC ruled that because "a substantially disproportionate percentage of persons convicted of 'serious crimes' are minority group persons" an employer's policy against employing anyone with a conviction for a serious crime "discriminates against Negroes."[76] Employers could retain this practice only if they could bear the burden of proof of the "job-relatedness of the conviction" and, in addition, take into account the employee's "recent" past employment history—to the *ex post* satisfaction of the EEOC."[77]

The EEOC defined which groups were "minorities" for legal purposes: Negroes, Indians, Orientals, and Hispanics.[78] Because this was an unconstrained choice by an unelected commission, it did not have to justify this selection to anyone, even though Orientals were included when they have higher incomes than other ethnic groups not included (such as Germans, Irish, Italians, or Polish-Americans[79])—and, in fact, had higher incomes and occupations than the average American.[80] The other officially designated ethnic minorities all have lower average ages and educational levels than the general population—a fact generally ignored in "representation" discussions. With the addition of women to the groups entitled to preferential (or "remedial") treatment, all the persons so entitled constitute about two-thirds of the total population of the United States. Looked at another way, discrimination is legally authorized against one-third of the U.S. population (Jewish, Italian, Irish, etc., males)—and for government contractors and subcontractors, it is not merely authorized but required.

The shifting of the burden of proof to the employer after a *prima facie* showing of statistical "underrepresentation" (as administratively defined) was paralleled by a shifting of the burden of proof to the employer whenever a test had differential impact on the officially designated minorities.[81] The apparently reasonable requirement that such tests be "validated" is in practice a virtual ban on tests for many employers, because the cost of such validation has been estimated by professional testers as "between $40,000 and $50,000 under favorable circumstances,"[82] and many employers simply do not have large enough numbers of employees in each job classification to achieve statistically significant results in any case, even if they were willing and able to spend the money. The EEOC has even gone beyond requiring "validation" to requiring *differential* validation for each ethnic group—still more costly where possible, and possible in fewer instances. The importance of costs and of placing the burden of proof on the government in legal transactions is amply illustrated by the results in the exceptional area of administrative law, where the accused can be presumed guilty after a meager *prima facie* case. Under "affirmative action," as administratively evolved, the *prima facie* case consists simply of systemic results ("underrepresentation") legally equated with intentional behavior ("discrimination"). As a well-known scholar in this area has observed: "One may review these enormous governmental reports and legal cases at length and find scarcely a single reference to any act of discrimination against an individual."[83]

However much "affirmative action" has come to *mean* quotas, administrative agencies cannot explicitly assign quotas, since the Civil Rights Act forbids that. What is done instead is to force an employer to confess to "under-utilization" and to design his own specific "affirmative action" plan as a precondition for retaining his eligibility for federal contracts or for doing subcontracting for anyone else receiving federal money. The agency does not tell him what numbers or percentages to hire from each group, but can only disapprove his particular mechanisms and goals until they agree. This raises the cost of communicating knowledge for the agency, the employer, and the economy. These costs are compounded by the overlapping jurisdictions of various federal agencies involved—the EEOC, the Justice Department, HEW, and the Labor Department. An "affirmative action" plan that is acceptable to one agency may not be acceptable to another agency, and even if it is acceptable to all the agencies simultaneously, an individual employee

252

can still sue the employer for "reverse discrimination." Indeed, federal agencies have sued each other under the Civil Rights Act.[84] In short, the policy fails to clearly prescribe in advance what an individual can and cannot do. Part of this ambiguity is inherent in administrative agencies' covert pursuit of policies that they are legally forbidden to follow.

The flouting of congressional intent brought attempts to return to the initial meaning of "affirmative action" as an attempt to "expand the pool of applicants."[85] This attempt to amend the law failed,[86] and its failure illustrates temporal bias as it affects special interest groups. Laws do not simply respond to pre-existing special interests. Laws also *create* special interests which then affect what is subsequently politically possible. As noted before, special interests are essentially people who have lower costs of knowledge of their own stake in government policy, and in this sense special interests include governmental personnel whose jobs and powers were created by given legislation. The "affirmative action" policy followed had enormous impact on the agencies administering such policies. For example, within a period of three years the EEOC's staff of lawyers increased tenfold.[87] The impact on minority employment has been found to be relatively minor.[88] Blacks have rejected preferential treatment 64 percent to 27 percent. Four-fifths of women also reject it. Indeed, no racial, regional, sex, income or educational group studied by the Gallup Poll favors preferential treatment.[89] Yet the drive of the administering agencies and the general acquiescense of the courts has been enough to continue policies never authorized by Congress and contrary to its plainly expressed legislative intent.

The insulation of administrative processes from political control is illustrated by the fact that (1) administrative agencies went beyond what was authorized by the two Democrats (Kennedy and Johnson) in the White House who first authorized "affirmative action" in a sense limited to decisions *without regard* to group identity, and (2) continue to do so despite the two Republican presidents (Nixon and Ford) who followed, who were positively opposed to the trends in agencies formally under their control as parts of the executive branch of government. This political insulation is illustrated even by the first major setback for "affirmative action"—which came from another non-elected branch of government, the Supreme Court, which after more than a decade of support for "affirmative action" was able to put a brake on the policy, which neither the public nor its elected representatives could reverse.

In a five to four decision, with fragmented partial concurrences and partial dissents, the Supreme Court ruled in the *Bakke* case (1978) that a university cannot establish minority admissions quotas which have the effect of "insulating each category of applicants . . . from competition with all other applicants."[90] It did not categorically forbid the voluntary use of race as a consideration, where this "does not insulate the individual from comparison with all other candidates,"[94] but emphasized that any uses of racial designations by the state were "inherently suspect and thus call for the most exacting judicial examination" under the Fourteenth Amendment.[91] The Supreme Court rejected the idea of group compensation for generalized "societal" wrongs—as distinguished from demonstrated discrimination by a given decision-making unit.[92] It pointed out that the Fourteenth Amendment grants "equal rights" to *individuals*—not group rights, and certainly not special rights to one group historically connected with the origin of the Amendment.[93] After more than a century of litigation under the Fourteenth Amendment, it is "far too late to argue that the guarantee of equal protection to *all* persons permits the recognition of special wards entitled to a degree of protection greater than that accorded others."[94] In a multi-ethnic society like the United States, the courts cannot assume the task of evaluating the historic "prejudice and consequent harm suffered by various minority groups."[95] Indeed, the very concepts "majority" and "minority" were challenged, since "the white 'majority' itself is composed of various ethnic groups, most of which can lay claim to a history of previous discrimination at the hands of the state and private individuals."[96] Any group rankings by harm suffered and remedies available would be transient, requiring repeated incremental adjustment as the judical remedies take effect, and the "variable sociological and political analysis" necessary for this "simply does not lie within the judicial competence"—even if it were otherwise politically feasible and socially desirable.[97]

While the above-cited court's decision written by Justice Lewis F. Powell directly addressed most of the major issues raised by "affirmative action" policies, the closeness of the vote and the partial concurrences that created different sets of majorities for different sections of the decision make the *Bakke* case less of a precedential landmark than it might be otherwise. That highly diverse and opposing groups greeted the decision as a victory for their particular viewpoints is further evidence of this. Moreover, the four justices who concurred with Powell in striking down the special minority admissions program *refused to concur in anything else* in his official opinion for the court,[98] and observed that "only a majority can speak for the court or determine what is the 'central meaning' of any judgment of the court.[99] The narrowly limited basis of the concurrence prevented any majority from existing over the range of issues addressed by Powell. The future legal implications of the *Bakke* decision were further clouded by the four dissenters, who tellingly pointed out how far the Supreme Court had already gone in the direction it was now rejecting.[100] The narrowness and tenuousness of the decision in the

Bakke case was underscored by an opposite decision in the *Weber* case just one year later.

After striking down admissions quotas at the University of California, the U.S. Supreme Court upheld job training quotas at a Kaiser Corporation plant in Louisiana. Following criticism of their employment patterns by the Office of Federal Contract Compliance, threatening loss of government contracts, Kaiser and the United Steelworkers Union jointly prepared an "affirmative action" plan modeled after a plan imposed on the steel industry by the government in a consent decree. Half of all places in the training program were reserved for blacks. One of the white workers excluded from the training program in favor of blacks with less seniority was Brian F. Weber, who instituted a lawsuit charging discrimination. Weber won in the trial court and in the Court of Appeals, but lost on a five-to-two decision by the Supreme Court. The four dissenting Justices in the *Bakke* case (Brennan, Marshall, White, and Blackmun) were joined by Justice Potter Stewart to form the new majority in the *Weber* case.

In *Weber* as in *Bakke*, the majority decision was based on the relevant statutory law—the Civil Rights Act of 1964—rather than on the Constitution. This meant that both cases avoided the establishment of a broad legal principle. Both cases also construed the applicability of even the statutory law very narrowly. In *Bakke*, the four concurring Justices declared:

> This is not a class action. The controversy is between two specific litigants.[101]

In *Weber* a very different majority likewise announced:

> We emphasize at the outset the narrowness of our inquiry. Since the Kaiser-USWA plan does not involve state action, this case does not present an alleged violation of the Equal Protection Clause of the Constitution.[102]

The traditional avoidance of unnecessary Constitutional decisions, when statutory law is sufficient, was in both cases carried to extremes by (1) ignoring government involvement in the substance of both quota decisions and (2) ignoring, and even boldly misstating, Congressional intent in the Civil Rights Act. Bakke had applied to a state-run medical school, and Weber had applied to a training program established under pressure from the Office of Federal Contract Compliance. Yet only Justice Powell addressed the issue of the Constitution's requirement that government provide "equal protection of the laws."

As for Congressional intent, the four concurring Justices in *Bakke* asserted that "Congress was not directly concerned with the legality of 'reverse discrimination' or 'affirmative action' programs"[103] when it was debating the Civil Rights Act of 1964. Yet one of those very same Justices (Rehnquist) later reported at great length, in a *Weber* case dissent, the numerous Congressional discussions of quotas and preferences, which were repeatedly, decisively, and emphatically rejected by Congress while writing the Civil Rights Act.[104] Why, then, the fictitious legislative history in *Bakke*? Its only effect was to provide a basis for judicial exegesis on a point allegedly neglected by Congress—in this case, creating a right to sue under the Civil Rights Act on a point for which no such right was provided in the Act itself.[105] This newly created right to sue made a statutory resolution of the issues possible, avoiding a constitutional precedent. Equally fictitious legislative history was invoked by a different set of Justices in the *Weber* case as a counterpoise to "a literal interpretation"[106] of what Congress had written in the Civil Rights Act, forbidding preferential treatment. Taking instead the "spirit" of that law and its "primary concern" for "the plight of the Negro in our economy,"[107] the *Weber* majority upheld the Kaiser quota which it repeatedly described as "voluntary," despite the obvious pressure from the OFCC noted by both the trial court and the Court of Appeals.[108] The Kaiser quota system was in fact simply the government's quota system imposed on a contractor.

In short, eight out of nine Justices—in two different cases before the identical court—chose to preserve the Court's options to pick and choose "affirmative action" plans it liked or disliked, even at the cost of (1) pretending to enforce Congressional intentions it was directly countering, and (2) ignoring government involvement in the creation of the programs at issue. This is a very consistent pattern underlying these differently decided cases, and may have more momentous implications than the actual decision in either case.

The central presumption behind "affirmative action" quotas has not been addressed directly by the courts or by the administrative agencies. That presumption is that systemic patterns ("representation") show either intentional actions ("discrimination") or, at the very least, the consequences of behavior by "society" at large—rather than actions for which the group in question may be in any way or to any degree responsible, or patterns arising from demographic or cultural causes, or statistical artifacts. The issue is not the categorical dichotomy between "blaming the victim" and blaming "society." It is an incremental question of multiple causation and perhaps multiple policy response.

More generally, the presumptive randomness of results selected as a baseline from which to measure discrimination is itself nowhere either empirically or logically demonstrated, and in many places and manners it is falsified. For example, even actions wholly within the descretion and control of each individual—choice of television programs to watch, card games to play, opinions to express to poll takers—show patterns that vary considerably by ethnicity, sex, region, educational level, etc. It is wholly arbitrary to exclude

256

variations which originate within the group from any influence on results for the group.[109] It is equally arbitrary to assume that those variables that are morally most important are causally most important.

A major nonmoral, nonsocietal variable that is routinely ignored is age. As already noted, median age differences among American ethnic groups range up to decades. The median age of American Indians is only one-half that of Polish-Americans (twenty versus forty); the median age of blacks is a little less than half that of Jews (twenty-two versus forty-six).[110] These differences affect everything from incomes and occupations to unemployment rates, fertility rates, crime rates, and death rates.[111] For example, Cuban-Americans average a higher income than Mexican-Americans, who are a decade younger, but in the same age brackets it is the Mexican-Americans who earn more.[112] Any attempt to explain gross income differences between these two groups in terms of either discrimination by "society" or by their respective "ability" runs into the hard fact that the gross difference is the opposite of the age-specific difference. Similarly, blacks have lower death rates than whites, but this in no way indicates better living conditions or medical care for blacks, much less any ability of blacks to discriminate against whites in these respects. Blacks are simply younger than whites, and younger people have lower death rates than older people; on an age-specific basis, whites have lower death rates than blacks.[113] Age differences also overshadow racial differences in unemployment rates: Blacks in the twenty-four to fourty-four-year-old brackets have consistently had lower unemployment rates than whites under twenty—every year for decades,[114] even though whites as a group have lower unemployment rates than blacks as a group. In short, the impact of age on statistical data is so great that to compare groups without taking age into account is like comparing apples and oranges. Yet "affirmative action" comparisons of group "representation" almost invariably ignore age differences.

Ages are important in another way related to "affirmative action" data. When prospective equality of opportunity is measured by retrospective results during a period of increasing opportunity, the gross statistics lump together different age-cohorts subject to the increased opportunities for varying proportions of their work careers—ranging from zero to one hundred percent. Older people whose careers began when there was less opportunity—or even total exclusion from some occupations—will have correspondingly less "human capital" with which to compete with their age peers in the general population. Younger members of the same ethnic group will be less handicapped in this respect, if opportunities have been increasing. Even if the ideal of equal prospective opportunity were achieved, retrospective data would not show statistical parity until decades later, after all members of the

o

older age-cohorts had passed from the scene. This is more than a theoretical point. Black income as a percentage of white income is progressively higher in younger age brackets,[115] and while the rate of return on education is lower for blacks than whites, the rate of return is slightly higher for younger blacks than for their white counterparts.[116]

Locational differences are another nonmoral variable having little relationship to the intentions of "society" but having a substantial impact on statistical data. No American ethnic group has income as low as one-half the national average, but two-to-one differences in incomes from one location to another exist, even within the same ethnic group. The 1970 census showed the average family income of blacks in New York State to be more than double the average family income of blacks in Mississippi. The average income of American Indians in Chicago, Detroit, or New York City was more than double what it is on most reservations. Mexican-Americans in the metropolitan area of Detroit earn more than double the income of Mexican-Americans in the metropolitan areas of Laredo or Brownsville, Texas.[117] Given the size and regional diversity of the United States, the geographic distribution of ethnic groups affects the statistical averages that are often blithely quoted, with as little regard for geographic as for demographic differences. Each ethnic group has its own geographic distribution pattern, reflecting a variety of historical and cultural influences,[118] and having little to do with the intentions of "society." Some indication of the combined influence of age and location is that young black working couples living outside the South had by 1971 achieved the same income as their white counterparts in the same region.[119] The disbelief and even denunciation which greeted publication of this fact indicates something of the vested interests that have built up in a different vision of the social process—and in programs built on that vision. Subsequent studies have reinforced the finding of income parity among these black and white younger age-cohorts with similar cultural characteristics.[120]

The point here is not that all is well. Far from it. The point is that both causal determination and policy prescription require coherent analysis, rather than gut feelings garnished with numbers. Many of the hypotheses behind "affirmative action" are not unreasonable as hypotheses. What is unreasonable is turning hypotheses into axioms. The preference for intentional variables ("discrimination") has virtually excluded systemic variables (age, location, culture) from even being considered. The practical consequences of this arbitrary theoretical exclusion extend far beyond the middlemen—employers—to much larger and more vulnerable groups, notably ethnic minorities themselves. Every false diagnosis of a condition is an obstacle to improvement. When recent studies show the still substantial black-white income differences to reflect conditions that existed before the younger age-cohorts ever reached the employer—reading (or nonreading) habits in the home, education, etc.[121]—this has implications for the effectiveness of programs which (1) postulate that discrepancies discovered at the work place are due to decisions made at the work place, and (2) establish legal processes centering on the work place.

The effect of "affirmative action" programs is viewed as axiomatically as its original process. In fact, however, studies have found little or no effect from affirmative action in advancing ethnic minorities, in either incomes or occupations.[122] In some particular places—prominent firms, public utilities, and others especially in need of appeasing federal administrative agencies—there have been some changes. But overall, the economic position of minorities changed little since "goals and timetables" (quotas) became mandatory in December 1971.

The ineffective record of "affirmative action" policies is in sharp contrast with the record of "equal opportunity" laws in the years immediately preceding. After passage of the Civil Rights Act of 1964—and before quotas in 1971—black income as a percentage of white income rose sharply, with blacks in white collar occupations also rising, along with rising proportions of blacks in skilled and professional jobs.[123] One reason for the difference was the different set of incentives presented by the two policies. "Equal opportunity" laws provided penalties for specifically proven discrimination. "Affirmative action" laws penalized numbers that disappointed administrative agencies, and made defenses against "rebuttable presumptions" costly and uncertain.

It might appear at first that "affirmative action" penalties—costs—were "stronger" (higher), but not when costs are recognized as opportunity costs, the difference between following one course of action rather than another. The general unattainability of many quotas means that penalties fall equally on discriminatory employers and nondiscriminatory employers. A discriminatory employer therefore has little to gain by becoming a nondiscriminatory employer, when the characteristics of the target population (age, education, etc.) insure that he will be unable to fill quotas anyway. Moreover, the ease with which a discrimination case can be made makes minorities and women more dangerous employees to have, in terms of future prospects of law suits if their subsequent pay, promotions, or other benefits do not match those of other employees or the expectations of administrative agencies. As in the case of other groups with special rights, as noted in Chapter 5, these rights have costs to the recipients themselves. In short, "affirmative action" provides opposing incentives to hire and not hire minorities and women. It is not surprising that it has been less effective than "equal opportunity" laws which provide incentives in only one direction.

Because "affirmative action" policies apply also to women, it should be noted that there has been a similar unwillingness to look beyond gross statistics for obviously systemic variables having little to do with intentional discrimination. With women the key variable is marriage. Even before "affirmative action" quotas, women in their thirties who worked continuously since high school earned slightly *more* than men in their thirties who worked continuously since high school.[124] In the academic world, where many discrimination charges have been filed under affirmative action, female academics earned slightly *more* than male academics when neither were married[125]—again even before "affirmative action"—and unmarried female Ph.D.'s who received their degrees in the 1930s and 1940s became full professors in the 1950s to a slightly *greater* extent than did unmarried male Ph.D.'s of the same vintage.[126] In short, the male-female differences in incomes and occupations are largely differences between married women and all other persons. Sometimes this is obscured in data for "single" women, many of whom are widowed, divorced, or separated—that is, have had domestic and maternal handicaps in pursuing their careers. The clear-cut income parity (or better) among women who never married suggests once again that systemic variables have more to do with the statistics than the intentional decisions at the work place at which the statistics were collected.

SCHOOL INTEGRATION

The 1954 Supreme Court decision in *Brown v. Board of Education* set in motion a chain of events that has resulted in a bitter controversy over what one side has characterized by its hoped-for results as "racial integration" in the public schools, and which the other side has characterized by its institutional mechanisms as "forced busing." Racial integration, in turn, sometimes implied more than statistical mixtures, and suggested at least some improved sense of mutual regard. Forced busing referred to busing categorically imposed by higher—more remote—authorities (usually appointed judges) on locally elected officials, parents, and children, as distinguished from such busing as the latter might voluntarily choose for themselves as incrementally justified by the benefits.

The *Brown* decision was historic in many respects. It outlawed as unconstitutional a whole political and legal pattern of racial segregation in the South, extending far beyond public schools. It pitted the Supreme Court against the whole political structure of that region for many years, and indeed put the court's general credibility and general effectiveness at stake on this particular issue. Had the Supreme Court been defied with impunity on this issue, its ability to enforce its other decisions in other areas could have been permanently jeopardized. Last but by no means least, it was the beginning of the era of Chief Justice Earl Warren and the increased judicial activism of the Supreme Court under his leadership. The high political and judicial stakes in the *Brown* decision are an integral part of the story of how school desegregation metamorphosed over the years into compulsory school busing to achieve prescribed racial proportions.[127] Even before the case was decided, Justice Frankfurter pointed out the great danger in a decision that might affirm a principle but be mocked in practice, through local defiance and evasion.[128] An immediate and categorical test of strength was avoided by announcing in the decision itself a delay for rehearings, followed by the conclusion after rehearing that the decision was to be implemented "with all deliberate speed"—i.e., incrementally, as political "realities" permitted. This highly unusual legal procedure[129] permitted lower courts and the Supreme Court to test the waters before proceeding, to assess and to some extent accommodate local circumstances, especially in the South. It also permitted time for opinion leaders to mobilize public support for "the law of the land," given that the high stakes included the basic legal framework of the nation and not simply the school system or even race relations alone.

Whatever the strategic merits of this approach, it also had momentous other consequences. It made the Supreme Court a party to an ongoing adversary relationship with institutions over whom it was established to have jurisdiction and to make rulings impartially. Moreover, it was a virtual invitation to evasions and delay, in as many forms as human ingenuity could devise. This in turn meant that the courts had to *monitor in detail* the laws, plans, regulations, and organizational patterns of institutions ranging all the way down to local school boards. Courts had to go beyond defining legality to determining "good faith." Among the evidences of good faith were the numbers of black children actually integrated into white schools—numbers that were often zero in some Southern states. For about a decade after the *Brown* decision, racial segregation by the state public schools remained entrenched in the Deep South.

As time went on, it became clear that courts could effectively enforce their orders on other institutions, that local, state or—if necessary—national government officials would use police or troops to prevent "the law of the land" from being openly defied. Time also permitted the most bitter opponents of racial desegregation to withdraw their children from public to private schools, or to move out to all-white suburban areas, weakening the effective opposition. As the balance of political power turned against their adversaries who had frustrated them for so long, the courts began to issue more and more sweeping orders, involving the courts more and more in the detailed operations of school systems.

Initially, the *Brown* decision required no more than that the state could no longer use race in assigning children to schools. This was reaffirmed in a later (1963) case where "racial classifications" were "held to be invalid." This position also appeared in the 1964 Civil Rights Act, which defined "desegregation" as the assignment of public school pupils "without regard to their race, color, religion, or national origin," and specified that it did *not* mean assignment "to overcome racial imbalance."[130] Indeed, such language appeared repeatedly in various provisions of the Civil Rights Act and in the congressional debates preceding its passage.[131] The congressional intent was, however, turned around in decisions by administrative agencies. The U.S. Civil Rights Commission urged upon the U.S. Office of Education the use of guidelines for the receipt of federal money by school districts, which required that the districts not merely "disestablish" segregated schools but achieve "integrated systems." These recommendations were acted on in administrative guidelines issued in 1966.[132] That same year, the Fifth Circuit Court of Appeals explicitly declared that the "racial mixing of students is a high priority educational goal."[133] This interpretation was unique to the Fifth Circuit, but the Supreme Court reversed the contrary interpretations of other circuits, obliquely establishing the Fifth Circuit decision as a precedent.[134] In short, a decision by administrative agencies in effect reversed congressional legislation,[135] and an appellate court's endorsement of that philosophy created a new "constitutional" requirement with neither congressional nor voter sanction and with no such requirement to be found in the Constitution. As a dissenting judge observed:

The English language simply could not be summoned to state any more clearly than does that very positive enactment of Congress, that these so-called 'guidelines' of this administrative agency . . . are actually promulgated and being used in opposition to and in violation of this positive statute.[136]

Such sweeping changes in policy by oblique means is difficult to explain as the actions of legal institutions impartially carrying out judicial functions, but is much more understandable as actions against long-time adversaries now being routed.

In the 1968 case of *Green v. County School Board*, the Supreme Court declared unconstitutional a "free choice" enrollment plan because there was now an "affirmative duty" to eliminate dual school systems "root and branch."[137] As in other areas, prospective equality of opportunity was tested by retrospective results. Because only about 15 percent of the black children had chosen to transfer to the formerly all-white school and no white children had chosen to transfer to the all-black school, there was not a desegregated or "unitary" school system, according to the Supreme Court.[138] The *Green* decision was as different from the *Brown* decision as the two colors in their titles. *Brown* required pupil assignment *without regard* to race and *Green* required pupil assignment specifically *with regard* to race, so as to eliminate statistical imbalances in the results. Yet the Supreme Court treated the 1968 decision as logically derived from the 1954 decision, though no such derivation was explained—the 1954 decision being only mentioned but not quoted. The *Green* decision has been aptly characterized as "a masterwork of indirection" and "a rarely equalled feat of sophistry."[139] The court simply pushed on from one victory to a further objective, in the manner of other unconstrained institutions continuing in a given direction, in disregard of diminishing or negative returns.

Under the Supreme Court umbrella provided by the *Green* decision, lower courts began requiring massive busing,[140] not only where there had once been legally segregated school systems,[141] but where there had never been legally separated school systems,[142] or even in places where racial segregation was forbidden by state law antedating the *Brown* decision.[143] Ability-grouping within schools was sometimes struck down because its statistical effects were different for blacks than whites, and the assignment of teachers by race upheld, along with the firing of white teachers who enrolled their own children in private schools.[144] Only with *Milliken v. Bradley* in 1971 did the Supreme Court put a limit on how widely a court could require busing. By a five to four decision, it overruled a lower court's order to bus between Detroit and its suburban school districts—an area as large as the state of Delaware and larger than the state of Rhode Island.[145] Still, the general principle of interdistrict busing was not repudiated,[146] and there was no reversal of the trend toward massive and pervasive retrospective court monitoring of the behavior of school officials, including putting burdens of proof on them to show their innocence after purely statistical *prima facie* evidence.

The ability of the courts to supersede the authority of other institutions is not the same as the ability to achieve the social results aimed at. The spread of court-imposed busing has been followed by massive withdrawals of white children from the affected schools,[147] increased racial polarization among the remaining "integrated" students,[148] heightened violence,[149] and opposition to busing by both the black and white populations at large.[150] None of this constitutes effective feedback to the Supreme Court, whose members have lifetime appointments. Legislative attempts to prevent compulsory busing to achieve racial statistical balance have been turned aside by the Supreme

Court by simply denying that the courts are seeking statistical balance[151] (though statistical imbalance is their operational definition of "segregation"), thereby implying that the law does not apply to the cases at hand.

The supposed educational or psychological benefits of school desegregation for black children have proved elusive, though many studies have been made to try to find them,[152] and some studies have triumphantly announced finding such benefits only to have the data evaporate when challenged.[153] The original premise of the historic *Brown* decision—that separate schools are inherently inferior—was neither supported by fact nor would it stand up under scrutiny. Within walking of the Supreme Court was an all-black high school whose eighty-year history prior to *Brown* denies that principle. As far back as 1899, it had higher test scores than any of the white schools in Washington,[154] and its average I.Q. was eleven points above the national average in 1939—fifteen years before the Supreme Court declared such things impossible.[155] There have been other such black schools elsewhere, and indeed NAACP attorney Thurgood Marshall in the *Brown* case was a graduate of such a school in Baltimore.[156] The history of all-Oriental and all-Jewish schools would reduce this ponderous finding to a laughingstock, instead of the revered "law of the land."

There was never a serious question whether black schools in general had lower average performances than white schools in general. What was an issue was the *cause* of this. A long history of highly unequal financial support for black and white schools led some to attribute the educational difference to this—but the *Coleman Report*[157] data showed (1) how little difference there was between black and white schools in this regard by the mid-twentieth century, and (2) how little difference financial resources or other characteristics of schools made in educational performances. Obvious genetic differences between blacks and whites led others to attribute educational differences to this,[158] but data on various European ethnic groups at a comparable stage of their social evolution in American schools showed I.Q.'s similar to—and in some cases, lower than—those of blacks, even though those European ethnic groups' I.Q.'s have now reached or surpassed the national average.[159] One of the problems in comparing any given group with the "national average" is that the national average is itself simply an amalgamation of highly varying individual and group averages. Therefore a group may vary greatly from the national average without being in any way unique.

Again, as in the case of "affirmative action," systemic explanations (residential concentration, cultural orientation, etc.) of such social phenomena were discounted in favor of intentional explanations ("segregation," "discrimination," etc.), even though black academic performance was not historically unique either in kind or degree. Huge statistical disparities existed among school performances of children from different cultural groups in the past, even when all the groups were white. As of 1911, for example, the proportion of Irish children in New York City who finished high school was less than one-one hundredth the proportion among Jewish children,[160] and the Italians did less well than the Irish.[161] Schools that were 99 percent Jewish were not uncommon, and attempts to bus the Jewish children from such schools to less crowded schools in Irish neighborhoods across town were bitterly resisted by Jewish parents[162] and the Jewish press.[163] These earlier busing reforms from above were subject to feedback because they originated with elected officials, unlike later busing schemes initiated by courts and administrative agencies.

The institutional settings and institutional incentives and constraints are crucial to understanding the thrust and persistence of school "integration" or "busing" trends—especially as it has proceeded over the opposition of blacks as well as whites. In the 1960s, Blacks were fairly evenly divided, with a slight majority opposed to busing.[164] In later polls in cities like Detroit and Atlanta, where busing has actually been tried on a massive scale, the majority of blacks against it was two-to-one.[165] In the well-known Boston busing case, a coalition of dozens of black community groups urged Judge Garrity to minimize busing of their children,[166] but neither he nor the NAACP Legal Defense Fund were deterred by such appeals. Indeed, the NAACP had gone against its own local chapters in Atlanta and San Francisco on school busing.[167] The head of the NAACP Legal Defense Fund said that his organization cannot poll "each and every black person" before instituting legal proceedings,[168] but this sidesteps the larger question of why the organization proceeded in a direction opposed by blacks in general. The answer may be instructive, not only as regards the NAACP Legal Defense Fund but so-called "public interest" law firms in general. The financial costs of the NAACP's litigation is not borne by its official clients but by third-parties, "middle class blacks or whites who believe fervently in integration."[169] In short, "the named plaintiffs are nominal only"[170] and the black population in whose name this is all done has little or no effective feedback. The NAACP lawyers "answer to a miniscule constituency while serving a massive clientele."[171]

To the outside white world, and especially the mass media, the image of the NAACP officials and lawyers is that of "spokesmen" for blacks as a whole—though there is no institutional mechanism to make that so, and much public opinion evidence on both busing and "affirmative action" to contradict that image. Institutionally, neither blacks as a whole nor even the particular plaintiffs have any control over, or effective input to, NAACP leaders or lawyers. Here, as elsewhere, firms defined by hoped-for results as "public interest" law firms are institutionally simply law firms financed by third party interests. In the case of the NAACP, these third party interests are well insulated from the costs of their activities by the fact that their own children are enrolled in private schools. This includes both direct participants in the school "integration" drive, like Thurgood Marshall and Kenneth B. Clark, political supporters like Senator Kennedy and Senator McGovern[172] and media supporters like Carl Rowan.[173]

The point here is not to make a categorical assessment of the NAACP. Such an assessment would undoubtedly include many valuable and heroic contributions of the NAACP in areas of crying injustices. The question at this point is the incremental movement of the NAACP, and whether that is in the area of diminishing or negative returns. One of the NAACP's Legal Defense Fund's staunch supporters and former officials recalls that by the mid-1960s "the long golden days of the civil rights movement had begun to wane"[174] and that legal "tools had been developed which now threatened to collect dust"[175] unless some new crusade was launched—as it was. Earlier, there was "simply too much else to do."[176] The progression from the urgent to the optional to the counterproductive is one already seen in other organizations with mandated jurisdiction and costs paid by third parties. There is no reason to expect the NAACP to be exempt from patterns discovered elsewhere under such incentives and constraints.

Where third party costs and benefits determine the actions of so-called "public interest" law firms, and where the administrative and judicial resolutions of the issues they raise are insulated from the feedback from those directly affected, then a major shift in political and legal power has occurred away from the actual experiences and desires of the general public and toward the beliefs and dreams of small self-anointed groups—and all this in the name of "democracy" and "the public interest."

THE SPECIALNESS OF RACE

Racial preferences and antipathies theoretically might be—and historically have been—dealt with by the whole range of social processes and institutions. This plain fact can be expressed, on the one hand, by saying that racism pervades American society, or can be expressed on the other hand by saying that race-based attitudes and behavior, which have affected mankind in every place and time, are handled with varying degrees of effectiveness by this society's decision-making processes and institutions as well. For "racism" to be an empirically meaningful category, there would have to be a nonracist alternative somewhere. Pending this discovery we are left with the age-old problem of judging institutions by how well they resolve the dilemmas that derive precisely from man's limitations in knowledge, power, and morality. Presumably, God and the angels do not need institutions.

Clearly, one reason for treating race as special is the historic and traumatic experience of blacks, subject to slavery, discrimination, and degradation in American society. But even if this might justify a special policy for blacks, that is quite different from justifying a *general principle*, applicable wherever racial differences exist, and readily extendable—logically or politically— to nonracially-defined subsets of the population who choose to call themselves "minorities" (in open defiance of statistical facts in the case of women). This "unreflective extension of policies deriving from America's racial dilemma to other areas"[177] is one of the costs of decision making through those processes which by their nature make their decisions in general and precedent-setting terms. Political, administrative, and especially judicial processes tend to operate in this way. Not only does this "trivialize the historic grievances"[178] which served as initial rationale; it multiplies the cost of any resolution of race problems by creating principles applicable beyond the special case used to justify them.

Even within the area of race, it is by no means clear that all historic grievances have a remedy, or who specifically should pay the cost of such remedies as might be attempted. If the purpose is to compensate the pain and suffering of slavery, those most deserving of such compensation are long dead. If the purpose is to restore their descendants to the position the latter would now occupy "but for" the enslavement of their ancestors, is that position the average income, status, and general well-being in their countries of origin? The former implicitly assumes what is highly unlikely—a voluntary immigration comparable to the forced shipment of blacks from Africa—and the latter raises the grotesque prospect of expecting blacks to compensate whites for the difference between American and African standards of living. If what is to be compensated is the unpaid economic contribution of slave ancestors to American development, this is an area in which controversies have raged for centuries over the effects of slavery on the American economy— not merely over its magnitude, but over whether slavery's contribution was positive or negative.[179] Without even attempting to resolve this continuing dispute among specialists, it can be pointed out that the case for a negative effect can hardly be dismissed *a priori*. The South was poorer than the North even before the Civil War, and those parts of the South in which slaves were most heavily concentrated have long been the poorest parts of the South, for whites as well as blacks. Compensation based on the economic contribution of slavery could turn out to be negative. Would anyone be sufficiently devoted to that principle to ask blacks to compensate whites? Or is this simply another "results-oriented" principle, taken seriously only when forwarding some other purpose?

If the basis for special or compensatory treatment of blacks is simply a desire of some segment of contemporary white society to rid itself of guilt for historic wrongs, the question arises as to why this must be done through institutions which extend the cost to other—perhaps much larger—segments of the society whose ancestors were not even in the United States when most of this happened, or were in no position to do anything about it. Even the argument that they or their ancestors were passive beneficiaries of racial oppression loses much of its force when it is unclear that there were any net social benefits beyond the immediate profits of a tiny group of slave owners. If there were ever any net social benefits, it is questionable whether they survived the Civil War, whose costs seemed to confirm Lincoln's fear that God's justice might require that the wealth from "unrequited toil shall be sunk" and "every drop of blood drawn with the lash shall be repaid by another drawn with the sword."[180]

Individual compassion or a sense of social responsibility for less fortunate fellow men does not depend upon theories of guilt or unjustified benefits, but without such theories it is harder to justify compulsory exactions upon others. Nor do the others accept such exactions without resentment: some "find it just a bit ironic when they demand that we feel guilty for what their ancestors did to the blacks. . . ."[181] Moreover, specific compensatory activities may be opposed by the intended beneficiaries themselves—as in public opinion polls which have repeatedly shown a majority of blacks opposed to quotas.[182] So it is not clear that guilt-reduction activity is a net social gain. The reduction of guilt, or the expression of social and humanitarian concern, can take place through any number of voluntary organizations, which have in fact made historic contributions to the advancement of black Americans.[183]

The question of who is to pay compensatory costs often has a perverse answer where such costs are imposed through administrative or judicial processes which permit little or no effective feedback. If compensation were awarded in the generalized form of money, it might at least be possible to make the costs bear some relationship to ability to pay. But much of the compensatory activity takes the form of specific transfers in kind—notably, exemption from standards applied to other applicants for jobs, college admissions, etc. In this form, costs are borne disproportionately by those members of the general population who meet those standards with the least margin, and are therefore most likely to be the ones displaced to make room for minority applicants. Those who meet the standards by the widest margin are not directly affected—that is, pay no costs. They are hired, admitted, or promoted as if blacks did not exist. People from families with the most general ability to pay also have the most ability to pay for the kind of education and training that makes such performance possible. The costs of special standards are paid by those who do not. Among the black population, those most likely to benefit from the lower standards are those closest to meeting the normal standards. It is essentially an implicit transfer of wealth among people least different in nonracial characteristics. For the white population, it is a regressively graduated tax in kind, imposed on those who are rising but not those already on top.

Where racial specialness extends beyond the historic black-white dichotomy, the anomalies are compounded. Americans of Oriental ancestry are often included in special categories. Biology and history may provide some basis for this, but economics does not. Chinese-Americans and Japanese-Americans have long earned a higher income than white Americans. *One-fourth* of all Chinese employed in the United States are in the highest occupational category of professional and technical workers.[184] Historically, Orientals have in years past suffered some of the most extreme discrimination and violence seen in America.[185] Past discrimination in schooling, for example, is still visible in the high levels of illiteracy among older Chinese, so that despite the above average education of Chinese-Americans, they also have rates of illiteracy several times that of blacks.[186] No amount of favoritism to the son of a Chinese doctor or mathematician is going to "compensate" some elderly illiterate Chinese whose life has been restricted to working in a laundry or washing dishes in a restaurant.

The racial and ethnic mixture of the American population poses still more dilemmas for any attempt to establish *institutionalized* "special" treatment for race or ethnicity as defined in categorical terms. About half the total American population cannot identify their ethnicity, presumably because of its mixture.[187] About 70 percent of black Americans have some Caucasian ancestor(s),[188] and a leading social historian estimates the number of whites with some black ancestors in the tens of millions.[189] Trying to undo history in this population is like trying to unscramble an egg. Doing justice to individuals in our own time may be more than enough challenge.

CRIME

Criminal law is basically a process for transmitting and evaluating knowledge about the guilt or innocence of individuals suspected of crime. It is also a process for transmitting to actual and potential criminals effective knowledge of the costs of their crimes to others, and the willingness of those others to shift those costs back, in the form of punishments, to the criminals who created them.[190] There are costs to the transmission of knowledge of individual guilt or innocence to the legal system, costs to individual defendants caught up in that system, costs to convicted criminals, and of course costs to the victims of crimes and to the general public whose anxieties and precautions against crime are very real costs, whether expressed in money or not. Ideally, the sum of these costs is to be minimized—though not necessarily any one cost in isolation.

In an ideal legal system, the costs of determining guilt or innocence would be held close to the minimum costs of gathering information and determining its veracity to some acceptable level of probability—"beyond a reasonable doubt" in the case of guilt, and to whatever level of probability would socially justify dismissing charges or discontinuing the investigation if the defendant or suspect appeared to be innocent. Since these costs are positive—indeed, substantial—even an ideally functioning legal system would not wholly eliminate crime, but there would be some optimal quantity of crime[191] based on costs of knowledge, costs of precautionary measures, and the inconveniences imposed on innocent parties as a result of rules, arrangements, investigations, and suspicions incident to crime-prevention or crime-detection. While the concept of an "optimal" quantity of crime may be uncomfortable, it is also clear that no one is prepared to devote half the Gross National Product to stamping out every residual trace of gambling. Nor are we even prepared to reduce the murder rate at all cost—when that would mean such stringent administration of homicide laws and such low levels of proof required for conviction as to cause some physicians to avoid accepting some or all patients who might die while under their care. There would be no social gain from allowing thousands to perish needlessly for lack of timely medical care, in order to reduce murders by one hundred. Obviously, no one would advocate going to such extremes regarding gambling, murder, or any other crimes, but the point here is to indicate the reasons why—reasons that apply, to some degree, across a much wider range of situations.

In crime control, as in other social processes, decisions and evaluations must be incremental rather than categorical. It is pointless to argue that this or that action will or will not *stop* this or that crime.[192] Nothing short of capital punishment will stop even the individual criminals already caught and convicted, much less others, and no one is prepared to use capital punishment for all crimes. The balancing of social costs implied by incremental decision making on crime control includes costs to all parties, including criminals. Virtually no one is prepared to impose unlimited costs—penalties—for petty crimes or disproportionate penalties even for serious ones. Costs (penalties) are imposed on criminals to reduce the costs they impose on others. If a wrist slap would deter murder, then that would be the socially optimal punishment, in the sense of minimizing the total social costs associated with crime. The argument for some harsher punishment is that a wrist slap will not reduce murders as much, if at all. That is, minimizing the costs to criminals is not minimizing social costs but only externalizing more costs to victims.

Changes in the criminal law change the effectiveness with which knowledge can be transmitted to those deciding innocence or guilt, to criminals contemplating crime, and to the voting public assessing their experience and assessing the protection offered—or not offered—by the criminal justice system.

There are many sources of knowledge, and the behavior of legal authorities puts a higher or lower cost on its transmission or effectiveness. The simple knowledge that a crime has been committed can vary in its availability to the criminal justice system according to the costs imposed on victims, witnesses, or informants. The costs of reporting rape can obviously be increased or decreased substantially by the way police respond to rape victims, by the way opposing attorneys are permitted to cross-examine the victim in court, and by the likelihood that a convicted rapist will be either turned loose soon (perhaps to retaliate against the plaintiff or witnesses) or given a retrial on a technicality. In the landmark *Mallory* rape case,[193] for example, the retrial ordered on appeal was the same as an acquittal, because the victim could not bear to go through the emotional trauma again. The *abstract* knowledge of guilt—from the defendant's confession as well as the victim's accusation—was not socially *effective* knowledge. Rape is a dramatic and readily understood example of a crime whose very existence can be socially and effectively known only according to the costs imposed by the legal institutions' behavior. But the same principle applies more generally, and includes laws and practices regarding publication of the identity of informants or the addresses of plaintiffs and witnesses.

The interpretation and administration of rules of evidence also controls or restricts the flow of knowledge necessary to determine innocence or guilt. American law is unique in the extent to which it excludes evidence.[194] Evidence can be excluded either because it is considered qualitatively less certain than other evidence, or because of the procedures by which it was obtained. Information that is incrementally less certain is often treated as categorically nonexistent under "hearsay" exclusionary rules in Anglo-Saxon law, though the same quality of evidence could be heard in courts in other Western countries or in Japan.[195] "Hearsay" does not mean simply gossip, but includes many official documents whose authenticity and veracity are unchallenged.[196] In addition to directly reducing the flow of knowledge into the criminal justice system, Anglo-Saxon "hearsay" rules have been held "responsible for most of the procedural quibbling that takes up so much time in American and British courts."[197] By adding to court congestion and trial delay, it indirectly reduces the flow of knowledge in other cases as well.

One of the most important ways in which knowledge is screened out of the criminal justice system is either by excluding it from trial or reversing the conviction in the appellate courts because it was not excluded. Evidence acquired without following minutely prescribed procedures can also be excluded, without regard to how accurate, verifiable, or relevant it may be. The great fear behind this initially was that police would beat confessions out of innocent people, reducing the reliablity of the confession as well as being a crime in itself. But even after coerced confessions were ruled inadmissible, the Supreme Court went further to exclude independent evidence of guilt, if that evidence was found as a result of information obtained from a coerced confession. The meaning of "coercion" was also expanded from physical beatings to psychological pressures to "unnecessary" detention to police failure to describe all the suspect's legal options.[198] There may be enough independent evidence to convict a murderer, if his confession leads police to the scene of the crime, where they find the corpse, and the murder weapon bearing the defendant's fingerprints all over it—but *all* of this evidence must be discarded by the criminal justice system if the original confession was procedurally incorrect.[199] Even the British do not go nearly that far.

In short, the social costs of effective knowledge of guilt or innocence is multiplied by the restrictions placed on gathering the knowledge in the first place, and by the many ways of having the effectiveness of the knowledge cancelled by appellate courts. It is the same net result if costs of knowledge are directly tripled or if only one-third the knowledge gathered survives the screening processes involved in restrictive rules of evidence, procedural technicalities, and the exhaustion of witnesses through delays and retrials.

In criminal law, as in other social processes, there are inherent constraints of circumstances and human beings, and these constraints entail trade-offs. The repugnance and pain which a conscientious person feels at the thought of imprisoning or executing an innocent man, or letting a guilty sadistic murderer go scot-free back into society on a technicality, in no way removes the constraints or relieves the essentiality of trade-offs. The ideal of "a government of laws and not of men" implies an established process rather than *ad hoc* judgments of what is right in each case. Inherent in this are deviations between the particular consequences of a systemic process and the individual results most in accord with the principles that the process was meant to embody. The more effective the legal processes, the smaller are these deviations, but in any process conceived and carried out by human beings there will be deviations—and in some cases, extreme deviations. Legal systems try

272

to reduce these extreme deviations by allowing appellate courts to review cases. But to some extent this recreates the original dilemmas of trial court systems at the appellate court level.

If appellate courts are to be part of a coherent legal system, rather than arbiters armed with power to decide each case anew in whatever way they choose, then what is decided in one case must be part of a legal pattern applicable to other cases with similar objective factors involved. What is decided in extreme cases becomes a precedent for other cases. In this kind of social package deal, often "hard cases make bad law" for the future. For example, blatant racial bias in trials and sentencing in some cases in some states may cause the whole federal legal system to involve itself in the minute details of state courts in all states.[200] As a result, a white, Anglo-Saxon criminal caught in the act in California may go free because of legal procedures created when an innocent black was railroaded to jail by an all-white jury in Mississippi. Appellate courts can adjust the application of their decisions to some extent, but there are limits to how far this can go and still retain the rule of law and the role of appellate courts as rule-making organizations, rather than roving commissions with sovereign powers to decide each case as they please. This is neither a criticism nor a defense of appellate courts, but simply an indication of the momentous legal trade-offs involved.

The Constitution of the United States limits how far these trade-offs can go in one direction—that is, how high the cost can go for a criminal defendant, or even for a convicted criminal. There are no comparable limits on the costs which the legal system can impose on a crime victim seeking to prosecute the criminal. In the case of rape victims these costs are obvious not only for the victim, but also for the larger society, which has its own interests in keeping rapists off the street. But there are no victim's counterpart of the defendant's constitutional protections against double jeopardy, self-incrimination, or cruel and unusual punishment. In particular, the right to a speedy trial applies only to the defendant, not to the victim or to witnesses who can become exhausted, disgusted, fearful, or forgetful in crucial details as repeated trial delays stretch out for months or even years. Indeed, victims or witnesses may die or move out of state as legal processes drag on, quite aside from the financial losses imposed in taking off from work repeatedly to go to court for a trial that is again and again postponed at the defendant's request. Criminal lawyers are well aware of the advantages of sheer delay in wearing down plaintiffs and witnesses, or even a district attorney with a limited budget and limited time. In short, "due process" has a social cost, and that cost can—in particular cases—rise to levels which in effect negate the law in question. This may or may not be inherent in any form of constitutional law. What is important here is to be aware of such cost relationships—the central reality of trade-offs—as we turn from this brief static sketch of criminal law and appellate courts to a consideration of the *trends* in criminal law in recent decades. These include trends in crime rates, in arrest procedures, in trials, and appeals.

CRIME RATES

Crime rates per 100,000 persons more than doubled during the decade of the 1960s—whether measured by total crime, violent crime, or property crime.[201] How much of this represents an actual rise in crime, and how much an increased reporting of crime, remains a matter of controversy. However, there is general agreement among people who agree on little else, that murder has generally been accurately reported, since it is hard to ignore a corpse or someone's sudden disappearance.[202] Trends in this widely reported crime are also rising dramatically. Murder rates in large cities doubled in less than a decade between 1963 and 1971. The probability that someone living his whole life in a large city today will be murdered is greater than the probability of an American soldier in World War II being killed in combat.[203]

Crime is no more random than any other social activities. Murder rates in the big cities are more than four times as high as in the suburbs.[204] More than half of all serious crime in the United States is committed by youths from ten to seventeen years old.[205] Moreover, juvenile crime rates are increasing faster than adult crime rates.[206] The number of murders committed by sixteen-year-olds tripled in four years in New York City.[207]

These patterns have some bearing on popular explanations for crime. For example, crime has been blamed on "poverty, racism and discrimination"[208] and on "the inhumanity of our prisons."[209] As already noted, poverty and racial discrimination (whether measured in incomes, education, or segregation laws) were greater in the past, and their continuing effects are more apparent among older blacks than the younger. Crime, however, is greatest among youthful blacks[210] and hostility to police is greatest among *upper* income blacks.[211] As for harsh punishment as a source of repeated crimes, (1) those persons arrested and released or acquitted are rearrested more often than those that are imprisoned[212] and (2) the escalation of crime rates during the 1960s occurred while smaller and smaller proportions of people were going to prison—indeed while the conviction rate was falling[213] and the prison population was going down as the crime rate soared.[214] Insofar as poverty, discrimination, and imprisonment are variables believed to be correlated with crime rates, the evidence refutes the hypothesis. Insofar as these constitute an axiom, it is of course immune to evidence.

The level and trend of American crime rates may be put in perspective by comparison with those of other nations. Murder rates in the United States have been several times those in such comparable societies as those of Western Europe and Japan.[215] Robbery rates are also higher.[216] Crime rates in general are only moderately higher in the United States than in Europe,[217] but it is in the violent crimes that the difference between the U.S. and other countries is greatest. For example, New York, London, and Tokyo have comparable numbers of inhabitants (Tokyo the most), but there are eight times as many murders in New York as in Tokyo,[218] and fifteen times as many murders as in London.[219] Intertemporal comparisons show a rise in crime rates around the world[220]—with the notable exception of Japan. What is different about Japan may provide some factual basis for testing competing theories of crime control.

The rising murder rate in the United States is largely a phenomenon dating from the mid-1960s, and continuing to escalate in the 1970s[221]—a rise generally coinciding with the sharp dropoff in executions.[222] This rise in murder rates reversed a long-term *decline* in the murder rate in the United States. The absolute number of murders in American urban centers of 25,000 or more remained relatively constant from 1937 through 1957,[223] even though the population in such centers was growing rapidly over that span.[224] Urbanization, as such, apparently had not entailed rising murder rates. Demographic and socioeconomic changes in the population have been too gradual to account for the sudden reversal of a downward trend and its replacement by an escalating upward trend. The only apparent variable that has changed dramatically in the 1960s and 1970s has been the procedures and practices of the criminal law.

CRIMINAL LAW PROCEDURE

One of the basic questions about criminal law procedure is simply how much of it there is, in purely quantitative terms. In England, the longest criminal trial on record lasted forty-eight days.[225] In the United States, there have been criminal trials in which the selection of a jury alone has taken months.[226] In England the selection of a jury "usually takes no more than a few minutes.[227] A criminal trial length that would be "routine" in California[228] would be record-breaking in England. The British example is particularly appropriate, not only because of general similarities between the two countries but more particularly because American law grew out of British law, the two countries have similar notions of fairness, and England is not regarded as either a police state or a place where innocent defendants are railroaded to jail.

Delays in American courts did not just happen. A procedural revolution in criminal law was created by the Supreme Court in the 1960s—the decade when crime rates more than doubled. Much attention has been focused on the specifics of these procedural changes—warnings to suspects, restrictions on evidence, etc.—but it is also worth noting the sheer multiplicity of new grounds for delay at every stage of criminal procedure, from jury selection all the way to appeals to the Supreme Court.

Contrary to a long legal tradition, the Warren Court interpreted the Fourteenth Amendment as applying many federal rights and practices to the states in general, and the state courts in particular.[229] Quite aside from the question of whether this was justified constitutional interpretation, or even whether the specific federal practices were better or worse than existing state practices, this created dual channels of legal appeal, between which a defendant could go back and forth—repeatedly adjudicating each of numerous new rights in two whole systems of multiple courts. The lowest federal district judge could now overturn the decision of a state supreme court, and the federal courts in general now assumed jurisdiction over procedures used in state trial and appellate courts. Moreover, some of these newly discovered or newly created rights were made retroactive, so that a criminal could, for example, challenge prior convictions on grounds that the state court could not *prove* that they had supplied him with a lawyer, thirty years before the Supreme Court required them to supply him with a lawyer—or to keep records of such things.[230] Similarly, the Supreme Court's 1968 ruling that it was unconstitutional to allow a jury to hear the unedited confession of a codefendant was made retroactive, and was then used in 1969 to overturn a 1938 felony conviction in which that had happened.[231]

The increased litigation made possible by the decisions of the Warren Court was litigation over *procedures*—not guilt or innocence. Premeditated murderers, witnessed in the act, were able to continue appeals for more than a decade without even *claiming* to be innocent, but merely challenging legal procedure.[232] A murderer-rapist of an eight-year-old child, whose confession was corroborated by both evidence and other testimony, was set free by federal courts on procedural grounds—and the state courts forbidden to re-try him—even though his confession was found to be voluntary, the facts of the crime undisputed, and the evidence "overwhelming" in the judgment of the state supreme court.[233] Nor were these procedural matters anything as serious as police beatings or even threats, but turned instead on fine legal points on which appellate judges often divided four to three or five to four.

The social costs of the Warren Court's procedural changes were not simply those particular instances of freeing dangerous criminals which outraged the public, but also included an exponential increase in litigation which backed up *other* criminal cases and necessitated plea bargaining. The number of state prisoners applying for writs of *habeas corpus* in the federal courts increased from less than 100 in 1940 to more than 12,000 in 1970.[234] Nor were these cases newly discovered miscarriages of justice. A federal appellate judge observed:

For all our work on thousands of state prisoner cases I have yet to hear of one where an innocent man had been convicted. The net result of our fruitless search for a non-existent needle in the ever-larger haystack has been a serious detriment to the administration of justice by the states.[235]

A California appellate judge likewise observed:

It is with almost melancholy nostalgia that we recall how only five years ago it was possible to sustain a judgment of conviction entered in such a clear case of unquestionable guilt and to accomplish it without undue strain. Today, however, the situation is vastly changed.[236]

While the extent to which procedural complexities and ambiguities impede criminal justice processes may be unique to the United States, elements of this trend have spread beyond the American borders. Even though the British courts do not exclude illegally seized evidence, and will not turn a felon loose merely because of police failure to follow procedural rules,[237] there has been some movement in the direction of "the 'Americanization' of English criminal justice":[238] less chance of imprisonment,[239] more lenient sentencing,[240] more release into the community,[241] and activities described by their hoped-for results as "rehabilitation" programs. How much things have changed in England may be indicated by the fact that in the 1930s a murder conviction meant a two-out-of-three chance of execution within two months,[242] whereas in 1975 the death penalty was abolished.[243] Along with these American procedures have come American results—court congestion,[244] delayed trials,[245] and rising crime rates.[246]

British intellectuals, like their American counterparts, have been preoccupied with the presumed social causes of crime[247]—the "root causes" in American intellectual terminology. The usually presumed social "causes" of crime—poverty, unemployment, and broken homes—are wholly uncorrelated with the rise in crime in Britain. There has been no increase in poverty or broken homes there, and there has been a reduction of income inequality and a "virtually nonexistent" unemployment rate in Britain during the period of rapidly increasing crime rates.[248] The criminal justice system has simply become slower and more uncertain.

By contrast, the only major nation in which crime rates have been going down over the past generation is Japan, where more than 90 percent of all violent crimes lead to arrest and 98 percent of all defendants are found guilty. Plea bargaining is illegal in Japan,[249] as it is in many other countries.

The sentences are no greater in Japan,[250] but the chance of getting away scot-free are less. Various supposed causes of crime—television violence, urbanization, crowding—are at least as prevalent in Japan as in the United States.[251] There are, however, far more policemen per square mile in Japan than in the United States, though somewhat fewer per number of people.[252] There is no evidence, however, that Japan has discovered the "root causes" of crime, much less eliminated them—or, indeed, is putting forth much effort in that direction.

Both international and intertemporal comparisons indicate that criminal law procedures affect crime in the way that common sense suggests: punishment which comes quicker and/or with higher probability deters more than punishment that can be delayed or evaded. The tendency of the Supreme Court in the Warren era has been to expand the number and scope of the grounds on which criminals can appeal—delaying (and thereby diluting) a given punishment, reducing the probability of conviction for the actual offense (more plea bargaining) and reducing the probability of being convicted at all. The fact that guilt becomes largely irrelevant when the police do not follow specified procedures allows corrupt policemen to convey legal immunity to criminals by deliberately violating such procedures.[253] The cost of groundless appeals to the criminal is zero if he has a lawyer supplied by the state or by third-party-financed ("public interest") law firms. Even if he has to act as his own attorney, the costs are negligible if he is in jail with nothing else to do. The repugnant task of rationing justice is no less inescapable for its repugnance. Unless unlimited resources are available for criminal justice procedures—and congested courts imply that they are not—then one man's right to appeal means a sacrifice of someone else's right to a speedy trial and/or the sacrifice of innocent third parties victimized by the backlog of other criminals free on bail while awaiting trial in a congested court system.

In recent years criminal law procedures have often been viewed, not as social institutions for transmitting knowledge about guilt or innocence, but as arenas for contests between combatants (prosecution and defendants) whose prospects must be to some degree equalized. In particular, the power of the state is depicted as so disproportionate to that of the defendant that some kind of equalization is in order. There is even great concern for intracriminal equity—equalizing the prospects of criminals with varying sophistication to escape prosecution or conviction. If experienced criminals, gang members, and Mafiosi know how to "stonewall" police questions, then "elemental fairness"[254] requires that similar sophistication be supplied by the government to less sophisticated criminals as a precondition for a guilty verdict to stand up in the appellate courts.[255] To do otherwise, according to this view, is to "take advantage of the poor, the ignorant, and the distracted."[256] Thus, intracriminal equity supersedes criminal-victim equity in this formula—or rather, the second kind of equity is ignored. This is a special case of the "fair contest" approach, which emphasizes the great power of the government vis-à-vis the individual criminal. But to judge "power" by physical artifacts—numbers of officials, sums of money, quantity of weapons, etc.—is to ignore the relationship of those things to their intended objects. A motor that is far too powerful for a lawn mower may be grossly inadequate for a truck. The individual criminal need only be concerned with saving himself from conviction, while the government must safeguard a whole population from his acts and the acts of other criminals, and from the fears and precautions due to those acts. Empirically, the evidence is that criminals as a group are more than able to hold their own against the government. Few crimes in the United States lead to anyone's being imprisoned.[257]

Intracriminal equity, like any form of equity, is equity only along a given dimension and conflicts with equity along other dimensions. For example, if people are to be paid according to an equitable principle of how much effort they put into their work, that conflicts with sharing equitably in the employer's earnings, or receiving an equitable portion of total national output—quite aside from the conflict of equity in general with various economic and other principles. Intracriminal equity likewise cannot be extended indefinitely without conflicting with equitable considerations regarding the victims of crime or the public in general. However, no institutional mechanism forces federal appellate courts to weigh these other considerations. And because federal courts supersede all state courts, the latter—though elective and therefore subject to feedback—are bound by the federal precedent. In short, the only constraints on how far intracriminal equity can be carried are constraints the federal judges choose to impose on themselves. When a U.S. Attorney General and a Chief Justice of the Supreme Court both argue for judicial equalization of legal prospects as between less sophisticated criminals and more sophisticated criminals, so that "hardened underworld types" will not have an unfair advantage over "unwary"[258] or "distracted"[259] criminals, clearly intracriminal equity is a principle enjoying a vogue in high places. The principle has been extended well beyond the idea that a court must not create categorical inequities of its own to the idea that it must redress certain preexisting inequities in criminal endowments of sophistication in eluding the law. Since courts cannot equalize downward by reducing the cleverness of the most accomplished criminals, all that is left is to equalize upward by increasing the ability of less clever criminals to evade punishment for their acts—regardless of what that means in terms of equity to victims and the public.

Intracriminal equity extends even to groundless appeals. If privately paid lawyers make frivolous appeals based on unsubstantiated claims of "insanity," then a court-appointed attorney who fails to do so for his client has, in this view, denied the client his constitutionally guaranteed right to counsel[260]—a right expanded during the Warren Court years to mean free provision of counsel, whose conduct of the defense can then be retrospectively evaluated by appellate courts to insure that he attempted enough technicalities to satisfy their conception of "competent" representation. It is not that the appellate court actually found the defendant insane—or even regarded that as a likely possibility—but that they second-guessed the defense strategy of the court-appointed attorney and thought that was a tactic he might have tried. Such extrapolations and improvisations from the simple constitutional right to use a lawyer illustrate again the law of diminishing returns, and the tendency of unconstrained institutions to extend themselves past the point of counterproductive inputs from the standpoint of their mandated purpose—in this case, determining guilt or innocence and meting out justice.

PUNISHMENT

Trends in the punishment of criminals can be readily summarized: over the past generation, punishments for convicted criminals have become less common, less severe, and less honestly reported to the public. In the American legal system, punishment is less common than in the British legal system from which it evolved. California alone has six times as many robbers as England, but more people were in prison for robbery in England than in California.[261] On paper, the United States has "the most severe set of criminal penalties in its law books of any advanced Western nation,"[262] but they are seldom put into practice. Less severe penalties—that are actually enforced—have produced a long-term reduction of serious crime (including hard drug usage) in Japan, over the same decades during which American crime rates have been soaring. Studies in various American cities show that most *felons with prior convictions* are placed on probation rather than going to jail.[263]

Harsh penalties on paper and probation in practice are part of a more general pattern of duplicity. "Life" sentences in many states mean "eligibility for parole in three to five years."[264] "First offenders" include long-term criminals whose prior convictions are not technically admissible in court because of the age at which these crimes were committed. Supposedly successful "rehabilitation" programs have repeatedly been found on closer scrutiny to have been ineffective, or even counterproductive.[265] These are not *random divergences* between theory and practice. They are *systematic biases* overstating to the public what punishment is being applied or understating either the crime (reduced charges under "plea bargaining") or the nature of the criminal ("first offender"). Concurrent sentences mean that there are *no* sentences for additional contemporaneous crimes. Parole boards mean that even the few sentences handed out in court are grossly overstated. So-called "supervised" probation or parole consists of "a 10- or 15-minute interview once or twice a month"[266] between a criminal who is on his own otherwise and an official who, in two-thirds of felony probations, is responsible for more than one hundred cases at a time.[267]

These systematic biases in the transmission of knowledge insulate decision makers, advisers, and others who influence the criminal justice system from feedback from the actual experience of the public with the fruits of their decisions. Central to the duplicity and the insulation are vast differences between the beliefs of criminal law "insiders" and the public—and the determination on the part of insiders that public influence is to be minimized. It is a point of honor to have ignored "public clamor." In short, criminal law decision making is insulated from feedback, not only institutionally but ideologically. No insulation is ever perfect, so that public outrage in some egregious cases that happen to come to light has occasional effect on the law. Nevertheless, the history of trends in criminal law over the past generation is essentially the history of intellectual fashions among a small group of theorists in law and sociology. These fashions include several key premises: (1) punishment is morally questionable, (2) punishment does not deter, and (3) sentences should be individualized to the criminal rather than generalized from the crime.

The moral questionability of punishment derives from the premise that "vengeance" is a "brutalizing throwback to the full horror of man's inhumanity in an earlier time . . . "[268] This argument from location in time is buttressed by claims that a personified "society" itself causes crime. According to this theory, "healthy, rational people will not injure others,"[269] so that crime is the result of a social failure to create such people or to rehabilitate the criminal into becoming someone who "will not have the capacity—cannot bring himself—to injure another to take or destroy property."[270] Neither blueprints nor examples are provided. Moreover, these quotations are not from a sophomore term paper, but from a book widely hailed by legal scholars, practicing lawyers, and leading newspapers and magazines.[271] In a similar vein, Chief Justice Earl Warren found crime "in our disturbed society" to be due to "root causes" such as "slum life in the ghettos, ignorance, poverty" and even—tautologically—the illegal drug traffic and organized crime.[272] "Root causes" are prominently featured in this literature,[273] and confidently spoken of as if they were well-documented facts, rather than arbitrary assertions at variance with the empirical relationship between the rising crime rates and reduced poverty and discrimination. The idea that people are *forced* to commit crimes by bad conditions of one sort or another also ignores thousands of years of history during which kings and emperors, raised in the midst of luxury, committed the most brutal atrocities against their subjects.

The argument that punishment does not deter takes many forms. At the most primitive level, failure of punishment to deter is claimed on the ground that various crimes—or crimes in general—have not been categorically eliminated. From this standpoint, the very existence of crime is proof of the futility of deterrence, for "criminals are still with us."[274] By parallel reasoning, we could demonstrate the futility of food as a cure for hunger, since people get hungry again and again despite having eaten. An old joke has a small child decrying baths as futile because "you only get dirty again." Similar reasoning by a grown man who was also the top law enforcement officer in the country seems somewhat less humorous, though no less ridiculous.[275]

The meaningful issue is not categorical deterrence but the incremental effect of punishment on crime rates. It is easy to become bogged down in the question as to how much the environment is responsible for crime as compared to individual volitional responsibility. But even if we accept, for the sake of argument, that environment is largely responsible—or even solely responsible—it does not follow that punishment is futile, either incrementally or categorically. Punishment is itself part of the environment. The argument that environmental forces influence or control the incidence of crime in no way precludes punishment from being effective, though that theory has often been put forth for that purpose. This is ultimately an empirical rather than a philosophical question, but commitment to the social reform or "root causes" approach has meant that few legal or sociological theorists "are even willing to entertain the possibility that penalties make a difference."[276] Only in relatively recent years have there been a few serious statistical analyses designed to test the empirical question—and they have indicated that punishment does deter.[277]

Arguments for "individualizing" the punishment to the criminal, rather than generalizing punishment from the crime, presuppose a result rather than specifying a process. Whether or not such a result is desirable, the question must first be faced whether courts can in fact do it. Merely varying sentences is easy, but to do so in a manner related to the actual personalities of each criminal is neither easy nor necessarily even feasible. As noted in Chapter 2, formal institutions have great difficulty acquiring accurate knowledge about individual personalities. Everything in the criminal justice setting provides incentives for concealment and deception on the part of the criminal, his family and friends—i.e., those actually possessed of the fullest and most accurate knowledge. Banks tend to leave the financing of new small businesses to their founders and the founders' family and friends for similar reasons. Courts are not institutionally constrained from speculating about personality traits, the way banks are constrained by the prospect of financial losses, but the social costs of such speculation can be even greater when courts rely on either mechanical criteria or psychological guesswork to "individualize" sentences. Moreover, so-called "individualized" sentences in practice mean *reduced* sentences. No psychological findings or other evidence will legally justify life imprisonment or execution for a petty thief, no matter what deadly personality characteristics are uncovered. It is a wholly asymmetrical process, and should be judged for what it is—one more way of reducing or eliminating punishment.

What are the social costs of this asymmetrical process of sentence-reduction? Insofar as sentences are reduced (or eliminated) to match the presumed personality of each offender, they do not convey as clear or as definite a message as deterrence to others. Moreover, even to the individual criminal, they present punishment not as their fellow man's assessment of the seriousness of their crime, but as a happenstance deriving from the personality or mood of a particular judge, or the criminal's own performance in impressing or maneuvering with psychiatrists, psychologists, or probation or parole officials. The social costs also include still more delay introduced into the courts, while all sorts of information, "findings," and "recommendations" are assembled—a process that can go on for months, even in relatively simple cases where all this activity does not change the end result.

As in other cases of attempted "fine tuning" of social decisions, the question in criminal justice is not what decision we should make if we were God, but what decisions we can make effectively, given that we are only human, with all that that implies in terms of limitations of individual knowledge. Juvenile criminal sentencing is particularly subject to "individualizing" tendencies—in some states, it is solely the well being of the individual young criminal that can be legally taken into account in the disposition of his case—and it is perhaps revealing that it is here that the failure of the system is most apparent in especially rapidly escalating crime rates.

In the emotion-laden area of capital punishment, a recent study indicates several murders deterred for every execution.[278] This conflicts with an earlier and cruder study, and the reception of the two kinds of studies by legal and social theorists is revealing. The earlier capital punishment study, by Thorsten Sellin, compared states with and without death penalty laws on their books.[279] The later study, by Isaac Ehrlich, compared actual executions rather than laws seldom put into effect. Clearly it is the executions rather than the words in law books which constitute capital punishment, and the question of deterrent effects is a question about executions. It is Ehrlich's study of actual executions that shows a deterrent effect. Yet the earlier and cruder study continues to be cited as proof that capital punishment is ineffective as a deterrent, while the later study is either ignored or subjected to far more critical scrutiny than the earlier.[280] It is clear which conclusion is preferred by legal and social theorists, but the policy preferences of "experts" do not become empirical facts by consensual approval or by sheer repetition.

Virtually all researchers on both sides of the capital punishment controversy are agreed that there are problems inherent in the data[281] and problems inherent in the choice of statistical techniques to analyze the data.[282] The very definition of "murder" creates problems. Data are usually available on "homicide," which includes accidental vehicular homicide and negligent manslaughter as well as murder and nonnegligent manslaughter, and "records are not generally separated according to the type of homicide committed."[283] No one expects the death penalty for first-degree murder to deter automobile accident fatalities, which are also included in the data being analyzed. Moreover, the drastic decline and—in some years—total disappearance of executions over the past generation[284] creates statistical problems due to small (or nonexistent) samples of one of the variables. There has been no period of history with both good data on first-degree murder and also a substantial number of executions. Finally, the period in which the death penalty declined and virtually disappeared was also a period when the risk of *any* punishment was also declining. In short, there is no factual proof either way, despite the consensual dogma that capital punishment does not deter.

As in other policy areas, however, the question is not *what* should be decided, but *who* should decide what should be done. Courts have largely appropriated that legislative function under the guise of "interpreting" the Constitution. What is far more clear is that a declining incidence of punishment in general (and capital punishment in particular) over the past generation—but especially during the 1960s—has been accompanied by a rising rate of violent crime in general, and murder in particular. International comparisons buttress this conclusion and are also consistent with the conclusion that it is not the words on law books which constitute deterrence. American laws are among the most severe in the Western world in theory and the least applied in practice, and the United States has far higher rates of violent crime (especially murder) than countries with less severe laws that are applied more often. Various historic, cultural and other differences among nations make international comparisons more difficult, but it is significant that the spread of American legal theories and practices to other countries has been accompanied by American results in court congestion and rises in crime rates. The influence of legal and social theorists on criminal law practices has also spread beyond the United States, and these "experts" are apparently no more open to factual evidence counter to their consensual beliefs abroad than in the United States.[285]

Throughout the Western world, capital punishment has been either explicitly abolished or has dwindled to the vanishing point in practice. The United States was already part of the general pattern of a declining use of capital punishment when the Supreme Court in 1972 declared the death penalty unconstitutional as "cruel and unusual punishment" forbidden by the Eighth Amendment—in some instances.[286] Since the Eighth Amendment consists of only one sentence[287] and contains no exceptions, the *partial* outlawing of the death penalty is even more obviously a judicial improvisation than the decision itself. The fallacy of confusing decisiveness with exactness runs through much of the Supreme Court testimony and questioning as to what exactly was meant by "cruel and unusual."[288] What clearly was *not* meant was the death penalty. The Fifth Amendment, passed at the same time as the Eighth Amendment, recognized the death penalty and required only that "due process" precede it. The states which ratified both amendments had death penalty laws which they—and others—applied for almost two centuries before they were stopped by a five to four Supreme Court decision (with nine separate opinions) saying that it was unconstitutional in some circumstances. The particular circumstances that would make it unconstitutional have themselves varied, so that in practice death penalties are unconstitutional when a particular Supreme Court chooses to object to the procedures used to reach verdicts. It is, in effect, the laws and the verdicts which have been ruled unconstitutional, under the guise of ruling the punishment unconstitutional as "disproportionate to the offense" or as capriciously applied—neither of which are characteristics of punishment itself.

Several arguments have been emphasized by opponents of the death penalty: (1) it is immoral for the state to deliberately kill, (2) capital punishment does not deter, (3) errors are irrevocable, (4) the application of the death penalty has been arbitrary and capricious in practice, and (5) blacks have been disproportionately overrepresented among those executed, showing the racial bias of the system.

The immorality of execution is based on a parallel between the first-degree murderer's premeditated killing of his victim and the law's subsequent premeditated killing of the murderer. In this view, we must "put behind us the notion that the second wrong makes a right. . . ."[289] The two events are certainly parallel as physical actions, but if that principle determines morality, it would be equally immoral to take back by force from a robber what he had taken by force in the first place. It would be equally immoral to imprison someone who had imprisoned someone else. It is another case of the physical fallacy—regarding things which are physically the same as being the same in value; in this case, moral value. By this standard a woman who uses force to resist rape would be as immoral as the would-be rapist. Insofar as he is successfully beaten off, all that has happened physically is that two people have been fighting each other. No one would regard the physical equivalence as moral equivalence. When the physical parallel involves human life, the stakes are higher, but the principle does not change. The morality of execution does not depend upon physical parallels.

Sometimes the claim of immorality is based on a supposedly inadvertent revelation of shame by the unwillingness of most people—even advocates of capital punishment—to witness an execution.[290] But most people would not want to witness an abdominal operation, and yet no one regards that as evidence of immorality in such operations. Nor would a philanthropist who donated money to a hospital to advance such operations be considered a hypocrite if he declined an invitation to watch the surgery. Such arguments are even more difficult to take seriously, when the very same proponents claim that it was immoral for people to watch executions when they did,[291] and that it is immoral for us not to watch them now.[292]

The argument that capital punishment does not deter glosses over some important distinctions. Any punishment may deter either by incapacitating the criminal (temporarily or permanently) from repeating his crime, or by using him as an example to deter others. Clearly capital punishment incapacitates as nothing else. The obviousness of this in no way reduces its importance. It is especially important because the attempt to incapacitate by so-called "life sentences" means nothing of the sort, and can mean that a first-degree murderer will be back on the street within five years legally, and of course sooner than that if he escapes. He can also kill in prison. Arguments about the supposedly low recidivism rates of murderers in general are beside the point. They would be relevant if the issue were whether all murderers must always be executed regardless of circumstances. But that is not the law at issue, nor have American judges and juries followed any practice approaching that. What is at issue is whether courts shall have that option to apply in those particular cases where that seems to be the only thing that makes sense.

The irrevocable error of executing the wrong person is a horror to anyone. The killing of innocent people by released or escaped murderers is no less a horror, and certainly no less common. The recidivism rate among murderers has never been zero, nor can the human error in capital cases ever be reduced to zero. *Innocent people will die either way.* If there were some alternative which would prevent the killing of innocent people, virtually anyone would take it. But such an alternative does not come into existence because we fervently wish it, or choose to assume it by closing our eyes to the inherent and bitter trade-off involved. Trying to escape these inherent constraints by arguments that "a society which is capable of putting a man on the moon" is "capable of keeping a murderer in jail and preventing him from killing while there"[293] is using an argument that would make us capable—seriatim, at least—of accomplishing almost anything we wanted to in any aspect of life. It is the democratic fallacy run wild.

Because executions take place in only a fraction of the convictions for capital crimes, opponents of capital punishment have claimed that the condemned were chosen "capriciously," "freakishly," "arbitrarily," or at random, or with no logic or justice.[294] Justice, of course, has many dimensions, of which intracriminal equity is only one; nor is it obvious why intracriminal equity should be the sole or overriding consideration. If this argument were taken seriously and applied seriously, it would be impossible to punish any criminals for any crime, in a system with different juries—which is to say, in all possible legal systems, as long as human beings are mortal. Barring a single, immortal, jury to hear all criminal cases, intracriminal equity can never be carried to perfection, but only into regions of negative returns, in any system of justice concerned also with other kinds of equity, including victims and the public.

To argue that the degree of intracriminal equity can be directly deduced from numbers and percentages is to repeat the fallacy in "affirmative action" cases of presupposing that numbers collected *at* a given institution are caused *by* that institution. If people differ in the quantity or manner of their crimes, they will differ also in their conviction and sentencing statistics, even if judges and juries were all totally impartial and just. We know that such perfection is not to be found among judges and juries, any more than among other groups of human beings, and in particular cases—blacks facing all-white juries in the South being the classic example—the reality has sometimes been very remote from the ideal. However, this is based on history and observations, not on the statistics cited as evidence and used to give it all a "scientific" appearance. If statistics, as such, are to be taken seriously, then a much ignored statistic must also be included: more black people are murdered than whites—that is, there are more black murder victims *in absolute numbers* than white murder victims,[295] even though blacks are only about 12 percent of the population. Moreover, murder is usually *not* across racial lines, involving as it often does family members and friends. Against that background, the statistic that blacks are overrepresented among those executed assumes a different dimension, since blacks are also grossly overrepresented among the victims. A recent study in the north found persons who commit murder about equally likely to be executed, whether they are black or white.[296] It is one thing to lament historic injustices; it is another to use them to misrepresent current empirical data.

Even in racially homogeneous societies there are undoubtedly differences in murder rates among very different social groups. Indeed, in the United States there are vast differences in murder rates between men and women.[297] Even in the absence of such evidence, however, anyone with any humility or sense of common humanity must recognize that, if raised under sufficiently bad conditions—taught no difference between right and wrong, and growing up in an environment where violence was not only accepted but admired— that he, too, could have grown up into the kind of person with whom no society can cope. In some ultimate ethical sense, "there but for the grace of God go I." It would be inexcusable even to shoot a mad dog if we knew how to catch him readily and safely, and cure him instantly. We shoot mad dogs only because of our own inherent limitations as human beings. There is no need to apologize for this—and certainly no need to pretend to more knowledge than we have, whether to "rehabilitate" a murderer or to eliminate "root causes" of crime. We do not play God when we act—as we must— within our limitations. We play God when we pretend to an omniscience and a range of options we do not in fact possess.

The notion that the death penalty is applied with caprice—as distinguished from bias—is an argument from ignorance. Observers do not know why some juries decided one thing and another jury decided something else. Since there is no institutional provision for juries to articulate their reasons— much less coordinate the articulation of one jury's findings with those of other juries—the absence of such a pattern is hardly surprising. To say that an observer does not see a pattern is not to say that there is no pattern. A motorist driving down a highway or through town may see no pattern in the location of hamburger strands, but an executive in the headquarters of McDonald's or Burger King might be able to show him that these locations are by no means random or capricious. Indeed, the mark of a specialist in any field is the ability to discern patterns which escape common observation. For many areas of human experience, there are no specialists or experts because no one is prepared to invest the time and effort needed to discover patterns in those areas. In an area such as jury verdicts, where reasons would be difficult to accurately articulate, where they are not required to be articulated, and where there are indeed restrictions on such articulation in public, to consider the absence of an apparent pattern among juries a sign of "freakish" decisions and arbitrary choices is the arrogance of asserting that what one does not discern does not exist. And to make that the basis of a constitutional ruling is to impose the arrogance of an elite on the rest of the country as "the law of the land."

CONSTITUTIONAL INTERPRETATION

Over and beyond questions of the wisdom, effectiveness, or efficiency of legal decisions regarding free speech, race, crime, and other vital concerns, is a larger question of the role of law, and particularly of "a government of laws and not of men." Considering the centuries of human suffering, struggle, and bloodshed to escape arbitrary tyranny, it is hardly surprising that there should be profound anxiety about the erosion or circumvention of that ideal. At sporadic intervals in history, the Supreme Court of the United States has been the center of storms of controversy, involving not only the merits of particular decisions, but also the fear that its role of constitutional interpretation was being expanded to judicial policy making—representing a threat to the very rule of law which it is supposed to epitomize. Such apprehensions go back to *Marbury v. Madison* in 1803, which established the Supreme Court's power to invalidate the laws of Congress as unconstitutional, and have surfaced again in such cases as the *Dred Scott* decision in 1857, the "court packing" controversy of the 1930s and *Brown v. Board of Education* in 1954. But while modern controversies surrounding the Supreme Court are not historically unique, what has been unique is the frequency, scope, and sustained bitterness of controversy engendered by a whole series of court decisions reaching into every area of American society. What has also been unique is that Warren Court partisans—notably in the law schools—have not only accepted but advocated judicial policy making as a Supreme Court function, urging it to more openly pass judgment on the wisdom and morality of congressional and presidential actions, under broadly conceived constitutional "values" rather than narrowly explicit constitutional rules.[298]

The issues involved in controversies over constitutional interpretation reach beyond the American legal system to questions about social processes and human freedom in general. The extent to which it is possible for central decision makers to wisely foresee and control the consequences of their decisions in a complex social process is seen very differently by those who want the court to act boldly from the way it is seen by those who want the court to construe the Constitution as a set of specific rules, interpreted as closely as possible to the sense in which they were written.[299] The extent to which either of these modes is desirable depends also on the value assigned to the freedom of the many as against the presumed wisdom of the few—though the latter presumption has itself been seriously challenged,[300] and the earlier discussion in this chapter may at least raise some questions in that regard. Finally, the substantive content of Supreme Court decisions has obviously influenced positions taken by observers or critics. Some Warren Court partisans have sweepingly dismissed its critics as "segregationists and security-mongers,"[301] "military fanatics,"[302] "reactionary interests,"[303] "bigots,"[304] or "crackers."[305] But historically, opponents of sweeping judicial interpretation have varied across the political spectrum, and in the wake of the *Dred Scott* decision, its opponents were among the strongest advocates of the cause of blacks, notably Thaddeus Stevens.[306] Even in our own time, severe critics of the Warren Court have included men who opposed racial segregation years before *Brown v. Board.*[307] Indeed, as the court pushed further and further into judicial activism, some of its own early partisans, such as Alexander Bickel, began to question its basic philosophy, and found themselves being heaped with the kind of scorn[308] which they had once poured onto others.[309] Even a dedicated civil rights lawyer who had braved the dangers of Mississippi violence[310] was denigrated as a sellout when he later questioned busing.[311] Legal insurgency has exhibited the same kind of pattern found in other forms of insurgency.

The constitutional provisions which provided the point of departure for the legal revolution of the Warren Court were the "due process" clauses of the Fifth and Fourteenth Amendments, and the "equal protection" clause of the latter. Those who favor "strict construction" of the Constitution find these technical legal phrases to have limited and highly specific meanings,[312] while those who favor "judicial activism" find them to be phrases which "were designed to have the chameleon's capacity to change their color with changing moods and circumstances."[313]

JUDICIAL ACTIVISM

The case for judicial latitude or activism in interpreting the Constitution rests on several assertions: (1) the specific application of constitutional generalities inherently requires judgments, including value judgments,[314] (2) the original meaning of intent of constitutional clauses are often lost in the mists of time, or were never intended to be very specific in the first place,[315] (3) even when the original, historical meaning is discernible, it need not be blindly accepted as against later insights and experience, (4) courts are in a better position than are legislative or executive institutions to judge the morality or the consequences of broad social principles,[316] (5) courts are "the least dangerous branch" of government because they lack the power of arms or money,[317] and (6) courts are a last resort for achieving social goals not achievable in other institutions.[318] These claims will be considered in order.

The limitations of language alone require some use of judgment in interpreting any set of rules, including the Constitution. At various times value judgments may also need to be made in finely balanced cases or when constitutional provisions conflict in a particular application. Virtually no one on either side of this controversy denies either of these points, though some proponents of judicial activism have set up as a straw man "literalists" who are "wedded" to "ever-irresistible simplicities."[319] But because certain inputs (judgments, value judgments) into the decision-making process are incrementally productive in some cases does not mean that they are categorically necessary or desirable in all cases or in general. An appellate court may be compelled to resort to these inputs in particular cases, but that in no way means that the Supreme Court has a general mandate to "evolve and apply"[320] such principles of its own as it finds "rational" or in the "spirit" of constitutional "values." Although the view that it does takes on an air of modernity, it is in fact quite old. Such ideas were set forth—and rejected—in the nineteenth century. In 1873 the Supreme Court declared that "vague notions of the spirit of the Constitution" are no basis on which to declare void "laws which do not square with those views," and the "spirit" of a constitution "is too abstract and intangible for application to courts of justice, and is, above all, dangerous as a ground on which to declare the legislation of Congress void by the decisions of a court."[321] The idea of applying the spirit or values instead of rules is not new. What is new is the extent to which the tendency to do so has been indulged. It rests ultimately on the non sequitur that what is necessary in some cases is authorized, justified, or beneficial as a general principle. It is as if an argument for the existence of justifiable homicide as a legal category proved that laws against first-degree murder were unnecessary.

The above argument that the Supreme Court *should* abandon the original meaning of the constitutional rules is often supplemented with the claim that it *cannot* follow the original meanings of those rules because they are too vague and imprecise, or their original meaning has somehow been lost in history. However, there are voluminous, detailed, verbatim records of the debates preceding the adoption of the Constitution and of its various amendments, so sheer lack of historical materials is not a real problem. The difficulties of ascertaining the original meaning or intention of constitutional provisions often turns on what can be called "the precisional fallacy"—the practice of asserting the necessity of a degree of precision exceeding that required for deciding the issue at hand. Ultimately there is no degree of precision—in words or numbers—that cannot be considered inadequate by simply demanding a *higher* degree of precision. If someone measures the distance from the Washington Monument to the Eiffel Tower accurately to a tenth of a mile, this can be rejected as imprecise simply by requiring it in inches, and if in inches, requiring it in millimeters, and so on *ad infinitum*. On the other hand, even a vague request by an employer for an employment agency to send him a "tall" man may be enough for us to determine that the agency has disregarded his instructions when it sends him a man who is 4 feet 3 inches tall. The vagueness of "tall" might be enough to cause interminable discussions about men who are 5 foot 11 or 6 foot 1, but if in the actual case at hand the man is "short" by any common standard, then vagueness is a red herring for that particular case.

The precisional fallacy is often used polemically. For example, an apologist for slavery raised the question as to where precisely one draws the line between freedom and involuntary servitude, citing such examples as divorced husbands who must work to pay alimony.[322] However fascinating these where-do-you-draw-the-line questions may be, they frequently have no bearing at all on the issue at hand. *Wherever* you draw the line in regard to freedom, to any rational person slavery is going to be on the other side of the line. On a spectrum where one color gradually blends into another, you cannot draw a line at all—but that in no way prevents us from telling red from blue (in the center of their respective regions). To argue that decisive distinctions necessarily require precision is to commit the precisional fallacy.

In the law, the question is not precisely what "due process" or other constitutional terms mean in all conceivable cases, but whether it *precludes* certain meanings in a given case. No one knows *precisely* the original meaning or boundaries of the constitutional ban on "cruel and unusual punishment"— but it is nevertheless clear from history that it was never intended to outlaw capital punishment. Therefore its "vagueness"[323] is not *carte blanche* to substitute any standard that Supreme Court justices happen to like. In the same vein, Chief Justice Earl Warren's remark in *Brown v. Board of Education* about the "inconclusive nature" of the Fourteenth Amendment's history "with respect to segregated schools"[324] confused the crucial point that there was *no* evidence that the writers of the Amendment intended to outlaw any kind of segregation, and much evidence that social policy issues were outside the scope of the Amendment.[325] Because we do not know *precisely* what the boundaries of the Fourteenth Amendment are does not mean that we cannot know that certain things are outside those boundaries. A border dispute between Greece and Yugoslavia does not prevent us from knowing that Athens is in one country and Belgrade in another. Decisiveness is not precision.

The precisional fallacy—the confusion of decisiveness with exactness— runs through the literature advocating judicial activism: the Constitution lacks "precision" or is not "exact,"[326] and is "muddy"[327] or "clothed in mystery."[328] The self-serving nature of "convenient vagueness" was exposed by Felix Frankfurter long before he became a Supreme Court Justice. The question he asked was "'convenient' for whom and to what end?"[329] While genuine agnosticism might be associated with caution, tolerance, or indecisiveness in the area of uncertainty, judicial avowals of agnosticism are frequently preludes to revolutionary changes in the interpretation of the Constitution. Even some supporters of judicial activism recognize the judicial tendency "to resort to bad legislative history" as an excuse to reinterpret the law.[330] A fictitious legislative history may even be fabricated out of whole cloth, as when the Supreme Court majority in *Bakke* claimed that Congress had not considered "reverse discrimination" when writing the Civil Rights Act of 1964,[331] even though it is a matter of record that reverse discrimination issues came up again and again during the debates.[332] Much of what has been done under the claim of vagueness has been directly counter to intentions that were quite clear as regards those particular interpretations, regardless of how unclear it might have been on other things. It is the kind of judicial approach that has been called "statesmanlike deviousness"[333] and "dissimulation" that is "unavoidable"[334] by a partisan of judicial activism and "merely window dressing"[335] by a critic who considers it "a Marxist-type perversion of the relation between truth and utility."[336]

More fundamental than the question as to whether original constitutional meanings and intentions can be discerned is the question *whether* those meanings and intentions should be sought and followed as rules for present-day judicial decisions. Admirers of judicial activism emphasize the need for "the evolution of principles in novel circumstances,"[337] that the Constitution is "a complex charter of government, lookng to unforeseeable future exigencies"[338] and virtually "an invitation to contemporary judgment."[339] The framers of the Constitution "did not believe in a static world"[340] or in a constitution "forever and specifically binding,"[341] and we must use "our own reasoned and revocable will not some idealized ancestral compulsion."[342] Therefore we must "update the Constitution"[343] to "keep the Constitution adjusted to the advancing needs of time."[344] In this context, the original interpretations of the framers of the Constitution are merely "artifacts of verbal archeology"[345] and to take them seriously is a "filiopietistic notion"[346] which would allow the founders of the republic "to rule us from their graves."[347]

As in the case of precision, so in the case of change, a great amount of effort (and airs of "realism") go as into arguing something that is both obvious and irrelevant to the conclusion actually reached, in the situations in which it is applied. To argue about "change" in generalized terms is to argue with oneself, for no sane person denies change since the writing of the Constitution. The question is—what kind of change: technological, verbal, philosophic, geographical, demographic, etc., and in what *specific* way does the change affect a *particular* constitutional provision or its application? This the activists shy away from. Clearly there are technological changes, such as electronic listening devices, which raise questions about the constitutional right to privacy in a context unforeseen by the writers of the Constitution. But the great controversies raging around the Warren Court's judicial activism have involved things that have existed for hundreds or thousands of years—the death penalty, the segregation of racial groups (the very word "ghetto" derives from the Jewish experience in centuries past), the arrest of criminals, the power of bureaucracy (both the Roman Empire and ancient China developed stifling bureaucracy), the gerrymandering of political districts, and the different weighting of votes. In this particular context, the constant reiteration of the word "change" is little more than a magic incantation. It is hard to imagine why the writers of the Constitution would have set up a congress or a president as decorative institutions if they thought there would be nothing for them to *do* in meeting the evolving needs of the nation. Incantations about "change" cannot drown out the central question in any social process—not *what* is to be done, but *who* is to decide what is to be done, and under what incentives and constraints? This question is at the heart of constitutional government, and no amount of insistence that *something* be done—or that something *new* be done—can be allowed to obscure it.

Words and "original intentions" become important as constraints—not as historical or archaeological artifacts, nor as pious ways of showing reverence for the Founding Fathers. Knowledge costs are crucial in conveying "the law of the land" across a vast and diverse nation, and through time across the centuries. What is crucially different about the *original* meaning of a given permutation of words in the Constitution (compared to alternative meanings that might accord just as well with a dictionary or a grammar book) is that that particular meaning has been documented, reiterated, analyzed and diffused throughout a vast decision-making network, and major public and private commitments made within the framework of that meaning. Frameworks sometimes have to be changed despite enormous losses, but the issue is *who* is to decide when and how. Shall it be elected officials subject to feedback from those who actually pay the many costs of changes in the social framework, or shall it be an appointed judiciary influenced only by those particular viewpoints to whom it is arbitrarily responsive (known as "moral conscience") and arbitrarily oblivious to other views (known as "public clamor")? Shall the change be made openly, weighing the costs and benefits in the light of all the knowledge and experience diffused among all the people, or shall it be accomplished by verbal sleight-of-hand in the Supreme Court chambers and in the light of the constricted experience of nine individuals? Important as these issues are in particular constitutional decisions, they are truly momentous when considering a general *policy* of judicial activism which throws doubt over the whole framework of laws, not merely those particular laws arbitrarily changed by judicial fiat. The "above the law" thinking implicit in judicial activism can also spread beyond the courts to other branches of government, as the Watergate episode illustrates. The very rhetoric of a "flexible" constitution which can be interpreted "in the light of modern needs" was used in the Nixon inner circle.[348] The extralegal transfer of the constitutional war-making power from Congress to the president, so bitterly resented during the Vietnam War, was in the same tradition. The selective indignation of the press and the intellectual community generally to these very similar usurpations for very different purposes is part of the environment within which judicial activism flourishes.

When it is not deemed sufficient to simply glide from the need for "change" to an assumption that courts are the chosen vehicles of change, arguments are advanced that courts are either the best or the only governmental institutions capable of making a certain necessary social change. In this approach, evolving social morality replaces explicit constitutional rules, as the court "makes value choices under the broad provisions" of the Constitution,[349] and this is deemed "a principled process"[350] of judicial decision making because judges are not simply making subjective rulings or even deciding issues *ad hoc*,[351] but are following some general rule, one sensed in society rather than found in the explicit language of a constitution. Even a justice so identified with "judicial restraint" as Felix Frankfurter reflected this view. Although Justice Frankfurter rejected any idea that he would "sit like a kadi under a tree dispensing justice according to considerations of individual expediency," he could still say that he was enforcing "society's opinion" rather than his "private view" and that society's opinion was the relevant standard "enjoined by the Constitution."[352] To sense the evolving social morality, Frankfurter felt that a judge should have "antennae registering feeling and judgment beyond logical, let alone quantitative, proof."[353] In this vision of judicial restraint, as further expressed by Frankfurter's former law clerk, Alexander Bickel, the court which is liberated from the explicit constraints of the written Constitution judicially restrains itself to be the mouthpiece of evolving social morality and makes "experiential judgment" on the state of society in making its rulings.[354]

It may seem strange that an institution deliberately insulated from the popular feedback which constrains the legislative and executive branches of government should choose to adopt that constraint for itself and to put it in place of the explicit constraints of the written Constitution. However, as in the case of the argument from precision or "change," this is simply not quite ingenuous. The judicially-restrained court is not binding itself to respond to the general public at large, by any means. Although there is some talk that the Supreme Court "represents the national will against local particularism"[355] the judiciary is more often spoken of by exponents of judicial activism as an "educational institution"[356] a "defender of the faith"[357] and "a leader of opinion, not a mere register of it."[358] In short, the court is to be in the vanguard of moral change, able to act when other institutions run by elected officials are constrained by an amorphous and somewhat tainted entity called political "reality," which among other things, makes amending the Constitution difficult. What all these lofty and vague phrases boil down to is that the court can impose things that the voters don't want and the Constitution does not require, but which are in vogue in circles to which the court responds. Paradoxically, these are called "democratic" things in terms of what people would, should, or ultimately will want, though perhaps "counter-majoritarian" at a given time.[359] The court is to cut itself off from both the words of the past and the public beliefs of the present and be general (principled) rather than *ad hoc* in its decisions. Thus, this approach can, with statesmanlike balance, reject the notion of direct, arbitrary, *ad hoc* rule by courts,[360] and the limited role of interpreting constitutional rules.

Perhaps the most telling commentary on this vision is that its most eloquent exponent, Alexander Bickel, turned against it after he saw it in action for a few years.[361] Instead of glorying in the courts' freedom to shape events, the later Bickel found it "a moral duty" to "obey the manifest constitution, unless it is altered by the amendment process it itself provides for."[362] Judicial amendment by "interpretation" and "educating" society were no longer envisioned, and the "benevolent quota" to which he had been sympathetic earlier[363] was now seen as "a divider of society, a creator of castes" and "all the worse for its racial base."[364] The events of the Watergate era were merely "the last straws" of a "results" oriented way of thinking that went back to the Warren Court.[365]

Ironically, the much-disdained "original intentions" of the framers of the Constitution foresaw the problems which the twentieth-century sophisticates had to discover from hard experience. Thomas Jefferson regarded judicially activist judges as a "subtle corps of sappers and miners" of the foundations of the American form of government,[366] who would concentrate power in the federal government, because that would "lay all things at their feet. . . . "[367]

DUE PROCESS

The Constitution of the United States twice declares that a person shall not be "deprived of life, liberty, or property, without due process of law"—either by the federal government (Fifth Amendment) or by state governments (Fourteenth Amendment). According to Alexander Hamilton, "the words 'due process' have a precise technical import, and are only applicable to the process and proceedings of the courts of justice; they can never be referred to an act of the legislature."[368] At the very least, the two fateful words already had a long history in Anglo-Saxon law as of the time they were first placed in the American Bill of Rights in 1791.[369] An even longer history of arbitrary power—of lands and even lives confiscated by royal or imperial decrees, and of heads cut off by peremptory order—lend momentous importance to the requirement that only prearranged legal procedures may deal with the fundamental rights of individuals. Centuries of struggle and bloodshed lay behind those two words.

The first historic attempt to make "due process" mean something more than adherence to legal procedures occurred in the *Dred Scott* case in 1857. The Supreme Court declared that "an Act of Congress which deprives a citizen of the United States of his liberty or property merely because he came himself or brought his property into a particular Territory of the United States, and who had committed no offense against the laws, could hardly be dignified with the name of due process of law."[370] Here the issue was not whether regularized *procedures* had been followed in the passage or administration of the law, but whether the *substance* of the legislation was valid. In many other very different issues, the battle would be joined again and again over the next century as to whether "procedural due process" was enough to satisfy the constitutional requirement, or whether the Supreme Court should also consider "substantive due process"—i.e., pass judgment on the validity of the substance of duly passed laws and duly established judicial proceedings.

The first historic judicial activist interpretation of "due process" as calling for Supreme Court approval of the *substance* of duly enacted legislation declared that property—a slave named Dred Scott—would be taken without due process of law if the slave were freed simply because he had been transported into a territory where Congress had outlawed slavery under the Missouri Compromise. Therefore it was ruled that it would be unconstitutional to set him free. The easy assumption that judicial activism is on the side that twentieth-century liberals regard as moral or socially forward-looking does not square with the history of the due process clause.

There was an historically brief respite from the "substantive due process" interpretation after the Supreme Court in 1873 refused to consider the substantive merits of a state-created slaughterhouse monopoly in Louisiana, on grounds that to rule on the substantive merits "would constitute this court a perpetual censor upon all legislation of the states."[371] It continued to resist the efforts of those unsuccessful elsewhere to use the Supreme Court to review the substantive justice of lower court decisions for "the merits of the legislation on which such a decision may be founded."[372] However, less than two decades later, a new Supreme Court declared in 1887 that it would look beyond "mere pretenses" to "the substance of things."[373] By the turn of the century, the era of "substantive due process" was launched—in which the Supreme Court repeatedly invalidated as unconstitutional laws regulating businesses or working conditions. The "substantive due process" era lasted longer than the Warren Court era. It was, of course, lamented in retrospect by those who supported the Warren Court's activism.

Courts in the "substantive due process" era—roughly 1905 to 1937—regarded property not as simply the physical things themselves, but as the options pertaining to those things, and recognized that to destroy options was exactly the same as confiscating property—even though the physical objects as such might be left in the possession of the owners. The economic validity of their reasoning is demonstrated perhaps most dramatically in the case of New York City rent-controlled buildings, whose value is often reduced to negative levels (note abandonment despite the risk of legal penalties), by simply reducing the landlord's options, while leaving him in sole possession of the physical structure itself. Conversely, working men possessing no physical property nevertheless had options of employment alternatives, and to reduce these alternatives was also considered by the Supreme Court to be a deprivation of property in violation of the Constitution.[374] The economic reasoning is as valid here as in the case of business property, for it is essentially the same principle that property rights are basically options rather than physical things. A more fundamental constitutional question regarding the Supreme Court's role in the "substantive due process" era was whether the protection of property under the Fifth and Fourteenth Amendments required the courts to monitor the economic substance of legislation. In short, the economic argument shows only that there has in fact been a confiscation of property, while the legal question is—was it under due process of law? Later decisions repudiating economic "substantive due process" either deny or sidestep the confiscation of property.

Post-1937 Supreme Court decisions somewhat ostentatiously cited decisions of the economic "substantive due process" era as examples of what it was *not* going to do.[375] Paradoxically, it was Justice William O. Douglas, a leading judicial activist, who wrote opinions sweepingly rejecting the use of "notions of public policy"[376] and declared that "we do not sit as a super-legislature to weigh the wisdom of legislation."[377] The apparent paradox turns on the addition of clauses restricting this judicial restraint to areas of "economic and social programs,"[378] "the business-labor field,"[379] or "business, economic, and social affairs,"[380] or "business and industrial conditions."[381] In short, a constitutional double standard was created by the court, relieving itself of the burden and the political responsibility for liberal social legislation, while pioneering in new judicial activism in criminal law, civil rights, and political power areas. Far from signalling a reduction in Supreme Court inquiry into the substance of "due process," it marked the expansion of such substantive issues on an unprecedented scale. "Due process" became the phrase by which federal restrictions—both explicit constitutional provisions and judicial extrapolations—were imposed on *state* courts and *state* law enforcement agencies,[382] in defiance of the Constitution and its judicial interpretations for nearly two hundred years. The exclusion of evidence,[383] the requirement of government paid defense lawyers,[384] restrictions on questioning suspects,[385] on search warrants,[386] on confessions,[387] and even the desegregation of the District of Columbia schools[388] and the nullification of Connecticut's anticontraception law,[389] were all based on substantive rather than procedural "due process." Only the *phrase* "substantive due process" had been stricken from judicial interpretation.

SUMMARY AND IMPLICATIONS

Trends in American law in the twentieth century—and especially in the Warren Court era—have included (1) a growing volume of law and litigation in general, and especially of laws and litigation growing out of decisions made by institutions insulated from feedback—especially administrative agencies and the federal judiciary, (2) a changing role of appellate courts from defining the boundaries of other institutions' discretion to second-guessing the substance of the decisions made by those other institutions, and (3) an ever more apparent social partisanship, as distinguished from biased principles, in applying the law.

Insulation from feedback takes many forms, not the least of which is duplicity. Administrative agencies have turned the Civil Rights Act's equal treatment provisions into preferential treatment practices. Laws prescribe severe criminal penalties vastly in excess of what is in fact carried out. A "results"-oriented Supreme Court creates constitutional "interpretations" that horrify even those who agree with the social policy announced. There is even duplicity imposed upon others, as when "affirmative action" requires employers to confess to being guilty of "under-utilization" of minorities and women, and to promise—in their "goals and timetables"—to achieve numbers or percentages which all parties may know to be impossible. Quite aside from the moral issues, doctrines which cannot be openly argued—quotas, judicial policy making, nonenforcement of criminal laws—cannot be subject to effective scrutiny.

Ironically, "results"-oriented legal policies have achieved largely intermediate institutional results, rather than their social goals. Appellate courts have successfully imposed their will on other institutions—school boards, trial courts, universities, employers—without achieving the social end results expected. For all the countless criminals freed on evidentiary technicalities, there is no evidence that the police practices the courts attacked have been eliminated or even reduced.[390] For all the costly and controversial procedures imposed by "affirmative action" quotas, there is little or no evidence that such policies have advanced blacks beyond what was achieved under the previous "equal opportunity" policy.[391] For all the bitterness surrounding the busing controversy, there is no overall evidence of any social, educational, or psychological gains from these policies,[392] and even purely statistical "integration" has been offset to a great extent by "white flight" to the suburbs.[393] In short, legal sacrifices of principles to get "results" have often been a one-way trade-off with no social gain, in terms of the avowed goals. That little or nothing has been achieved does not mean that there has been no cost. The purely financial costs of busing can run into the hundreds of millions of dollars for just one school system,[394] not to mention the hundreds of millions of dollars nationally in school closings alone,[395] and such social costs as *increased* racial antagonism,[396] and a disruption of school children's social life and reduced parental input into local schools.[397] An "affirmative action" *report* can cost an employer hundreds of thousands of dollars, not to mention its costs in morale to officials,[398] white male employees, and even minority and female employees feeling the backlash.

None of this is evidence of special ignorance or culpability in the individuals in appellate courts and administrative agencies who impose these policies. Rather, it is evidence of the inherent limitations of such institutions, and ultimately of human knowledge, as it exists in any one place. The elaborate, overlapping, knowledge-transmitting networks which constitute the various institutions of a complex society demonstrate both the wide diffusion of relevant knowledge and the high cost and high value of its transmission and coordination. For political institutions, especially for those insulated from effective feedback, to persistently override the decisions of other institutions and millions of individuals is virtually to insure results that are unproductive or counterproductive, even in terms of the preferences of the overriding institutions.

The virtual impossibility, in many circumstances, of having any real knowledge beforehand has created a demand for surrogates for knowledge—

the so-called "findings" of "experts." In *Brown v. Board of Education*, for example, Chief Justice Earl Warren confidently referred to psychological findings "amply supported by modern authority,"[399] and cited as his particular authority a study subsequently devastated as invalid, if not fraudulent.[400] Even the attorneys who used the study regarded it skeptically among themselves, and one said, years later, "I may have used the word 'crap'. . . ."[401] Courts, like other institutions, often fail to make the crucial distinction between (1) opinions in vogue among intellectuals, and (2) empirical evidence, based on recognized analytical procedures, such as controlling for variables other than the ones at issue. "Affirmative action," for example, abounds with numbers and percentages which consistently ignore such gross demographic differences as age, and discussions of capital punishment repeat as dogma the findings of a superseded study which defined "capital punishment" as words in law books, rather than executions. To lump all these things together under the ponderous name of "expertise" is to add self-deception to insulation from the firsthand knowledge so readily dismissed as "public clamor."

The purely institutional, factual, or methodological, deficiencies of legal decision making might explain random variations but not systematic bias. Indeed, bias is not quite the right word, insofar as it implies a preference for a particular principle, such as a Marxist's preference for socialism or a teetotaler's preference for non-alcoholic drinks. A court with a biased approach might, for example, consistently insist on an extremely stringent standard of proof, or—if biased in the other direction—consistently accept rather low levels of evidence as proof. The courts have done neither of these things. They have applied extreme standards of proof before accepting the convictions of some categories of defendants and have made other categories of defendants virtually have to prove their innocence. This is not a principled bias but social partisanship.

A court that believed in the *principle* of either "procedural" due process or "substantive" due process might consider following either principle or—if unable to make up its mind—vacillate randomly between them. The courts have done neither of these things. They have applied the principle of procedural due process to some social categories of litigants (property owners, for example) and substantive due process to others (criminals, for example). A court biased in principle for or against overriding the decisions of other institutions might consistently move in either of these directions, but the Supreme Court's consistency is only in which kinds of institutional processes it would defer to (administrative agencies), and which kinds it would review and monitor in detail (state courts, businesses). Courts biased for or against the principle of extended accountability for the consequences of one's actions might go in either of these directions, but only socially partisan courts would

301

extend the principle to unprecedented lengths of "product liability" for businessmen[402] while reducing it by unprecedented amounts in libel immunity for newspapers.[403] When the post-1937 Supreme Court ostentatiously repudiated the "substantive due process" doctrine in economic matters, it simultaneously began an extensive and unprecedented expansion of its scrutiny of the substantive nature of "due process" in criminal, civil liberties, and racial cases. This might appear to be "compartmentalized thinking"[404] from the standpoint of reconciling principles, but it is perfectly consistent as social partisanship. Indeed, there is remarkable consistency in social partisanship across the various areas of inconsistent principles.

Repudiation of the economic version of substantive due process meant allowing politically liberal legislation and administrative agencies a free hand to control businessmen with little judicial scrutiny of constitutional issues, such as confiscation of property. Relaxed standards of proof—including *de facto* burdens of proof on the accused—facilitated the same policy at the expense of the same social group, with judicial "deference" to the "expert" findings of administrative agencies in issues from antitrust to "affirmative action." The findings of trial courts of judges and jurors selected for impartiality were given no such deference as the findings of administrative agencies staffed by personnel selected for their zeal on one side of an issue. Even proof of a criminal defendant's guilt in court was not enough to sustain a conviction at the appellate level if any of a number of newly created and sometimes retroactive technicalities were not observed—even though the technicalities might be a matter of close dispute among expert appellate judges,[405] and therefore far from obvious to policemen on the street.

The problem with social partisanship is not simply the particular selection of groups to be favored or disfavored, but (1) its general inappropriateness in a system of law, (2) the duplicity necessary to sustain it in the guise of legal principles which appear and disappear rapidly and unpredictably, (3) uncertainty and demoralization where the legal system provides, not a framework within which to place and utilize knowledge best known to those involved, but instead a continual threat of second guessing which may cause decision makers to act in ways most likely to appear plausible to outsiders, rather than in ways judged best by those who actually know. Even those groups supposedly favored by the social partisanship of the courts lose as members of the general society, so that what is involved is not simply a judicial transfer of benefits but a set of policies which can become so counterproductive that everyone loses. It is perhaps indicative when polls show blacks opposed to busing or to "preferential" treatment (quotas), and declaring that the law is too "lenient" with criminals.[406]

Despite the tendency of intellectuals, "experts," and policy makers to view the functioning of society as a series of issues and problems to be directly "solved" from an implicitly unitary viewpoint, the real problem is to locate decision-making discretion in the respective social processes most able to resolve the particular considerations arising in different areas of human life. The same diversity of values which makes this desirable also makes it difficult to achieve. Those in the higher, more powerful, and more remote institutions face the constant temptation to prescribe results rather than define the boundaries of other institutions' discretion. Nothing is easier than to confuse broader powers with deeper insight. But, almost by definition, those with the broadest powers are the most remote from the specific knowledge needed for either deciding or for knowing the actual consequences of their decisions.

Various feedback mechanisms serve to limit the impact of errors, moderate the presumptions of the powerful, and remedy the essential ignorance of social "expertise." These feedback mechanisms may be formal or informal, and social, economic, or political. Their effectiveness varies with the extent to which they convey not only information, but also a degree of persuasion or coercion which cannot be ignored by those whose decisions must be reconsidered. In the intimacy of the family, or in other important informal relationships, the value of the relationship itself forces some mutual accommodation. In economic organizations, the life-and-death power diffused among customers makes ignoring their preferences a folly in which few can indulge, and which even fewer can survive. Political organizations are constrained by elections, but the courts—which is to say, ultimately, the Supreme Court— are constrained only by history and by "a decent respect for the opinions of mankind."

Because history is by definition tardy, and the opinions that matter to judges may be far more restricted than those of mankind, courts are especially inappropriate for making "results"-oriented decisions, as distinguished from decisions of principle or decisions which demarcate the boundaries of other institutions' discretion. The relative lack of flexibility of courts is an asset for decision making in those areas where we want very little flexibility— i.e., in areas dealing with the security of our persons, possessions, and freedom. In venturing beyond such areas, courts are venturing beyond their institutional advantages.

As the legislative and executive branches of government demarcate the boundaries of private decision making, so the courts have confined the scope of the government's activities. Constitutional guarantees encumber the state precisely so that the state may not encumber the citizen. Imposing outsiders' rules to supersede insiders' understanding and flexibility is questionable even as social policy, aside from its constitutional problems. When something similar was suggested for the Supreme Court itself, in the modest form of a case prescreening panel to reduce its work load, the institutional needs of the court were expressed in terms which go to the heart of what the court's own decisions have done to other institutions across the country. According to Justice Brennan, "flexibility would be lost"[407] in an "inherently subjective" process[408] with "intangible factors"[409] that are "more a matter of 'feel' than of precisely ascertainable facts,"[410] and which involve a "delicate interplay" of "discretionary forces."[411] The tragedy is that he apparently considered this to be an institutional peculiarity of the Supreme Court,[412] rather than a pervasive fact of decision making in general.

Chapter 10

Trends in Politics

Among the prominent political currents of the twentieth century are (1) a worldwide growth in the size and scope of government, (2) the rise of ideological politics, and (3) the growing political role of intellectuals. In addition, it has been an "American century" in terms of the growing role of the United States on the world stage, particularly during two world wars and in the nuclear age. This does not imply that international events have followed an American blueprint or have even been favorable on the whole to American interests or desires. It does imply that the fate of the United States has become of world historic, rather than purely national, significance. These developments will be considered here in terms of their implications for the effective use of knowledge in social processes, and in terms of the even more important question of their implications for human freedom.

THE SIZE AND SCOPE OF GOVERNMENT

SIZE

By almost any index, government has grown in size and in the range of its activities and powers over the past century, throughout the Western world. This has been true of governments at all levels, but particularly of central or national government. In the United States, there were less than half a million civilian employees of the federal government as late as the onset of World

War I, but there are now more than six times that number,[1] and even this understates the growth of the federal payroll, because "most government activities are carried out by workers who are not included in the federal employment statistics"[2]—employees of federal contractors or subcontractors, and state and local programs financed and controlled from Washington. In addition, "about one person in every four in the U.S. population receives *workless* pay from government sources"[3]—relief, unemployment compensation, and innumerable benefits of various other social programs. The expenditures of the federal government in 1975 were more than double what they were in 1965, and these in turn were nearly twice what they were in 1955.[4] To compare this with pre-New Deal expenditure patterns, 1975 federal spending was more than one hundred times federal spending in 1925.[5] Moreover, the budget of HEW alone is roughly equal to that of all fifty state governments combined.[6]

One of the problems in trying to comprehend federal spending is that the units involved—billions of dollars—are so large as to be almost meaningless to many citizens. To visualize what a billion dollars means, imagine that some organization had been spending a thousand dollars a day *every day since the birth of Christ*. They would not yet have spent a billion dollars.[7] In the year 2000 they would still be more than 250 million dollars short of one billion dollars. Government agencies of course spend not one but many billions of dollars annually. HEW alone spends about 182 billion dollars annually.[8] To get a figure comparable to what the entire federal government spends annually, change the one thousand dollars per day to *half a million dollars per day*, every day since the birth of Christ. At the end of two thousand years the grand total would amount to less than three quarters of what the federal government spent in 1978 alone.

The size of government has grown, not simply by doing more of the same things but by expanding the scope of what it does. At the extreme of this development, a new political phenomenon has made its appearance in the twentieth century—the totalitarian state. Undemocratic, despotic, or tyrannical governments have existed down through the ages, but the totalitarian state is more than this.

TOTALITARIANISM

It is not simply the origin or basis of political power that defines totalitarianism, nor even the amount of power or its ruthless application. A tyrant is not automatically a totalitarian. It is the political blanketing of the vast range of human activities—from intimate personal relations to philosophical beliefs—that constitutes "totalitarianism." The founder of fascism and originator of the term "totalitarianism," Benito Mussolini, summed it up: "All through the state, all for the state, nothing against the state, and nothing outside the state."[9] Totalitarianism "recognizes the individual only insofar as his interests coincide with those of the State." Nongovernmental entities, whether formal or informal, had no place. "No individuals or groups, political parties, associations, economic unions, social classes are to exist apart from the state."[10] It is the exclusion or suppression of autonomous sources of orientation that is the defining characteristic of totalitarianism.

A military dictator may hold power through force of arms and mercilessly kill every political rival, and yet care little how children are raised, or whether the people are religious or not. In the Roman Empire before Christianity became the state religion, religious toleration was widespread,[11] as was a certain amount of general toleration, accommodation, and social mobility in a large multiracial, multicultural domain.[12] At this juncture, the Judeo-Christian religions were dealt with harshly precisely because they refused to accommodate other religions, which they denounced as idolatry.[13] Yet the Roman Empire was an autocracy, and at various times a military dictatorship in which the emperor exercised arbitrary powers of life and death over the masses and the aristocracy alike. It was not totalitarian, however.

Totalitarian governments reach into every nook and cranny of private life, among the masses as well as the elite. Children are indoctrinated with the official ideology, taught to betray even their parents to the state, and as adults live in an atmosphere in which even the most intimate relationships are subject to state scrutiny and carry the threat of mutual betrayal or official retaliation against lovers or family members for the actions of an individual who has displeased the political authorities. History, science, and the arts are all made subject to political direction. Hitler's "pseudoauthoritative judgments about everything under the sun"[14] were matched by Stalin's pronouncements that extended to linguistics and his disastrous imposition of Lysenko's genetic theories on Soviet agriculture, and by Mao's "sayings" which seemed to cover every aspect of human existence. It is not the source or the ruthlessness of power alone which defines totalitarianism, but the unprecedented scope of the activities subjected to political control.

A concentration camp is the ultimate in totalitarianism, with political decisions determining such routine things as eating and sleeping, as well as personal relations (dehumanization) and death (extermination). Slave plantations in the antebellum South have been analogized to concentration camps,[15] but their paramount *nonpolitical* objective of economic gain meant that slave owners had to make far more concessions to slaves than concentration camp commanders ever made to their inmates. Concentration camps in both Nazi Germany and the Soviet Union were far less economically efficient than the totalitarian societies of which they were a part,[16] but they were maintained despite this, for political purposes. Slave plantations were profit-making enterprises,[17] inherently limited by that fact in how far they could go in oppressing or destroying the sources of their wealth. Whatever moral equivalence may have existed between the two kinds of institutions, they were neither politically nor economically equivalent.

A unifying ideology is essential in a totalitarian state, if only so that its multitudes of organizations do not work at cross purposes to such an extent as to be self-destructive. In the intentional terms of totalitarian belief or propaganda, power is exercised in the service of the ideology. However, in view of the ease with which Nazi officials became Communist officials after World War II, it is also possible that the ideology is exercised in the service of power. Certainly it is hard to imagine totalitarian state power without a unifying ideological theme, and history presents no examples.

The particular ideology may be a creation of the totalitarian leader, as in Hitler's National Socialism, or may have an historical tradition, as in Marxism. However, even in the latter case, the ideology may still be instrumental rather than controlling. Certainly people *following* Marxism—as distinguished from *using* Marxism—could never set up a totalitarian state. Marx and Engels opposed autocracy, much less totalitarianism.[18] The whole point of the proletarian revolution—i.e., a revolution from the bottom up—was that revolution from the top down implied a post-revolutionary dictatorship *over* the proletariat.[19] Lenin's revolution from the top down confirmed the Marxian fears, but Lenin was not bound by the "original meaning" of Marxism and in fact reinterpreted Marx to justify what he had done.[20]

Ideology is not only instrumental, or a producer's good, for the government; it is also a consumer good for the populace, or segments thereof. Totalitarian ideology typically features (1) the *localization of evil*—in Jews, capitalists, or some other group—so that comprehensive political solutions to age-old human problems seem feasible within a reasonable time horizon by surgically removing the offending group, leaving a healthy body politic intact, (2) the *localization of wisdom*, to explain why this miraculous cure has escaped so many minds for so many centuries, as well as explaining the necessity for superseding democratic institutions and beliefs, (3) a *single scale of values* by which priorities may be arranged in every field of human endeavor, to be achieved "at all cost," (4) the *presupposition of sufficient knowledge* to achieve whatever goal may be projected, (5) the *urgency* of the "problem" to be "solved" so that ruthlessness is the lesser of two evils, and (6) a *psychic identification* with millions, whose opinions may nevertheless be disregarded and whose lives may be sacrificed in the cause, without feelings of guilt. Finally, the totalitarian ideology must be a self-enclosed system, to exclude alternative views and visions which are—regardless of their substance—inherently antithetical to a single totalitarian ideology. It is therefore central to totalitarian ideology that it convert questions of fact into questions of motive.[21] Facts are a threat because they are independent of the ideology, and questioning the motives of whoever reports discordant facts is a low-cost way of disposing of them.

An ideology may be viewed as a knowledge-economizing device, for it explains complex empirical data with a few simple and familiar variables. It is hardly surprising that ideological explanations should have a special appeal to those with higher costs of alternative knowledge—the inexperienced ("youth") and the previously politically apathetic ("masses"). As a leading student of totalitarianism has observed:

It was characteristic of the rise of the Nazi movement in Germany and of the Communist movements in Europe after 1930 that they recruited their members from this mass of apparently indifferent people whom all other parties had given up as too apathetic or too stupid for their attention.[22]

It is also in keeping with the concept of ideology as a knowledge-economizing device that there should be defections with age as discordant knowledge forces itself on one's attention, until a point is reached where the cost of reconciling it with the ideological vision exceeds the cost of discarding the vision itself. Explaining complex reality with simple and familiar variables is a low-cost process initially, but this cost tends to rise over time, as ever more complex relationships must be postulated between the simple variables and the accumulating complex reality—much like the Flat Earth Society explaining away phenomena which have long ago convinced others that the earth is round. Indeed, when theories are viewed instrumentally, rather than as literal reconstructions of reality, the reason for preferring the round earth theory is basically an intellectual economizing process: the incremental investment in a slightly more complex initial assumption than a flat earth is later repaid by lesser intellectual effort in reconciling the results with empirical observation. It is a question of cost-effectiveness rather than of reaching ultimate, immutable truth. For the initiate in totalitarian ideology, however, cost-effectiveness may lie with the simple assumptions, because authentication is a sequential process in which the full costs will be revealed only in the course of time. He may also be more interested in the power than in the cognitive advantages to be derived from totalitarianism—or may become so oriented in the course of time.

This consumer good aspect of totalitarian ideology is an essential part of the phenomenon. The hypnotic fascination and exhilaration with which Hitler's followers listened to his speeches was an integral part of Nazism. Among Communists, the vision of the ideology itself—the "wretched of the earth" creating "a new world"—substitutes for oratorical genius, and has in fact proven far more effective with intellectuals. The "intellectual delight" and "intellectual bliss" on reading the Marxian vision,[23] the sense of revelation when "the whole universe falls into a pattern like the stray pieces of a jigsaw puzzle assembled by magic at one stroke,"[24] the thrill when the "revolutionary words leaped from the printed page and struck me with tremendous force"[25]—these are part of the psychic rewards for the total commitment that characterizes totalitarian movements.

Because Marx and Engels had already paid the high fixed costs of creating the vision, latter-day Marxists could achieve ideological results at lower incremental costs. They need not possess Hitler's genius for oratory or for discerning exploitable human susceptibilities. It is only in the light of such ideological visions that it is possible to understand the "confessions" to nonexistent crimes which have been produced not only in Soviet courts but even in Communist movements in Western democracies—movements possessing no tangible power to punish their members. The ideological context dwarfs the particular characteristics of the particular individual, as in this description of an internal party "trial" among American Communists in the 1930s:

... there had to be established in the minds of all present a vivid picture of mankind under oppression.... At last, the world, the national, and the local picture had been fused into one overwhelming drama of moral struggle in which everybody in the hall was participating. This presentation had lasted for more than three hours, but it had enthroned a new sense of reality in the hearts of those present, a sense of man on Earth.... Toward evening the direct charges against Ross were made....

The moment came for Ross to defend himself. I had been told that he had arranged for friends to testify in his behalf, but he called upon no one. He stood, trembling; he tried to talk and his words would not come. The hall was as still as death. Guilt was written in every pore of his black skin. His hands shook, he held onto the edge of the table to keep on his feet. His personality, his sense of himself, had been obliterated. Yet he could not have been so humbled unless he had shared and accepted the vision that had crushed him, the common vision that bound us all together.

"Comrades," he said in a low, charged voice, "I'm guilty of all the charges, all of them."

His voice broke in a sob. No one prodded him. No one tortured him. No one threatened him. He was free to go out of the hall and never see another Communist. But he did not want to. He could not. The vision of a communal world had sunk into his soul and it would never leave him until life left him.[26]

Conversely, without the commitment to the ideological vision, even the horrors of slave labor camps could not silence Solzhenitsyn, Sakharov, or other Soviet opponents of totalitarianism.

Ironically, the first book that Marx and Engels wrote together, in 1843, contained a scathing indictment of the practice of first breaking down individual self-respect and personality, and then attempting to reconstruct a human being according to some preconceived plan. The hero of a contemporary novel had made a religious conversion in that way. Marx and Engels pointed out that with his "smooth, honeyed curse" he had first "to soil her in her own eyes" in order to make her receptive to the redemption he would offer.[27] The lofty motives with which this was done were simply camouflage for the zealot's "lust" for "the self-humiliation of man"[28] Even in a political context, Marx had no use for the idea of state indoctrination.[29]

"Confessions" to nonexistent crimes illustrate another characteristic of totalitarianism—the concept of "political truth." Not only people and organizations are subject to total control, so too is the truth. Hitler's use of the reiterated big lie, and numerous Soviet revisions of official history (complete with air brush erasures in historic photographs) are part of a pattern of control that extends to the basic data itself. This is more than the usual political lying common to systems of various sorts. It is monopolistic lying, with the exclusion of alternative sources of information. Moreover, it is lying on principle—or rather, it is a philosophy that regards what is said as largely instrumental, so that the very distinction between lying and the truth becomes blurred or even regarded as trivial or naive.[30] Political truth is whatever will advance the interests of the cause or movement. Quite aside from ethical questions, this approach makes the same assumption of omnicompetence that is central to totalitarianism as a whole.

The philosophic postulate that statements are instrumental may be necessary, but by no means sufficient, as the basis for lying as a principle. It is not that philosophical postulate but the empirical presupposition of virtually zero incremental knowledge costs (omniscience) for some subset of people ("leaders") that is crucial for the conclusion. Even viewed from a wholly instrumental perspective, the ethical norm of truth is a cost-saving social institution for people for whom knowledge is not a free good. If the set of such people includes all of humanity, then instrumental lying has social costs which cannot be assumed to be less than whatever benefits are contemplated—either for society at large or even for the subset who engage in this wholesale disinvestment in credibility. The presumption is indeed the other way. The systemic evolution of ethical norms of truthfulness in the most diverse and separated cultures—around the world and down through history—suggests something of the instrumental value of truth. Similar ethical norms in this regard originating in the prehistory of the human race, when the species was even more separated and fragmented than today, hardly seem the product of coincidental philosophic intentions rather than of systemic universalistic experience. It is difficult even to conceive theoretically of a society that could survive if statements had no more probability of being true than if they were generated by a process that was random with respect to truth as a value in itself. Even totalitarian governments invest substantially in the production of truth, including secret police and torture, from an instrumental point of view.

The substitution of instrumental consequences for empirical truth as the criterion for statements is by no means the substitution of a more manageable standard. "The usefulness of an opinion is itself matter of opinion: as disputable, as open to discussion and requiring discussion as much as the opinion itself."[31] The sweeping scope and arbitrariness of the assumption that one can trace the instrumental consequences of particular words and deeds may be indicated by asking whether anyone could have foreseen the consequences of a certain Italian explorer's theory that he could reach India by sailing west—a set of words and deeds that led to the discovery of half the planet and changed the course of history in both halves. It is especially ironic for totalitarianism to assume such omniscience, since it was precisely totalitarian oppression which drove from Germany and Italy the men who gave America the decisive military weapon of World War II and ushered in the nuclear age—Albert Einstein and Enrico Fermi.

Conversely, imagine a being with zero incremental knowledge cost—someone able to discern the remotest ramifications of his every statement. Why should such a being be bound by ethical norms of truth, either from the standpoint of self-interest or even if making the interests of humanity the paramount determinant of his behavior? If he knows to a certainty that saying A would on net balance (in all its ramifications) be more beneficial to mankind than saying B, would it not be blind, fetishistic, traditionalism for him to say B? Would it not be self-indulgence to say B in order to salve his own conscience at the known expense of perhaps millions of his fellow creatures, now and in the future? This is only to say that if human beings were entirely different creatures, entirely different principles might well apply. More practically, a choice among principles involves an understanding of the inherent limitations of the species and its surrounding circumstances, rather than a comparison of what would be the best mode of operation in an unconstrained world.

The instrumental case for truth is the instrumental case for human institutions in general—ultimately knowledge costs, which is to say, the unattainability of omniscience. Courts are preferred to lynch mobs even when it is known to a certainty in the particular case that the accused is guilty, and even if the lynch mob inflicts exactly the same punishment that the court would have inflicted. The philosophic principle that we "should not take the law into our own hands" can be viewed instrumentally as the statement that, however great our certainty in the particular case, we cannot supplant legal institutions as cost-saving devices because we cannot assume equal certainty in future cases. If we *could* know with certainty (zero incremental knowledge cost) in all cases who was guilty, would it not be blind, fetishistic traditionalism to maintain legal institutions to determine such matters? If man were indeed able to take in all existence at a glance—including past, present and future existence—would there be any reason for *any* institutions? Even if some of these omniscient beings preferred antisocial behavior, why would it be necessary to have rules existing beforehand (and that is what institutions are) to deal with them, when the necessary actions to deal with them could be determined *ad hoc*—and indeed the potentially antisocial people would know this themselves and be deterred.

Totalitarian institutions would be a contradiciton in terms, if the central assumption of omnicompetence were universalistic. But totalitarian movements and institutions are based on a belief in *differential* knowledge costs (their leader or doctrine supposedly giving them vast advantages over others) and therefore *one-way* lying. The instrumental value of truth in the other direction is recognized by totalitarian nations' pervasive surveillance of the population, monitoring of the effectiveness of their indoctrination, and sorting and labeling of the populace according to their perceived instrumental value to the state. All these assessments are intended to be as true as possible, even by the most lying totalitarian state. Soviet economic statistics are generally assumed to be technically correct, even if selectively and misleadingly published,[32] simply because it is instrumentally essential that Soviet decision makers have the truth as far as they can get it themselves, and a multitude of copies of two different sets of statistics (one true for internal use and one false for the outside world) would be unfeasible, just from the virtual certainty of leaks in such a massive undertaking in duplicity.

The instrumental case for truthfulness rests ultimately on the same assumption as the instrumental case for human institutions in general, and for free institutions in particular. That assumption is that, because we cannot know all the ramifications of whatever we say or do, we must put our faith in certain general or systemic processes (morality, constitutions, the family, etc.), whose authentication by social experience over the centuries is more substantial than any particular individual revelation or articulation. This is not to say that no social processes should be changed or even abandoned. On the contrary, their history has been largely a history of change—usually based on social experience, even when marked by individual revelation or articulation. What is at issue is: *who should decide* the nature of these changes, subject to what incentives and contraints? An enduring framework—morality or a constitution—does not preclude change but may well facilitate it, by reducing the fears that might otherwise be aroused by reforms if their full ramifications were literally unbounded and unimaginable.

TRENDS AND ISSUES

Countries may change faster because they have certain institutional limitations, just as cars travel faster because they have brakes.

The social and political differences between the United States today and two centuries ago are staggering, though all within the same general legal and moral framework. Totalitarian governments can make more rapid changes of personnel ("purges") and policies (the Nazi-Soviet pact, changes in Sino-Soviet relations, etc.) as of a given time, but the fixed purposes of all such changes may mean less fundamental social and political change within the country than in a democratic or conventionally autocratic system. Certainly it would be difficult to argue that the Soviet Union today is as socially and politically different from the Soviet Union fifty years ago as is the contemporary United States from what it was half a century ago. The change in the status of the American black population alone has been dramatic, in addition to changes in the role of government in the economy and society, and countless shifts in the balance of social and political power among a variety of regional, economic, and philosophic groups.

Change is one of the great promises of totalitarian movements—whether Hitler's "New Order," Mussolini's "new departure in history,"[33] or a variety of Marxist-Leninist-Stalinist variations on the same theme. Initially profound changes in political power are indeed characteristic of totalitarianism. But whatever the intentional forces at work among the original insurgents, the systemic effects have been centered on retaining the totalitarian power, at whatever cost in terms of violating the original program or ideology. This has typically necessitated, at some point, a purge of those attracted by the original insurgent program that is now being discarded when in power. Hitler's 1934 purge of his storm trooper leaders from insurgent days[34] and Stalin's purge of Trotsky (and many others) were part of a pattern that has been characteristic of totalitarian governments around the world. While national dangers have been used to justify such actions, they have in fact typically occurred *after* a consolidation of power, when there was considerable evidence (including statements within the regime) that the dangers to the government had lessened.[35] Perhaps these events mark the transition from a totalitarian movement's seeking of power for a purpose to a situation in which power has itself become the purpose. For at least some unfortunate segments of totalitarian movements, it is clear that they could not predict the ramifications of the forces they set in motion as insurgents.

CONSTITUTIONAL DEMOCRACY

As noted in Chapter 5, a government whose source of power is democratic may promote either freedom or tyranny. The rise of popularly elected government in the American South toward the end of the nineteenth century marked the spread of Jim Crow laws and an unprecedented terror against the black population, both inside and outside the law. By contrast, most of the personal rights which are loosely referred to as "democratic" rights were pioneered in England under governments that were democratically elected only within the past century—the popular franchise being a consequence rather than the cause of these developments, which go back to Magna Carta. In short, despite a general, historical association of freedom and democracy, they can be independent of each other in theory, and have at times been so in practice. Indeed, Hitler came to power through democratic and constitutional processes.

Freedom cannot be made definitionally a part of democracy. The democratic process is a mode of political decision making. Freedom may occur under this or other modes. The more autocratic the government, however, the more freedom depends on the benevolence, indifference, or inefficiency of the authorities. Such freedom can readily be suspended or revoked when it threatens the existing authorities or the existing form of government. By contrast, democratic freedom typically means recognition as a practical matter—and/or as an ethical principle—that freedom is difficult to maintain for most when it is not maintained for all. Thus democratic freedoms include the freedom to denounce freedom and to advocate and even carry out its destruction, as in the rise of Hitler in the Weimar Republic. In short, the movement from freedom to totalitarianism tends institutionally to be a one-way movement, since despotism recognizes no popular right to move back toward freedom. Historically, the movement from despotism to freedom has taken place after despotism's self-destruction (Hitler being the clearest example) through either internal or external force, aroused by the excesses of despotism itself. The immediate incremental costs of moving in the totalitarian direction are, however, asymmetrical. It is easy to give up freedom and hard to get it back. Only a general horror of loss of freedom acts to convey these future costs into present-day decision-making processes.

In the perspective of world history, constitutional democracy is a very late arrival. Autocratic, aristocratic, and dynastic governments all go back for thousands of years, but the first time in history when a national government voluntarily relinquished power to an alternative set of political leaders as a result of a popular vote was 1800, when the Federalists turned power over to Jefferson's Democratic Republicans. Constitutional democracy is a new—and indeed, fragile—form of government. Yet its appeal is so widespread that even some totalitarian governments create its outward appearances to win supporters (or at least, neutralize critics) at home and abroad.[36]

While freedom antedates constitutional democracy, both are rooted in a division of power. A constitution intentionally creates institutionally what has occurred fortuitously or systemically at various times in history—such a division of the decision-making power as to preclude one faction's complete domination and to necessitate their courting of popularity. "Despotism itself is forced to truck and huckster," under such circumstances, and even an absolute monarch "governs with a loose rein that he may govern at all . . ."[37] Freedom as a result of division prevailed among the Arabs before Mohammed united them,[38] and religious freedom existed among the diverse peoples of the Roman Empire before Christianity united them by conversion or through force. Much of the freedom of colonial America and the early United States was a fortuitous freedom, born of the sheer diversity of local despotisms, too numerous and widespread to unite or overcome one another. A leading American historian has observed: "In none of the colonies was there anything that would today be recognized as 'freedom of the press.' "[39] Religious freedom was equally scarce. In 1637 the Massachusetts Bay Colony "passed an ordinance prohibiting anyone from settling within the colony without first having his orthodoxy approved by the magistrates."[40] A Puritan leader declared that other religionists "shall have free Liberty to keep away from us."[41] The banishment of Roger Williams,[42] and the public whippings and brutal imprisonment of the Quakers who came to Massachusetts[43] indicate that this was no idle statement. Nor was Massachusetts unique, or Quakerism the only proscribed religion. In late colonial America, "the only place where the public exercise of Catholic rites was permitted was Pennsylvania, and this was over the protest of the last governor."[44] It was from this "decentralized authoritarianism" that a "great diversity of opinion" came, *not* from toleration in principle but from "the existence of many communities within the society each with its own rigid canons of orthodoxy."[45]

Systemically evolved freedom in colonial American later became intentionally preserved freedom, in the Constitution of the United States. The Constitution relied on institutionalized divisions of power to preserve the freedom created by fortuitous divisions of power. It was the social equivalent of a chance mutation being preserved because it proved valuable. In addition to the classic division of powers into legislative, executive, and judicial, the Constitution divided powers into federal and state—with the state power being the predominant power in most areas, superseded by federal power primarily in interstate or international matters. This created as many independent power centers as there were states. States' rights, like some other rights, exist not so much to benefit the actual holders of these rights, but to serve larger social purposes.

The dominant theme of the Constitution itself and of the writings of those who created it was the danger of power concentrated in a single decision-making unit or in a few decision making units operating in concert. What Madison called a system of "opposite and rival interests"[46] was built into the American government. Each branch of government was given "the necessary constitutional means and personal motives to resist encroachments of the others."[47] Freedom was not trusted to the morality of leaders but to their conflicting drives: "Ambition must be made to counter ambition."[48] Government was not to *create* divisiveness but to utilize the inherent conflicts "sown in the nature of man" as a means of preserving freedom.[49] Perhaps the point is most easily illustrated in reverse: the one area in which a united national majority was easily identified in colonial America was race, and it was here that the loss of freedom was carried to its extreme in slavery. Although it is known when Africans were first brought to America (in 1619), it is not known when slavery began, because the first captured Africans became indentured servants, like an even larger number of contemporary whites.[50] But slavery evolved as systemically for blacks as freedom for whites, and in both cases the legal system later ratified what was already an accomplished fact. In short, the connection between freedom and the presence of offsetting powers is shown both by the presence and the absence of freedom in colonial America.

Over the years, but especially in the twentieth century, the constitutional division of powers has been eroded or destroyed in a number of ways. The intentional combination of the constitutionally-divided legislative, executive, and judicial powers in administrative agencies is only one of these ways, though perhaps the most blatant. The Civil War and its aftermath for generations set up federal-state confrontations in which "states' rights "were almost invariably interwoven with racial oppressions increasingly rejected by the country at large. The preservation of the historic division of powers has been dependent upon the interpretation of the Constitution by a Supreme Court which itself stands to benefit from the concentration of power in the federal government, and by extending judicial power into executive and legislative areas. Moreover, the sheer growth in size of the federal government has given it new powers derived neither from the Constitution nor from any statutes, but inherent in the disposition of vast sums of money, many important jobs, and great discretionary powers of enforcing a massive and ever growing amount of laws and regulations. Finally, the ideologizing of politics has made the preservation of the constitutional framework a matter of reduced importance in the face of passionately felt urgencies. These various forces can be summed up as the moral and the institutional reasons for the erosion of the constitutional divisions of power.

How does the sheer size of government affect constitutional democracy or freedom? First of all, the size of the government affects the ability of the citizens to monitor what it does—or even the ability of their elected political surrogates to monitor the activities of a far-flung administrative empire, with officials who may dispose of sums of money greater than the gross national products of many nations. The congressional committee system attempts to cope with the problem by assigning a segment of each house to concentrate on particular policy issues—banking and currency, the military, labor, etc.— and make reports to the full Senate or House of Representatives, to guide the votes of individual members. However, as the government has expanded the scope of its activities, each Senator or Representative has to serve on so many committees and subcommittees (about ten subcommittees per Senator, for example[51]) dealing with matters of such complexity that no unaided individual could stay abreast of it all. This in turn means that political surrogates themselves are forced to resort to other surrogates—their staff aides, whose influence is so pervasive that they have been referred to as a second set of lawmakers.[52] Committee staffs do not simply acquire factual information; they influence the substance and thrust of legislation, and often write its provisions. The high cost of knowledge also adds weight to lobbyists for special interests, who have incentives to become knowledgeable in a narrow but often complex area. Like the committee staffs and lobbyists, career bureaucrats owe much of their influence to the high cost of knowledge. The career bureaucrats both write and interpret federal regulations, which in 1975 occupied more than 60,000 pages of the *Federal Register*—three times the number of pages in 1970.[53] In short, escalating knowledge costs reduce the representativeness of government. There are also huge financial costs of government programs, which tend to be argued over in terms of their individual merits or demerits, without regard to their effect on the size and responsiveness of government.

The growth of administrative agencies is not merely the growth of an arm of government performing assigned tasks. It is the growth of a sector with its own political initiatives and its own external constituencies developed as a result of its initial mandate, constantly pushing for an expansion of its activities and benefits. It is the creation of an external constituency that is politically crucial, and this means that one segment of the electorate receives—in addition to whatever current direct benefits are involved—the enduring advantage of mutual knowledge of who constitues the beneficiaries at a lower cost than the average citizen's cost of knowledge of who pays in money and in other ways. The net result is that programs whose costs exceed their benefits may not only continue but expand, due to different costs of knowledge between the created constituency and the general public. In the light of these different knowledge costs, it is understandable that between 1950 and 1970 government payments to farmers increased tenfold, even though the number of farms was reduced about 50 percent,[54] that heavily criticized programs like Urban Renewal had their appropriations tripled in less than a decade,[55] or that expenditures on elementary and secondary education have risen exponentially while both the numbers and performances of students have been declining.[56] It is difficult to imagine any of these things happening in a world of zero knowledge cost or even of *equal* knowledge cost as between bureaucratic constituencies and the voting public.

The knowledge cost differential is exploited in various ways. One is the "entering wedge" approach to political innovation, in which the initial stakes are so low as to cause opposition fears to seem so exaggerated as to be discredited as outlandish. Later, the scope of the innovation can manifest itself in growing sums of money and/or burgeoning powers, after public interest has waned or turned to other things. For example, HEW began with less than a six billion dollar appropriation, which has since increased to more than thirty times that amount. The income tax began in 1913 with a maximum tax rate of 6 percent on incomes of a million dollars per year and over; now higher rates than that are paid on incomes of two thousand dollars per year.[57] Temporary concealment pays big political dividends because of the high cost—and *differential* costs per unit of benefit—to the public of trying to continuously monitor all ongoing programs. Building subsidies in various government housing programs are routinely understated at the outset, even though it will obviously be impossible to conceal them indefinitely, because, as one federal official said (in justification), "if you put these huge capital contributions up front there's no way any administration would propose it or any Congress would approve it."[58] In other words, the voters would never stand for it if they knew. That it will eventually become "public knowledge" in some sense means little in practical political decision-making terms, if "eventually" lies beyond the time horizon of political incumbents and/or if the "public" which eventually knows the facts is substantially less than the electorate.

Many economic devices and accounting tricks which do nothing more than postpone the transmission of financial knowledge to the public depend for their political effectiveness on knowledge cost differentials between the public and "insiders." One such device is simply mislabeling as "loans" expenditures which no one expects to be repaid. These may be "loans" to individuals, businesses, municipalities, other nations, or international organizations. Even better for concealment purposes are "loan guarantees" in which both the federal government and the recipient can boldly state (without fear of immediate demonstrable contradiction) that there is "no handout" involved but only federal good offices used in obtaining private loans from banks. Everyone directly involved may know—as in the case of federal loan guarantees to New York City—that there is no rational hope that the private loans will ever be repaid, and that the banks will collect from the U.S. Treasury, *eventually.* In the meantime, it is not carried on the books as an expenditure or as a liability (economically or politically) of the incumbent administration. This is not a new phenomenon historically. It has long been commonplace in the deficit financing of Italian cities by the central government in Rome.[59] Its political acceptance in America is relatively new because previously there was a strong but generalized and largely unarticulated suspicion of subsidies in any form. With the emergence of an onus of articulated rationality for all positions taken, such low-cost political protection was no longer available to the public.

The political advantages to "insiders" of postponed knowledge availability are more readily seen in economic terms, but the same principle applies in noneconomic policy areas as well. One can produce "peace in our time" as British Prime Minister Neville Chamberlain did in 1938, at costs that become manifest in later times—though not late enough for Chamberlain's political career in this particular case. Japan's militarists produced exhilarating triumphs at Pearl Harbor and Bataan, whose ultimate costs were paid at Hiroshima and Nagasaki. Hitler likewise produced a great national exhilaration with a series of triumphs for Germany at later costs that included German cities *more* devastated than Hiroshima or Nagasaki, though by pre-nuclear technology. It was not simply that Tojo or Hitler miscalculated. Rather, they took calculated risks whose magnitudes (costs) were insufficiently understood by their respective peoples during the decision-making period. More politically successful cost concealments abound, however. On a smaller scale, social experiments of various sorts have produced immediate political benefits for their partisans at costs only much later manifested in demonstrable consequences.

The classical criticism of the growth of government has been that it threatens both efficiency and freedom—that it is "the road to serfdom."[60] While many inefficiencies of government are too blatant to deny, the big-government threat to freedom has been denied and ridiculed. It is claimed that "nothing of the sort has happened."[61] "Nor need we fear" that "increased government intervention" will mean "serfdom."[62] It is pointed out that "in none of the welfare states has government control of the economy—regardless of the wisdom and feasibility of the regulatory measures—prevented the electorate from voting the governing political party out of power."[63] Such views are not confined to the liberal-left portion of the political spectrum. A leading economist of the "Chicago School" has stated: "hardly anyone believes that any basic liberties are seriously infringed today."[64]

Part of the problem with the argument that freedom has not been impaired by big government is the arbitrarily restrictive definition of "freedom" as those particular freedoms central to the activities of intellectuals as a social class. But the right to be free of govermment-imposed disabilities in seeking a job or an education are rights of great value, not only to racial or ethnic minorities—as shown by the civil rights movements of the 1960s—but also to the population at large, as shown in their outraged (but largely futile) reaction to "affirmative action" and "busing" in the 1970s. Even aside from the question of the substantive merits or demerits of these policies, clearly people perceive their *freedom* impaired when such vital concerns as their work and their children are controlled by governmental decisions repugnant to, but insulated from, the desires of themselves and the population at large. This loss of freedom is no less real when others make the case for the merits of the various social policies involved or denounce as immoral the opposition to them. Freedom is precisely the right to behave contrary to the values, desires or beliefs of others. To say that this right can never be absolute is only to say that freedom itself can never be absolute. Much of the loss of freedom with the growth of big government has been concealed because the direct losses have been suffered by intermediary decision-makers—notably businessmen—and it is only after the process has gone on for a long time that it becomes blatantly obvious to the public that an employer's loss of freedom in choosing whom to hire is the worker's loss of freedom in getting a job on his merits, that a university's loss of freedom in selecting faculty or students is their children's loss of freedom in seeking admission or in seeking the best minds to be taught by. The passions aroused by these issues go well beyond what would be involved in a simple question of efficiency, as distinguished from freedom. Nor can the passionate opposition be waved aside as mere "racism." Not only are minorities themselves opposed to quotas and busing: so are others who have fought for racial equality long before it became popular. Nor are racial issues unique in arousing passions. Even such an apparently small issue as mandatory seat belt buzzers created a storm of protest against government encroachment on the freedom of the individual. The quiescence of intellectuals as long as their freedom to write and lecture remained safe may be less an indication of the preeminence of these particular freedoms than of the insularity of intellectuals.

The argument that the ability to vote to put political leaders out of office remains unimpaired by the growth of government is somewhat beside the point. Democracy is not simply the right to change political personnel, but the right to change *policies*. The reduced ability of the electorate to change policy is one of the consequences of growing government—and particularly of government whose power is growing most in its most insulated institutions, the federal courts and administrative agencies. The judicial and administrative nullification of congressional attempts to stop quotas and bus-ing[65] are only the most striking contemporary examples. The undeclared war in Vietnam was another short-circuiting of public control over major national policy. Public opinion against leniency to criminals has had little effect, and the growing public support for capital punishment[66] has paralleled a growing outlawing of its use by the Supreme Court. Even policies nominally under the control of elected officials have gone counter to the philosophy of those officials. "Affirmative action" quotas and massive school busing both devel-oped under the Nixon-Ford administrations which were opposed to them. So too did the rapid growth of federal welfare expenditures, which finally sur-passed military expenditures under Nixon.[67] The substantive merits of these developments are not at issue here. The point is that this illustrates the in-creasing difficulty of public control of governmental policies, even with changes of officials, even at the highest elected levels.

None of this is historically unique. In the late stages of the Roman Empire its civil servants "felt able to exhibit a serene defiance of the emperor."[68] Ro-man emperors had the power of life and death, but Roman bureaucrats knew how to run a vast empire that had grown beyond the effective control (or even knowledge) of any individual. The same was later true of Czarist Russia, for John Stuart Mill declared: "The Czar himself is powerless against the bureaucratic body; he can send any one of them to Siberia, but he cannot govern without them, or against their will."[69] The experience of imperial China was very much the same.[70]

Freedom to act in economic matters is neither a negligible kind of free-dom in itself nor unrelated to other freedoms. The "McCarthy era" attacks on people associated with left-wing causes was primarily an attack or their jobs rather than any attempt to get direct government prohibitions or restric-tions on what people could say or believe. Yet both sides recognized the high political stakes in this basically economic restriction. But even as regards is-sues where both the ends and the means are economic, freedom may yet be involved. When people living in homes and neighborhoods that pose no threat to themselves or others are forced to uproot themselves and scatter against their will, leaving their homes to be destroyed by bulldozers, they have lost freedom as well as houses and personal relationships. This loss of freedom would be no less real if it were justifiable by some national emer-gency (military action) or locally urgent conditions (epidemic). That it is more likely to be a result of some administrative agency's preference for see-ing a shopping mall where the neighborhood once stood only adds economic and sociological issues. It does not eliminate the issue of freedom. Indeed, serfdom itself was largely an economic relationship, but that did not prevent its disappearance from being a milestone in the development of freedom.

The oft-noted political "cowardice" of big business corporations may in fact be prudence in light of the many costly processes through which government can run them. The constitutional protections against government punishment-by-processing (independent of ultimate verdicts) do not apply where economically punitive actions are not legally interpreted as punishments, or where administrative agencies can drain their time and money, subject neither to restrictions of impartial judiciary concepts nor to governmental bearing of burdens of proof. What is "euphemistically called social responsibility" may in fact be simply the "threat of law"[71]—or of extralegal powers derived from institutions set up for entirely different purposes. For example, the Internal Revenue Service can (and has) threatened to revoke the tax-exempt status of organizations whose policies displease the government, even though such organizations violated no explicit statute. In addition, political hostility to philanthropic foundations found expression in the 1969 Tax Reform Act which both drained and constrained the use of foundations' financial resources.[72]

Though the Constitution was intended as a barrier against the concentration of power in the federal government, it has been construed by the Supreme Court in ways that facilitate such concentration. Despite the impartiality expected of the judiciary, the Supreme Court is itself an interested party in any case concerning the constitutional division of power, either between state and federal governments or among the executive, legislative, and judicial branches of the latter. Public opinion long stood as a barrier to judicial activism, and the "court-packing" threat of Franklin D. Roosevelt in the 1930s which forced the Court to retreat from "substantive due process" doctrines was evidence of the limits of political toleration and the Court's reluctance to face a constitutional showdown. Less than twenty years later, however, the Supreme Court was launched on a course of judicial activism which made the earlier courts seem very tame—and there was no similar reaction of public opinion on political leaders. Attempts at restraining the Court or impeaching particular justices—Warren and Douglas being prime targets— were ridiculed for their futility. Partly this may have been due to the fact that the courts were, initially at least, moving with the currents of the time, especially in desegregation. Partly, too, it reflected the growing influence of political and legal "realism" about the impossibility of objective "interpretation" of the Constitution as distinguished from judicial policy-making. As in other contexts, "realism" here meant the acceptance of incremental defects as categorical precedents. A continuum between objective "interpretation" and subjective policy-making was arbitrarily dichotomized in such a way that everything fell on the subjective side. Having proven the impossibility of *perfect* universally objective and neutral interpretation, it was a short step to acceptance of a growing subjective component in what was increasingly regarded by even the Supreme Court's friends and partisans as judicial policymaking. It was another triumph of the precisional fallacy, that because a line could not be precisely drawn, there were no decisive distinctions among any parts of the relevant continuum.

Whatever the mixture of reasons and their respective weights, the courts were no constitutional barrier to the concentration of power. In the jargon of the times, they were not part of the solution, but part of the problem.

Historic events also promoted the concentration of power. The Civil War and its racial aftermath, in the South especially, ranged many of the most conscientious people in the nation on the side of federal power against "states' rights." The principle of "states' rights" was generally available only in a "package deal" with racial bigotry, cynical discrimination, and lynchings. In such a package, the principle had no chance of long-run-survival on its own merit vis-à-vis the principle of unrestrained federalism. But every decision increasing federal power at the expense of state power applies to *all* the states—not just the South—and reduces the states from autonomous power centers toward the status of administrative units of the national government. This is most apparent in federal-state joint programs, ranging from "revenue sharing" to specific "matching grants" or other Washington-financed and Washington-controlled activities in which federal money sustains state activities—*contingent* on state subordination of its decision-making discretion to federal "guidelines." However, even in activities solely administered by the state or local government—public schools, for example—federal "guidelines" control not only the hiring of teachers and the placement of students but a host of other decisions down to such minute considerations as the number of cheerleaders for girls' and boys' athletic teams.[73] That the physical administration remains wholly in state and local hands in no way changes the fact that the *decision making* has moved to Washington. In this way the physical fallacy conceals an historic shift of power.

Even more of an historic landmark in political development was the Great Depression of the 1930s. Though liberal and conservative scholars alike have traced the origin of the Depression to catastrophic governmental monetary policies,[74] the popular interpretation and the political consensus both treat the Great Depression as showing the failure of the economic market and the inherent flaws of capitalism, demonstrating an "objective" need for government economic intervention. However disputable this belief, what is not seriously disputable is that the belief itself marked a turning point in the political and economic thinking of an age. It would be hard to explain how post-World War II America, in an age of unprecedented prosperity, widening opportunities, and virtually nonexistent unemployment became preoccupied with government guaranteed security, without realizing that only a decade earlier this generation went through a traumatic economic and social experience. The 1930s left more than a psychic legacy, however. *Enduring institutions were created to deal with an episodic crisis.* The severity of that crisis need not be underestimated because it was episodic. Millions of American farmers and homeowners found themselves on the verge of losing what they had worked and sacrificed for a lifetime to have, when monetary contractions beyond their control or foresight increased the real burden of their mortgages at a time when their incomes were sharply cut or lost altogether. When mortgage foreclosures were resisted by armed and desperate people, the government's options were bloodshed or relief measures. However prudent, wise, or humane it may have been to aid destitute farmers, for example, to aid them by establishing enduring institutions meant that, decades later, billions of dollars would still be spent under entirely different conditions—much of it going to agricultural corporations.

Agriculture was, of course, only one of many areas in which permanent institutions were established to cope with an episodic crisis. Labor, aviation, electric power generation, public housing, dairy products, and a host of "fair-traded" items all became subjects of newly created federal agencies. The fiscal policies of the federal government were also permanently altered. Whereas years of government budget surpluses outnumber years of deficits in both the eighteenth and nineteenth centuries, and though the 1920s were a solid decade of surpluses, the 1930s were a solid decade of deficits—setting the stage for the general prevalence of deficits ever since.[75] The inflationary effects of these deficits can be seen in the doubling of the wholesale price level between 1931 and 1948, whereas it declined between 1831 and 1848, and, in fact, prices were lower at the end of the 19th century than they were at the beginning.[76] But aside from their economic effects, budget deficits have the political effect of insulating expenditures from immediate taxpayer knowledge.

The New Deal administration of the 1930s also introduced intellectuals into the government on a large scale—enlisting in the process not only those intellectuals actually in office but to a considerable extent also enlisting as natural partisans their fellow-intellectuals in the academy and elsewhere. This too has remained an enduring and expanding feature of political decision-making. The beliefs and fashions of intellectuals entered political decision-making, not under the open and challengeable banner of interest or ideology, but in the insulated guise of "expertise." In short, it was another force tending toward the insulation of governmental decision making from effective public feedback. The opening of political careers (usually nonelective) to intellectuals also provided intellectuals inside and outside of government with an incentive for favoring the concentration of power. As Tocqueville observed more than a century ago:

It may easily be foreseen that almost all the able and ambitious members of a democratic community will labor unceasingly to extend the powers of government, because they all hope at some time or other to wield those powers themselves. It would be a waste of time to attempt to prove to them that extreme centralization may be injurious to the state, since they are centralizing it for their own benefit. Among the public men of democracies, there are hardly any but men of great disinterestedness or extreme mediocrity who seek to oppose the centralization of government; the former are scarce, the latter powerless.[77]

RATIONALES FOR POWER

The discussion thus far has been primarily in terms of the *manner* in which government has expanded more so than the underlying *rationales* behind such changes. Perhaps the simplest rationale for expansion of the areas and powers of governmental decision-making is that a crisis has thrust new responsibilities upon the government, and it would be derelict in its duty if it did not expand its powers to meet them. Among the more prominent ideological rationales for expanded government is a "maldistribution" of status, rights, or benefits—any existing process or result constituting "maldistribution" to those who would prefer something else. For example, equality can be a maldistribution of status from the standpoint of racists, and the correction of this "maldistribution" was in fact a central feature of Hitler's program. Power may also be sought on the rationale that it is needed to offset already existing power. Yet another rationale for expanded government is the creation of national "purpose"—consensus being viewed as a consumer good (implicitly, worth its cost).

CRISIS

Even the most democratic and constitutional governments tend to expand their powers during wartime, and in natural disaster areas it is common to station troops and declare martial law even in peacetime. Such buildups of governmental power tend to dissipate with the passage of the emergency, which is generally easily recognized by the public at large.

An enduring concentration of governmental power requires either that the public perception of crisis be deliberately prolonged or that the crisis be used to establish institutions which will outlast the crisis itself.

A deliberately prolonged crisis atmosphere can be managed indefinitely only by a totalitarian state, able to depict itself to its people as threatened on all sides by enemies—and able to exclude contrary interpretations of events. This has in fact been the basic posture of totalitarian states in general. For example, the reiterated theme of "peace," renunciations of expansionism in general and in particular, and an outright ridicule of foreign fears to the contrary were common to Hitler[78] and to Stalin in the 1930s—though the latter annexed even more territory than the former from the beginning of World War II to the Nazi's invasion of the U.S.S.R.[79] Even the most aggressive totalitarian state can claim to be threatened by others—and can even cite evidence, since its aggressive military preparations are sure to stimulate at least some military preparedness on the part of other countries. Hitler in the 1930s was perhaps the classic example of this propaganda inversion of cause and effect, though certainly not the last.

In a constitutional democracy, a crisis cannot be made to last indefinitely because alternative versions of events cannot be suppressed. Real crises must be utilized to establish enduring institutions. The Great Depression of the 1930s was a landmark in this respect. The monetary system—the gold standard—was permanently changed. Labor-management relations were permanently changed by the Wagner Act, adding legal sanctions against employers to other union powers. The permissible limits of price competition were permanently reduced by the Robinson-Patman Act, "fair trade" laws, and a host of special restrictions and subsidies applying to sugar, the maritime industry, and others. All these political developments enhanced governmental power, either directly, as with regulatory laws, or indirectly by freeing government from previously existing restraints, as with the abandonment of the gold standard and relaxed standards of constitutionality or the hybrid executive-legislative-judicial agencies created by the New Deal. There was not only an extraordinary growth of governmental power but an unprecedented political swing. Roosevelt's electoral victory in 1936 was the greatest ever achieved at that point: he carried all but two states. Moreover, it was part of a larger, historical pattern, which ultimately included an unheard of string of four successful presidential elections, along with one political party's control of both houses of congress for more than a decade—also unprecedented in American history.

The demonstrable political value of crises was not lost upon subsequent governments or politicians. So many things have since been called a "crisis" that the word has virtually become a political synonym for "situation," and indicates little more than something that someone wants to change.

In recent decades, there has been a trend toward superseding individual decision making based on behavioral assessments with decision making based on ascribed status. There have been laws proposed and enacted, administrative rulings, judicial decisions, and other political directives prohibiting various kinds of private decision makers from sorting and labeling on the basis of innate biological characteristics (race, sex), transient conditions (childhood, old age) or even volitional behavior (homosexuality, drug use, criminal record). In addition, there have been costs of various sorts and magnitudes imposed by government on those attempting to sort people by various performance characteristics (test scores, work evaluations). For example, letters of reference have been forced to become *non*confidential, and together with the increasing ease of initiating lawsuits, this means that they have become so bland and noncommittal as to lose much of their value as transmissions of information on which to sort and label job applicants or seekers after various other kinds of benefits. The imposition of "due process" concepts on public school administrators has similarly reduced the ability of decision makers on the scene to sort out students preventing other children from learning, either by direct disruption of classes or by creating an atmosphere of random terrorism and/or systematic extortion.[80]

Sometimes these governmental activities have been accompanied by admonitions to judge each person individually, rather than by sorting and labeling selected characteristics, but such advice is little more than gratuitous salt in the wound, given the cost differentials involved in these two methods. Sometimes the ascribed status is preferential, so that sorting and labeling that is biased in the prescribed direction is legal but any bias in a different direction is not.

Many decisions which involve status ascription might be regarded from some other points of view as ordinary social decisions involving efficiency or other such mundane considerations. However, what is striking about recent times is precisely the growth of an ideological passion which regards particular decisions and decision making processes as symbolic of status rather than simply instruments of social expediency. One of the more extreme examples of this was the insistence of French-Canadian authorities in Canada's Quebec Province that airline pilots landing at their airports converse with the control towers only in French. Even though hundreds of lives are at stake in conversations between pilots and control towers, this social expediency consideration was subordinated to status ascription issues involved—the general controversy over the preeminence of French language and culture in Quebec. Only a concerted refusal of international airline pilots to fly into Quebec forced the government to reconsider this policy. In the United States, various groups have regarded various laws and policies (private and public) as involving the status of its members—their ultimate value as human beings—rather than simply questions about the best way to get a given job done or the social expediency of particular processes. Even where there are demonstrable *behavioral* differences between groups—e.g., a decade's difference in longevity between men and women—the law has forbidden employee pension plans to treat men and women differently, as a violation of their equal *status*.[81] The separation of boys and girls in athletic and social activities is also challengeable in courts, even where such separation is by nongovernmental, voluntary organizations like the Boys Club, and even though there are numerous demonstrable behavioral differences between boys and girls, including not only physical strength but maturation rates as some of the more obvious examples. Yet the passion behind objections to differences in treatment turns on *status* questions rather than behavioral questions. Moreover, the issue is often posed as if it were inherently and solely a status issue—as if there is no conflict between behavior-based and status-based decisions, and therefore opponents of particular status-based decisions are depicted as advocates of *inferior* status for a group in question. Even groups *defined* by behavioral differences (homosexuals, alcoholics) claim denial of their equal status when treated differently by others. Carried to its logical conclusions, this trend would argue that social processes should make decisions solely on the basis of status rather than behavior: if there are homes for unwed mothers, there should be homes for unwed fathers. While few would go that far, the point is that the principle invoked—and the categorical way it is invoked and its opponents smeared—provides no logical stopping point short of that. The only practical limit is what status ascription advocates find intuitively plausible or politically feasible at a given time—and neither of these considerations provides any long-run constraint on carrying the principle into regions of diminishing or negative returns.

The link between status ascription and political power is apparent in the "redistribution" of income and other economic benefits. While growing governmental control over the output generated by private activity is often described by its hoped for result as "income redistribution," statistical data show that the actual "redistribution" of money and power from the public to the government vastly exceeds any "redistribution" from one income class to another. The percentage of the aggregate American income earned by the top fifth, bottom fifth, etc., has remained almost unchanged for decades[82] while governmental powers and welfare state expenditures have expanded tremendously. There has been "less a redistribution of free income from the richer to the poorer, as we imagined, than a redistribution of power from the individual to the State."[83] International comparisons show the same result as intertemporal comparisons: "In all the Western nations—the United States, Sweden, the United Kingdom, France, Germany—despite the varieties of social and economic policies of their governments, the distribution "of income is strikingly similar."[84] What the national differences in "welfare state" policies actually affect is the distribution of money and power between the public and the government.

So-called "income redistribution" schemes substitute status for behavior as the basis for receipt of income: Because of one's status as an equal citizen of the country, one has a "right" to at least a "decent income," and perhaps an "equitable share" in the nation's output or even an "equal share" where this doctrine is carried to its logical conclusion. In short, personal income should not be based on behavioral assessments by users of one's services but by ascribed status as determined by a given set of political authorities. Implicit in this latter process is a concentration of power, for "distributive justice" as a hoped-for ideal means *distributor's justice* as a social process.

In an uncontrolled economy it is possible for all individuals to become more prosperous, each acquiring more of his own preferred mixture of goods. But because "justice" is inherently interpersonal, it is not similarly possible for everyone to acquire more justice. More "social justice" necessarily means more of one conception of justice overriding all others. The economic inefficiencies involved in such a process are less important politically for their own sake than from their effect on freedom. An imposed social pattern that leaves many unrealized economic gains to be made from mutually beneficial transactions must devote much political power to preventing these transactions from taking place, and must pay the cost not only economically and in loss of freedom, but in a demoralization of the social fabric as duplicity and/or corruption become ways of life. The demoralizing experience of attempting to prevent mutually preferred transactions in only one commodity—alcoholic beverages under Prohibition—suggests something of the magnitude of the problem involved.

Justice of any sort—criminal justice as well as so-called "social justice"—implies the imposition of a given standard on people with different standards. Ironically, many of those politically most in favor of "social justice" are most critical of the loss of personal freedom under the authority of criminal justice, and most prone to restrict the discretion and power of police and trial judges in order to safeguard or enhance personal freedom. The imposition of criminal justice standards, however, usually involves far more agreement on values—the undesirableness of murder or robbery, for example—than is involved in standards of "social justice," and should therefore require less loss of freedom in imposing one standard on all. Certainly it would be hard to argue the opposite, in view of the broad similarity of criminal justice across nations and ages, and their disparities as regards the distribution of income and power ("social justice").

What is in fact being sought and achieved under the banner of "social justice" is a redistribution of decision-making authority. Decision makers acting as surrogates for others in exchange for money or votes are being either replaced or superseded by decision makers responsible largely or solely to the pervasive social vision of their clique. This redistribution is often advocated or justified on the basis of the supposed amorality of the first decision makers, who are depicted as solely interested in money or votes. But insofar as this depiction is correct, such decision makers are only transmitters of the preferences of the public, not originators of their own preferences, and so exercise no real "power," however much their decisions affect social processes. It is the second—more moral or ideological—set of decision makers who originate and impose standards, i.e., who reduce freedom. Their passionate arguments for particular social results tend to obscure or distract attention from the question of the social *processes* by which these hoped-for results are to be pursued.

This is nowhere better illustrated than in John Rawls' *Justice*, which speaks of having a society *somehow* "arrange"[85] social results according to a given conception of justice—the bland and innocuous word "arrange" covering a pervasive exercise of power necessary to supersede innumerable individual decisions throughout the society by sufficient force or threat of force to make people stop doing what they want to do and do instead what some given principle imposes. Even Rawls' principle of restricting "economic and social inequalities to those in everyone's interests"[86] requires forcible intervention in all transactions, quite aside from the difficulties of the principle as a principle. On a sinking ship with fewer life preservers than passengers, the only *just* solution is for everyone to drown. Yet virtually anyone would prefer to save lives, even if those saved had no more just claim to such preference than anyone else. This example is extreme only in the starkness of the alternatives. More generally, social decisions are not a zero-sum process, so the "distribution" of benefits ("justice") cannot be categorically more important than the benefits themselves, as Rawls' central thesis suggests. There must be some prior value to the things distributed in order to have their distribution mean anything. No one cares if we each leave the beach with different numbers of grains of sand in our hair.

THE POLITICAL ROLE OF INTELLECTUALS

One of the fundamental problems in any analysis of intellectuals is to define the group in such a way as to distinguish a class of people from a qualitative judgment about cognitive activity. Intellectuals will be defined here as the social class of persons whose economic output consists of generalized ideas, and whose economic rewards come from the transmission of those generalized ideas. This in no way implies any qualitative cognitive judgment concerning the originality, creativity, intelligence, or authenticity of the ideas transmitted. Intellectuals are simply defined in a sociological sense, and a transmitter of shallow, confused, or wholly unsubstantiated ideas is as much of an intellectual in this sense as Einstein. It is an occupational description. Just as an ineffective, corrupt, or otherwise counterproductive policeman is still regarded as having the same occupational duties and authority as the finest policeman on the force, so the inept or confused intellectuals cannot be arbitrarily reclassified as a "pseudo-intellectual" in an occupational sense, however much he might deserve that classification in a qualitative cognitive sense. Qualitative questions about the intellectual *process* are another matter entirely, and will also be considered—but separately.

The distinction between the intellectual class and the intellectual process is crucial. One might, for example, be anti-intellectual in the sense of opposing the social views of that particular class of people, and yet be very intellectual in the sense of having exacting standards in the cognitive process. Conversely, a totalitarian dictator might be anti-intellectual in the sense of disdaining and discrediting cognitive processes that would otherwise undermine the ideological mind conditioning that is central to totalitarianism, and yet provide unprecedented political power and/or economic rewards to those intellectuals willing to serve the regime. Lysenko achieved a degree of prominence and dominance under Stalin that no contemporary geneticist could achieve in a free society.

The hoped-for results of the intellectual occupation—creativity, objectivity, authenticated knowledge, or penetrating intelligence—cannot be incorporated into the very definition of the occupation. Whether or to what degree they in fact exist in the occupation are empirical questions. One definition of intellectuals is that they are "professional second-hand dealers in ideas"[87]—incorporating a negative assessment of their creativity in the very definition. Truly creative intellectuals may in fact be rare, but empirical results of whatever sort do not belong in the definition itself. Intellectuals may choose to believe that they are purveyors of knowledge, but there is no reason to assume that the bulk of what they say or write consists of ideas sufficiently authenticated in either empirical or analytic terms to qualify as "knowledge." Such a general assumption would itself be cognitively unsubstantiated, and (as social policy) politically dangerous.

Many occupations deal with ideas, and even with ideas of a complex or profound order, without the practitioners being considered intellectuals. The output of an athletic coach or advertising executive consists of ideas, but these are not the kind of people that come to mind when "intellectuals" are mentioned. Even the designers of television circuits, mining equipment, or parlor games like "Monopoly" are less likely to come to mind than professors, authors, or lecturers. Those occupations which involve the *application* of ideas, however complex, seem less likely to be regarded as intellectual than occupations which consist primarily of *transmitting* ideas. Moreover, even those transmitting ideas that are highly specific—a boxing manager telling his fighter how to counter a left jab, or a printer explaining the complexities of his craft—are not considered to be intellectuals in the same sense as those who deal with more sweepingly general ideas such as political theory, economics, or mathematics. The most narrowly specialized physicist bases his work on generalized systems of analytic procedures and symbolic manipulations common to economics, chemistry, and numerous other fields. He is an intellectual because his work deals in generalized ideas, however narrow the focus of his particular interest. By the same token, a drugstore clerk is not considered an intellectual, though dealing with a wide range of products and people, but with the work itself not requiring mastery of a generalized scheme of abstractions. Nor is it complexity or intelligence that is central. Even if we believe (like the present writer) that being a photographic technician requires more intelligence and authenticated knowledge than being a sociologist, nevertheless the sociologist is an intellectual and the photographic technician is not, because one transmits generalities and the other uses ideas that are far less general.

The point here is not to illustrate an arbitrary definition, but to show that the definition is far from arbitrary, and reflects what is a general pattern of usage, even if unarticulated. Moreover, as will be seen, these definitional distinctions correspond to empirical distinctions in the political and social viewpoints of the various groups as categorized. Even on university faculties, agronomists and engineers have very different political opinions from those of sociologists or the humanities faculty.[88] In defining the intellectual occupation, the purpose is not so much to make hard-and-fast boundaries as to define a central conception and to recognize different degrees of approximation to it. Thus there is some sense in which an agronomist or engineer is less likely to be classified as an "intellectual" than is a sociologist or a literary critic, or is thought to fit in the category less fully or less well.

The incentives and constraints of intellectual processes are quite different from the incentives and constraints of intellectual activity as an occupation. For example, intellectual processes are highly restrictive as to the conclusions that may be reached, requiring painstaking care in the formulation of theories, rigorous discipline in the design and carrying out of experiments, and strict limitations of conclusions to what the evidence can logically support.

By contrast, intellectuals as a social class are rewarded for presenting numerous, sweeping, plausible, popular and policy-relevant conclusions. Criminology may be at a stage of highly disparate speculation,[89] but public policy pressures to "solve" the crime "problem" mean that large sums of government money are available to criminologists who will claim to know how to "rehabilitate" criminals or discover the "root causes" of crime. How many criminologists or intellectuals in general succumb to the incentives of their class, as distinguished from the incentives of their cognitive process, is not at issue here. The point is that they are very different incentives.

THE INTELLECTUAL PROCESS

Intelligence may take many forms, from the incrementally imperceptible and partially unconscious modifications of behavior over the years that we call "experience" to the elaborately articulated arguments and conclusions that are central to the intellectual process. Intelligence and the intellectual are two different things. The hoped-for result is that the latter will incorporate the former, but whatever the facts may be about their overlap, they are not conceptually congruent.

Explicit *articulation*—in words or symbols—is central to the intellectual process. By contrast the enormously complex information required to make life itself possible, which has systemically evolved and exists in unarticulated form in the genetic code, is not intellectual, though the efforts to transform the genetic code into an articulated form is a challenging if uncompleted intellectual process. Conversely, the forms of articulation may be elaborate and impressive and yet the substance of what is elaborated simple or even trivial. There is nothing either instrinsically difficult or profound about the proposition that LIX times XXXIII equals MCMXLVII. Children in the fourth grade perform this kind of arithmetic every day. The symbols alone make it formidable. Graphs, Latin phrases, and mathematical symbols likewise create an air of complexity or profundity in the process of elaborating ideas that may contain little of complexity or substance, much less validity.

However limited the scope of articulation, within those limits it serves a vital role in the intellectual process. A mere isolated idea, or arbitrary constellation of ideas—a vision—is metamorphosed into an empirically meaningful theory by the systematic articulation of its premises and the logical deduction of their implications. This does not in itself produce either truth or creativity. It aids in detecting error or meaningless rhetoric. The more rigorously formalized the reasoning, the more readily detectable are shifting premises or other internal inconsistencies, or a discord between the implications of the theory and observable events. In short, articulation is crucial to the intellectual process, however limited (and sometimes confusing) it may be in the social decision making process.

Articulation, indeed, readily *loses* information, as noted in Chapter 8 in discussions of price control and central planning. The definition or articulation of product characteristics by third parties seldom covers as many dimensions as are unconsciously coordinated in unarticulated market processes, so that (for example) an apartment typically has more auxiliary services when there is less articulation (in private housing markets) than when there are more elaborate articulations (in public housing regulations). The characteristics of even relatively simple things like an apartment or a can of peas cannot be exhaustively articulated, or even articulated enough in most cases to match the systemic control of characteristics through voluntary transactions. In more elaborate or subtle things, such as deeply felt emotions, articulation often seems so wholly inadequate as to be discarded for symbolic gestures, looks, and tones of voice, which may be less explicit and yet convey more meaning. Resort to poetry, music, and flowers on highly emotional occasions is evidence of the limited transmission capacity of articulation.

Because nothing can be literally exhaustively articulated, the process of articulation is necessarily to some extent also a process of abstraction. Some characteristics are defined, to the neglect of others which may be present but which are deemed less significant for the matter at issue. This purely judgmental decision may of course prove to be right or wrong. The point is that abstract intellectual models—"mimic and fabulous worlds"[90] as Bacon characterized them—are inherent in intellectual activity, whether these models be explicit and highly formalized (as in systems of mathematical equations) or informal or even implicit. In the implicit models, however, it is possible to ignore the fact that one is abstracting and theorizing, to call the premises or conclusions "common sense" and to shift one's premises without being aware oneself and without alerting others to the shift. For example, one may use the public witnessing of executions as evidence for the immorality of capital punishment in one part of an informal and implicit argument, and pages later also use the public's *not* witnessing executions as more evidence for its immorality. Were all the arguments reduced to equations, the inconsistent premises would at the very least be located nearer one another in a more condensed presentation, would be more readily detectable and more conclusively demonstrable by universally recognized mathematical principles. In a celebrated episode in the development of modern economic theory, a set of instructions given to a draftsman preparing a graph proved impossible to execute, leading to the later discovery of a substantive economic principle inherent in that impossibility.[91] Had the same theory been presented in a purely informal and verbal manner, nothing would have compelled the recognition of the inconsistency. Indeed the particular inconsistency in question is still common among "practical" men, though analytically discredited decades ago.[92]

The enormous value of articulation, abstraction, and formalized rationality in the intellectual process is as part of the *authentication* process. They are neither part of the creative act nor of the empirical evidence which determines its ultimate applicability. The essentially negative role of articulated rationality in filtering, modifying, and eliminating ideas on their way to becoming knowledge is teachable in schools because it is formally demonstrable. But the creative performance—the "preanalytic cognitive act"[93] as it has been called—is not. The most highly trained products of the leading universities are therefore better equipped to demolish ideas than to generate them. This is a systemic characteristic to be understood rather than an intentional choice to be criticized. It must be kept in mind, however, when considering such people as potential creators of "solutions" for social "problems." Insofar as they are being creative, they are not doing what they were taught, but are instead professionals acting in an amateur capacity. The maxim that "experts" should be "on tap but not on top" expresses an appreciation of their valuable but largely negative role in filtering policy alternatives.

The very concept of "solving" social "problems" extends academic practices to a completely different process. The academic process is a process of pre-arrangement by persons already in possession of knowledge which they intend to articulate and convey unilaterally. Social processes are processes of systemic discovery of knowledge and of its multilateral communication in a variety of largely unarticulated forms. To "solve" an academic "problem" is to deal with pre-selected variables in a prescribed manner to reach a pre-arranged solution. To apply the academic paradigm to the real world is to arbitrarily preconceive social processes—the whole complex of economic, social, legal, etc., activities—as already comprehended or comprehensible to a given decision maker, when in fact these very processes themselves are often largely mechanisms for coping with pervasive uncertainty and economizing on scarce and fragmented knowledge. Resolutions of conflicting desires and beliefs may emerge from social processes, through the communication and coordination of scattered and fragmented knowledge, but that is wholly different from a solution being imposed from above as "best" by a given overriding standard in the light of a given fragment of knowledge.

What is a social "problem"? It is generally a situation which someone finds less preferable than another situation that is incrementally costlier to achieve. If the alternative situation is no costlier, it would already have been chosen, and there would be no tangible "problem" remaining. In both theory and practice, a social problem is likely to be one of the higher valued unfulfilled desires—one that is *almost but not quite* worth the cost of satisfying. Such situations are inherent in the incremental balancing of costs and benefits, which is itself inherent in the condition of scarcity and trade-off. A "solution" to such "problems" is a contradiction in terms. It is of course always possible to eliminate all unfulfilled desires of a given sort—that is, extend the consumption of some benefit to the point where its incremental value is zero—but in a system of inherent scarcity (i.e., unlimited human desires) that means denying some other benefit(s) even more. Much political discussion of problem-solving consists of elaborately demonstrating the truism that extending a given benefit would be beneficial in that particular regard—more airports, day-care centers, rental housing, etc.—without any concern with the incremental value of sacrificed alternatives. A variation on this theme is that some set of people "need" a particular benefit but cannot "afford" it—i.e., its incremental value to group A exceeds its incremental cost to group B. Whatever the plausibility or perhaps even merit of this argument with particular benefits and particular descriptions of people, it clearly loses validity as group A approaches a state of being identical with group B. Yet very similar political arguments for "solving" some "problems" are used when A and B are identical. For example, the Amercan people cannot afford the medical care they need, and so should have national health insurance (paid for by the American people).

To "solve" some social "problem" is (1) to move the locus of social decision making from systemic processes of reciprocal interaction to intentional processes of unilateral or hierarchical directives, (2) to change the mode of communication and control from fungible and therefore incrementally variable media (emotional ties, money, etc.) to categorical priorities selected by a subset of a population for the whole population, and (3) because of the diversity of human values, which make any given set of tangible results highly disparate in value terms (financial or moral), pervasive uncompensated changes through force are likely to elicit pervasive resistance and evasion, which can only be overcome by more force—which is to say, less freedom. Moreover, the very concept of a "solution" involves some given standard by which one situation will be regarded as a "solution" of another. These standards may be moral or material, or anywhere in between, but there must be a standard for there to be a "solution." With diverse people making diverse trade-offs, however satisfying the results they reach may be for them respectively, it can only be "chaos" or a "problem" requiring "solution" to anyone applying a single standard.

The undemocratic implications of applying the academic paradigm in politics are exacerbated by the tendency of many intellectuals to favor—or indirectly insist upon—decision making processes cast solely in the mold of explicit articulation. In this view, social decisions must require articulation before government commissions, administrative agencies, courts, parole boards, school committees, advisory groups to corporations, police departments, and all other social decision makers. Unarticulated decision making is equated with "irrationality." "Why do we need four gas stations at a single intersection?" asks an intellectual painting a picture of "wasteful" decision making in America by "a thousand little kings" motivated by "greed."[94] The more fundamental question is why articulated justification to third parties must be the mode of determining business location or any other decisions by any other segment of the population? To the extent that decision makers are motivated by "greed" rather than an *a priori* preference pattern, their decisions are constrained by the decisions of competing bidders who are in turn surrogates for alternative sets of particular resources, including locations.

That a set of decisions is not articulated is not evidence that they are either irrational or undemocratic. On the contrary, the need to articulate to a tribunal of third parties applying their own standards is a reduction in both democracy and freedom, and often involves a loss of effective knowledge transmission in decision making. Moreover, it is socially biased in favor of those more skilled in articulation, even if their skills in other respects are lacking. Given the advantages of specialization, there is no reason to expect that those skilled in articulation will be more skilled in particular fields than those specialized in those fields. Systematic location patterns—gas stations and doctors offices being near each other and liquor stores and stationery shops often being dispersed from one another—suggests that there is nothing as random as "irrationality" behind it, nor anything as widespread as the desire for an improved economic condition responsible for one particular pattern. That a decision is called "greed" when it is found in some groups but "aspirations" or "need" in others is an incidental characteristic of fashions among intellectuals.

The virtues of the intellectual process are virtues *within* the intellectual process, and not necessarily virtues when universalized as paramount in other social processes. Articulation, formalized rationality, and fact-supported conclusions are central features of the intellectual process when determined by its own inner incentives and constraints. To what extent such considerations characterize the behavior of intellectuals as a social class in the political arena is another question. So too is the extent to which these intellectual virtues survive even in intellectual matters when the personal or political rewards available to intellectuals as a social class provide incentives to do otherwise.

338

INTELLECTUALS AS A SOCIAL CLASS

Intellectuals—persons who earn their living by transmitting generalized ideas—have incentives and constraints determined by the peculiarities of their social class, as well as incentives deriving from the nature of the intellectual process. Questions about resolving conflicts between the two—how to be honest while political, ethical while an advocate—only highlight the existence of two disparate sets of incentives and constraints. Such conflicts are defined out of existence when intellecutals are categorized as people who "live for rather than off ideas."[95] Such may be the hoped-for ideal, but the actual observable characteristic of the group is that they live off ideas. The extent to which they ignore that fact and regard purely cognitive incentives as overriding is an empirical question that can be examined after first determining the incentives created by their social class and those created by their cognitive activity.

It is to the self-interest of intellectuals as a social class to benefit themselves economically, politically, and psychically, and for each intellectual to benefit himself similarly. Among the ways in which this can be done is by increasing the demand for the sources of intellectuals and increasing the supply of raw material used in their work. The output of intellectuals—ideas—is a product supplied in abundance by all other members of society, so that a prerequisite for increasing the demand for specifically intellectuals' ideas is to differentiate their product. Certificates from authenticating institutions (universities, learned societies, research institutes, etc.) help, but the intellectual differentiates his product most distinctively by its manner of packaging—the choice of words, organization of the material, and observance of cognitive principles and scholarly form. The intellectual who does these things can even dispense with degrees entirely, as John Stuart Mill did, or they may be wholly incidental, as in the case of Karl Marx (a legal degree) and Adam Smith (a degree in philosophy). It may well be that most contemporary intellectuals are degree-holders, but that is hardly their defining characteristic.

The conflict between cognitive and occupational incentives is particularly clear in the choice between existing knowledge and newly created ideas. An intellectual is rewarded not so much for reaching the truth as for demonstrating his own mental ability. Recourse to well-established and widely accepted ideas will never demonstrate the mental ability of the intellectual, however valid its application to a particular question or issue. The intellectual's virtuosity is shown by recourse to the new, the esoteric, and if possible his own originality in concept or application—whether or not its conclusions are more or less valid than the received wisdom. Intellectuals have an incentive to "study more the reputation of their own wit than the success of another's business," as Hobbes observed more than three centuries ago.[96] As part of this product differentiation, it is essential that alternative (competing) social inputs be discredited cognitively ("irrational") or morally ("biased," "corrupt"), that competing elites be discredited ("greedy," "power hungry"), and that the issues at hand be depicted as too unprecedented for application of existing knowledge inputs available to intellectuals and nonintellectuals alike, and too urgent (a "crisis") to wait for systemic responses, which are also alternatives that compete with intentional intellectual "expertise." More generally, the meaning of knowledge must be narrowed to only those particular kinds of formalized generalities peculiar to intellectuals. Assertions of the gross inadequacy of existing institutions and ideas likewise increase the demand for intellectuals by discrediting alternatives. The rewards are both psychic and financial.

The demand for intellectuals' services is also increased by developing preferences for such political and social processes as commonly use more of intellectuals' inputs—e.g., political control and status ascription from the top down, "education" or "more research" as the answers to the world's ills, and "participation" and institutional articulation as the way to better decisions.

The occupational self-interest of intellectuals is served not only by product differentiation, but by "relevance." Many cognitively intellectual productions are of no immediate applicability, because (1) they have not yet been subjected to empirical validation or cannot be in the real world, or (2) their very nature and thrust are different from political discussions on the same subject matter, or (3) the time horizon of the scholarly endeavor may far exceed that of politics, so that no cognitively authenticated conclusion may be available within the time in which a political decision has to be made, and (4) such articulated knowledge as may be available may go counter to what is politically desired. Making intellectual output "relevant" involves resolving such dilemmas. Cognitive incentives mean less relevance and lower occupational rewards in money, status, power, popularity, etc. Occupational incentives obviously mean more of such rewards and less cognitive authenticity.

The incentives sketched are intended to depict the behavior of an intellectual motivated solely by occupational rewards, and prepared to trade off as expendable considerations such competing incentives as cognitive principles, ethical standards, and democratic freedoms. The point here is not to define *a priori* how many intellectuals will behave what way but to provide a framework within which to judge the observable behavior of actual intellectuals in a variety of social, political and historical settings.

"RELEVANCE"

Intellectuals have long sought to be politically "relevant." More than three centuries ago, Hobbes expressed the hope that his *Leviathan* would someday "fall into the hands of a sovereign" who would "convert this truth of speculation into the utility of practice."[97] Karl Marx eloquently expressed the psychic importance of "relevance" to the intellectual:

... the time must come when philosophy not only internally by its content but externally by its appearance comes into contact and mutual reaction with the real contemporary world ... Philosophy is introduced into the world by the clamour of its enemies who betray their internal infection by their desperate appeals for help against the blaze of ideas. These cries of its enemies mean as much for philosophy as the first cry of a child for the anxious ear of the mother, they are the cry of life of the ideas which have burst open the orderly hieroglyphic husk of the system and become citizens of the world.[98]

It is noteworthy that this was *not* an expression of the satisfaction of promoting a particular doctrine or cause. Marx at this point had not yet met Engels, who converted him to communism, and so there was not yet a Marxian theory to promote. It expressed simply the general joy of intellectuals at being taken seriously and talking about big things.

Nor is it solely in political subjects that political "relevance" is sought. Demography was heavily involved in politics literally from the first page of the first edition of Malthus' *Essay on Population* in 1798.[99] Biology was made the basis for political theory in the nineteenth and early twentieth century intellectual vogue called "social Darwinism."[100] Psychology was politicized in the decades long controversies preceding the drastic revision of American immigration laws in the 1920s. In the political crisis of the Great Depression, virtually all of the so-called "social sciences" attempted to be politically "relevant" rather than simply cognitively valid, and the rise of the welfare state institutionalized this tendency of applied intellectual activity among "social scientists." In totalitarian nations, virtually every intellectual field is politicized. Genetics and economics acquire ideological significance in the Soviet Union,[101] and Nazi Germany proclaimed the existence of such intellectual entities as *German* physics, *German* chemistry, and *German* mathematics.[102] The concern here, however, is not so much with what governments have done to the intellectual process, but what intellectuals themselves have done in the quest for "relevance."

Malthus' population theory was openly intended to counter contemporary revolutionary political theories, notably those of Godwin and Condorcet. After these theories faded with the years, later editions of Malthus' *Essay on*

Population turned its thrust toward other policy issues, the aim being not so much policy solutions as moral justification of the existing institutions:

... it is evident that every man in the lower classes of society who became acquainted with these truths, would be disposed to bear the distresses in which he might be involved with more patience; would feel less discontent and irritation at the government and the higher classes of society, on account of his poverty ... The mere knowledge of these truths, even if they did not operate sufficiently to produce any marked changes in the prudential habits of the poor with regard to marriage, would still have a most beneficial effect on their conduct in a political light.[103]

While the mere intentions or applications of a doctrine, in themselves, have no necessary effect on its cognitive validity, the Malthusian theory's many intellectual flaws related directly to its political goals. Like many other intellectual productions with political "relevance," its most fundamental flaw was not a particular conclusion but an inadequate basis for any conclusion. On a theoretical level, the Malthusian doctrine inconsistently compared one variable defined as an abstract potentiality (population growth) with another variable defined as an historical generalization (food growth).[104] On an empirical level, there was grossly inadequate evidence for the postulated behavior of either variable. The supposed doubling of the population in colonial America every 25 years was based on a guess by Benjamin Franklin, repeated by a British clergyman named Price and obtained third-hand by Malthus. The first American census was published after Franklin's death and the first British census was taken three years after Malthus' book was published. The theoretical argument depended on shifting usages of the word "tendency," to sometimes mean (1) what was abstractly possible, (2) what was causally probable, or (3) what was historically observable—each according to the polemical convenience of the moment. Though contemporaries criticized this shifting ambiguity that was central to the Malthusian doctrine, Malthus refused to be pinned down to any given meaning.[105] Empirically, the successive censuses after Malthus' book was published revealed that in fact the food supply was growing *faster* than the population, and that most of the population growth was not due to reckless marriages and childbearing among the poor, as Malthus claimed, but to reduced death rates.[106] The Malthusian theory boils down to the proposition that population growth increases with prosperity—an empirical relationship that is demonstrably false from both the history of given countries over time and from comparisons of countries at a given time. As countries become more prosperous, their birth rates and population growth rates generally decline. At a given time, prosperous countries typically do not have higher population growth rates than poorer countries. In purely cognitive terms, it may well be that the Malthusian theory has received one of the most thorough refutations of any theory in the social sciences,[107] but in social and political terms, the Malthusian doctrine is still going strong almost two centuries after its first appearance. Like so many other political-intellectual productions, its triumph is largely a triumph of reiteration. Malthus' crucial success was in *identifying* poverty with "overpopulation" in the public mind, so that to deny the latter is deemed tantamount to denying the former.

One of the elements in the public success of the Malthusian doctrine which has proved equally serviceable in other politically "relevant" doctrines has been the display of cognitively irrelevant statistics. The second edition of Malthus' *Essay on Population* was several times larger than the first, due to the addition of masses of data. These data were never used to *test* the Malthusian theory but to illustrate or apply it. In Malthus' own words, the data are intended to "elucidate the manner" in which his theory operates, to "examine the effects of one great cause"—the population principle—but *not* to test the principle itself. Any population size or growth rate would be consistent with the principle: "The natural tendency to increase is everywhere so great that it will generally be easy to account for the height at which the population is found in any country."[108] No matter what the data show, he would be "right."

This decorative display of numbers which in no way test the central premise continues in modern, more sophisticated, statistical studies. A noted study of the economic effects of racial discrimination begins by simply defining "discrimination" as *all* intergroup differences in economic prospects.[109] It then proceeds to elaborate mathematically and statistically in the light of that premise, but never testing the premise itself. All intergroup differences in cultural orientation toward education, work, risk, management, etc., are simply banished from consideration by definition. Discrimination in this context becomes simply a word denoting statistical results, though of course the very reason we are interested in discrimination, in its usual sense, is because it refers to intentional behavior whose moral, political, and social implications concern us. That social and political concern is implicitly appropriated for statistical results that depend on numerous other factors as well.

Such arbitrary attribution of causation by definition is a special case of a more general problem that plagues statistical analysis. Whenever outcome A is due to factors B and C, by holding B constant, one can determine the residual effect of C on A. The problem is that A may also be affected by factors D, E, or F, etc., and if they are not specified in the analysis, then all of their effect is wrongly attributed to C. Moreover, even the attempt to hold B constant may fail in practice. Theoretical variables may be continuously divisible, but actual statistics may be available only in discrete categories. In comparing two groups who differ on a particular variable (male and female differences in height, for example), attempts to hold that variable constant by comparing individuals with the same value of the variable (the same height) may mean in practice comparing individuals who fall in the same discrete intervals (between five and six feet, for example). But groups whose distributions differ across specified intervals can also differ within those respective intervals. The average height of males and females who fall in the interval from five feet to six feet is probably different (males in that interval being taller than females in the same interval), despite the attempt to hold them constant. Therefore some of the effect of the variable supposedly held constant will appear statistically as the effect of some residual variable(s). This residual method of analysis has great potential for misstating causation, through inadequate specification of the variables involved, either inadvertently or deliberately. Whether one's preferred residual explanation is discrimination, genetics, schooling, etc., deficiencies in the specification of alternative variables are rewarded with more apparent effect from the preferred residual variable. The ultimate extreme of this is to implicitly hold all other variables constant by arbitrarily *defining* one variable as *the* variable and using this definition as if it were a fact about the real world, by using the same *word* normally used to describe that fact—"discrimination" in this case. The political benefits of this cognitive deficiency may be illustrated not only by the reliance of national political figures and institutions on the advice of the economist using this technique, but also his academic success in promoting a conclusion consonant with academics' social and political vision, however cognitively questionable. It is a technique—and a result—common in other fields, as will be noted again.

A similar pattern of disregarding alternative variables is followed in discussions of "income distribution," where statistical results about people in various phases of their economic life cycle are spoken of as if they referred to socioeconomic classes in the usual sense of people stratified in a certain way across their lifetimes. The "top 10 percent" of wealth holders may conjure up visions of Rockefellers or Kennedys, but they are more likely to be elderly individuals who have finally paid off their mortgages, and who may well have been among the statistical "poor" in data collected when they were younger. The point here is not whether income or wealth differences are greater or less than might be desired from some point of view or other. The more basic question is whether there is sufficient congruence between the statistical categories and the social realities to make any conclusion viable. To declare that "dry statistics translate into workers with poverty-level incomes"[110] may be politically effective but it asserts what is very much open to question.

The negative cognitive effects of political "relevance" can be further illustrated with Darwin's theory of evolution. The political application of Darwin's biological concept of "survival of the fittest" involved not simply an extension but a distortion of the concept. What was in Darwin a *causal* principle of biological evolution pertaining to species became in its political application an *evaluative* principle pertaining to individuals. The systemic tendency toward adaptation of organisms to their respective environments became an intentional triumph of individuals evaluated as superior not merely within a particular set of social environmental circumstances, but politically justifying one set of circumstances rather than another.[111] This political application distorted the Darwinian principle. Lazy amorality might be the "fittest" quality to survive in a sufficiently extreme welfare state, for example, or ruthless ambition in a sufficiently extreme *laissez-faire* economy without adequate law enforcement. Darwin himself did not make the political applications and distortions known as "social Darwinism." It was Herbert Spencer in England, William Graham Sumner in America, and countless disciples in both countries who turned the Darwinian principle of biological change into a political principle justifying the status quo.

Darwinism at least retained its integrity within biology. But the young field of psychology was not so fortunate in its rush to establish its claims to scientific stature and political "relevance." Intelligence tests began in France in 1905 with a politically defined policy goal—the sorting out of students with low academic aptitudes to be placed in special schools. The test developed for that purpose by Alfred Binet in France was translated and adapted for American youths by Lewis Terman of Stanford University as the Stanford-Binet I.Q. Test. It was also politically adapted to American issues— the controversies then raging over American immigration policy.

Unlike earlier generations of immigrants, the immigrant groups ariving in the United States in the 1880s and afterwards were no longer of northern and western European stock, but largely eastern and southern Europeans who differed culturally, religiously (many being Catholic or Jewish) and genetically from the American population at large, as well as from earlier immigrants. The serious social stresses associated with the emergence of every new ethnic minority in the urban economy and society were seen as peculiarities of these new and "unassimilable" immigrants. Vast amounts of data showed that these "new" immigrant groups had higher incidences of social pathology—and lower I.Q.'s. To the new field of psychology, the immigrants' low I.Q.'s were an opportunity to establish the political "relevance" of their profession along with its cognitive ("scientific") claims.

The leading test "experts" of the era—including Terman, Goddard, and Yerkes—insisted that they were presenting "not theory or opinions but facts" and facts of relevance "above all to our law-makers."[112] They were "measuring *native or inborn intelligence.*"[113] Their results indicated "the fixed character of mental levels."[114] Intelligence tests would "bring tens of thousands" of "defectives" under "the surveillance and protection of society."[115] All of this was said at a time when the I.Q. test had existed for less than a decade in the United States.

The leading I.Q. "experts" were also members of eugenics societies devoted to preventing the reproduction of "inferior" stocks.[116] However, the political impossibility "at present" of convincing "society" that low I.Q. groups "should not be allowed to reproduce"[117] made the "experts" predict a "decline in American intelligence" over time.[118] After a later survey of data generated by the mass testing of soldiers in World War I, testing expert Carl Brigham—later creator of the College Board SAT—concluded that "public action" and "legal steps" were needed to prevent the "decline of American intelligence." Such steps should be "dictated by science and not by political expediency," and included immigration laws that would be not only "restrictive" but "highly selective," and other policies for "prevention of the continued propagation of defective strains in the present population."[119] Virtually identical conclusions were reached at the same time by Rudolf Pintner, another leading authority and also the creator of a well-known mental test: "Mental ability is inherited. . . . The country cannot afford to admit year after year large numbers of mentally inferior people, who will continue to multiply and lower the level of intelligence of the whole nation."[120]

These were not the views of the village racist. They were the conclusions of the top contemporary authorities in the field, based on masses of statistical data, and virtually unchallenged either intellectually, morally, or politically within the profession at the time. Controversies raged between the "experts" and others—notably Walter Lippman[121]—but such critics' conclusions were contemptuously dismissed as "sentiment and opinion" as contrasted with the "quantitative methods" of the new science.[122]

In many ways this episode illustrates far more general characteristics of intellectual-political "relevance": (1) the almost casual ease with which vast expansions of the amount and scope of government power were called for by intellectuals to be used against their fellow citizens and fellow human beings, for purposes of implementing the intellectuals' vision, (2) the automatic presumption that differences between the current views of the relevant intellectuals ("experts") and the views of others reflect only the misguided ignorance of the latter, who are to be either "educated," dismissed, or discredited, rather than being argued with directly in terms of cognitive substance (that is, the intellectual *process* was involved primarily in giving one side sufficient reputation *not* to have to engage in it with non-"experts"), (3) the confidence with which predictions were made, without reference to any prior record of correct predictions nor to any monitoring processes to confirm the future validity of current predictions, (4) the moral as well as intellectual superiority that accompanied the implicit faith that the current views of the "experts" represented the objective, inescapable conclusions of scientific evidence and logic, and their direct applicability for the public good, rather than either the vogues or the professional self-interest of these "experts," and (5) a concentration on determining the most likely alternative conclusions rather than whether *any* of the conclusions had sufficient basis to go beyond tentative cognitive results to sweeping policy prescription.

What was the compelling evidence that led the early test experts to conclude that southern and eastern Europeans—including Jews[123]—were innately intellectually inferior to other European "races"? They scored lower on mental tests—averaging I.Q.'s of about 85, the same as blacks today nationally, and slightly lower than northern blacks.[124] What was controlled or held constant in these statistical comparisons? Practically nothing. The new immigrants (Jews, Italians, Slovaks, etc.) almost by definition averaged fewer years in the United States than most of the older immigrant groups (Germans, Irish, Britons, etc.), spoke correspondingly less English, and lived in commensurably lower socioeconomic conditions. When years of residence in the United States were held constant, the mental test differences disappeared.[125] In the massive World War I testing program, the results on many subsets of the tests showed the modal number of correct answers to be *zero*— indicating little understanding of the instructions.[126] On those subsections where special efforts were made to elaborate instructions or to demonstrate what was expected, zero scores were less common, even when the questions themselves were more complex (the same was true of black soldiers).[127] Some "intelligence" test questions dealt with such peculiarly American phenomena as the name of the Brooklyn National League baseball team, Lee's surrender at Appomattox, and the author of *Huckleberry Finn*.[128] As for controlled samples, the methods of selecting which soldiers would take which test "varied from camp to camp, and sometimes from week to week at the same camp."[129]

These defects in testing were known to the "experts" who sweepingly labeled great portions of the human race as innately inferior. One rationale for accepting the results was offered by Carl Brigham:

The adjustment to test conditions is a part of the intelligence test. . . . If the tests used included some mysterious type of situation that was "typically American," we are indeed fortunate, for this is America, and the purpose of our inquiry is that of obtaining a measure of the character of our immigration. Inability to respond to a "typically American" situation is obviously an undesirable trait.[130]

Whatever merit this kind of reasoning might have as a justification of the purely empirical predictive validity of a test, that is wholly different from reaching conclusions about genetic mental capacity as it must unfold in subsequent generations of American-born offspring—especially in the context of draconian proposals to forcibly control the reproduction of these groups. As for the correlation between immigrants' mental test scores and their years of residence in the United States, this was dismissed by showing that immigrants with five years of residence taking the nonverbal test still did not reach native American test score levels[131]—five years being presumably sufficient to change life-long cultural patterns, and a nonverbal test being presumed to be culturally unbiased. The ominous prediction of a declining national I.Q.—a prediction common in the literature in the United States and in other countries—had no empirical evidence, and as evidence accumulated over the years, it showed the national I.Q.'s in the United States and elsewhere either remaining constant or drifting upward, forcing later upward revisions of I.Q. standards.[132]

The point here is not that particular results in a particular field during a particular era were wrong. The point rather is that a certain general pattern of behavior appeared that has been far more general, a pattern later reappearing when psychological fashions changed and equality of the races was now deemed to be proven by "evidence" equally as shaky. Moreover, it is a pattern apparent in many other areas having nothing to do with I.Q. or race.

The dogmatic conclusions about racial inferiority which reigned supreme among "experts" in the 1910s and 1920s were replaced with equally dogmatic conclusions about scientific proof of racial equality in the same field by the 1940s and 1950s. By the 1960s official government agencies could declare it "demonstrable"—without demonstration—that "the talent pool in any one ethnic group is substantially the same as that in any other ethnic group."[133] According to the new dogma, "Intellectual potential is distributed among Negro infants in the same proportion and pattern as among Icelanders or Chinese, or any other group."[134] These statements may someday be shown to be true, but that is wholly different from claiming that any such evidence or proof exists today. Both in the earlier and the later dogmatism, the cognitive question is simply not open for discussion, and the ideologically preferred position becomes a moral touchstone rather than a tentative cognitive conclusion. Unlike the earlier period, the present dogmatism has some challenge within the profession—notably by Arthur R. Jensen[135]—but the efforts to discredit his conclusions ("racist") rather than confront his analysis, and sometimes to physically prevent his speaking,[136] indicate that the new dogma is no more willing to treat issues according to intellectual processes than was the old. It is as if beliefs in the psychological field of mental testing have gone through the phases of adolescent fads—fiercely obligatory while in vogue and wholly beyond consideration once the vogue has passed. At least one of the leaders of the older dogmatism—Carl Brigham—later soberly recanted, after the vogue had passed, repudiating the reasoning of the earlier studies and declaring that his own earlier conclusions were "without foundation."[137] Not mistaken, exaggerated, or inconsistent, but *without foundation*.

Both phases of the innate intelligence controversy illustrate a more general characteristic of socially and politically "relevant" intellectual activity—an unwillingness or inability to say, "we don't know," or even to admit that conclusions are tentative. Such admissions would be wholly consonant with intellectual *processes* but not with the interests of intellectuals as a social class. The distinction must be insisted upon, in part because even otherwise worldly thinkers often proceed as if intellectuals have *no* self-interests involved but act solely on cognitive bases or in the policy interest of society at large. Even Voltaire could naively say: "The philosophers having no particular interest to defend, can only speak up in favor of reason and the public interest."[138] That belief—in their own minds or in the minds of others—is itself one of their greatest assets in furthering their own self-interests under protective coloration.

POWER

Intellectuals have for centuries promoted the abrogation of ordinary people's freedom, and romanticized despotism. The shocking record of Western intellectuals glorifying Stalinism in the 1930s was no isolated aberration.

Religious intellectuals in the later Roman Empire, after it became Christian, created a "systematic, active intolerance" that was "something hitherto unknown in the Mediterranean world."[139] There had been "transient persecutions"[140] of early Christians, whose doctrinal abhorrence of "idolatry" had led them to disdain, insult, and even disrupt other religions.[141] But it was only with the triumph of Christianity, and especially of theological intellectuals like Augustine, that intolerance and persecution became pervasive in the Roman Empire. Pagan sacred books were burned,[142] pagan traditions persecuted,[143] and a "forced Christianization"[144] imposed on the Roman Empire, which had long had religious diversity and tolerance as a means of preserving political tranquility and unity. The attempt to impose a particular intellectual (religious) unity or orthodoxy created political disunity as "the bands of civil society were torn asunder by the fury of religious factions."[145] A theoretical controversy among Christian intellectuals over the nature of the Trinity "successively penetrated into every part of the Christian world."[146] In the wake of this and other theological disputes followed violence and atrocities by Christians on other Christians deemed heretical.[147] In many provinces, "towns and villages were laid waste and utterly destroyed."[148] After a respite of tolerance under the Emperor Julian,[149] persecution was resumed under his successors.[150] The internecine violence among various denominations of Christians took far more lives than all the earlier persecutions of Christians in the Roman Empire.[151] Like later totalitarian persecutions in the twentieth century, the persecutions by the Christians produced the emigration of some of the "most industrious subjects" of the Roman Empire, taking with them "the arts both of peace and war."[152] Centuries later, the Reformation brought forth freedom—not by intention but systemically, from the new diversity of power sources. The Protestant Reformation was as intolerant and bloody as any Catholic inquisition.[153] Freedom "was the consequence rather than the design of the Reformation."[154]

In the Roman Empire, as with later persecutions, the abstruse issues involved were matters of moment only to intellectuals. Yet the rival intellectuals' attempts to impose their own vision by force produced mass devastation and a divisiveness that contributed to the decline and fall of the empire.[155] Its immediate effect was to vastly expand the scope of government power into an area—religion—which had once been a realm of freedom.

Such patterns—intellectuals promoting government power and intolerant divisiveness—were not peculiar to the Roman Empire, nor even to Western civilization. In the later dynasties of the Chinese empire, intellectuals also rose to dominance, producing a similar pattern in a very different setting. Beginning with the Sung dynasty (960–1127 A.D.), "scholar-officials," chosen by examinations, dominated the Chinese government and society.[156] Rulers became more autocratic, and government powers more centralized and pervasive in their scope, including "smothering government control of large scale business"[157] and a "secret police almost unfettered by legal restraints."[158] Later, the "recurrent factional controversies" among the intellectuals running the government became "a major factor in the decline of the Ming dynasty."[159] As in ancient Rome, so in the later Chinese empire, the military profession was downgraded[160] and the army "declined in strength and fighting ability."[161] As in ancient Rome, this was the prelude to the Chinese empire's being overwhelmed militarily by foreign peoples once disdained as barbarians.

Prior to its decline and fall, imperial China was the preeminent nation in the world in technology, organization, commerce, and literature,[162] and had the highest standard of living in the world, as late as the sixteenth century.[163] As in the case of Rome in its decline, so in the last century of the Ming dynasty, many people emigrated from China.[164] These "overseas Chinese" have flourished economically in numerous countries from southeast Asia to the

Caribbean, while their native land languished in poverty and weakness, for lack of the practical skills and abilities of those driven out by the oppressions of governments dominated by intellectuals. These intellectuals, "applying the principles they learned from ancient Chinese writings to the realm of practical governance,"[165] promoted "a strong sense of social-welfare activism" in which "central governments assumed responsibility for the total well-being of all Chinese and asserted regulatory authority over all aspects of Chinese life."[166] In short, Chinese intellectuals in power were impelled by Neo-Confucian ideals that would today be called "social justice." But whatever the hoped-for results, the actual processes led to despotism, decline, and defeat.

Intellectuals' promotion of despotism has not been confined to situations, like those in the Roman or Chinese empires, where they themselves were directly involved in wielding power or instigating violence. Even such admirers of freedom in principle as the eighteenth-century French *philosophes* were also admirers of contemporary Russian and Chinese despotism,[167] much like their twentieth-century counterparts. The reasons were also quite similar. The despotisms in question were seen as vehicles for the imposition of intellectuals' designs on society at large. In the eighteenth-century despotisms "the men of letters served in places of eminence, at the very center of things."[168] Class self-interest was, however, seen as the public interest. According to D'Alembert, "the greatest happiness of a nation is realized when those who govern agree with those who instruct it."[169] In the nineteenth century free nations as well, as John Stuart Mill observed, "impatient reformers, thinking it easier to get possession of the government than of the intellects and dispositions of the people," proposed to expand "the power of government."[170]

The French Revolution gave the eighteenth-century intellectuals a chance to rule directly, rather than by their influence on existing despots. Though disciples of the freedom-extolling *philosophes* and ostensibly concerned only with the public interest, their "all-powerful Committee of Public Safety ruled France absolutely as no monarch had ever been able to rule it."[171] The brief rule of Jacobin intellectuals was not only despotic and bloody, but totalitarian in its pervasiveness. The very names of months and years were changed to correspond with their ideology, as were the names of streets, people, and even playing cards.[172] Their regulations extended to friendship and marriage: each adult male had to publicly declare who his friends were, and any married couple who did not either have children or adopt children within a specified time were to have their marriage dissolved and be separated by the government.[173] To administer all this control of individuals, the intellectual-politicians created a vast bureaucracy—never dismantled, and the enduring legacy of the Revolution long after the ideologues were replaced by

Napoleon and then by innumerable other French governments. It was one of the earliest demonstrations of what it meant in practice to "arrange" a society according to "justice."

Although there were despotic governments in the nineteenth century, it was not until twentieth-century totalitarianism that anything like the Committee of Public Safety emerged again. Once more, it was intellectuals who created it—Lenin, Trotsky, and their successors and offshoots carrying out a vision descended from Marx, and Hitler carrying out his own vision from *Mein Kampf*. Whether or not any of these political leaders were intellectuals in the qualitatively cognitive sense, all owed their power precisely to their transmission of ideas, rather than to other political routes to power from dynastic succession, economic achievements, hierarchical progression, or technical expertise. The characteristics of these modern totalitarian governments have already been noted. The support, apologetics, and glorification of foreign totalitarianism among intellectuals in the democratic nations must also be noted, however. The glorification of the Stalin regime by democratic Fabian socialists Sidney and Beatrice Webb is perhaps the classic example,[174] but they are part of a long line of intellectuals including Jean-Paul Sartre,[175] George Bernard Shaw,[176] and G. D. H. Cole,[177] who extolled the virtues of Stalinist Russia, joined by the *Nation, The New Republic,* and (in England) *The New Statesman*.[178] The supporters of an American Communist for President of the United States in 1932 included John Dos Passos, Sherwood Anderson, Edmund Wilson, and Granville Hicks.[179] Fascism also did not lack for apologists and romanticizers, including Irving Babbitt, Charles Beard, George Santayana, and Ezra Pound.[180]

Most American intellectuals of the 1930s were, however, content to support a vast expansion of governmental power in more conventional terms under the New Deal. Disillusionment with Stalin and the Soviet Union eventually led many intellectuals to return to the liberal-left. It has not prevented a similar cycle of romantic glorification of Mao, Castro, and other totalitarians.

THE INTELLECTUAL VISION

Virtually everyone has political opinions, but not everyone has a political vision—a central set of premises from which particular positions can be deduced as corollaries. These premises may be religious, tribal, or ideological. What makes them a coherent vision is the high degree of correlation among the particular conclusions reached on highly disparate subjects. To a racist, for example, the color of an individual's skin may determine a whole host of intellectual, moral, aesthetic, political, and even etiquette questions pertaining to that individual.

An ideological vision is more than belief in a principle. It is a belief that that principle is crucial or overriding, so that other principles or even empirical facts must give way when in conflict with it. The Inquisition had to reject Galileo's astronomical findings in the interests of a higher vision, as the Nazis had to reject Einstein in spite of any evidence about his theories or his individual abilities.

An ideology has been defined as a "systematic and self-contained set of ideas supposedly dealing with the nature of reality (usually social reality), or some segment of reality, and of man's relation (attitude, conduct) toward it; and calling for a commitment independent of specific experience or events." [181] The intellectual process might seem to be a counterforce against generalized, ideological visions, since its canons imply following the particular consequences of its cognitive procedures wherever those consequences (truth) lead in specific instances. Insofar as intellectuals as a social class are motivated by the intellectual process, their positions might be expected to be as diverse as the different readings possible on the complexities of political issues. In short, intellectuals as a social class might be expected to show less of a "herd instinct" pattern as regards group conformity, and at the individual level to dissect issues on their respective specific merits, leading to less correlation among their various political positions than among people who "vote the straight ticket" in either a partisan or an ideological sense. Actual studies of opinions among academics, however, show "exceptionally high correlations among opinions across a broad array of issues," [182] even when the specifics involve such disparate matters as foreign policy, marijuana, and race. These cohesive beliefs among intellectuals have been politically to the left of the general public for as long as such surveys have been taken. [183] This is true not only in the United States, but internationally. [184] What is important at this point, however, is not so much where the intellectuals are politically, but how cohesively the various positions fit together as principles deduced from an underlying vision.

The coherence of a vision may derive from an accurate depiction of a coherent set of relationships empirically observed in the real world, or from the deduction of various conclusions from a given set of premises without much regard to observed facts. As noted in earlier chapters, many political policies are neither based on hard evidence as to causation nor monitor hard evidence on subsequent effects, and especially not negative effects. Antitrust laws, schools busing, rent control, and minimum wage laws, are all based on their consonance with a general vision of the social process, rather than on empirical tests of their positive and negative effects. That crime is caused by poverty and/or discrimination is also part of the same vision, but the empirical evidence is hardly overwhelming, or even unambiguous, since violent crime *declined* in the 1930s[185] during the greatest depression in history and skyrocketed during the affluent 1960s. In England, the crime rate rose as unemployment was reduced to the vanishing point. What Earl Warren called "our disturbed society"[186] had a downwardly trending urban murder rate for about twenty years until the 1960s, when it suddenly doubled in less than a decade, as the Warren Court changed the rules of criminal justice. Sex education in the public schools was another part of the same social vision, and was promoted as a means of reducing teenage pregnancy and venereal disease—but reconsideration of its wisdom or effectiveness has been made in the light of steep increases in both. The percentage of the *public* disavowing sex education in the public schools has increased,[187] but among intellectuals there is no such reconsideration in the light of evidence. Public support of the death penalty, which was declining prior to the increase in the murder rate in the 1960s, rose again as the murder rate rose. Again, this suggests a public more responsive to empirical evidence than intellectuals—i.e., less ideological. A critic has said of liberal intellectuals that their responses to public issues "are as predictable as the salivation of Pavlovian dogs" and can be predicted "with the same comforting assurance with which you expect the sun to rise tomorrow."[188] The data show this to be an overstatement—but not otherwise an incorrect statement.

If the existence of the intellectual vision raises questions about whether it is a product of intellectual processes or of intellectuals' occupational self-interest, the specific contents of the prevailing intellectual vision raise the same question even more sharply. These may be summarized, and to some extent simplified, as follows:

1. There is vast unhappiness ("social problems") caused by other elites with whom intellectual elites are competing—notably businessmen, the military, and politicians.
2. Those who are empirically less fortunate are morally and causally "victims" of those competing elites, and their salvation lies in more utilization of the services of intellectuals as "educators" (literally or figuratively), as designers of programs (or societies), and as political leaders and decision-making surrogates.
3. Articulated rationality—the occupational characteristic of intellectuals—is the best mode of social decision making.
4. Existing knowledge—whether scattered in fragments through society or collected together in traditions, the Constitution, etc.—is inadequate for decision making, so that "solving" the society's "problems" depends on the specific fragment of knowledge held by intellectuals.

Egocentric visions of the world do not imply deliberate attempts at deception and self-aggrandizement. The mechanisms of human rationalization are too complex for any attempt here to say how such views emerged. It is enough for present purposes that such views of social organization are concentrated among intellectuals, and the question is how these views compare with ascertainable facts.

As a necessarily limited sampling of what has been called a "litany of woe and crisis," there have been recent assertions by intellectuals that "human society is in a stage of comprehensive breakdown,"[189] that the United States "disintegrates,"[190] that the nation is "essentially evil and the evil can be exorcised only by turning the system upside down,"[191] that "the civil rights legislation is absolutely meaningless, and it was meant to be meaningless,"[192] and that "life has broken down in this country."[193] Although intellectuals often pose as articulators of a general malaise, in fact neither the general public nor the designated "victims" share this vision of the intellectuals. Among the supposedly embittered and disenchanted youth, 90 percent describe their past life as happy and 93 percent expect their future life to be so.[194] From 80 to 90 percent of the supposedly alienated workers with "dehumanizing" jobs describe themselves as satisfied with their work.[195] Significantly, about half felt that *others* were dissatisfied with their work;[196] the intellectuals' outpourings were not ineffective, in matters outside people's direct experience. More blacks were satisfied than dissatisfied in such areas as work, housing, and education.[197] In contrast to the intellectuals' preoccupation with "distributive justice," there were four times as many blacks who thought that people with more ability should earn more as there were who believed in even approximate equality of earnings.[198] As for "women's liberation," fewer women than men were sympathetic to it.[199] For Americans as a whole, only 12 percent would like to live in another country—less than in Sweden, Holland, Brazil, or Greece, and less than half as many as in West Germany or Great Britain.[200] Among those in foreign countries who would like to live somewhere else, the United States was either the first or second choice in Sweden, West Germany, Greece, Brazil, Finland and Uruguay.[201]

Where the public differs from intellectuals, it is often taken as axiomatic that that demonstrates the misguided ignorance of the public and their need to be "educated." However, the supposed "alienation" of workers, "black rage," and the opinion of women are subjects on which these respective groups are themselves the experts. Moreover, insofar as there are hard data on such matters, these data almost invariably support public opinion rather than the intellectual vision. The supposedly "meaningless" civil rights revolution saw black family income double in the 1960s while white family income rose by only 69 percent,[202] black college enrollment almost doubled in less than a decade,[203] and the number of black foremen and policemen more than doubled during the 1960s.[204] While statisticians keep large-scale poverty alive with data limited to cash income, in-kind transfers (food stamps, housing subsidies, free medical care, etc.) have reduced it drastically in fact.[205]

The tripling of government welfare spending from 1965 to 1973 provided a total value of resources consumed by the poor in 1973 which was "enough to raise every officially poor family 30 percent above its poverty line."[206] Yet the official census data are based on samples in which people "are not even asked if they receive food stamps, live in public housing, or are eligible for medicaid."[207] Independent private researchers who count in-kind transfers find only 3 to 6 percent of the American population poor[208] by the same standards as the government uses. One perhaps revealing statistic is that 30 percent of the families with official incomes under $3,000 have air conditioners and 29 percent have color televisions.[209]

Intellectuals almost automatically explain the misfortunes of groups in terms of victimization by elites who are rivals of intellectuals. By asserting or defining (seldom testing) misfortune as victimization, all other possible explanations are arbitrarily ruled out of order, and with them perhaps hopes of in fact remedying the misfortune. The victimhood approach also requires ignoring, suppressing, or deemphasizing successful initiatives already undertaken by the disadvantaged group or portions thereof—thereby sacrificing accumulated human capital in terms of know-how, morale, and a favorable public image of groups usually portrayed as a "problem." In the victimization approach, intergroup statistical differences become "inequities," though in particular cases they may be due to group differences in age, geographical distribution, or other variables with no moral implications.

Victimhood as an explanation of intergroup differences extends internationally to the Third World—typically countries that were poor before Western nations arrived, remained poor while they were there, and have continued poor after they left. The explanation of their poverty? Western exploitation! An economist who treats this as a testable hypothesis notes that "throughout the underdeveloped world the most prosperous areas are those with which the West has established closest contact" and contrasts this with "the extreme backwardness of societies and regions without external contacts."[210] But like other victimhood approaches, Third-Worldism is not really an hypothesis but an axiom, not so much argued explicitly as insinuated by the words chosen ("the web of capitalism,"[211] "the imperialist network"[212]) and established by reiteration.

What is the function of victimhood for intellectuals? It hardly derives from rigorous application of intellectual processes. It does, however, greatly enhance the role of intellectuals as a social class—as consultants, advisors, planners, experimenters, authorities, etc. At a minimum, the victimhood approach presents intellectuals with psychic gratifications[213] (including denouncing rival elites). Beyond that are influence, power, visibility, and money—ample incentives for most people in most times. The victimhood concept is at least a rational approach, and perhaps an optimal approach, to social questions from the standpoint of intellectuals as a social class, however little it does for anyone else and however counterproductive it may be for society at large. The victimhood approach is also consonant with a more general, intellectual approach to human beings, abstracting from tangible natural or cultural differences—and being left highly suspicious of intergroup differences in socioeconomic results, which are indeed inexplicable, once major variables have been assumed away.

Behind this questionable cognitive procedure may lie a desire to establish the equality of man and perhaps a sense of "there but for the grace of God go I." This may be a laudable objective as a counterpoise to the egoistic ideology of individual or group "merit." But both approaches confuse causation with morality. If individual A has characteristic X, and individual B does not, then it is important for both to know whether X is an advantage or a disadvantage, even if neither "deserves" it and even if both are completely creatures of circumstances beyond their control as regards that characteristic. Nothing is gained by pretending that it doesn't matter when it does, or by leaving it out of account in explaining differences between them. That only opens the way to concocting mythical reasons for their differences.

The victimhood axiom is based on little more than a minute scrutiny of rival elites and a reporting of their numerous sins and shortcomings—such as could be found in equally close scrutiny of any other group of human beings—elite or otherwise. That multinational corporations have cheated here and bribed there is neither startling as information nor a causal explanation of Third World poverty, however morally deplorable or legally actionable it may be. If prosperity could come only from the united efforts of upright and noble-minded people, all of mankind would still be sunk in poverty. It is always true, at least in the short run, that those poorly fed would be better fed if the well-fed shared some of their food. That is wholly different from saying that people are starving in India *because* overfed Americans somehow took their food.

The dissonance between the intellectual vision and the experience and opinions of the public has led to a new phenomenon in recent years, sometimes called "totalitarian democracy." Whereas in earlier times—the New Deal era, for example—the "intelligentsia saw The People as its ally in the struggle for power,"[214] and "a plebiscitary interpretation of democracy"[215] was considered a hallmark of liberalism, they now see public opinion and democratic processes as obstacles to be overcome. While intellectuals still speak in the name of The People and espouse democratic ideals, "their ceaseless strategy is inconsistent with their professed thought."[216] Such strategy features "rules that minimize majority participation, thereby permitting a small faction to gain control."[217] Whether within political party caucuses, environmental agencies, or other social decision-making institutions, complex rules and tiresome procedures are sorting devices that ensure the differential survival of intellectuals in decision-making processes. These procedures are, in effect, "the poll tax that the New Elite has been imposing on everyone else."[218] Recourse to courts and administrative agencies as the preferred mechanisms of decision making also favors the chances of intellectuals in imposing their vision on the rest of society. As a leader in the fight for eliminating capital punishment observed, there was "an unmistakable preference for the courts," because reform through democratic legislation requires either "public consensus or a powerful minority lobby,"[219] as contrasted with the greater ease of attempts to "market new constitutional protections to judges."[220] A bow toward democracy is made with claims that the newly created "constitutional" rights are "a response to deeply rooted social conflicts that elected representatives have not addressed" because "the interests that the Court protected could not mobilize sufficient power,"[221] but these vague references to "deeply rooted social conflicts" and "power" boil down to the simple fact that a majority of the public—indeed, "a twenty-year high"— supported the death penalty in the midst of the intellectuals' crusade to abolish it.[222] Appeals to a higher moral code—of which they are axiomatically the keepers—not only justifies the superseding of the democratic will or the constitutional processes, but justifies calling it "democracy," for it is what the people *would* want, if only they knew better, if only they shared the intellectuals' vision. This approach has been aptly called "totalitarian democracy." Sometimes the moral superiority of intellectuals is put even more bluntly, as in the assertion that "a more equal society is a better society even if its citizens prefer inequality."[223]

Political intellectuals attempt to supersede not only political processes but also cognitive processes. Although they may specialize in cognitive skills, the impersonal or "objective" nature of this skill makes it politically unreliable at any given juncture. What is far more reliable is to use the intellectuals' *general* superiority in cognitive matters as a reason for dismissing—rather than arguing with—opposing views on a particular matter. Terman did not in any substantive sense *argue* with Walter Lippman over the issue of racially innate intelligence. Rather he used his position as an "expert" in the field to dismiss Lippman's ideas as "sentiment and opinion," contrasted with his own "quantitative methods"—which he *referred to* but in no way exhibited. Keynes, in a book devoted to comparing capitalisn and communism, sweepingly dismissed Marxism as a doctrine "which I know to be not only scientifically erroneous but without interest or application for the modern world[224]—

without ever telling us *why* it was wrong, or even offering a hint. James Baldwin similarly asserted that Americans are "the most dishonorable and violent people in the world,"[225] without any reference to others whose claim to that title included the wholesale extermination of more people than were denied civil rights in the United States. More generally, intellectuals' personal preferences and beliefs tend to become axioms rather than hypotheses. The notion that minority progress can only occur through governmental intervention is a typical such axiom—even though (1) low-income American Indians have long had much government involvement, while more financially successful groups such as Orientals and Jews have had little government involvement in their rise from poverty to affluence, (2) the very existence of northern urban black communities is due almost exclusively to private transfers of property through market mechanisms, and (3) the education of black youngsters was initially almost solely nongovernmental (or even antigovernmental, in defiance of laws against their education in the antebellum South), and it was 1916 before the number of black youngsters educated in public high schools equalled the number educated privately.[226] The point is not that these particular facts are determining as far as the relative importance of contemporary political and nonpolitical alternatives. Rather, the point is that opposite facts have been arbitrarily postulated or implicitly assumed, as if *they* were determining.

Intellectuals' attempts to depict the less fortunate as victims of some competing elite—especially businessmen—is likewise seldom subject to any empirical test or even specification of alternative hypotheses. If lowpaid workers were exploited, for example, we might expect to find their employers unusually prosperous rather than finding, as we generally do, high rates of bankruptcy among low-wage firms. The point is not that this particular test has not been used, but that the whole discussion avoided any test, and relied instead on axioms. It is ideological rather than cognitive thinking: "When we discover that certain ideas about man, history and society seem, to those who believe in them, to be either self-evident or so manifestly correct that opposing them is a mark of stupidity or malice, then we may be fairly sure we are dealing with an *ideology* and ideological thinking."[227]

The intellectual vision of victimhood makes the Third World the source of the wealth of the industrial countries, when in fact the bulk of American investments, for example, are in other industrial countries rather than the poorer nations. The rhetoric of victimhood extends even to those who prosper from so-called "underground" publications which are sold openly everywhere, including in government buildings. Often the nonempirical assertions assume the camouflage of empirical statements by the use of modifying words which reduce their meaningfulness "immeasureably," "invariably," "profoundly," etc.—which simply "indicates that the writer has no data, has done no research, and has merely transmuted perceptions into 'facts.' "[228]

Sometimes this transmuting of notions into "facts" includes an exaggeration of the advancement of foreign totalitarians rather than a denigration of that of democratic nations. For example, the supposed economic triumphs of the Bolsheviks are often based on the belief that czarist Russia had advanced unusually slowly, when in fact it had become one of the fastest growing economies in Europe. The military might of the U.S.S.R. is not proportional to its economic development, but to the ability of its government to appropriate a higher share of its output for military purposes.

Articulated rationality as a process and the delegation of decision making to "experts" have become the central features of the intellectuals' vision of political and social decision making. Where there is no compellingly articulated rationality, then there is irrationality, from this viewpoint. The experiential, systemic, traditional, or other forms of authentication are not even considered. Thus "Americans have an irrational commitment to private ownership"[229] to which they are "addicted"[230] and *social* goals are built into the very definition of "rational" policy,[231] in the approach of two well-known scholars who unsurprisingly declare: "Delegation to experts has become an indispensible aid to rational calculation in modern life."[232] To them bureaucracy "is a method for bringing scientific judgments to bear on policy decisions,"[233] and a "triumph for the deliberate, calculated, conscious attempt to adapt means to ends in the most rational manner."[234] Like Max Weber's assertion of the "indubitable technical superiority" of bureaucracy[235] and Thorstein Veblen's assertions of the supposed efficiency of a technocratic economy,[236] this argument ignores the fact that there is *no such thing as efficiency independent of values*. Processes are efficient or inefficient at reaching specified values—e.g., an engine in moving a car forward, rather than dissipating its power in random shaking. No amount of bureaucratic or technological expertise can produce "efficiency" by numerous and disparate individual standards, however much they may facilitate the substitution of other standards by "experts" to whom power has been delegated.

Perhaps the most important policy question is not how or why intellectuals have sought power but how and why others have granted them as much power and influence as they have. It has seldom been because of any demonstrated success. Crime rates have soared as the theories of criminologists were put into practice; educational test scores have plummeted as new educational theories were tried. Indeed, no small part of the intellectuals' achievement has been in keeping empirical verification processes off the agenda. Moreover, those who are more essentially intellectual in occupation—primarily producers of ideas—have been both more avid and more favored in power terms than those who produce tangible benefits in verifiable form. It is not the agronomists, physicians, or engineers who have risen to power, but the sociologists, psychologists, and legal theorists. It is the latter groups who have transformed the political and social landscape of the United States and much of the Western world. Not only is much of their cognitive output inherently unverifiable empirically; they have by various definitions and axiomatic procedures made their output even less susceptible of authentication than it would be otherwise. The jargon alone in these fields makes their substance largely inaccessible to outsiders. Transitionism explains away all disastrous consequences as the short-run price for a long-run triumph. They have conquered by faith rather than works. This is hardly surprising in the light of similar achievements by religious intellectuals who preceded them by centuries. Whatever has made human beings eager to hear those who claim to know the future has worked for modern as well as ancient intellectuals.

The modern equivalent of the ancient seer to whom men submitted their credulity is the "expert." Deference to "experts" generally does not depend upon any consideraton of (1) whether there is in fact any expertise on the particular issue (often there is not, especially in the social sciences), (2) whether the individuals selected have in fact any such expertise, as contrasted with an assortment of miscellaneous information, or (3) whether those who have expertise are in fact applying it, as distinguished from using it as a means of imposing personal preferences or group fashions. Politicians may also take issues to "experts" as a means of escaping political responsibility for unpredictable or controversial outcomes. Finally, there are "experts" whose expertise consists largely of detailed knowledge of some particular governmental program, whose institutional complexities and jargon make them incomprehensible to others. The enormous investment of time and effort required to acquire familiarity with intricate regulations and labyrinthine administrative procedures is unlikely to be made by someone unsympathetic to a program, both because the philosophic or cognitive interest would not be sufficient and because such an investment offers large payoffs only to those whom the particular bureaucracy would employ as consultants or officials— obviously *not* those unsympathetic to its programs. Even among "experts" in institutional detail who are unaffiliated with the program, their expertise has value only so long as the program itself exists. They would become experts in nothing if the programs were abolished, and a costly investment on their part would be destroyed. Under this set of incentives and constraints, it may be a truism that "all the experts" favor this or that program, but that may indicate very little about its value to the larger society. "Experts" of this sort can often devastate critics by exposing the latter's misunderstandings of particular details, terminology, or legal technicalities—none of which may be crucial to the issue but all of which establish politically the superior knowledge of those favoring the program, and enable them to dismiss critics as "misinformed."

It is not so much the bias of "expert" intellectuals that is crucial, but the *difference* between their perceived "objective" expertise and the reality which makes the political process vulnerable to their influence. Publicly recognized special interest groups—landlords discussing rent control, oil companies discussing energy, etc.—may have similar incentives and constraints, but are far less effective in getting their social viewpoints accepted as objective truth or social concern. But when an academic intellectual appears as an "expert" witness before a congressional committee, no one ever asks if he has been a recipient of large research grants or lucrative consulting fees from the very agency whose programs he is about to "objectively" assess in terms of the public interest. While special interest advertising carries not only that explicit designation but a heavy price tag as well, talk show hosts eagerly welcome "experts" extolling the virtues of this or that program, or raising alarms about the dire consequences of its possible curtailment or extinction. Such experts are then thanked warmly for "taking time out from your busy schedule" to come "inform" the public—i.e., to get free advertising for their special interest, with an audience in the millions. The print media are equally likely to bill such "experts'" statements as news rather than advertising.

As noted in Chapter 8, special interests can serve a useful social purpose in airing issues—especially when there are *competing* special interests and they are all recognized for what they are. The political advantages of intellectuals derive precisely from their not being recognized as interested parties. It is this *difference* in the public's cost of knowledge of the personal stakes of the spokesman involved when businessmen, academic intellectuals, and others dispute that gives the intellectuals their decisive advantage. In many issues, there are no competing organized interests to challenge the intellectuals, as when it is a question of taking tax money and using it to create or support programs that intellectuals favor on ideological grounds or for personal gain. Vast governmental research funds, controlled by the very agencies whose performances and impact are being evaluated, ensure that any politically sophisticated agency can field a battalion of precommitted "experts" from among its academic grant recipients and consultants. Not all of the latter are simply "hired guns." As long as the agency involved can select among grant recipients, they can choose people sincerely committed to their viewpoint and not those sincerely committed to opposite views. The former will have massive research to back up their viewpoint; the latter may be reduced to speaking in generalities or raising methodological questions about others' research, neither of which is very effective politically. The net result is that tax money is used to subsidize campaigns to get more tax money. More important, from the standpoint of freedom, central government power is used to promote more central government power, with intellectuals a major force in these efforts.

Despite their acceptance as independent "experts" giving objective judgements, intellectuals have enormous personal stakes. In addition to their immediate personal gains as individuals, intellectuals as a class are dependent upon the backing of political power to impose their visions on the underlying population. The history of intellectuals from the Roman and Chinese empires to the French Revolution to modern totalitarianism shows how compelling a goal that has been, and how readily the freedom of others is sacrificed to such visions—whether of religious salvation, or "social justice." Totalitarianism is only a carrying to its logical conclusion of the view that the vision—ideals, principles, religion, etc.—is paramount and flesh-and-blood human beings expendable.

Ironically, despite intellectuals' power concentrating role and their insulation of that power from public feedback, among their justifications is that *other* decision-making elites possess concentrated power, and are unaccountable in its use. Attempts to depict nonintellectual decision makers as both powerful and socially irresponsible are clearly in the class interest of intellectuals. Moreover, it is easy for intellectuals to conceive of rival elites as unaccountable powers because their accountability is often *not* in terms of articulated rationality, the central modality of intellectuals. Corporate executives' decisions may reflect very little articulated input from the public and may be accompanied by very little discussion of their own reasons, or may even be obfuscated by public relations statements—and yet be responsive to public opinion to the point of paranoia about offending, boring, or otherwise losing their customers. The extreme sensitivity of television networks to program ratings is a classic case of corporate hyperresponsiveness in a situation where there is virtually no articulate consumer-producer interaction. The Edsel was not dropped, nor the W.T. Grant department store chain liquidated because of articualtion in either direction, but because customer choices forced such decisions.

In short, the absence of *articulated* accountability is not an absence of accountability as such. Conversely, the presence of articulation, and of phrases about "the public interest" or "the people" does not imply accountability, whether such phrases are used by intellectuals, politicians, or corporate press agents copying their styles to convey a fashionable image of "corporate responsibility." The decisive knowledge that is conveyed, and responded to, is transmitted financially. Accountability is apparent not only in the dramatic cases where famous products or companies disappear, but more pervasively in the constant changing of products, corporate policies and/or managements to accomodate changing consumer preferences and changing technological and organizational possibilities.

That intellectuals tend to conceive of accountability solely in terms of their own processes of articulated rationality says more about the myopia or egocentricity of intellectuals than about the functioning of social processes. A businessman whose whole economic future is staked on the correctness of his assessments of consumer desires or technological possibilities is regarded by intellectuals as unaccountable, because he does not articulate to anyone. Conversely, psychiatrists, psychologists and social workers whose articulated assessments lead to dangerous criminals being turned loose are *not* accused of being unaccountable, even though they suffer no penalties for the robberies, assaults, or murders committed by those released—not even the embarrassment of having a personal box score kept on the criminals released on their recommendations.

Many of the same intellectuals who depict business as unaccountable to the public also deplore such things as television ratings and the proliferation of product models differing by nuances (automobiles, telephones, airline passenger sections)—all representing attempts to cater to public taste(s). Intellectuals' conceptions of making business accountable almost invariably involve making more *articulation* necessary—at stockholders' meetings, before government agencies, or public disclosures about internal business processes. Unarticulated accountability by *results*—product characteristics and prices—is either ignored or arbitrarily subordinated to articulation about processes, despite the fact that (almost by definition) a lay public is more likely to be able to judge tangible end results than to monitor complex specialized processes. Often proposals for accountability in the *name* of the public mean in practice articulation to intellectuals placed on corporate boards by government (or under threat of government action) as "public" representatives. Here the self-interest of intellectuals is even more apparent, and the claim of responsiveness to the desires of the general public even more questionable.

Nowhere is the meaning of "public" representation better illustrated than in so-called "public" television, where the tastes actually served are not those of the public but of atypical elites, favoring sports (soccer, tennis) different from those preferred by the public (baseball, football), favoring *British* soap operas ("Poldark," "Upstairs, Downstairs") rather than American, and rescuing performers who lost out in public popularity (Dick Cavett) compared to their competitors (Johnny Carson), but who happen to be favored by intellectuals. The issue here is not about the artistic merits of these various enter-tainment productions, but about what "public" accountability means in practice, when conceived of as articulation rather than alternative processes for conveying public preferences.

Sometimes the supposed lack of "accountability" of corporate manage-ment is vis-à-vis stockholders, rather than the general public. The "separa-tion of ownership and control" has long been regarded as a social "problem" to be "solved"—almost invariably by more articulation and/or political con-trol. The possibility that such separation may be *desired* by stockholders themselves is ignored. Yet many stockholders have sufficient investments to form their own business and manage it—if they wanted to. Their preference for having someone else carry out the managerial functions is revealed by their purchase of stock. As stockholders, they monitor end-results—divi-dends—rather than attempt to monitor managerial processes. To allow other stockholders or "public" representatives to monitor managerial processes would be to deprive stockholders in general of the option of choosing to whom to entrust their investments. Those stockholders who might prefer be-ing involved in management can of course hold stock in such corporations as choose to attract them by offering such terms, if such arrangements are suffi-ciently viable to allow such corporations to compete and survive.

Sometimes the business "concentration" that is attacked is based on the percentage of the market served ("controlled") by some small number of companies or the proportion of wealth or land owned by some given number or percent of businesses, families, or individuals. As noted in earlier discus-sions of so-called "income distribution," much of the individual and family data reflect different stages of a life cycle rather than people in one class rather than another—some of today's upper bracket people being yesterday's lower bracket people and some of today's lower bracket people being the children of today's upper bracket people. Business concentration figures are even trickier. Statements that, for example, 568 companies control 11 per-cent of the land area[237] convey insinuations but no economic conclusion or even allegation, since 568 companies are not a decision-making unit, nor even a basis for a viable conspiracy—even if 11 percent of the land were enough to conspire with. To claim, as Ralph Nader does, that twenty-five landowners own more than 61 percent of California's private land[238] is com-pletely misleading. Not only do state and national government own a sub-stantial part of California—reducing the true percentage well below the 61 percent figure—it is also important to realize that the so-called twenty-five "landowners" include thousands or millions of *people*, because of organiza-tional ownership by corporations with vast numbers of stockholders. The full facts reveal not so much a concentration of land ownership among few people as a preference of many people to have their assets managed for them by professional managers.

Given the advantages of specialization, it is hard to imagine how various activities could fail to be "concentrated." Business concentration is simply arbitrarily singled out for detailed scrutiny and exposé-style treatment, fraught with insinuations but devoid of empirically testable conclusions. The implicit premise is that there is something strange, unique, or sinister in such numerical relationships representing "concentration," when in fact such numerical relationships are commonplace throughout human endeavors. Anyone who watches professional basketball knows that less than 12 percent of the population supplies over half the basketball stars. Only 3 percent of the population grows all of the food, less than 1 percent of the population runs all of the post offices or drives all of the taxicabs. Indeed, far less than 1 percent of the population writes all the stories about small percentages of people controlling large percentages of activities. All the authors, editors and reporters in the country add up to much less than one percent of the population—and in fact less than one-twentieth as many people as proprietors, managers, and officials in business, who are supposed to represent "concentration" dangers.[239] The simple underlying fact of advantages of specialization can be looked at in many ways, including the sinister insinuations chosen by intellectuals when discussing competing elites.

The discussion here of the political role of intellectuals has been almost exclusively a discussion of the role of politically liberal intellectuals because (1) the predominant political orientation of American intellectuals has been liberal and left, and (2) the small, politically far less influential, nonliberal intellectuals are a heterogeneous group, consisting of followers of specific economic or social principles—the "Chicago School" of economists (Milton Friedman, George Stigler, etc.), the sociologically oriented "Neo-conservatives" (Irving Kristol, James Q. Wilson, etc.) and conservatives in the more usual sense of people who follow traditional values (William F. Buckley, Russell Kirk, etc.). Unlike political liberalism, which can be reduced to a body of values, postulates or inferences,[240] "conservatism," as the term is usually applied (to include all the varieties itemized above, for example), has little or no determinate content. If a conservative is someone who wants to conserve, then what specifically he wants to conserve depends upon what happens to exist, and this might be anything from the social-political system of eighteenth-century England to the contemporary Soviet Union. In short, the broad label "conservative" is itself virtually devoid of content, however much specific content there may be in each of the groupings and individuals to whom that label is loosely applied.

Because the great majority of intellectuals are liberal, it is essentially liberals who define what is meant by the term "conservative." In the liberal vision, conservatives are people who want to either preserve the status quo or go back to some earlier and "simpler" times. However politically effective such conceptions may be, in putting alternatives out of court, there are great cognitive difficulties with such characterizations. For example, there is not a speck of evidence that earlier times were in fact "simpler," though of course our knowledge of such times may be cruder. Moreover, the status quo in the United States and throughout much of Western Europe is a liberal-left status quo, entrenched for at least a generation. Alternatives to this are arbitrarily called "going back," even when these alternatives refer to social arrangements that have never existed (the monetary proposals of Chicago economists, for example), while proposals to continue or accelerate existing political-economic trends are called "innovative" or even "radical." Conservers of liberal or socialist institutions are never called by the perjorative term, "conservative." Neither are those who espouse the ideals, or repeat the very phrases, of 1789 France. In the broad sweep of history, the systemic advantages of decentralized decision making are a far more recent conception than the idea that salvation lies in concentrating power in the hands of the right people with the right principles. Adam Smith came two thousand years after Plato, but contemporary versions of the philosopher-king approach are considered new and revolutionary, while contemporary versions of systemic decentralization are considered "outmoded." Such expressions are themselves part of a vision in which ideas may be judged temporally rather than cognitively—what was adequate to older and simpler times being inadequate for the complexities of modern life.

The characteristics of the intellectual vision are strikingly similar to the characteristics of totalitarian ideology—especially the localization of evil and of wisdom, and psychic identification with the interests of great masses, whose actual preferences are ignored in favor of the overriding preferences of intellectuals. It is consistent with this that intellectuals have supported and indeed spearheaded the movement toward a centralization of political power in democratic nations and have apologized for foreign despotisms and totalitarianisms which featured like-minded people. Democratic traditions may create either internal ideological conflicts or an external pragmatic need to rhetorically paper over the totalitarian thrust of the intellectual vision. Here intellectual processes—definitional clarity, logical consistency, canons of evidence—are often sacrificed to the intellectual vision or the self-interest of the intellectual class. For example, antidemocratic processes may be described by democratic rhetoric as "participation" or "public" representation. Presumption may be substituted for evidence—past, present, or future—as in numerous arguments that the national I.Q. was declining, or existing evidence may be resolutely disregarded, as in claims that crime rates reflect social "root causes," or that "innovative" educational methods are more effective, or that sex education reduces the incidence of teenage pregnancy and venereal disease. In short, there is little to suggest that intellectuals' political positions reflect the intellectual process, and much to suggest that their positions reflect a vision and a set of interests peculiar to the intellectual class.

SUMMARY: EMBATTLED FREEDOM

Freedom has always been embattled, where it has not been wholly crushed. The desire for freedom and for its opposite, power, are as universal as any human attributes. The nuclear age has added a new dimension to the struggle between them. So too has the rise to prominence of intellectuals as a social class with growing political aspirations, influence and/or dominance.

Almost by definition, the movement to totalitarianism is a one-way movement. No totalitarian government has ever chosen to become free or democratic, though a free and democratic nation may choose to move toward totalitarianism, as Germany did in 1933. If governmental choice were the only variable, the eventual worldwide triumph of totalitarianism would be inevitable, since choices in one direction are reversible and choices in the other direction are not. Nazi totalitarianism was smashed by external military power and its empire liberated by invading armies. But the invasion of Normandy that led to the liberation of Western Europe can hardly find a new counterpart to liberate Eastern Europe in a nuclear age. That the Western democracies had to stand by helplessly while Soviet tanks crushed Eastern European uprisings in the 1950s was grim proof of the new realities of nuclear annihilation. Perhaps in a very long run, political erosions might sap the vitality of totalitarianism or economic efficiency claims modify it incrementally (as it has already in agriculture) to the point where ultimately it no longer resembles its present centralized model. But even these remote hopes are lessened if the surviving examples of free and democratic nations are lost before this can happen.

In the nuclear era, the international survival of the nontotalitarian world rests ultimately on an American nuclear deterrent. Otherwise the nuclear power of the Soviet Union would be irresistible as a threat in international power politics, whether or not it was ever actually used. Seldom has the survival of human freedom rested so decisively in the hands of one government, or the survival of the species in just two.

The spread of totalitarianism—communism since World War II—has been at the expense of all kinds of nontotalitarian governments: a democracy in Czechoslovakia, a kingdom in Laos, a Latin American autocracy in Cuba. These various forms of government, whatever their merits or demerits otherwise, tend to be changeable. A dictatorship like Spain could liberalize after Franco, and Portugal could swing to the left after Salazar. As of any given moment, some of these governments might seem not very different in their degrees of freedom from communist dictatorships. But a communist dictatorship has a permanence that these other forms of government cannot approach. Inasmuch as most of the governments on the planet are nondemocratic as well as noncommunist, stemming the spread of totalitarianism necessarily means American cooperation with nondemocratic nations. To some Americans, but especially intellectuals, such cooperation appears as a violation of the democratic creed, and should be contingent on the nondemocratic nation's adoption of democratic institutions. This is a special case of the general implicit assumption of a single scale of values applicable to all. The historical recency and rarity of constitutional democracy makes the universal application of such a model especially egocentric and arbitrary. As a precondition for cooperation to stem the tide of an irreversible totalitarianism, it suggests either a low estimate of the threat or an unwillingness to face the historic responsibility implied by it. The central assumption of a single scale of values applicable to all is a force in domestic as well as international politics. It has facilitated the imposition of many specific laws and policies resented by the population, and—more important—it has altered the enduring political framework to make such impositions possible through courts, administrative agencies, and other institutions and processes insulated from public feedback and responsive to smaller, more zealous constituencies. Domestically as well as internationally, freedom as the general preservation of options gives way to the imposition of one group's preferred option. Their influence greatly exceeds their numbers, partly because they are perceived as objective "experts" and partly because of the moral nature of their arguments and the apparently moral high ground that they themselves occupy (as contrasted with the arguments of conventional special interest groups in these respects).

The moralistic approach to public policy is not merely a political advantage to those seeking greater concentration of power. Moralism in itself implies a concentration of power. More justice for all is a contradiction in terms, in a world of diverse values and disparate conceptions of justice itself.

"More" justice in such a world means more forcible imposition of one particular brand of justice—i.e., less freedom. Perfect justice in this context means perfect tyranny. The point is not merely semantic or theoretical. The reach of national political power into every nook and cranny has proceeded in step with campaigns for greater "social justice." A parent forced by the law and income to send his child off to a public school where he is abused or terrorized by other children is painfully aware of a loss of freedom, however much distant theoreticians talk of justice as they forcibly unsort people, and however safe the occupational advantages of intellectuals remain from governmental power.

The myopic conception of freedom as those freedoms peculiar to intellectuals, or formal constitutional guarantees, ignores the many ways in which options can be forcibly removed by administrative or judicial fiat, or by the government's ability to structure financial or other incentives in such a way as to impose high costs or grant high rewards according to whether individuals and organizations do what the government wants done—*whether or not the government has any explicit statutory or constitutional authority for controlling such behavior*. More than a century ago, John Stuart Mill saw the dangers in the growth of the extralegal powers of government:

Every function superadded to those already exercised by the government causes its influence over hopes and fears to be more widely diffused, and converts, more and more, the active and ambitious part of the public into hangers-on of the government, or of some part which aims at becoming the government. If the roads, the railways, the banks, the insurance offices, the great joint-stock companies, the universities, and the public charities were all of them branches of the government; if, in addition, the municipal corporations and local boards, with all that now devolves on them, became departments of the central administration; if the employees of all these different enterprises were appointed and paid by the government, and looked to the government for every rise in life; not all the freedom of the press and popular constitution of the legislature would make this or any other country free otherwise than in name.[241]

Freedom is endangered both internationally and domestically. The international danger turns ultimately on military power, and the domestic danger on ideology. It is not merely that an ideology may be wrong—everything human is imperfect—but that the zeal, the urgency, and the moral certitude behind it create special dangers to a free constitutional government of checks and balances, for maintaining that constitutional freedom often seems less important than scoring a victory for "justice" as envisioned by zealots. When a segment of these zealots are able to pose as disinterested "experts" the dangers are compounded.

The United States of America is a central battleground for both kinds of dangers to freedom, domestic and international. Militarily, the whole Western world is dependent on American nuclear power. Politically, the power-centralizing forces have advanced much further toward their goals in other Western countries than in America, where a variety of autonomous forces are still able to oppose these trends. Intellectuals have never been as cohesive in the United States as in smaller, more socially homogeneous countries,[242] and the public has never been as thoroughly awed by them. One symptom of this is the utter failure of socialist movements to take root in the United States, while they are strong in Western Europe. Socialist movements (and communist movements) have—in every period of history and around the world—been the creation of middle class intellectuals, though the ceaseless reiteration of the "working class" theme in socialist rhetoric may verbally obscure this plain fact. Where socialist intellectuals have allied themselves politically with labor unions—as in the British Labor Party, for example—it is the intellectuals who lead the alliance to the left, with varying degrees of resistance or acquiescence by the working class segment of the alliance. The very same pattern has been attempted at various times in American history, but American workers have historically been far less deferential to their "betters"—whether employers or intellectuals—than European workers. The intellectuals have been more successfully rebuffed here.

Certainly if the trend toward centralization of power—and the corresponding erosion of freedom—can be stopped anywhere, it can be stopped in America. But in a nuclear age, even the momentous question of human freedom must be considered in the light of military realities.

THE MILITARY "BALANCE"

For a brief period at the end of World War II, the United States stood in a military power position perhaps unparalleled in human history. The Roman Empire at its height was not as unchallengeable. In addition to its monopoly of the greatest military weapon in history, the United States alone of the industrial nations had its entire productive capacity intact, unscathed by war, and producing more than all the rest of the world put together.[243] Its people were united behind the government as seldom before or since. In sheer power terms, the United States could have imposed an American empire or at least a modern version of the *Pax Britannica* that kept Europe and most of the world free of major wars for generations. The point here is not to argue that either of these things should have been done. The point is to show the situation, the possibilities, and to compare these with what in fact happened.

What actually happened was that three-quarters of the total American military force demobilized in one year—9 million men and women from 1945 to 1946, and the remaining 3 million military personnel were reduced by half again by 1947.[244] By 1948 the American military force was smaller than it had been at the time of Pearl Harbor. Nations from which the American army drove the Nazis were forthwith restored to their own sovereignty. The American occupation army that entered Japan in 1945 was ordered to neither take nor even buy food from the Japanese, as that would reduce food badly needed by the Japanese civilian population. For what may have been the first time in history, a conquering army was put on short rations until food arrived from their homeland, so that a conquered people would not be deprived. The humane treatment of conquered enemy nations made Germany and Japan two of the most pro-American nations in the world, both politically and culturally. These actions are noteworthy in themselves, remarkable against the historical background of other conquering nations, incongruous with the image of a "sick" society, and in particular contrast with the record of the Soviet Union.

Over the years since World War II, the military supremacy of the United States has disappeared, and what has been called the "nuclear stalemate" has emerged. Both the United States and the Soviet Union have enough nuclear weapons to annihilate the major population centers of the other nation several times over—"overkill," as it is called. However, nuclear "overkill" may not be as unprecedented as it appears nor decisive as an indication of negligible incremental returns to continued military development. It may well be that when France surrendered to Nazi Germany in 1940, it had enough bullets left to kill every German soldier twice over, but such theoretical calculations would have meant little to a conquered nation. Would anyone say that a lone policeman confronting three criminals had "overkill" because his revolver contained enough bullets to kill them all twice over? On the contrary, depending on how close they were, and with what weapons they were armed, he might be in a very precarious position.

In an era of sophisticated radar defenses and missile interceptor systems, the only way to actually deliver a nuclear weapon on target might be to saturate the enemy defense system with more incoming missiles than it can handle—that is, with a number of missiles representing extravagant "overkill" in terms of what would be theoretically necessary if the enemy were as defenseless as a sitting duck. Since both the United States and the Soviet Union have missile defense systems, theoretical examples of "overkill"—if taken literally—represent either naiveté or demagoguery, depending upon how they are used. As long as the technology of attack and defense systems keeps advancing, there is no point at which we can comfortably say, "enough," because it is not the size of the arsenal that matters but the ability to deliver it through enemy defense systems that matters. Military forces have always had overkill. It is doubtful if most of the bullets fired in most wars ever hit anybody, and a substantial number of soldiers never fire at all. Yet no one would claim that it is futile to arm soldiers going into combat or that it is a waste to issue more bullets than there are enemy soldiers.

The history of the Soviet-American military balance has been essentially a history of the relative decline of the American position. Whereas the United States in 1965 had several hundred more nuclear missiles than the U.S.S.R., by 1975 the Soviets had more than a thousand more nuclear missiles than the United States.[245] Whereas the United States in 1965 had more military personnel in both conventional and nuclear attack forces than the U.S.S.R., by 1975 that too had been reversed.[246] Most other components of nuclear military power had also changed to the detriment of the United States in this decade.[247] In Europe, the Soviet bloc Warsaw Pact outnumbers the Western NATO allies in troops (50 percent more), tanks (three times as many), airplanes (40 percent more) and artillery pieces (three times as many), with the lone Western military advantage being in tactical nuclear weapons (twice as many).[248] Tactical nuclear weapons—the West's one advantage—have the serious disadvantage that a defending nation risks endangering its own people with radioactive fallout if it uses the weapon against an invader. The invading forces face no comparable risk, since its tactical nuclear weapons would be used near someone else's civilian population.

Western attempts to redress this imbalance by developing a tactical nuclear weapon with reduced and more transient fallout—the so-called "neutron bomb" (actually an artillery shell) were met by a massive worldwide propaganda campaign, centering on an incidental feature of the weapon, its lack of destruction of physical structures. That it would "kill people but not destroy property" became the theme of Soviet propaganda, echoed in the West, creating the impression that this demonstrated the capitalist mentality of concern for things rather than people. That the Soviets would argue this way is unsurprising, but that it should find such a responsive echo on the political left in Western countries—especially on a matter of national survival rather than political ideology—proved politically decisive. Antineutron "bomb" demonstrations swept across the Western would, and at the eleventh hour in the NATO negotiations, the American President withdrew plans for this tactical weapon, whose chief military characteristic was that it equalized *defensive* forces with offensive forces by not requiring defensive forces to destroy their own civilians to repel an invader. Existing tactical nuclear weapons, for example, would kill an estimated five million civilians in West Germany alone if used to repel an invader.[249] The credibility of such a weapon as a deterrent could be discounted in advance by any invader, aware that it could literally hurt defenders worse than it would hurt an invading army. That emotional or ideological predispositions should influence decisions of this grim magnitude is an indication of the greater political as well as military vulnerability of the West. Such political reactions on the political left in Europe were far stronger than in the United States, the left itself being stronger in Western Europe. In America, the leading liberal spokesman, Senator Hubert Humphrey, threw his support behind the weapon.[250] Western governments were apparently also in favor of the weapon, but often more so privately than publicly, given the political furor.[251]

How did the present military imbalance develop, given the initial Western predominance? Quite simply by political decisions to trade off defense spending for domestic welfare programs. In 1952 military expenditures were 66 percent of the federal budget, but this declined to 24 percent by 1977 while social welfare expenditures rose from 17 percent to 50 percent over the same span.[252] Inflationary dollar figures maintain the political illusion that defense spending is rising, but in constant purchasing power terms military expenditures in the United States declined not only relatively but absolutely. Moreover, much of today's military spending represents simply higher pay for military personnel—a fourfold increase in cost per soldier since 1952[253]— rather than for weapons. More than half of all current American military expenditures are for personnel costs. The Soviet government has maintained and increased its military expenditures as the United States has reduced its. In short, the relative decline of American military power has been largely self-imposed, and "arms race" talk simply ignores the Soviet military build-up that has proceeded while American military resources were being diverted to social programs.

There is a striking parallel here with the decline and fall of the Roman Empire. In its early years the Romans "preserved the peace by a constant preparedness for war."[254] Their soldiers were rigorously trained[255] and carried heavy armor and weaponry,[256] and were commanded by the Roman aristocracy and led in battle by emperors.[257] Their morale was supported by the pride of being Roman.[258] Later, discipline relaxed,[259] and the soldiers carried less armor and weaponry, as a result of their complaints about carrying burdens that had been carried in earlier generations.[260] They were defeated by barbarian armies smaller than other barbarian armies that had been routed by Roman legions in earlier times.[261] Behind the self-weakening of Rome lay forces similar to those at work today in the United States and in the Western world at large: internal divisiveness[262] and demoralization,[263] rising welfare expenditures,[264] a growing and stifling bureaucracy[265]—and a rising political influence of intellectuals.[266] In Rome, as in later Western countries, both the zealotry and the power were concentrated precisely in those particular intellectuals who dealt in nonverifiable theories—religious theories in the case of Rome; "social justice" in the contemporary West.

374

The longer time horizon of a one-party totalitarian state is a military as well as political advantage. In the short run, elected officials in a democratic country have incentives to convert military expenditures into social welfare expenditures, since the former involve long-run national interests and the latter have short-run political payoff. This is especially so in an era when high levels of fixed governmental obligations and voter resistance to higher taxes leave little room for financial maneuvering, other than cutting the military share of the budget. In the United States that share has already been reduced by more than 40 percentage points in the past quarter century.[267] A totalitarian government like the Soviet Union need make no such reductions, nor has it.

Not only are there political dividends in cutting defense spending—defense "waste" by either allegation or definition—to finance social programs; there are also more direct political dividends from advancing toward "peace" through military agreements with the Soviet Union, regardless of the long-run consequences of the specific terms of those agreements. The political advantages of such agreements fall within the time horizon of elected incumbents, while any later consequences are left for future administrations or generations to cope with. Again, this is not to claim that such explicitly cynical calculations are made. The point is that this is the tendency of the incentives, and human rationalization in the face of tempting incentives is a common phenomenon. As Congressman Les Aspin remarked, "you've got to cut the defense budget if you want sufficient money for your own programs."[268] The net result is an asymmetry in the bargaining power of the U.S. and the U.S.S.R. Politically, American elected officials need to make such agreements moreso than do Soviet officials, who are in a position to hold out for terms which neutralize those weapons in which the U.S. has an advantage and enhance the prospects for those weapons in which the U.S.S.R. has an advantage. At any given time, the results need not be a blatant imbalance. The cumulative effect over time is what matters.

The history of the West in general and the United States in particular is not encouraging as regards military preparedness. In the 1930s, the American army was only the sixteenth largest in the world, behind Portugal and Greece. In 1934, despite the aggressions of Japan in the Orient and the rise of Hitler in Europe, the budget of the U.S. army was cut 51 percent, to help finance New Deal programs.[269] Overall military expenditures were reduced 23 percent in one year,[270] and total military personnel on active duty fell below a quarter of a million in the early 1930s, drifting downward each year from 1930 through 1934.[271] The Civilian Conservation Corps of young men working in forests was larger than the army—and the CCC recruits were paid more.[272] Attempts to train them militarily were defeated politically by a pacifist protest led by intellectuals—John Dewey and Reinhold Neibuhr.[273] Later, attempts to build some semblance of military defense for the Philippines were criticized by the editor of the *Nation*, who asked why the islands' people were not being taught to live rather than to kill.[274] This lofty assumption of unconstrained choice—three years before Pearl Harbor—takes on a grim or even hideous aspect as an historical background to the devastation of the Philippines and massive, unspeakable atrocities against its people by invading Japanese armies. American soldiers in the Philippines vainly attempted to defend themselves with obsolete rifles, mortars a quarter of a century old, and mortar shells so old that they proved to be duds in 70 percent of the cases.[275] On Bataan, four out of five American hand grenades failed to explode.[276] Attempts to break through the Japanese blockade of the Philippines had to be made "with banana boats hired from the United Fruit Company, and with converted World War I destroyers."[277] These were among the long-run costs of the "savings" on military expenditures during the previous decade. Actually it was not a saving but a disinvestment—a current consumption of future resources.

The uncontrolled political climate of a free nation allows the development of ideological currents inimical to national defense—the so-called "neutron bomb" episode being but one example—or even the orchestration of propaganda campaigns by foreign powers with an obvious vested interest in reduced Western military defense. Moreover, the unverified nature of arguments about nuclear prospects—prospects that no sane person *wants* verified—gives a special political advantage to the verbally adept, that is, to intellectuals, who have tended to be antimilitary at least as far back as the Roman Empire.[278] It was precisely at the leading British universities that young men took the "Oxford Pledge" in the 1930s never to defend their own country in warfare.[279] Such pacifist reaction to the carnage of World War I may have been understandable, like the current American reaction to the bitterness of Vietnam. However, such attitudes were a crucial element in the Western powers' appeasement of Hitler at a time when they had superior military force but were politically incapable of using it.[280] By the time Hitler's rearmament policy, annexations, and conquests had changed Britain's attitude, he now had superior military force. When the young men who took the "Oxford Pledge" saw Hitler's armies marching and the bombs falling on their own homes, they vindicated themselves in the skies over Britain and later on the beaches at Normandy. But it was still a desperately close brush with subjugation by one of the greatest barbarians in human history. Hitler's outrages put a pacifist intellectual like Einstein in the ironic position of initiating the development of the most destructive military weapon ever used.

But now that the nuclear age is here, such changes of mind as a result of crisis experience may no longer be possible—or at least, not in time to change policy and change history. The timetable of a nuclear war—or nuclear blackmail—may not permit second thoughts about what should have been done when we had the chance.

For a richer and technologically more advanced nation to fall behind militarily, when national survival and the survival of democratic freedom internationally are among the stakes, requires a certain amount of demoralization. No one supplies this demoralization more constantly or effectively than intellectuals. Again, this is not, historically, a new role for intellectuals, The intellectuals' vision has long taken precedence over any tangible reality. In the Roman Empire, the vision was religious salvation, and if divisiveness was engendered by persecutions of pagans, thereby weakening a whole civilization in the face of barbarian invaders, so be it. If the social visions behind the French Revolution required the execution of tens of thousands of human beings (including revolutionary philosophers like Condorcet), so be it. If the vision of proletarian communism or German racial purity required that millions be slain, so be it. Against this background, there is hardly any reason for surprise if current visions of "social justice" do not moderate to accommodate military necessity, or if campaigns to discredit rival elites like businessmen or the military are so all-out that the consequences are the demoralization of a whole civilization and a weakening of the will to defend it.

In this context, it is understandable how an *American* official can speak of the military arms race as something for which "all of us here in America are to blame," how "the United States has led the way in arms escalation" and how "the lion's share of the blame," within the U.S. "belongs to the business sector of society" which is seeking "the profits of doom."[281] It is a remarkable statement from an official representative of the United States to the U.N. Disarmament Session, and particularly for the representative of a country that demobilized almost 90 percent of its armed forces in three years and has voluntarily relinquished military supremacy over the years by cutting back the resources devoted to it. But it is no more remarkable than statements by former U.N. Ambassador Andrew Young equating massive slave labor camps in the Soviet Union with individual miscarriages of justice in American courts, calling the victims of both "political prisoners." Both officials are extreme examples of a more general tendency toward national demoralization, without which such people could not survive in their official positions. The public's outrage is a sign that the battle is not over, but that American officials can continue in office after making anti-American propaganda on an international stage is also a sign of the political climate.

TRENDS AND ISSUES

THE FUTURE OF FREEDOM

Hobbes defined freedom as the absence of opposition or impediments.[282] Freedom may be constrained by political power or informal influences, but as long as diverse human beings constitute a society, their disparate values must somehow be reconciled and therefore someone's—or everyone's—freedom must be curtailed. When these mutual reconciliations are affected through informal channels, reciprocal advantages may be traded off, so that the disparate values of individuals permit them to incrementally relinquish what they value least for what they value most, even though physically what one relinquishes is identical to what another receives. When reconciliations are made by the decisions of formal hierarchies, one scheme of values is offered, and if the hierarchy is a monopoly—such as government—imposed. A choice among hierarchies (churches, employers, associations) preserved freedom through the inevitable differences among human beings as individuals or groups.

Where the differences among people are least—in the desire to be safe from violence and secure in their possessions, for example—there is less sacrifice of freedom in assigning to a monopoly the power to punish individual violence or robbery. Were the same monopoly to determine the "best" size(s) or style(s) of shoes, the result would be mass discomfort, and were it to determine more and weightier matters the results would be even less satisfactory in terms of the differing values of individuals, however "better" it might be in terms of the particular values of the monopoly.

This brief summary of various "efficiency" arguments already elaborated in earlier chapters is relevant here to freedom as a separate value in its own right. It is the difference between the preferred and the imposed values that necessitates the use of force—the curtailment (or extinction) of freedom. In this context, an ideology of categorically transcendant values—whether religious salvation or "social justice"—is an ideology of crushing power. The logic of transcendant values drives even the humane toward the use of force, as those not imbued with the same values prove recalcitrant, evasive, or undermining—provoking indignant anger and confronting decision makers with a choice between accepting defeat for sacred causes or applying more power. This systemic logic rather than intentional design drove Robespierre—"a man of great sweetness of character"[283]—to mass executions as flesh-and-blood human beings repeatedly acted at cross purposes with the ideals of the French Revolution. "Moralism is fatal to freedom," wrote a former friend of Robespierre, while awaiting the guillotine.[284] It was not a principle unique to the French Revolution. Much milder political changes have been driven by similar logic to exert far more power than originally contemplated in pursuit of a transcendant goal. No one expected *Brown v. Board of Education* to lead to federal judges taking over local school systems and ordering the massive busing of children, in disregard of both initial opposition and subsequent consequences. Indeed, no one expected the humane social programs initiated by the New Deal to lead to bureaucratic empires issuing their own laws—more laws than Congress—unilaterally, outside the constitutional framework, and almost immune to either electoral correction or judicial oversight. Where, whether and how we can build a roof over our heads is determined by an anonymous zoning commission; whether we dare walk the streets near our home is determined by decisions of equally unknown parole board members; and how long we can live in our neighborhood depends on the grand designs of urban redevelopment administrators.

These are of course not attacks on *intellectual* freedom; merely on some of the most precious concerns of ordinary human beings down through the ages. Just how far the myopic view of freedom can go may be illustrated by the behavior of musicians under Nazi rule. As various ethnic, political, and cultural groups successively fled Nazi persecution, the musicians—including, notably, conductor Kurt Furtwangler and composer Richard Strauss—remained behind to collaborate with the Hitler regime, because there were no comparable restrictions on *musicians'* freedom.[285] Against this background, it may be less surprising that intellectuals living in affluent suburbs (or in "security buildings" in the cities) and/or with their children in private schools, can see no reason for working class people's resentment of "progressive" political developments other than benighted ignorance, blind reaction, or vicious racism. Evidence that these are not, in fact, the attitudes of most working people is ignored, for these are the only explanations consonant with the intellectual vision. That businessmen—large or small—are in effect conscripted to be part-time, unpaid administrators for the Internal Revenue Service, the Social Security Administration, and numerous other federal agencies will occasion even less concern.

Past erosions of freedom are less critical than current trends which have implications for the future of freedom. Some of these trends amount to little less than the quiet, piecemeal, repeal of the American Revolution.

The American Revolution was very different from the French Revolution of the same era. The French Revolution was based on abstract speculation on the nature of man by intellectuals, and on the potentiality of government as a means of human improvement. The American Revolution was based on historical experience of man as he is and has been, and on the shortcomings and dangers of government as actually observed. *Experience*—personal and historical—was the last court of appeal of the founders of the United States and the writers of the Constitution. Their constantly reiterated references were to "experience, the least fallible guide of human opinions,"[286] to "the

379

accumulated experience of ages,"[287] to "the uniform course of human events,"[288] to the history of ancient Rome,[289] to "the popular governments of antiquity,"[290] and the history, economics, and geography of contemporary European nations.[291] They explicitly rejected "Utopian speculations,"[292] "the fallacy and extravagance" of "idle theories" with their "deceitful dream of a golden age."[293] In contrast to Robespierre, who said that revolutionary bloodshed would end "when all people will have become equally devoted to their country and its laws,"[294] *The Federalist* regarded the idea of individual actions "unbiased by considerations not connected with the public good" to be an eventuality "more ardently to be wished than seriously to be expected."[295] They were establishing a government for such flesh-and-blood people as they knew about, not such creatures as they might hope to create by their activities.

The opposing policies of the two revolutions—and their very different historical fates—were related to their very different premises about the nature of knowledge and the nature of man. To the men who made the American Revolution and wrote the Constitution, knowledge derived from experience—personal and historical—and not from speculation or rhetorical virtuosity. Their own backgrounds before the Revolution were as men of affairs, personally responsible for economic outcomes, whether commercial or agricultural. By contrast, the French *philosophes* were denizens of literary salons where style, wit, and rhetoric were crucial[296]—and whose whole lives were lived under circumstances in which the only authentication process consisted of impressing readers or listeners. In the modern vernacular, they "never met a payroll"—or a scoreboard, or a laboratory experiment, or a military campaign, or any other authentication process whose empirical results could not be talked away. They were masters of the world of unverified plausibilities.

Man, as he appeared in the writings of the American revolutionaries, was very different from man as he appeared in the writings of the French revolutionaries. In contrast with the "perfectability of man" in contemporary French thinking, *The Federalist* speaks of "the constitution of man" as an inherent barrier to objective decision making or administration.[297] While the French revolutionaries put their faith in selecting the most dedicated leaders—"the brightest and the best" in modern terms—and entrusting them with vast powers, the Americans argued that the very reason why government existed at all was because "the passions of men will not conform to the dictates of reason and justice" otherwise,[298] and that governments, like individuals, have a pride which "naturally disposes them to justify all their actions, and opposes their acknowledging, correcting, or repairing their errors and offenses."[299] Though there were American leaders "tried and justly approved for patriotism and abilities,"[300] the future of the country could not be left to depend on such leaders: "Enlightened statesmen will not always be at the helm."[301] Moreover, there are "endless diversities in the opinions of men,"[302] so that "latent cases of faction are thus sown in the nature of man," and mankind has a propensity "to fall into mutual animosities."[303] Men "are ambitious, vindictive, and rapacious." They have a "love of power or the desire of pre-eminence and dominion."[304] The question facing the founders of the American government was not how to give expression to the ideas of those presumed to be morally or intellectually superior, but how to guard freedom from the inherent weaknesses and destructive characteristics of men in general. Their answer was a series of checks and balances in which ambitions would counter ambition and power counter power, with all powers not explicitly granted retained by the people themselves or dispersed among state and local governments. Nor were they prepared to rely on pious hopes in the Constituion—"parchment barriers against the encroaching spirit of power," as Madison called them[305]—but relied instead on so structuring the institutions that they will "be the means of keeping each other in their proper places."[306] Such separation of powers was "essential to the preservation of liberty"[307] and their coalescence in any branch was "precisely the definition of despotic government."[308] They did not trust *anyone*. If freedom was to exist, it had to be systemic rather than intentional, "supplying by opposite and rival interests, the defect of better motives," and arranging things so that "the private interest of every individual may be a sentinel over the public rights."[309] That all this implied a negative view of man did not stop the writers of the Constitution:

It may be a reflection on human nature that such devices should be necessary to control the abuses of government. But what is government itself but the greatest of all reflections on human nature? If men were angels, no government would be necessary. If angels were to govern men, neither external nor internal controls on government would be necessary. In framing a government which is to be administered by men over men, the great difficulty lies in this: you must first enable the government to control the governed; and in the next place oblige it to control itself.[310]

Like a judo expert using an opponent's strength against him, so the writers of the Constitution hoped to use the strong, if negative, motivations of man for the purpose of preserving the political benefits of freedom. As a modern writer has observed: "A system built on sin is built on very solid foundations indeed."[311] This is true of both economic and political systems. Neither constitutional democracy nor a market economy relies on decision makers to have superior wisdom or morality. Both put in the hands of the mass of ordinary people the ultimate power to thwart or topple decision makers. Historically, it was—and is—a revolutionary concept, rejecting theories going back thousands of years which insist that what matters is which persons and which doctrines rule, rather than the systemic incentives and constraints that control whoever rules under whatever doctrine. The American Constitution left little room for philosopher-kings or messiahs.

The great vulnerability of the Constitution today is that it is an obstacle in the path of groups that are growing in size, influence, and impatience. The most striking, and perhaps most important, of these are the intellectuals, especially in the politicized "social sciences." Politicians, once constrained by national (voter) reverence for constitutional guarantees, now operate more freely in an atmosphere where intellectuals make all reverence suspect and make "social justice" imperative. The decline in political party control ("machine politics") has given the individual politician more scope to be charismatic and entrepreneurial about causes and issues. Politicians ambitious for themselves as individuals and intellectuals ambitious for recognition as a class must discredit existing social processes, alternative decision-making elites, and the accumulated human capital of national experience and tradition which competes with their product, newly minted social salvation. However much they may emphasize the special virtues of their particular schemes, it is unnecessary here to go into them, for the point is that *whatever* the current specifics, they are certain to be superseded by new specifics in a few years to perform the same political function for the careers of new politicians and intellectuals. The danger to the Constitution is not so much in particular laws as in the general climate of opinion in which law and government are no longer seen as a framework within which individuals make changes incrementally, but as themselves means of making categorical changes directly, according to the preferences of whoever happens to have control of these institutions. One symptom of how far this has gone is that the first peacetime imposition of federal wage and price controls in American history occurred in 1971 under an administration widely regarded as "conservative"—as indeed it was. But that even "liberal" administrations in the past had not dared to do the same thing was one indication of how much the political climate had changed.

The "crisis" orientation of politicians and intellectuals is accepted and amplified by the mass media. *Today's* "problems" are news; neither the long-run implications nor the inherent constraints can be photographed by the television camera, or even discussed in the brief minutes between commercials. Moreover, with print and broadcast journalists as part of the intellectual class, grounded largely in the so-called "social sciences," few questions may be raised about the cognitive processes they employ.

The rise of goal-oriented imperatives has meant the undermining or superseding of process-oriented constitutionalism. The imperatives of economic recovery from the Great Depression of the 1930s spawned numerous hybrid agencies combining the very powers which the Constitution had so carefully separated. Military imperatives, beginning in World War II and continuing into the nuclear age, have sanctioned an increase of the presidential powers as commander-in-chief of the armed forces, to the point where they include the *de facto* power to declare war without congress, as demonstrated in Vietnam. Finally, moral imperatives concerning the less fortunate segments of society (farmers and industrial workers in the 1930s, blacks in the 1960s, miscellaneous other groups in the 1970s) have expanded the scope of the judiciary beyond anything ever contemplated when the Constitution was written. Along with this has developed a philosophy that it is not merely expedient but legitimate to circumvent the democratic process in the interest of "higher" moral goals—ending the death penalty, integrating the schools, redistributing income, and other forms of "social justice."

While the new trends in the political climate are easiest to notice, there is no need to extrapolate them as an inevitable "wave of the future." There are ample signs that the public has had more than enough, and even signs that some of this disenchantment has begun to penetrate the insulation of courts, bureaucracies, and other institutions. The Burger Court is not the Warren Court, though it is hardly the pre-Warren Court either. Deregulation moves by the Civil Aeronautics Board, stronger criminal sentencing laws in various states, and the defeat of school bond issues that were once passed easily are all signs that nothing is inevitable. Whether this particular period is merely a pause in a long march or a time of reassessment for new directions is something that only the future can tell. The point here is not to prophesy but to consider what is at stake, in terms of human freedom.

Historically, freedom is a rare and fragile thing. It has emerged out of the stalemates of would-be oppressors. Freedom has cost the blood of millions in obscure places and in historic sites ranging from Gettysburg to the Gulag Archipelago. A frontal assault on freedom is still impossible in America and in most of Western civilization. Perhaps nowhere in the world is anyone frankly against it, though everywhere there are those prepared to scrap it for other things that shine more brightly for the moment. That something that cost so much in human lives should be surrendered piecemeal in exchange for visions or rhetoric seems grotesque. Freedom is not simply the right of intellectuals to circulate their merchandise. It is, above all, the right of ordinary people to find elbow room for themselves and a refuge from the rampaging presumptions of their "betters."

NOTES

Chapter 1

1. Milton Friedman, "The Methodology of Positive Economics," *Essays in Positive Economics* (University of Chicago Press, 1953), pp. 32–34.
2. Kenneth Fearing, *Collected Poems of Kenneth Fearing* (Random House, 1940), p. 7.
3. Eugene Genovese, *Roll, Jordan, Roll* (Pantheon Books, 1974), pp. 587–621.
4. Thomas Sowell, *Race and Economics* (David McKay Co., 1975), pp. 11–15.

Chapter 2

1. George J. Stigler of the University of Chicago, after leaving a committee meeting.
2. Theodore Caplow and Reece J. McGee, *The Academic Marketplace* (Science Editions, Inc., 1961), pp. 238–255; Gerald G. Somers, "The Functioning of the Market for Economists," *American Economic Review*, May 1962, pp. 516–518; David G. Brown, *The Mobile Professors* (Council on Education, 1967), pp. 170–187.
3. Richard A. Lester, *Antibias Regulation of Universities* (McGraw-Hill Book Company, 1974), pp. 13–29.
4. Gerald G. Somers, *op. cit.*, p. 517; Kathleen Brook and F. Ray Marshall, "The Labor Market for Economists," *American Economic Review*, May 1974, pp. 505–506, 508.
5. David G. Brown, *op. cit.*, Chapter 4.
6. F. A. Hayek, "The Use of Knowledge in Society," *American Economic Review*, September 1945, pp. 519–530.
7. Richard Gambino, *Blood of My Blood* (Anchor Books, 1974), pp. 7–8.
8. Robert W. Fogel and Stanley L. Engerman, *Time on the Cross* (Little, Brown and Company, 1974). pp. 214–215.
9. *Loc. cit.*, Eugene D. Genovese, *Roll, Jordan Roll: The World the Slaves Made* (Pantheon Books, 1974), pp. 14–20.
10. The probability of being correct on all three variables at the same time is the probability of being correct on each variable separately multiplied by the probability of being correct on each of the other variables: $\frac{3}{4} \times \frac{3}{4} \times \frac{3}{4} = 27/64$. See W. Allen Wallis, and Harry V. Roberts, *Statistics: A New Approach* (The Free Press, 1956), pp. 324–325.
11. R. H. Coase, "The Problem of Social Cost," *Journal of Law and Economics*, Vol. III (October 1960), pp. 1–44.
12. Harold Demsetz, "Toward a Theory of Property Rights," *American Economic Review*, Vol. LVII, No. 2 (May 1967), pp. 347–359.
13. Robert A. Dahl and Charles E. Lindblom, *Politics, Economics and Welfare*, (University of Chicago Press, 1976), p. xxii.

Chapter 3

1. The two kinds of knowledge that are differently weighed are not merely different amounts of expertise on *how* to administer municipal affairs, but knowledge of the different specific effects of policy on different people with different values. Ideally, those with the great-

est expertise can manage a city in such a way as to maximize the satisfaction of the values of all, including those denied a direct (or fully weighted) input or feedback to the decision-making process. Under such an ideal arrangement, those disfranchised would achieve higher levels of satisfaction of their own values, because the same values would be as fully represented in the decision-making process as if they were voting, but would be pursued with greater expertise by administrative surrogates chosen for their ability rather than their political articulateness or charisma. In reality, however, the city manager form is also a tempting arrangement for substituting the values of some for the values of the disfranchised. Viewed as a knowledge-conveying device, it screens out some knowledge of both values and effects and provides no institutional incentive to take them into account, even vicariously, though some decision makers might choose to do so out of conscience.

2. In other words, only cost-constrained decision-making units can be assured of not proceeding into the region of absolutely diminishing returns—and then only if the cost constraints relate to the particular input in question. Most profit-and-loss enterprises are automatically kept out of that region in most of their activities. Enterprises that are institutionally neither impelled by profit nor constrained by losses can often proceed a considerable distance into the region of absolutely diminishing returns—government agencies and such "nonprofit" (and non-loss) organizations as universities, hospitals, and foundations being pominent examples. As of any given time, almost all activities and institutions have a limited budget, but expansion of that budget over time may cost non-profit institutions only the effort to make a plausible case for increased "need."

3. This can also be stated preposterously, as it has been by some economists, by saying that roundabout production is more valuable. Actually, the additional cost of time-consuming production is paid only because the thing produced is already more valuable.

4. Hamlet's soliloquy.

5. Peter F. Drucker, "Pension Fund 'Socialism'," *The Public Interest*, Winter 1976, pp. 3–46.

6. St. Thomas Aquinas, "Summa Theologica," *Early Economic Thought*, ed. Eli Monroe (Harvard University Press, 1951), pp. 53–64.

7. R.A. Radford, "The Economic Organization of a Prisoner of War Camp," *Economica*, November 1945, pp. 189–201.

8. Adam Smith, *An Inquiry into the Nature and Causes of the Wealth of Nations* (Random House, 1937), pp. lvii, 79.

9. See Christopher Finch, *The Art of Walt Disney*, New Concise N.A.L. Edition (Walt Disney Productions, 1975), pp. 21–24.

10. U. S. Bureau of the Census, *Social Indicators, 1976* (U.S. Government Printing Office, 1977), p. 455.

11. *Ibid.*, p. 462.

Chapter 4

1. James M. McPherson, *The Struggle for Equality* (Princeton University Press, 1964), pp. 103, 109. See also pp. 27, 95.

2. Edward C. Banfield, *The Unheavenly City Revisited* (Little, Brown and Co., 1974), p. 204.

3. *Ibid.*, p. 198.

4. Adam Smith, *The Wealth of Nations*, p. 460.

5. *Ibid.*, p. 423.

6. Karl Marx, *Capital*, Vol. I.

7. Karl Marx and Friedrich Engels, *Basic Writings on Politics and Philosophy* (Anchor Books, 1959), p. 399.

8. See, for example, Oscar Handlin, *Boston's Immigrants* (Antheneum, 1970), chapter IV; Carl Wittke, *The Irish in America* (Russell & Russell, 1956), chapter III; Diane Ravitch, *The Great School Wars* (Harper and Row, 1974), pp. 27–29.

9. Diane Ravitch, *op. cit.*, pp. 178, 311; E. C. Banfield, *op. cit.*, pp. 65–66, 68; Herbert J. Gans, *The Urban Villagers* (The Free Press, 1962), p. 241.

10. Compare Richard Gambino, *Blood of My Blood* (Garden City: Doubleday Anchor Books, 1974), pp. 245–273; Louis Wirth, *The Ghetto* (Chicago: University of Chicago Press, 1956), pp. 76–77, 82, 148; Nathan Glazer and Daniel Patrick Moynihan, *Beyond the Melting Pot* (MIT Press, 1963) pp. 155–159, 199.

11. Maldwyn Allen Jones, *American Immigration* (University of Chicago Press) pp. 212–213.

12. Anthony Downs, *An Economic Theory of Democracy* (Harper and Row, 1957), p. 4.

13. Thorstein Veblen, *The Place of Science in Modern Civilization* (Russell & Russell, 1961), p. 251.

14. Edmund Burke, *Reflections on the Revolution in France* (Everyman's Library, 1967), p. 84.

15. *Loc. cit.*

16. Quoted in F. A. Hayek, *Law, Legislation and Liberty* (University of Chicago Press, 1973), Vol. I, p. 26.

17. Edmund Burke, *op. cit.*, p. 84.

18. Perhaps the classic case is the citing of Kenneth B. Clark's "study" of segregation in *Brown v. Board of Education* in 1954. Subsequent criticism has devastated Clark's "findings." See, for example, E. van den Haag, "Social Science Testimony in the Desegregation Cases," *Villanova Law Review*, Fall 1960, pp. 69–79.

19. Adam Smith, *op. cit.*, p. 423.

20. For example, by Dahl and Lindblom, *op. cit.*, p. 392, and Richard A. Lester, "Shortcomings of Marginal Analysis for Wage Employment Problems," *American Economic Review*, March 1946, pp. 62–82.

21. F. A. Hayek, *Individualism and Economic Order* (University of Chicago Press, 1948), p. 32.

22. Eugene Genovese, *op. cit.*, p. 471.

23. *Ibid.*, p. 622.

24. *Ibid.*, pp. 379, 380–381, 382, 619.

25. *Ibid.*, pp. 450–458; see also Herbert G. Gutman, *The Black Family in Slavery and Freedom, 1750-1925* (Pantheon, 1976) *passim*.

26. See, for example, Hans Mühlestein, "Marx and the Utopian Wilhelm Weitling," *Science & Society*, Winter 1948, pp. 128–129.

27. Adam Smith, *The Theory of Moral Sentiments* (Liberty Classics, 1976), p. 381.

28. *Ibid.*, p. 379.

29. *Ibid.*, p. 380.

Chapter 5

1. Daniel Patrick Moynihan, *Maximum Feasible Misunderstanding* (The Free Press, 1970), p. lvii.

2. Richard Posner, *Antitrust Law* (University of Chicago Press, 1976), p. 230.

3. *Loc. cit.*; Nathan Glazer, *Affirmative Discrimination* (Basic Books, Inc., 1975), pp. 212–214.

4. For example, Dahl and Lindblom assert that the government "cannot keep its hands off" wage negotiations because so "much is at stake" (*op. cit.*, p. 185); government regulation is used to "remedy deficiencies in the price system" (p. 213), war "compels the abandonment of the price system" (p. 374), because "of course the price system cannot perform well" (p. 381); medical care, housing, and other activities are "collectivized because of particular shortcomings in the price system" (p. 419). In none of these examples is the possibility of political incentives for taking such actions even mentioned, much less seriously considered. Similar assertions and avoidances are found in Adolph A. Berle, *Power* (Harcourt, Brace and World., Inc., 1969), where the government "had to be called in" in education (p. 195); "cannot avoid" expansion of economic controls (p. 261); France "found it necessary" to have government control capital markets (p. 214); government control of consumption is "the only practicable escape from unendurable congestion and confusion, if not chaos" (p. 252).

5. Anthony Downs, *An Economic Theory of Democracy*, p. 28.

NOTES

6. Quoted in F. A. Hayek, *The Constitution of Freedom* (University of Chicago Press, 1960), p. 11.

7. Edmund Burke, *Reflections on the Revolution in France* (J. M. Dent & Sons, Ltd., 1967); Alexander Hamilton, James Madison and John Jay, *The Federalist Papers* (New American Library, 1961), pp. 310–311; Alexis de Tocqueville, *Democracy in America* (Alfred A. Knopf 1966), Vol. II, Fourth Book. chapter III.

8. Robert Higgs, *Competition and Coercion* (Cambridge University Press, 1977), *passim*.

9. Gunnar Myrdal, *An American Dilemma*.

10. Richard Kluger, *Simple Justice* (Alfred A. Knopf, 1976), *passim*.

11. Dahl and Lindblom, *op. cit.*, p. 29; Anthony Downs, *Inside Bureaucracy* (Boston: Little, Brown and Co., 1966), p. 259; Karl Marx and Friedrich Engels, *The Holy Family* (Foreign Languages Publishing House, USSR, 1950), p. 176; Karl Marx and Friedrich Engels, *Basic Writings on Politics & Philosophy*, p. 222.

12. Adam Smith, *The Theory of Moral Sentiments*, Pt. I., Section II, Ch. 3, p. 166; John Rawls, *A Theory of Justice* (The Belknap Press, 1971), p. 3.

13. *Loc. cit.*

14. *Ibid.*, Part II, Section II, Chapter 2, pp. 380–381.

15. Rawls, *op. cit.*, p. 3–4.

16. Dahl and Lindblom, *op. cit.*, p. 49.

17. This is denied by F. A. Hayek in *The Road to Serfdom* (University of Chicago Press, 1944), p. 80, on the ground that something is not a privilege if everyone can acquire it. This says prospectively that access is not a privilege, which in no way denies that retrospective possession may be a privilege. Surely the President of the United States is a privileged office, even though the Constitution makes it prospectively attainable by almost anyone (and some of the incumbents reinforce the reality of this). A function, such as the presidency or property rights, may be a privilege without the individual who ends up exercising that function having reached that point as a result of personal advantages or privileges. The emperor of the Roman Empire was an enormously privileged office, though many individuals who achieved that position rose from modest or even disadvantaged positions in society.

18. In this context, the expression "property rights versus human rights" loses much of its meaning. Property itself has *no* rights. Only human beings have rights. The only meaningful choice is between alternative decision-making mechanisms for resolving conflicts between people regarding trade-offs among alternative goods. Some urgency of the moment may or may not outrank the importance of a particular property right. But here, as with freedom, individual questions of ranking need not be allowed to overshadow or confuse the central question of distinguishing.

19. Even a ninety-year-old owner of a forest need not cut it all down if he wants immediate gain. The future value of trees that will mature long after his death are reflected in the present value of his forest in the market. The value of the forest is not limited by his use of it, but by others' use of it. However limited the ninety-year-old man's time horizon may be, there are others with longer time horizons to whom it will have correspondingly greater value. A life insurance company may be quite interested in trees (or other assets) that will mature in fifty years, when many of its current policy holders' claims will have to be paid off.

20. Quoted in Joseph S. Berliner, "Prospects for Technological Progress," *Soviet Economy in a New Perspective*, Joint Economic Committee, Congress of the United States (Government Printing Office, 1976), p. 437

21. See, for example, Richard Posner, *Economic Analysis of Law* (Little, Brown and Company, 1972), Chapter 2; Henry G. Manne, ed., *The Economics of Legal Relationships* (West Publishing Co., 1975), Part I, Section B.

22. Alec Nove, *The Soviet Economy* (Frederick A. Praeger, 1961), p. 234.

23. Walter E. Williams, *Youth and Minority Unemployment* (Hoover Institution Press, 1977), pp. 34–35.

24. Oliver MacDonagh, "The Irish Famine Emigration to the United States," *Perspectives in American History*, Vol. X (1976), p. 412.

25. If the patient is dying from a condition that is only incrementally different from a condition from which people are recovering every day, documenting the *degree* of his illness may be a more formidable task.

26. Edward F. Denison, *The Sources of Economic Growth in the United States* (Committee for Economic Development), p. 17.

27. *Loc. cit.*

28. George F. Will, "Rah, Rah, Rah! Sis, Boom, Bah! Let's Hear It for Title IX!" *Los Angeles Times*, March 6, 1978, Part II, p. 7.

29. Anthony Downs, *Inside Bureaucracy*, p. 258.

30. Dahl and Lindblom, *op. cit.*, p. 27.

31. *Ibid.*, p. 213.

32. *Ibid.*, p. 419.

33. *Ibid.*, p. 465.

34. *Ibid.*, p. 467.

35. *Ibid.*, p. 185.

36. *Ibid.*, p. 374

37. *Ibid.*, p. 467.

38. *Ibid.*, p. 185.

39. *Ibid.*, p. 374.

40. Roger Freeman, *The Growth of American Government*, p. 10.

41. Marver H. Bernstein, "The Life Cycle of Regulatory Commissions," *The Politics of Regulation*, ed., Samuel Krislov and Lloyd D. Musolf (Houghton Mifflin Co., 1964), pp. 80–87.

Chapter 6

1. The explicitness of a trade-off may range from a consumer's comparison of products, sitting side by side on a shelf with price tags on each, to the implicit systemic trade-off involved when the dinosaur's size and strength failed to preserve their existence in competition with smaller, more agile, intelligent or otherwise environmentally more adaptable creatures.

2. See, for example, the celebrated Lester-Machlup controversy of a generation ago in economics. Lester challenged the systemic effects predicted by marginal productivity theory by sending questionnaires to businessmen asking if they intentionally did those kinds of things. When they replied that they did not, he considered this systemic theory disproved! Richard A. Lester, "Shortcomings of Marginal Analysis for Wage-Employment Problems," *American Economic Review*, March 1946, pp. 63–82; Fritz Machlup, "Marginal Analysis and Empirical Research," *American Economic Review*, September 1946, pp. 519–554.

3. Adam Smith, *The Wealth of Nations* (Modern Library, 1937), p. 423.

4. *Ibid.*, pp. 128, 249–250, 402–403, 429, 438, 460, 579.

5. Karl Marx, *Capital* (Charles H. Kerr & Co., 1906), Vol. I, p. 15.

6. See Thomas Sowell, "Adam Smith in Theory and Practice," *Adam Smith and Modern Political Economy*, ed. Gerald P. O'Driscoll (Iowa State University Press, 1979), pp. 7, 16; Thomas Sowell, "Karl Marx and the Freedom of the Individual," *Ethics*, January 1963, p. 121.

7. Marx and Beard are contrasted, *Loc. cit.*

8. Edmund Burke, *Burke's Politics*, ed. Ross J. S. Hoffman and Paul Levack (Alfred A. Knopf, 1949), p. 36.

9. *Ibid.*, p. 290.

10. *Ibid.*, p. 38.

11. *Ibid.*, p. 57.

12. *Ibid.*, p. 58.

13. Friedrich Engels, "Socialism: Utopian and Scientific," Karl Marx and Friedrich Engels, *Basic Writings on Politics and Philosophy*, ed. Lewis S. Fever (Anchor Books, 1959), pp. 107–108.

14. See, for example, Karl Marx, "The British Rule in India," *Ibid.*, pp. 479–481. See also *Ibid.*, pp. 450–452.

15. *Cf.* Horace B. Davis, "Nations, Colonies and Social Classes: The Position of Marx and Engels," *Science & Society*, Winter 1965, pp. 26–43.

16. Eugene D. Genovese, *Roll, Jordan, Roll*, pp. 13–14; Alec Nove, "Soviet Agriculture Marks Time," *Foreign Affairs*, July 1962, pp. 589–590.

NOTES

Chapter 7

1. Everett C. Ladd, Jr., and Seymour Martin Lipset, *The Divided Academy* (McGraw Hill, 1975), Chapter 1.
2. See, for example, Milton Friedman and Anna J. Schwartz, *A Monetary History of the United States, 1876–1960* (Princeton University Press, 1963), Chapter 7, especially pp. 407–419.

Chapter 8

1. *Utah Pie Co. v. Continental Baking Co., et al.*, 386 U.S. 685 (1967) at 698.
2. A. Lawrence Chickering, "The God that Cannot Fail," *The Politics of Planning*, ed. A. L. Chickering (Institute for Contemporary Studies, 1976), p, 332.
3. Dahl and Lindblom, *op. cit.*, p. 204.
4. *Ibid.*, p. 206.
5. *Ibid.*, pp 205, 206.
6. "A second group of difficulties is the measurement of cost and demand and those which arise from *the impossibility of getting statistical equivalents to theoretical concepts,*" *Ibid.*, p. 206 (italics in the original).
7. As claimed *Ibid.*, pp. 207–209. Perhaps the classic example of this animistic fallacy is Richard A. Lester, "Shortcomings of Marginal Analysis for Wage-Employment Problems," *American Economic Review*, March 1946, pp. 63–82. Among the many replies to Lester is Fritz Machlup, "Marginal Analysis and Empirical Research," *American Economic Review*, September 1946. See also Milton Friedman, *Essays in Positive Economics* (Univ. of Chicago Press, 1953), pp. 3–43).
8. It would be a real minimum wage law if it guaranteed that such a wage could be earned, such as by making jobs available at that wage. Pointing this out does not of course constitute advocacy of such a scheme, the merits and demerits of which would require further exploration. For a sketch of some objections to such a policy, see Thomas Sowell, "Beneficiaries and Victims," *The Washington Star*, February 24, 1978, p. A-7.
9. Walter E. Williams, *Youth and Minority Unemployment* (Hoover Institution Press, 1978).
10. U. S. Bureau of the Census, *Historical Statistics of the United States, Colonial Times to 1957* (U. S. Government Printing Office, 1961), p. 72.
11. Walter E. Williams, *Youth and Minority Unemployment*, pp. 16–18.
12. See Albert Rees, *The Economics of Trade Unions* (University of Chicago, 1962), pp. 34–35.
13. But not always. See Walter E. Williams, *Youth and Minority Unemployment*, pp. 23–24; W. H. Hutt, *The Economics of the Colour Bar* (Andre Deutsch, Ltd., 1964), p. 71; P. T. Bauer, "Regulated Wages in Under-developed Countries," *The Public Stake in Union Power*, ed. Philip D. Bradley (University of Virginia Press, 1959), pp. 346–347.
14. Lorenzo J. Green and Carter G. Woodson, *The Negro Wage Earner* (Columbia University Press, 1930), pp. 34–35.
15. Thomas Sowell, "Three Black Histories," *American Ethnic Groups*, ed. Thomas Sowell, (Urban Institute, 1978), pp. 19–20.
16. Irving Howe, *World of Our Fathers* (Harcourt, Brace, Jovanovich, 1976), pp. 177–179; Kathleen Neils Conzen, *Immigrant Milwaukee, 1836-1860*, (Harvard University Press, 1976), pp. 57–59, 80–81; Gunnar Myrdal, *An American Dilemma* (McGraw-Hill, 1964), vol. 1, p. 376.
17. Senator Thomas F. Eagleton, "Why Rent Controls Don't Work," *Reader's Digest*, August 1977, p. 111.
18. "Gas Crisis in New York: One Fact, Many Notions," *New York Times*, July 29, 1979, p. 30.
19. George W. Hilton, "American Transportation Planning," *The Politics of Planning*, ed. A. Lawrence Chickering, p. 152.
20. *Ibid.*, pp. 153–154.
21. *Ibid.*, pp. 167, 170, 172.
22. *Ibid.*, p. 154.

23. George J. Stigler, *The Citizen and the State*, p. 19.
24. See, for example, Clair Wilcox, *Public Policies Toward Business* (Richard D. Irwin, Inc., 1971), pp. 452–453.
25. George W. Hilton, *op. cit.*, p. 163.
26. *Ibid.*, p. 147.
27. *Ibid.*, p. 149.
28. Senator Charles Percy, *Congressional Record*, Vol. 125, No. 20, February 3, 1977, p. S2133.
29. *Loc. cit.*
30. *Loc. cit.*
31. Martin Anderson, *The Federal Bulldozer* (M.I.T. Press, 1965), pp. 67, 220, 221.
32. This is obvious with artificially high prices, but even artificially low prices can persist only so long as either (1) products with deteriorated quality under price controls need not compete with higher quality uncontrolled products, or (2) the subsidy which makes other low prices possible is concealed or politically insulated from feedback from those forced to subsidize these prices.
33. In a sense, this is no more than a special case of the common principle underlying all property rights—namely, that two entirely different independently run activities cannot go on unrestrictedly in the same place and time without interfering with one another. Therefore one party is legally permitted to exclude all others, not ultimately for *his* benefit but so that *some* activity can go on effectively, to the ultimate benefit of society. This right to exclude others from the use of a given resource is all that makes any resource usable in practice. A socialist state must exercise this right as rigorously as a private capitalist or nothing could be produced (e.g., with a baseball game going on in a glass factory while fun lovers conduct pistol practice on the same site).
34. Walter Adams, "The Role of Competition in the Regulated Industries," *American Economic Review*, May 1958, p. 539.
35. *Ibid.*, p. 529.
36. *Loc. cit.*
37. Simat, Helliesen and Eichner, Inc., "The Intrastate Air Regulation Experience in Texas and California," *Regulation of Passenger Fares and Competition among the Airlines*, ed. Paul W. MacAroy and John W. Snow (American Enterprise Institute, 1977), pp. 42–44.
38. *Ibid.*, p. 44.
39. *Loc. cit.*
40. Armen A. Alchian and Reuben A. Kessel, "Competition, Monopoly, and the Pursuit of Money," *Aspects of Labor Economics*, ed. H. Gregg Lewis (Princeton University Press, 1962), pp. 157–183.
41. Harry Averich and L. L. Johnson, "The Behavior of the Firm Under Regulatory Constraint," *American Economic Review*, December 1962, pp. 1052–1069.
42. Walter Adams., *op. cit.*, p. 537. These rulings were later overturned in court.
43. *Ibid.*, p. 541.
44. Simon Rottenberg, "The Economics of Occupational Licensing," *Aspects of Labor Economics*, ed. H. Gregg Lewis, pp. 11–12.
45. Walter E. Williams, "Government Sanctioned Restraints that Reduce Economic Opportunities for Minorities," *Policy Review*, July 1978, p. 22.
46. Morris K. Udall, "Land Use: Why We Need Federal Legislation," *No Land Is an Island*, p. 59.
47. *Ibid.*, p. 65.
48. *Ibid.*, p. 70.
49. *Ibid.*, p. 74.
50. A. Lawrence Chickering, "Land Use Controls and Low Income Groups: Why Are There No Poor People in the Sierra Club," *Ibid.*, pp. 87–91.
51. Bernard Siegan, "No Zoning is the Best Zoning." *Ibid.*, pp. 160–161.
52. Benjamin F. Bobo, "The Effects of Land Use Controls on Low Income and Minority Groups: Court Actions and Economic Implications," *Ibid.*, p. 95.
53. B. Bruce-Briggs, "Land Use and the Environment," *Ibid.*, p. 9.
54. *Loc. cit.*
55. Jean Gottman, *Megalopolis* (M.I.T. Press, 1962), p. 3.
56. B. Bruce-Briggs, *op. cit.*, p. 13.

NOTES

57. Bernard H. Siegan, "No Zoning is the Best Zoning," *California Real Estate Magazine*, February 1975, p. 38.

58. Robert H. Bork and Ward S. Bowman, "The Crisis in Antitrust," *Columbia Law Review*. Vol. 65, No. 3 (March 1965), pp. 363–376; Frederick M. Rowe, "The Federal Trade Commission's Administration of the Anti-Price Discrimination Policy," *Columbia Law Review*, Vol. 64, No. 3 (March 1964), pp. 415–438; Richard Posner, *Antitrust Law: An Economic Perspective* (University of Chicago Press, 1976).

59. Robert H. Bork, "Contrasts in Antitrust Theory: I," *Columbia Law Review*, Vol. 65, No. 3 (March 1965), p. 401.

60. Donald J. Dewey, "The New Learning: One Man's View," *Industrial Concentration: The New Learning*, ed. Harvey J. Goldschmidt, H. Michael Mann, J. Fred Weston, (Boston: Little, Brown and Co., 1974), p. 3.

61. Richard A. Posner, *Antitrust Law: An Economic Perspective* (Chicago: University of Chicago Press, 1976), p. 228.

62. *United States v. Von's Grocery Co.*, 384 U. S. 270 (1965) at 301.

63. F. M. Scherer, "Economies of Scale and Industrial Concentration," *Industrial Concentration: The New Learning*, ed. H. J. Goldschmidt, *et al.* p. 21.

64. *Ibid.*, p. 26.

65. *Ibid.*, p. 31.

66. Harold Demsetz, *The Market Concentration Doctrine* (American Enterprise Institute, 1973).

67. "Dialogue," *Industrial Concentration: The New Learning*, pp. 244–245; see also Posner, *op. cit.*, p. 89.

68. *Federal Trade Commission v. Proctor & Gamble Co.*, 386 U. S. 568 (1967) at 572.

69. *Ibid.*, pp. 603n–604n.

70. *Utah Pie Co. v. Continental Baking Co., et al.*, 386 U. S. 685 (1967) at 690, 695.

71. See Posner, *op. cit.*, p. 119.

72. *United States v. Aluminum Co. of America*, 148 F. 2d 416 (2d Cir. 1945) at 426.

73. *Ibid.*, at 431.

74. *Brown Shoe Co., Inc., v. United States* 370 U. S. 294 (1962) at 303.

75. *United States v. Pabst Brewing Co.*, 384 U. S. 546 (1966) at 550.

76. *United States v. Von's Grocery Co.*, 384 U. S. 270 (1966) at 272.

77. "The Act is really referring to the effect upon competition and not merely upon competitors . . . " *Anheuser-Busch, Inc. v. Federal Trade Commission*, 289 F 2d 835 (7th Cir. 1961), at 840.

78. *Federal Trade Commission v. Morton Salt Co.*, 334 U. S. 37 (1948) at 50.

79. *Ibid.* at 46–47.

80. *Automatic Canteen Co. v. Federal Trade Commission*, 346 U. S. 61 (1953) at 79.

81. *Utah Pie Co. v. Continental Baking Co., et al.*, 386 U. S. 685 (1967) at 697.

82. *Ibid.*, at 691n.

83. *Ibid.*, at 699.

84. *Robinson Patman Act*, Section 2(a).

85. *United States v. Borden Co.*, 370 U. S. 460 (1962) at 469. See also pp. 470–471.

86. *Ibid.*, at 470.

87. *Anheuser-Busch, Inc. v. Federal Trade Commission*, 289 F. 2d 835 (7th Cir. 1961), at 843.

88. *Loc. cit.*

89. *Ibid.*, at 842.

90. Frederick M. Rowe, *op. cit.*, p. 416n.

91. The nineteenth-century activities of the Standard Oil Company have been repeatedly cited by twentieth-century exponents of the "predatory pricing" theory (suggesting a dearth of more timely examples). However, the authenticity of even that one ancient example has been challenged. John S. McGee, "Predatory Price Cutting: The Standard Oil (N.J.) Case," *Journal of Law & Economics*, October 1958, pp. 137–169.

92. "The Empty Truck Syndrome," *Wall Street Journal*, July 15, 1977, p. 6.

93. Frederick M. Rowe, *op. cit.*, p. 427.

94. *Ibid.*, p. 436n.

95. Frederick M. Rowe, *op. cit.*, p. 430.

96. Areeda, *op. cit.*, pp. 847–848.

97. Wassily Leontief and Leonard Woodcock, "The Case for Planning," *The Politics of Planning*, p. 348.

98. *Ibid.*, p. 352.

99. David K. Shipler, "Pravda Points Up Continuing Problems in Providing Goods That Are in Demand," *New York Times*, December 4, 1977, p. 3.

100. Alec Nove, "The Problem of 'Success Indicators' in Soviet Industry," *Economica*, February 1958, p. 5; Alec Nove, *The Soviet Economic System* (George Allen & Unwin, Ltd., 1977), pp. 97–99.

101. "Some manufacturers inflate their production statistics by dividing their assembly lines among various enterprises and then counting the value of a part several times as it moves from one factory to another." David K. Shipler, op. cit.

102. Alec Nove, "The Problem of 'Success Indicators'," *op. cit.*, p. 6; David Granick, *The Red Executive* (Anchor Books, 1961), pp. 132–134.

103. David Granick, *op. cit.*, p. 134.

104. Ralph Harris, "Great Britain: The Lessons of Socialist Planning," *The Politics of Planning*, p. 58.

105. *Ibid.*, p. 59.

106. Walter Eucken, "On the Theory of the Centrally Administered Economy: An Analysis of the German Experiment," *Comparative Economic System*, ed. Morris Bornstein (Richard D. Irwin, Inc., 1969), pp. 132, 135.

107. Hubert H. Humphrey in *National Economic Planning: Right or Wrong for the U. S.?* (American Enterprise Institute, 1976), p. 3.

108. *Ibid.*, p. 6.

109. Wassily Leontief in *Ibid.*, p. 9.

110. *Loc. cit.*

111. Hubert Humphrey in *Ibid.*, p. 7.

112. Wassily Leontief in *Ibid.*, pp. 14–15.

113. *Ibid.*, p. 20.

114. Hubert Humphrey in *Ibid.*, p. 19.

115. *Ibid.*, p. 37.

116. Karl Marx, *The Poverty of Philosophy* (International Publishers Co., Inc., 1963), pp. 60–61.

117. Frederich Engels, "Preface to the First German Edition," *Ibid.*, p. 19.

118. Oskar Lange, "On the Economic Theory of Socialism," *On the Economic Theory of Socialism*, ed. Benjamin E. Lippincott (New York: McGraw-Hill, 1964), pp. 57–143; Abba P. Lerner, *The Economics of Control* (The Macmillan Co., 1944).

119. Svetozar Pejovich, "The End of Planning: The Soviet Union and East European Experiences," *The Politics of Planning*, p. 109.

120. *Ibid.*, p. 99.

121. *Loc. cit.*

122. Alec Nove, "The Problem of 'Success Indicators'," *op. cit.*, p. 4.

123. Joseph S. Berliner, "Managerial Incentives and Decision-Making: A Comparison of the United States and the Soviet Union," *Comparison of the United States and Soviet Economics*, Subcommittee on Economic Statistics, Joint Economic Committee of the United States, 1959, Part I, p. 361.

124. Alec Nove, "Soviet Agriculture Marks Time," *Foreign Affairs*, July 1962, p. 588.

125. *Ibid.*, p. 581.

126. *Ibid.*, pp. 582–583.

127. Daniel J. Boorstin, *The Americans*, Vol. I: *The Colonial Experience* (New York: Random House, 1958), pp. 87, 88.

128. *Ibid.*, p. 95.

129. The physical characteristics of the land in Georgia would have remained unchanged, but the average size of a farm would have moved toward the optimum level, and the distribution of land among people with different amounts of agricultural knowledge would have made the total land more productive after this sorting process.

130. Daniel Boorstin, *op. cit.*

131. *Ibid.*, p. 90.

132. *Ibid.*, p. 83.

133. *Ibid.*, p. 93.

NOTES

134. *Loc. cit.*

135. *Loc. cit.*

136. George Bernard Shaw, *The Intelligent Woman's Guide to Socialism* (Brentano's Publishers, 1928), p. 334.

137. *Ibid.*, p. 137.

138. Joseph S. Berliner, "Prospects for Technological Progress," *op. cit.*, p. 440. Centralized inventories and the "middleman" in charge of them are an alternative (at least incrementally) to individual inventories held by consumers and producers. One of the problems chronically plaguing the Soviet economy has been the hoarding of raw materials and equipment by individual Soviet factories. Ideally, central planners allocate the amount of inputs each producer needs for his output, but the omniscience implicit in that theory is seldom realized in practice. A bottleneck at one point can result in a chain reaction of unfulfilled production quotas, unless there are inventories available to the individual producer without going through the long bureaucratic process of articulating feedback to central planners "through channels." Yet without channels to authenticate, sort and label requests, the central planners would be swamped with requests—ranging from desperate to frivolous—for more of everything, from all over a vast nation. Experimental Soviet middlemen are able to respond to local demands without central authorization, a procedure which in effect "denies the value of centralized planning" (*loc. cit.*)—or at least makes explicit its limitations, which may explain politically why it remains experimental.

139. Karl Marx, "Wage Labour and Capital," Karl Marx and Frederich Engels, *Selected Works* (Foreign Languages Publishing House, Moscow, 1955), Vo. I, pp. 99–105.

140. Karl Marx, *Capital* (Charles H. Kerr & Co., 1906), Vol. I, pp. 207–220.

141. *Ibid.*, pp. 207–255.

142. Eugene D. Genovese in "Capitalism, Socialism, and Democracy: A Symposium," *Commentary*, April 1978, p. 41.

143. U. S. Bureau of the Census, *Historical Statistics of the United States, Colonial Times to 1970*, p. 870.

144. V. I. Lenin, *Imperialism: The Highest Stage of Capitalism* (International Publishers, 1963), p. 64.

145. Robert L. Schuettinger, "Four Thousand Years of Wage and Price Controls," *Policy Review*, Summer 1978, p. 74.

Chapter 9

1. "Those Lawyers," *Time*, April 10, 1978, p. 59.

2. J. Anthony Kline, "Curbing California's Colossal Legal Appetite," *Los Angeles Times*, February 12, 1978, Part VI, p. 1.

3. "Too Much Law?" *Newsweek*, January 10, 1977, p. 45.

4. *Wheeler v. St. Joseph Hospital*, App. 133 Cal. Rptr. 775, at 794.

5. Robert J. Glennon, Jr. and John E. Nowak, "A Functional Analysis of the Fourteenth Amendment 'State Action' Requirement," *The Supreme Court Review 1976*, ed. Philip B. Kurland (University of Chicago Press, 1977), p. 247; Harold W. Horowitz and Kenneth L. Karst, "The Proposition Fourteen Cases: Justice in Search of a Justification," *UCLA Law Review*, Vol. 14, No. 1 (November 1966), pp. 37–51.

6. Richard A. Maidment, "Policy in Search of Law: The Warren Court from *Brown* to *Miranda*," *Journal of American Studies*, Vol. 9, No. 3 (December 1975), pp. 301–320; Raoul Berger, *Government by Judiciary: The Transformation of the Fourteenth Amendment* (Harvard University Press, 1977); Philip B. Kurland, *Politics, The Constitution and the Warren Court* (University of Chicago Press, 1970).

7. Robert J. Glennon Jr. and John E. Nowak, "A Functional Analysis of the Fourteenth Amendment 'State Action' Requirement," *The Supreme Court Review 1976*, ed. Philip B. Kurland (University of Chicago Press, 1977), p. 247.

8. *Ibid.*, p. 260.

9. William Lilley III and Jame C. Miller III, "The New 'Social Regulation,'" *The Public Interest*, Spring 1977, p. 51.

10. U. S. Bureau of the Census, *Historical Statistics of the United States: From Colonial Times to 1970*, Vo. II, p. 1081.

11. U. S. Senator Gary Hart, on numerous occasions.

NOTES

12. Frederick M. Rowe, "The Federal Trade Commission's Administration of the Anti-Price Discrimination Law—A Paradox of Antitrust Policy," *Columbia Law Review*, Vol. 64, No. 3 (March 1964), pp. 415–438; Richard A. Posner, *The Robinson Patman Act: Federal Regulation of Price Differences* (American Enterprise Institute, 1976), pp. 31, 46.

13. Thomas Sowell, *Affirmative Action Reconsidered* (American Enterprise Institute, 1975), p. 7.

14. Eugene Bardach and Lucian Pugliaresi, "The Environmental-Impact Statement vs. The Real World," *The Public Interest*, Fall 1977, pp. 29–31; Gary Sands Miller, "Environmental Report May Have Little Value in Predicting Impact," *Wall Street Journal*, June 1, 1978, pp. 1 ff.

15. *Abrams v. United States*, 250 U.S. 616 (1919) at 659.

16. *Ibid.*, at 661.

17. *Schenck v. United States*, 249 U. S. 47 (1919) 655.

18. Adam Smith, *The Wealth of Nations*, pp. 128. 249–250, 402–403, 429, 438, 579.

19. *Thornhill v. Alabama*, 310 U. S. 88.

20. *Milk Wagon Drivers Union v. Meadowmoor Dairies*, 312 U. S. 287 (1941) at 193.

21. *Bakery Drivers Local v. Wohl*, 315 U. S. 769 at 776.

22. See Raoul Berger, *Government by Judiciary: The Transformation of the Fourteenth Amendment* (Harvard University Press, 1977), Chapter 8.

23. *Marsh v. Alabama*, 326 U. S. 501 (1946) at 507.

24. *Amalgamated Food Employees Union Local 590, et al. v. Logan Valley Plaza, Inc., et al.*, 391 U. S. 308 (1968) at 330.

25. For example, the daily rental fee for a Rolls-Royce is well within the budgets of most Americans, though most could also think of better uses for the money.

26. *Marsh v. Alabama*, 326 U. S. 501 (1946) at 512–517, *passim.*

27. Customers pay through higher prices in shops with "better" atmosphere.

28. Harold W. Horowitz and Kenneth L. Karst, *op. cit.* p. 38.

29. Herbert Wechsler, "Toward Neutral Principles of Constitutional Law," *Harvard Law Review*, Vol. 73, No. 1 (1959), pp. 19, 24.

30. *Marsh v. Alabama*, 326 U. S. 501 (1946) at 503.

31. *Amalgamated Food Employees Union Local 590, et at. v. Logan Valley Plaza Inc., et al.*, 391 U. S. 308 (1968) at 318.

32. *Ibid.*, at 324–325.

33. *Ibid.*, at 309, 313, 324, 326, "Naked title is all that is at issue," *Ibid.*, p. 324.

34. *Ibid.*, p. 324.

35. *Lloyd Corp., Ltd., v. Tanner, et al.*, 407 U. S. 551 (1972), at 563.

36. *Ibid.*, at 580.

37. *Evans et al. v. Newton et al.*, 382 U. S. 296 (1966) at 322.

38. Public utility companies may not be set up without state authorization as being conducive to "the public necessity and convenience"—which it never is deemed to be when an existing utility is serving the same community, however well or badly.

39. Thomas Sowell, *Economics: Analysis and Issues* (Scott, Foresman & Co., 1977), pp. 120–121.

40. Thomas Sowell, "Three Black Histories," *American Ethnic Groups* (Urban Institute, 1978), p. 21.

41. Raoul Berger, *Government by Judiciary* (Harvard University Press, 1977), Chapter 2.

42. *Ibid.*, p. 30.

43. *Civil Rights Cases*, 109 U. S. 3 (1883) at 11.

44. *Ibid.*, at 26–27.

45. *United States v. Cruikshank*, 92 U. S. 542 (1875); *United States v. Harris*, 106 U. S. 629 (1882).

46. *Nixon v. Herndon*, 273 U. S. 536 (1927); *Smith v. Allwright*, 321 U. S. 649 (1944).

47. *Shelley v. Kraemer*, 334 U. S. 1 (1948) at 13.

48. *Ibid.*, at 19.

49. *Peterson v. Greenville*, 373 U. S. 244 (1956); *Lombard v. Louisiana*, 373 U. S. 267 (1963).

50. *Reitman, et al., v. Mulkey, et al.*, 387 U. S. 369 (1967) at 375, approvingly quoting the California Supreme Court decision which the U. S. Supreme Court affirmed.

51. *Burton v. Wilmington Parking Authority, et al.*, 365 U. S. 715 (1961), at 722.

52. *Moose Lodge No. 107 v. Irvin*, 407 U. S. 163 (1972).

NOTES

53. *Jackson v. Metropolitan Edison Co.*, 419 U. S. 345 (1974).

54. *Burton v. Wilmington Parking Authority, et al.*, 365 U. S. 715 (1961), at 728.

55. *Marsh v. Alabama*, 326 U. S. 501 (1946); *Amalgamated Food Employees Union v. Logan Valley Plaza*, 391 U. S. 308 (1968).

56. *Burton v. Wilmington Parking Authority, et al.*, 365 U. S. 715 (1961).

57. *Evans, et al. v. Newton, et al.*, 382 U. S. 296 (1966).

58. *Burton v. Wilmington Parking Authority, et al.*, 365 U. S. 715 (1961), at 725.

59. *Jackson v. Metropolitan Edison Co.*, 419 U. S. 345 (1974) at 357.

60. See notes 6 and 7 above and Charles L. Black quoted in Raoul Berger, *op. cit.*, pp. 346–350, *passim*.

61. Section 10(c), *National Labor Relations Act of 1935*.

62. Harry A. Millis and Emily Clark Brown, *From the Wagner Act to Taft-Hartley* (University of Chicago Press, 1950), p. 97.

63. Nathan Glazer, *Affirmative Discrimination: Ethnic Inequality and Public Policy* (Basic Books, Inc., 1975), p. 46.

63a. See U. S. Equal Employment Opportunity Commission, *Legislative History of Titles VII and XI of Civil Rights Act of 1964*, (Washington, D.C.: U. S. Government Printing Office, no date), p. 4.

64. Quoted in Richard A. Lester, *Antibias Regulation of Universities* (McGraw-Hill Book Co., 1974), p. 62.

65. *The Civil Rights Act of 1964*, Section 401(b) uses the phrase "without regard to their race, color, religion, sex, or national origin," and other sections declare that various decisions or exclusions cannot be "on the ground of race, color, religion, or national origin" (Section 202; see also Section 601), "on account of" such designations (Section 301[a]) or "because of" similar designations (Section 703).

66. U. S. Equal Employment Opportunity Commission, *Legislative History of Titles VII and XI of Civil Rights Act of 1964*, p. 3005.

67. *Ibid.*, p. 3006.

68. *Ibid.*, pp. 3160, 3161.

69. *Ibid.*, p. 3015.

70. Quoted in Glazer, *Affirmative Discrimination*, p. 45.

71. "Nothing contained in this title shall be interpreted to require any employer, employment agency, labor organization, or joint labor-management committee subject to this title to grant preferential treatment to any individual or any group because of the race, color, religion, sex, or national origin of such individual or group on account of an imbalance which may exist with respect to the total number or percentage of persons of any race, color, religion, sex, or national origin employed . . ." Section 703(j), *Civil Rights Act of 1964*.

72. U. S. Department of Labor guidelines issued December 4, 1971, quoted in Glazer, *Affirmative Discrimination*, p. 49.

73. Thomas Sowell, "Ethnicity in a Changing America," *Daedalus*, Winter 1978, p. 221.

74. *Ibid.*, pp. 213–237.

75. *Hearings before the Equal Employment Opportunity Commission on Utilization of Minority and Women Workers in Certain Major Industries* (Hearings held in Los Angeles, California, March 12–14, 1969), p. 303.

76. Quoted in Glazer, *op. cit.*, p. 56.

77. *Ibid.*, p. 57.

78. *Ibid.*, p. 47.

79. Sowell, "Ethnicity in a Changing America," *op. cit.*, pp. 214, 215.

80. *Ibid.*, p. 214.

81. Glazer, *op. cit.*, pp. 51–56.

82. *Ibid.*, p. 57.

83. *Ibid.*, p. 67.

84. Francis Ward, "U. S. Agencies Clash in Rights Lawsuit, *Los Angeles Times*, April 27, 1975, Part IV, p. 1 ff.

85. James L. Buckley, *Congressional Record*, March 2, 1976, Vol. 127, No. 28.

86. *Congressional Record*, 94th Congress, Second Session, Vol. 122, No. 28.

87. Nathan Glazer, *op. cit.*, p. 38.

88. James P. Smith and Finis Welch, *Race Differences in Earnings: A Survey and New Evidence* (Rand Corporation, 1978), p. 1.

89. *Gallup Opinion Index,* June 1977, Report 143, p. 23.
90. *Regents of the University of California v. Allan Bakke,* 46 U. S. *Law Week* 4896 at 4909.
91. *Ibid.,* at 4902.
92. *Ibid.,* at 4906.
93. *Ibid.,* at 4901.
94. *Ibid.,* at 4903.
95. *Loc. cit.*
96. *Ibid.*
97. *Ibid.*
98. *Ibid.,* at 4935.
99. *Ibid.,* footnote 1 at 4933.
100. *Ibid.,* at 4918–4922, *passim.*
101. *Ibid.,* at 4933.
102. *United Steelworkers of America v. Brian F. Weber,* 47 *U.S. Law Week* 4851, at 4853.
103. *Regents of the University of California v. Allan Bakke,* 46 *U.S. Law Week* 4896, at 4934.
104. *United Steelworkers of America v. Brian F. Weber,* 47 *U.S. Law Week* 4851, at 4861–4866.
105. *Regents of the University of California v. Allan Bakke,* 46 *U.S. Law Week* 4896, at 4936.
106. *United Steelworkers of America v. Brian F. Weber,* 47 *U.S. Law Week* 4851, at 4853.
107. *Loc. cit.*
108. *Ibid.,* at 4853, 4854, 4859.
109. Moreover, using negative differences from the national average (in income, occupational "representation," etc.) as a measure of discrimination implicitly excludes *a priori* the possibility of any group's ever having overcome discrimination to any degree.
110. Thomas Sowell, "Ethnicity in a Changing America," *op. cit.,* p. 221.
111. *Ibid.,* pp. 221–225.
112. U. S. Bureau of the Census, *Current Population Reports,* Series P–20, No. 213, p. 6.
113. Ben Wattenberg, *The Real America* (Doubleday, 1974), p. 136.
114. *Employment and Training Report of the President,* 1976 (Government Printing Office, 1976), p. 241–243.
115. James P. Welch and Finis Welch, *Race Differences in Earnings: A Survey and New Evidence* (Rand Corporation, 1978), p. 7.
116. Finis Welch, "Black-White Differences in Returns to Schooling," *American Economic Review,* Vol. LXIII, No. 5 (December 1973), pp. 893–907.
117. U. S. Bureau of the Census, *U. S. Census of Population, 1970: Subject Reports* PC (2)-7C, pp. 170, 171.
118. Thomas Sowell, "Ethnicity in a Changing America," *op. cit.,* pp. 225–226.
119. U. S. Bureau of the Census, *Current Population Reports,* Series P–23, No. 46, p. 22.
120. Richard B. Freeman, *Black Elite,* pp. 88, 107; Thomas Sowell, *Affirmative Action Reconsidered,* pp. 21–22.
121. Freeman, *Loc. cit.*
122. James P. Smith and Finis Welch, *Race Differences in Earnings,* pp. 21, 47–50; Orley Ashenfelter, "Comments," *Frontiers of Quantitative Economics,* ed. M. D. Intriligator and D. A. Kendrick (North-Holland Publishing Company, 1974), Vol. 2, p. 508; Thomas Sowell, *Affirmative Action Reconsidered,* pp. 23, 41–42.
123. Ben Wattenberg, *op. cit.,* pp. 131–132.
124. "The Economic Role of Women," in *The Economic Report of the President, 1973* (U. S. Government Printing Office, 1973), p. 103.
125. Thomas Sowell, *Affirmative Action Reconsidered,* pp. 32–33.
126. Helen S. Astin, "Career Profiles of Women Doctorates," *Academic Women on the Move,* ed. Alice S. Rossi and Ann Calderwood (Russell Sage Foundation, 1973), p. 153.
127. Lino A. Graglia, *Disaster by Decree: The Supreme Court Decisions on Race and the Schools* (Cornell University Press, 1976), Chapter 3.
128. Richard Kluger, *Simple Justice: The History of Brown v. Board of Education and Black America's Struggle for Equality* (Alfred A. Knopf, 1976), p. 572.
129. Lino A. Graglia, *op. cit.,* p. 34.

130. *Ibid.*, p. 46.
131. *Ibid.*, pp. 46–52.
132. *Ibid.*, p. 55.
133. *Ibid.*, p. 59.
134. *Ibid.*, p. 66.
135. Thomas Sowell, *Affirmative Action Reconsidered*, pp. 4–7.
136. *Bell v. School City of Gary, Indiana*, 372 F2d 910 at 906.
137. *Green v. County School Board of New Kent County* 391 U. S. 430 (1968), at 437–438.
138. *Ibid.*, at 441.
139. Lino A. Graglia, *op. cit.*, p. 71.
140. *Ibid.*, *passim*.
141. *Ibid.*, p. 105.
142. *Ibid.*, pp. 129, 132, 203.
143. *Ibid*, pp. 160, 161.
144. *Ibid.*, pp. 145, 223; Glazer, *op. cit.*, pp. 92–93.
145. *Ibid.*, p. 216.
146. *Ibid.*, p. 257.
147. *Ibid.*, p. 132; David Armor, *White Flight, Demographic Transition, and the Future of School Desegregation* (The Rand Corporation, 1978).
148. Lino A. Graglia, *op. cit.*, p. 276; David Armor "The Evidence on Busing," *The Public Interest*, Summer 1972, pp. 90–126; "On Busing: An Exchange," *The Public Interest*, Winter 1973, pp. 88–134.
149. Graglia, *op. cit.*, p. 269; Langerton, *op. cit.*, pp. 15–16.
150. David J. Armor, *Sociology and School Busing Policy* (The Rand Corporation, 1978), p. 2; Graglia, *op. cit.*, p. 277; Langerton, *op. cit.*, p. 3.
151. Graglia, *op. cit.*, pp. 153–154.
152. *Ibid.*, pp. 272–273.
153. Langerton, *op. cit.*, pp. 51–57, 72.
154. Constance McLaughlin Green, *The Secret City* (Princeton University Press, 1967), p. 137.
155. Thomas Sowell, "Black Excellence—the Case of Dunbar High School," *The Public Interest*, Spring 1974, p. 8.
156. Thomas Sowell, "Patterns of Black Excellence," *The Public Interest*, Spring 1976, p. 8. See also pp. 35–37.
157. James S. Coleman, et. al., *Equality of Educational Opportunity* (Government Printing Office, 1966).
158. Arthur R. Jensen, "How Much Can We Boost IQ and Scholastic Achievement?" *Harvard Educational Review*, Vol. 39, No. 1 (Winter 1969), pp. 1–123.
159. Thomas Sowell, "Race and IQ Reconsidered," *Essays and Data on American Ethnic Groups*, pp. 203–238.
160. Diane Ravitch, *The Great School Wars* (Basic Books, Inc., 1974), p. 178.
161. *Loc. cit.*
162. *Ibid.*, p. 176.
163. Irving Howe, *World of Our Fathers*, (Harcourt Brace Jovanovich, 1976), p. 278.
164. Langerton, *op. cit.*, p. 37.
165. *Ibid.*, pp. 37, 42.
166. Derrick A. Bell, Jr., "Serving Two Masters: Integration Ideals and Client Interests in School Desegregation Litigation," *Yale Law Journal* Vol. 85, No. 4 (March 1976), p. 470, 482.
167. *Ibid.*, p. 486; Glazer, *op. cit.*
168. Quoted in *Ibid.*, p. 492.
169. Derrick A. Bell, *op. cit.*, p. 489.
170. *Ibid.*, p. 491n.
171. Ronald R. Edmonds, "Advocating Inequity: A Critique of the Civil Rights Attorney in Class Action Desegregation Cases," *The Black Law Journal*, Vol. 3, Nos. 2, 3 (1974), p. 178.
172. Graglia, *op. cit.*, p. 334–335.
173. Langerton, *op. cit.*, pp. 152–153.
174. Michael Meltsner, *Cruel and Unusual: The Supreme Court and Capital Punishment* (Random House, 1973), p. 36.
175. *Ibid.*, p. 37.

176. *Ibid.*, p. 15.

177. Peter L. Berger and Richard John Neuhaus, *To Empower People: The Role of Mediating Structures in Public Policy* (American Enterprise Institute, 1977), p. 12.

178. *Loc. cit.*

179. Harold B. Woodman, "The Profitability of Slavery: A Historical Perennial," *Journal of Southern History,* August 1963, pp. 303–325.

180. Second Inaugural Address of Abraham Lincoln.

181. Andrew M. Greeley, *That Most Distressful Nation* (Quadrangle Books, 1972), p. 40. See also Antonin Scalia, "The Disease as Cure," *Washington University Law Quarterly,* Winter 1979, p. 152.

182. Gallup Opinion Index, June 1977, Report 143, p. 23.

183. James M. McPherson, *The Abolitionist Legacy* (Princeton University Press, 1975), Chapters 9–11.

184. Thomas Sowell, ed., *Essays and Data on American Ethnic Groups* (Urban Institute, 1978), p. 300.

185. Stanford M. Lyman, *Chinese Americans* (Random House, Inc., 1974), Chapters 4, 5; William Petersen, *Japanese Americans* (Random House, 1971), Chapters 3, 4.

186. Betty Lee Sung, *The Story of the Chinese in America* (Collier Books, 1967), p. 125.

187. U. S. Bureau of the Census, *Current Population Reports,* (Government Printing Office, 1973), Series P–20, No. 249, p. 1.

188. Gunnar Myrdal, *An American Dilemma* (McGraw-Hill Book Company, 1964), Vol. I, p. 133.

189. J. C. Furnas, *The Americans* (G. P. Putnam's Sons, 1969), p. 406, "State laws carefully defined those with up to seven-eighths white ancestry as 'Negroes.' To have pushed the definition any further would have embarrassed too many prominent 'white' families." Eugene Genovese, *op. cit.*, p. 420.

190. There is no illusion that each criminal can be punished for his crime, but this simply makes the application of the principle depend on probability like the search for oil wells, the purchase of life insurance, or other individual or social decisions involving probabilities.

191. Gary S. Becker and William M. Landes, eds., *Essays in the Economics of Crime and Punishment* (Columbia University Press, 1974), pp. 55–67.

192. ". . . these practices will not be stopped by mere force." Ramsey Clark, *op. cit.*, p. 118.

193. 354 U. S. 449 (1957)

194. Gordon Tullock, *The Logic of the Law,* p. 93; Steven Schlesinger, *Exclusionary Injustice* (Marcel Dekker, Inc., 1977), pp. 4, 107–108.

195. Gordon Tullock, *op. cit.*, p. 94.

196. *Ibid.*, pp. 93–97.

197. *Ibid.*, p. 96.

198. See *Escobido v. Illinois,* 378 U. S. 748 (1964); *Miranda v. Arizona,* 384 U. S. 436 (1966).

199. Macklin Fleming, *The Price of Perfect Justice,* pp. 123–124; Steven R. Schlesinger, *Exclusionary Injustice,* pp. 31–32.

200. The extent of such involvement is discussed in Macklin Fleming, *op. cit.,* Chapters 3–7.

201. U. S. Bureau of the Census, *Historical Statistics of the United States, Colonial Times to 1970* (U. S. Government Printing Office, 1974), p. 413.

202. Ramsey Clark, *op. cit.*, p. 31.

203. James Q. Wilson, *Thinking About Crime* (Basic Books, Inc., 1975), p. 17.

204. Ramsey Clark, *op. cit.*, p. 34.

205. "The Youth Crime Plague," *Time,* January 11, 1977, p. 18.

206. "All Kinds of Crime—Growing . . . Growing . . . Growing," *U. S. News and World Report,* December 16, 1974, p. 33.

207. Ernest van den Haag, *Punishing Criminals* (Basic Books, Inc., 1975), p. 146.

208. Ramsey Clark, *Crime in America,* p. 35.

209. *Ibid.*, p. 195.

210. Ernest van den Haag, *op. cit.*, p. 100.

211. James Q. Wilson, *Thinking About Crime,* p. 104.

212. Charles R. Tittle, "Punishment and Deterrence of Deviance," *The Economics of Crime and Punishment,* ed. Simon Rottenberg (American Enterprise Institute, 1973), p. 89.

213. Ernest van den Haag, *op. cit.*, p. 158.

214. U. S. Bureau of the Census, *Historical Statistics of the United States, From Colonial Times to 1970*, pp. 413, 420.

215. Ernest van den Haag, *Punishing Criminals*, p. 222.

216. James Q. Wilson, *Thinking About Crime*, p. 199; Ernest van den Haag, *Punishing Criminals*, p. 5n.

217. James Q. Wilson, "Crime and Punishment in England," *The Public Interest*, Spring 1976, p. 5.

218. Ernest van den Haag, *op. cit.*, p. 5n.

219. James Q. Wilson, "Crime and Punishment in England," *op. cit.*, p. 6.

220. *Ibid.*, p. 10.

221. U. S. Bureau of the Census, *Pocket Data Books USA 1976* (Government Printing Office, 1976), p. 142.

222. *Loc. cit.* See also U. S. Bureau of the Census, *Historical Statistics of the United States, Colonial Times to 1970*, p. 422.

223. *Ibid.*, p. 413.

224. *Ibid.*, p. 11.

225. Ernest van den Haag, *op. cit.*, p. 166.

226. Macklin Fleming, *op. cit.*, p. 64; Ernest van den Haag, *op. cit.*, p. 166.

227. Macklin Fleming, *Loc. cit.*

228. *Ibid.*, p. 65.

229. Raoul Berger, *Government by Judiciary: The Transformation of the Fourteenth Amendment* (Harvard University Press, 1977), Chapter 8; Philip B. Kurland, *Politics and the Warren Court* (University of Chicago Press, 1970), Chapter 3.

230. Macklin Fleming, *op. cit.*, p. 16.

231. *Ibid.*, pp. 17–18.

232. *Ibid.*, pp. 28–29.

233. *Ibid.*, pp. 31–35.

234. *Ibid.*, p. 27.

235. *Loc. cit.*

236. *Ibid.*, p. 17.

237. James Q. Wilson, "Crime and Punishment in England," *op. cit.*, pp. 13–14.

238. *Ibid.*, p. 5.

239. *Ibid.*, p. 20.

240. *Ibid.*, p. 21.

241. *Ibid.*, p. 22.

242. Gordon Tullock, "Does Punishment Deter Crime?" *The Public Interest*, Summer 1974, p. 108.

243. James Q. Wilson, "Crime and Punishment in England," *op. cit.* p. 25.

244. *Ibid.*, p. 5.

245. *Ibid.*, p. 25.

246. *Ibid.*, pp. 4, 6.

247. *Ibid.*, p. 10.

248. *Ibid.*, pp. 9–10.

249. Ernest van den Haag, *Punishing Criminals*, p. 157.

250. David Bayley, "Learning About Crime—The Japanese Experience," *The Public Interest*, Summer 1976, p. 60.

251. *Ibid.*, pp. 58–60.

252. *Ibid.*, pp. 58–59.

253. Jonathan Rubinstein, *City Police* (Ballantine Books, 1973), p. 378; Steven R. Schlesinger, *Exclusionary Injustice*, p. 57.

254. Ramsey Clark, *Crime in America*, p. 297.

255. Such considerations appeared in quoted statements in the landmark case of *Miranda v. Arizona*, 384 U. S. 436 (1966), at 470, 471.

256. Ramsey Clark, *op. cit.*, p. 298.

257. The exact percentage varies with the definition—one out of sixty according to Gordon Tullock, *The Logic of the Law*, p. 171. A much higher percentage is cited in Charles E. Silberman, *Criminal Violence, Criminal Justice*, (Random House, 1978), pp. 257–260. Silberman first excludes more than a quarter of a million juveniles from his statistics (p. 259) and then proceeds

to refer to the remainder of the criminals as "the total" and "all," in figuring his percentages. He also defends the Warren Court's criminal law decisions by (1) basing his analysis of 1970s national crime rates on extrapolations from California statistics for the early 1960s (pp. 257–258), *before* many of the controversial Warren Court decisions, and (2) uses 1920s data as before-and-after evidence of the Warren Court's effect on crime rates (pp. 261–262)—even though the Warren Court era did not begin until 1953 and its major criminal decisions date from the mid to late 1960s. Such desperate statistical maneuvers are revealing, not only as regards the vulnerability of the Warren Court's record, but also its partisans' will to believe.

258. Earl Warren, *The Memoirs of Earl Warren*, (Doubleday & Co., Inc., 1977), p. 316.

259. Ramsey Clark, *op. cit.*, p. 298.

260. Macklin Fleming, *op. cit.*, pp. 75–76.

261. James Q. Wilson, "Crime and Punishment in England." *op. cit.*, p. 19.

262. James Q. Wilson, *Thinking About Crime*, p. xiv.

263. *Ibid.*, pp. 165, 173.

264. *Ibid.*, p. 186.

265. *Ibid.*, pp. 168–169, 186–187. See also p. 172.

266. *The Challenge of Crime in a Free Society*, A report by the President's Commission on Law Enforcement and Administration of Justice (Government Printing Office, 1967), p. 165.

267. *Ibid.*, p. 169.

268. Ramsey Clark, *Crime in America*, p. 199.

269. *Ibid.*, p. 200.

270. *Loc. cit.*

271. *Ibid.*, p. i and back cover.

272. Earl Warren, *op. cit.*, p. 317.

273. *Ibid.*, p. 317; Michael Meltsner, *Cruel and Unusual: The Supreme Court and Capital Punishment* (Random House, 1973), p. 40.

274. Anthony G. Amsterdam, "Capital Punishment," *The Stanford Magazine*, Fall/Winter 1977, p. 47.

275. Ramsey Clark, op. cit., pp. 117–118.

276. James Q. Wilson, *Thinking About Crime*, p. 175.

277. *Ibid.*, pp. 174–175.

278. Isaac Ehrlich, "The Deterrent Effect of Capital Punishment: A Question of Life or Death," *American Economic Review*, 1975, p. 39.

279. Thorsten Sellin, "The Death Penalty," *Model Penal Code* (American Law Institute, 1959).

280. David C. Baldus and James W. L. Cole, "A Comparison of the Work of Thorsten Sellin and Isaac Ehrlich on the Deterrent Effect of Capital Punishment," *Yale Law Journal*, Vol. 85, No. 2 (December 1975), pp. 170–186; William J. Bowers and Glenn L. Pierce, "The Illusion of Deterrence in Isaac Ehrlich's Research on Capital Punishment," *Ibid.*, pp. 187–208; Hans Zeisel. "The Deterrent Effect of the Death Penalty: Facts v. Faiths," *The Supreme Court Review*, 1976 (University of Chicago Press, 1977) pp. 326–327.

281. Hans Zeisel, *op. cit.*, pp. 326–327; *Furman v. Georgia*, 408 U. S. 238 (1972), at 349.

282. Hans Zeisel, *op. cit.*, p. 333.

283. *Ibid.*, p. 326.

284. U. S. Bureau of the Census, *Historical Statistics of the United States, From Colonial Times to 1970*, p. 422.

285. James Q. Wilson, "Crime and Punishment in England," *op. cit.*, p. 23.

286. *Furman v. Georgia*, 408 U. S. 238 (1972).

287. "Excessive bail shall not be required, nor excessive fines imposed, nor cruel and unusual punishments inflicted."

288. Quoted in Michael Meltsner, *op. cit.*, pp. 268–278.

289. Michael Meltsner, *op. cit.*, p. 316. See also Anthony Amsterdam, *op. cit.*, p. 43.

290. Michael Meltsner, *op. cit.*, pp. 62. 181.

291. *Ibid.*, p. 61.

292. *Ibid.*, pp. 62, 181.

293. Amsterdam, *op. cit.*, p. 46. See also *Furman v. Georgia*, 408 U. S. 238 (1972), at 300–301.

294. *Furman v. Georgia*, 408 U. S. 238 (1972), at 293, 295, 300, 304, 309, 310.

295. Ben Wattenberg, *The Real America*, (Doubleday & Co., Inc., 1974), p. 142.

296. James Q. Wilson, *Thinking About Crime*, pp. 188–189.

297. U. S. Bureau of the Census, *Historical Statistics of the United States, Colonial Times to 1970*, p. 414.

298. "The constitutional function of the Court is to define values and proclaim principles." Alexander M. Bickel, *The Least Dangerous Branch* (Bobbs-Merrill Co., Inc., 1962), p. 68. See also *Ibid.*, pp. 27, 39, 48, 50, 55, 58, 71; Robert J. Glennon and John E. Nowak, "Functional Analysis of the Fourteenth Amendment 'State Action' Requirement," *The Supreme Court Review* 1976, pp. 227, 261.

299. For the latter view, see Raoul Berger, *Government by Judiciary, passim.*

300. See *infra*, Chapters 8 and 9, *passim.*

301. Alexander M. Bickel, *The Least Dangerous Branch*, p. 46.

302. Earl Warren, *op. cit.*, p. 325.

303. *Ibid.*, p. 330.

304. *Ibid.*, p. 293.

305. Richard Kluger, *Simple Justice*, p. 747.

306. Raoul Berger, *Government by Judiciary*, p. 222.

307. *Ibid.*, p. 4.

308. *Ibid.*, p. 322.

309. Alexander M. Bickel, *The Least Dangerous Branch*, pp. 46. 74, 75.

310. Derrick A. Bell. See Michael Meltsner, *Cruel and Unusual*, p. 12.

311. Nathaniel R. Jones, "Is Brown Obsolete? No!" *Integrated Education*, May–June 1976, p. 29.

312. "Study of what the terms meant to the framers indicates that there was no mystery," Raoul Berger, *Government by Judiciary*, p. 18; See also *Ibid.*, Chapters 2, 10, 11.

313. *Ibid.*, p. 100n.

314. Alexander M. Bickel, *The Least Dangerous Branch*, pp. 43, 48, 58, 68, 71.

315. *Ibid.*, pp. 15, 49, 93, 103, 104.

316. *Ibid.*, pp. 33.

317. *Ibid.*, Chapter 5.

318. Michael Meltsner, *Cruel and Unusual*, pp. 25–26.

319. Alexander M. Bickel, *The Least Dangerous Branch*, p. 75.

320. *Ibid.*, p. 55.

321. *Hepburn v. Griswold*, 75 U. S. 603 (1869) at 638.

322. Ulrich Bonnell Phillips, *Life and Labor in the Old South*, (Little, Brown and Co., 1957), p. 160.

323. Michael Meltsner, *op. cit.*, p. 269.

324. *Brown v. Board of Education of Topeka*, 347 U. S. 483.

325. Raoul Berger, *op. cit.*, pp. 117–133.

326. Alexander M. Bickel, *The Least Dangerous Branch* , p. 36.

327. See Raoul Berger, *op. cit.*, p. 343.

328. See *Ibid.*, p. 368n.

329. *Ibid.*, p. 193n.

330. *Ibid.*, p. 387.

331. *Regents of the University of California v. Allan Bakke*, 46 U. S. Law Week, 4896, at 4934.

332. U. S. Equal Employment Opportunity Commission, *Legislative History of Titles VII and XI of Civil Rights Act of 1964* (U. S. Government Printing Office, no date), pp. 3005, 3006, 3015, 3131, 3134, 3160, 3161.

333. Alexander M. Bickel, *The Least Dangerous Branch*, p. 14.

334. *Ibid.*, p. 96.

335. Raoul Berger, *Government by Judiciary*, p. 244.

336. *Ibid.*, p. 319.

337. Alexander M. Bickel, *The Least Dangerous Branch*, p. 25.

338. *Ibid.*, p. 35.

339. *Ibid.*, p. 93.

340. *Ibid.*, p. 103.

341. *Ibid.*, p. 106.

342. *Ibid.*, p. 110.

343. See Raoul Berger, *op. cit.*, p. 282.

344. *Ibid.*, p. 363n.
345. *Ibid.*, p. 288.
346. *Loc. cit.*
347. *Ibid.*, p. 314.
348. *Ibid.*, p. 329.
349. Alexander M. Bickel, *The Least Dangerous Branch*, p. 48.
350. *Ibid.*, p. 58.
351. *Ibid.*, p. 59.
352. *Louisiana ex rel, Francis v. Resweber* 329 U. S. 459 (1947), at 471.
353. Quoted in Raoul Berger, *Government by Judiciary*, 261n.
354. Alexander M. Bickel, *The Least Dangerous Branch*, p. 57.
355. *Ibid.*, p. 33.
356. *Ibid.*, p. 33.
357. *Ibid.*, p. 70.
358. *Ibid.*, p. 239.
359. *Ibid.*, p. 16.
360. *Ibid.*, pp. 43. 244.
361. Alexander M. Bickel, *The Morality of Consent* (Yale University Press, 1975), pp. 27–30.
362. *Ibid.*, p. 30.
363. *Ibid.*, p. 60.
364. *Ibid.*, p. 133.
365. *Ibid.*, pp. 119–120.
366. Quoted in Philip B. Kurland, *Politics, the Constitution and the Warren Court* (University of Chicago Press, 1970), p. 56.
367. *Ibid.*, p. 57.
368. Raoul Berger, *op. cit.*, p. 194.
369. *Ibid.*, p. 196n, "The words 'due process of law,' were undoubtedly intended to convey the same meaning as the words, 'by the law of the land,' in Magna Carta." *Murray's Lessee v. Hoboken Land Co.*, 59 U. S. 272 (1856);
370. *Dred Scott v. Sanford*, 60 U. S. 393 (1857).
371. *Slaughter-House Cases*, 21 L. Ed. 394 (1873).
372. *Davidson v. New Orleans*, 96 U. S. 97 (1877).
373. *Mugler v. Kansas*, 123 U. S. 623 (1877).
374. *Lochner v. New York*, 198 U. S. 452 S. Ct. 539.
375. *Olsen v. Nebraska*, 313 U. S. 236 (1941), at 247; *Lincoln Federal Labor Union v. Northwestern Iron & Metal Co.*, 335 U. S. 525 (1949), at 535–537; *Ferguson v. Skrupa*, 372 U. S. 726 (1963), at 729–731; *Day-Brite Lighting, Inc. v. Missouri*, 342 U. S. 421 (1952) at 423; *Williamson v. Lee Optical Co.*, 348 U. S. 483 (1955), at 488; *Griswold v. Connecticut*, 381 U. S. 479 (1965), at 482.
376. *Olsen v. Nebraska*, 313 U.S. 236 (1941), at 247.
377. *Day-Brite Lighting, Inc. v. Missouri*, 342 U. S. 421 (1952), at 423.
378. *Olsen v. Nebraska*, 313 U. S. 236 (1941), at 247.
379. *Day-Brite Lighting, Inc. v. Missouri* 342 U. S. 421 (1952), at 423.
380. *Ibid.*, at 425.
381. *Williamson v. Lee Optical Co.*, 348 U. S. 483 (1955), at 488.
382. Macklin Fleming, *op. cit.*, p. 93; Raoul Berger, *op. cit.*, Chapter 8.
383. *Mapp v. Ohio*, 367 U.S. 643 (1961).
384. *Gideon v. Wainright*, 372 U.S. 335 (1963).
385. *Escobido v. Illinois*, 378 U. S. 748 (1964); *Miranda v. Arizona*, 348 U. S. 436 (1966).
386. *Ker v. California*, 374 U.S. 23 (1963).
387. See footnote 385, above.
388. *Bolling v. Sharpe*, 347 U.S. 497 (1954).
389. *Griswold v. Connecticut*, 381 U.S. 479 (1965).
390. *Bivens v. Six Unknown Federal Narcotics Agents*, 403 U.S. 388 (1971), at 411.
391. James P. Smith and Finis Welch, *Race Differences in Earnings*, pp. 47–54; Orley Ashenfelter, "Comments," *Frontiers of Quantitative Economics*, ed. M. D. Intriligator and D. A. Kendrick (North-Holland Publishing Co., 1974), Vol. 2, p. 558; Thomas Sowell, *Affirmative Action Reconsidered* (American Enterprise Institute, 1975), p. 23.

NOTES

392. See footnotes 148–150 above.
393. See footnote 147 above.
394. Lino A. Graglia, *Disaster by Decree*, p. 264.
395. *Ibid.*, pp. 264–265.
396. *Ibid.*, p. 276.
397. Nathan Glazer, *Affirmative Discrimination*, p. 104.
398. See, for example, Joseph Adelson, "Living with Quotas" *Commentary*, May 1978, pp. 23–29.
399. *Brown v. Board of Education of Topeka*, 347 U.S. 483 (1954), at 494.
400. See, for example, Ernest van den Haag, "Social Science Testimony in the Desegregation Cases—A Reply to Professor Kenneth Clark," *Villanova Law Review*, Vol. 6, No. 1 (Fall 1960), pp. 69–79; James Gregor, "The Law, Social Science, and School Segregation: An Assessment," *Western Reserve Law Review*, Vol. 14, No. 4 (September 1963), pp. 621–636.
401. Richard Kluger, *Simple Justice*, p. 555.
402. See, for example, *Henningsen v. Bloomfield Motors, Inc.*, N.J. 358 A. 2d (1960); *Collins v. Uniroyal*, 64 N.J. 260, 315A. 2d. 16 (1974). See also James A. Henderson, Jr. "Judicial Review of Manufacturers' Conscious Design Choices: The Limits of Adjudication." *Columbia Law Review*, Vol. 73, No. 4 (December 1973), pp. 1531–1578.
403. *New York Times Co, v. Sullivan*, 376 U.S. 254 (1964).
404. Raoul Berger, *op. cit.*, p. 303.
405. Macklin Fleming, *The Price of Perfect Justice*, p. 123.
406. Gallop Opinion Index, June 1977, Report 143, p. 23; Ben Wattenberg, *The Real America*, p. 278.
407. William J. Brennan, Jr., "The National Court of Appeals: Another Dissent," *University of Chicago Law Review*, Vol. 40, No. 3 (Spring 1973), p. 480.
408. *Ibid.*, p. 481.
409. *Ibid.*, p. 482.
410. *Ibid.*, p. 479.
411. *Ibid.*, p. 484.
412. *Loc. cit.*

Chapter 10

1. U. S. Bureau of the Census, *Historical Statistics of the United States, From Colonial Times to 1970*, p. 1102.
2. Roger Freeman, *The Growth of American Government* (Hoover Institution, 1977), p. 5.
3. *Ibid.*, p. 6.
4. U. S. Bureau of the Census, *Pocket Data Book, 1976*, p. 99; *idem, Historical Statistics of the United States: From Colonial Times to 1970*, p. 1105.
5. *Idem, Historical Statistics of the United States, Colonial Times to 1970*, p. 1104.
6. "The Beneficent Monster," *Time*, June 12, 1978, p. 24.
7. A thousand dollars a day for 365 days a year is $365,000 annually. For a thousand years that adds up to $365 million, and for two thousand years $730 million. A billion dollars are a thousand million, so $730 million is less than three-quarters of a billion.
8. "The Beneficent Monster," *op. cit.*
9. Quoted in Bertram D. Wolfe, *An Ideology in Power* (Stein and Day, 1969), p. 162n.
10. *Loc. cit.*
11. Edward Gibbon, *The Decline and Fall of the Roman Empire* (Modern Library, no date), Vol. I, pp. 25–26, 28, *Ibid.*, Vol.II, pp. 49, 464–465.
12. *Ibid.*, Vol. I, pp. 29–35, 240–241, 303, 945; *Ibid.*, Vol. II, p. 79, 196, 885.
13. *Ibid.*, Vol. I, pp. 383–385, 406, 448.
14. Hannah Arendt, *The Origins of Totalitarianism* (Harcourt Brace Jovanovich, Inc., 1973), p. 305.
15. Stanley Elkins, *Slavery* (University of Chicago Press, 1969).
16. Hannah Arendt, *The Origins of Totalitarianism*, p. 00.
17. Alfred H. Conrad and John R. Meyer, "The Economics of Slavery in the Antebellum South," *Journal of Political Economy*, April 1958, pp. 95–130; Robert W. Fogel and Stanley L. Engerman, *Time on the Cross* (Little Brown and Co., 1974), pp. 59–106, 174, 184–190.

18. See Thomas Sowell, "Karl Marx and the Freedom of the Individual," *Ethics*, January 1963, pp. 119–125.

19. *Ibid.*, pp. 122–123.

20. *Ibid.*, p. 123.

21. Totalitarian elites "dissolve every statement of fact into a declaration of purpose." Hannah Arendt, *The Origins of Totalitarianism*, p. 385.

22. *Ibid.*, p. 311.

23. Richard Crossman, ed., *The God that Failed* (Bantam Books, 1949), p. 16.

24. *Ibid.*, p. 19.

25. *Ibid.*, p. 125.

26. *Ibid.*, pp. 140–141.

27. Karl Marx and Friedrich Engels, *The Holy Family* (Foreign Languages Publishing House, Moscow 1956), pp. 230, 232.

28. *Ibid.*, p. 240.

29. Karl Marx, "Critique of the Gotha Programme," Karl Marx and Friedrich Engels, *Basic Writings on Politics and Philosophy*, ed. Lewis S. Fever (Anchor Books, 1959), p. 130.

30. Richard Crossman, ed., *The God that Failed*, pp. 92–100.

31. John Stuart Mill, "On Liberty," *The English Philosophers from Bacon to Mill*, ed. Edwin A. Burtt (Modern Library, 1939), p. 966.

32. Abram Bergson, "Reliability and Usability of Soviet Statistics: A Summary Appraisal," *American Statistician*, June–July 1953, pp. 19–23.

33. Bertram Wolfe, *op. cit.*, p. 162n.

34. William L. Shirer, *The Rise and Fall of the Third Reich* (Fawcett Publications, 1960), pp. 307–308.

35. Hannah Arendt. *op. cit.*, p. 390n.

36. Svetozar Pejovich, "The End of Planning: The Soviet Union and East European Experiences," *The Politics of Planning*, ed. A. Lawrence Chickering (Institute for Contemporary Studies, 1976), p. 96.

37. Edmund Burke, "On Conciliation with the Colonies," *Speeches and Letters on American Affairs*, ed. Peter McKevitt (J. M. Dent & Sons, Ltd., 1961), p. 96.

38. Edward Gibbon, *The Decline and Fall of the Roman Empire*, pp. 65–67.

39. Daniel Boorstin, *The Americans*, Vol. I: *The Colonial Experience* (Random House, 1958), p. 329.

40. *Ibid.*, p. 7.

41. *Loc. cit.*

42. *Ibid.*, p. 8.

43. *Ibid.*, p. 37.

44. John P. Roche, *Shadow and Substance* (Collier Books, 1969), p. 10.

45. *Ibid.*, p. 41.

46. Alexander Hamilton, James Madison, and John Jay, *The Federalist Papers*, No. 51 (New American Library of World Literature, Inc., 1961), p. 322.

47. *Ibid.*, pp. 321–322.

48. *Ibid.*, p. 322.

49. *Ibid.*, p. 79.

50 Maldwyn Allan Jones, *American Immigration* (University of Chicago Press, 1960), pp. 13, 32.

51. Michael J. Malbin, "Congressional Committee Staffs: Who's in Charge Here?" *The Public Interest*, Spring 1977, p. 36.

52. "Capitol Hill Staffs: Hidden Government in Washington," *U. S. News & World Report*, April 4, 1977, p. 37; "Reflections of a Senate Aide," *The Public Interest*, Spring 1977, p. 42.

53. William Lilley III & James C. Miller III, "The New 'Social Regulation'," *The Public Interest*, Spring 1977, p. 50.

54. James Q. Wilson, "The Rise of the Bureaucratic State," *The Public Interest* Fall 1975, p. 92.

55. *Loc. cit.*.

56. "Quest for Better Schools," *U. S. News & World Report*, September 11, 1978, p. 51.

57. U. S. Bureau of the Census, *Historical Statistics of the United States: From Colonial Times to 1970*, p. 1111.

58. Martin Mayer, *The Builders* (W. W. Norton & Co., Inc., 1978), p. 417.

NOTES

59. "New York City—Italian Style," *Wall Street Journal*, July 21, 1978, p. 8.

60. F. A. Hayek, *The Road to Serfdom* (University of Chicago Press, 1957).

61. "Capitalism, Socialism, and Democracy," *Commentary*, April 1978, p. 31.

62. *Loc. cit.*

63. *Ibid.*, p. 49.

64. George J. Stigler, *The Citizen and the State* (University of Chicago Press, 1975), p. 5.

65. See Nathan Glazer, *Affirmative Discrimination*, Chapters 1–3.

66. Michael Meltsner, *Cruel and Unusual*, p. 308.

67. Martin Anderson, *Welfare* (Hoover Institution Press, 1978), pp. 26–27.

68. Michael Grant, *The Fall of the Roman Empire*, (Annenberg School Press, 1976), p. 147.

69. John Stuart Mill, "On Liberty,"*op. cit.*, p. 1038.

70. Charles O. Hucker, *China's Imperial Past* (Stanford University Press, 1975), p. 306.

71. Michael C. Jensen and William H. Meckling, "Can the Corporation Survive?" *Public Policy Working Paper Series*, pps. 76–4 (May 1976) Graduate School of Management, University of Rochester, p. 3.

72. Gerald D. Keim and Roger E. Meiners, "Corporate Social Responsibility: Private Means for Public Wants?" *Policy Review*, Summer 1978, p. 92.

73. George F. Will, "Rah, Rah, Rah! Sis, Boom, Bah! Let's Hear It for Title IX!" *Los Angeles Times*, March 6, 1978, Part II, p. 7.

74. See, for example, John Kenneth Galbraith *The Great Crash* (Houghton-Mifflin Co., 1961), Chapter III; Milton Friedman and Anna Schwartz, *A Monetary History of the United States* (Princeton University Press, 1963), Chapter 7, especially pp. 407–409.

75. U.S. Bureau of the Census, *Historical Statistics of the United States, From Colonial Times to 1970*, pp. 1104–1105.

76. *Ibid.*, pp. 200–202.

77. Alexis de Tocqueville, *Democracy in America* (Alfred A. Knopf, 1956) Vol. II, pp. 307–308.

78. William L. Shirer, *The Rise and Fall of the Third Reich*, pp. 291–292, 394, 632–633.

79. See, for example, Alexander Werth, *Russia at War* (Barrie and Rockliff, 1969), Part One, Chapters III, IV, V.

80. See *Goss, et al. v. Lopez, et al.* 419 U. S. 565 (1975).

81. *City of Los Angeles v. Manhart*, 435 U.S. 702 (1978).

82. U. S. Bureau of the Census, *Historical Statistics of the United States, From Colonial Times to 1970*, p. 293.

83. Irving Kristol, *Two Cheers for Capitalism*, p. 224.

84. *Ibid.*, p. 185.

85. John Rawls, *A Theory of Justice* (Harvard University Press, 1971), p. 43.

86. *Ibid.*, p. 30.

87. F. A. Hayek, *Studies in Philosophy, Politics and Economics* (Simon and Schuster, 1967), p. 178.

88. Everett C. Ladd, Jr. and Seymour Martin Lipset, *The Divided Academy* (McGraw-Hill Book Co., 1975), Chapter 3.

89. "One recent textbook devotes 82 pages to what the author terms a very condensed summary of current theories of crime causation." *The Economics of Crime and Punishment*, ed. Simon Rottenberg, p. 13. Also James Q. Wilson, *Thinking About Crime*, see Chapter 3.

90. Francis Bacon, "The Great Instauration," *The English Philosophers from Bacon to Mill*, ed. Edwin A. Burtt, p. 19.

91. See Jacob Viner, *The Long View and the Short* (The Free Press, 1958), pp. 79–84.

92. "Practical" (i.e., non-analytical) men often fail to recognize that utilizing given equipment to its optimal extent (Producing that quantity of output for which average cost is lowest) is *not* the same as producing a given level of output (even that same level of output) at its lowest cost. An obvious example is that most automobiles are idle 90 percent of the time, and yet that may be the most efficient mode of transportation in many cases.

93. J. A. Schumpeter, *History of Economic Analysis* (Oxford University Press, 1954), p. 4.

94. Howard Sherman, *Radical Political Economy* (Basic Books, 1972), p. 73.

95. Lewis Coser, *Men of Ideas* (The Free Press, 1970), p. viii.

96. Thomas Hobbes, "Leviathan," *The English Philosophers from Bacon to Mill*, ed. Edwin A. Burtt, p. 148.

97. *Ibid.*, p. 220.

98. Karl Marx, "The Leading Article of No. 179 of *Kölnische Zeitung*," K. Marx and F. Engels, *On Religion* (Foreign Languages Publishing House, Moscow, 1955), p. 31.

99. Thomas Robert Malthus, *Population: The First Essay*, ed. Kenneth E. Boulding (University of Michigan, 1959), pp. xiii, 1.

100. See Richard Hofstadter, *Social Darwinism in American Thought* (The Beacon Press, 1955).

101. Alec Nove, *The Soviet Economic System*, pp. 127. 312–313.

102. William L. Shirer, *The Rise and Fall of the Third Reich*, p. 345.

103. T. R. Malthus, *An Essay on the Principle of Population* (J. M. Dent & Sons, Ltd.), Vol. II, p. 260.

104. See Thomas Sowell, *Classical Economics Reconsidered* (Princeton University Press, 1974), pp. 88–89.

105. See Nassau William Senior, *Two Lectures on Population* (Saunders and Ottley, 1829), Appendix.

106. See Thomas Sowell, "Sismondi: A Neglected Pioneer," *History of Poitical Economy*, Spring 1972, p. 82.

107. George J. Stigler, "The Ricardian Theory of Value and Distribution," *Journal of Political Economy*, June 1952.

108. T. R. Malthus, *An Essay on the Principle of Population*, Vol. I, p. 131.

109. Lester C. Thurow, *Poverty and Discrimination* (The Brookings Institution, 1969), p. 2.

110. Howard Sherman, *Radical Political Economy*, p. 74.

111. See Richard Hofstadter, *Social Darwinism in American Thought* (University of Pennsylvania Press, 1945).

112. Carl Brigham, *A Study of American Intelligence* (Princeton University Press, 1923), p. viii.

113. *Ibid.*, p. 100.

114. Quoted in Leon Kamin, *The Science and Politics of I.Q.* (Erlbaum Associates, 1974), p. 8.

115. *Ibid.*, p. 6.

116. *Loc. cit.*

117. *Loc. cit.*

118. *Ibid.*, p. 21.

119. Carl Brigham, *op. cit.*, p. 210.

120. Rudolf Pintner, *Intelligence Testing: Methods and Results* (Henry Holt & Co., 1923), p. 361.

121. See N. J. Block and Gerald Dworkin, *The I.Q. Controversy* (Pantheon Books, 1976), pp. 4–44.

122. *Ibid.*, p. 31.

123. Thomas Sowell, "Race and I.Q. Reconsidered," *Essays and Data on American Ethnic Groups*, ed. T. Sowell (Urban Institute, 1978), pp. 208.

124. *Ibid.*, p. 207.

125. Oscar Handlin, *Race and Nationality in American Life*.

126. Thomas Sowell, "Race and I.Q. Reconsidered," *op. cit.*, pp. 226–227.

127. *Ibid.*, p. 227.

128. Carl Brigham, *op. cit.*, p. 29.

129. *Ibid.*, p. 57.

130. *Ibid.*, p. 90.

131. *Ibid.*, p. 102.

132. John C. Loehlin, Gardiner Lindsey, and J. N. Spuhler, *Race Differences in Intelligence* (W. H. Freeman and Co., 1975), Chapter 6.

133. Arthur R. Jensen, *Educability and Group Differences* (Methuem, 1973), p. 215n.

134. *Loc. cit.*

135. Arthur R. Jensen, "How Much Can We Boost I.Q. and Scholastic Achievement?" *Harvard Educational Review*, Vol. 39, No. 1 (Winter 1969) pp.1–123.

136. Arthur R. Jensen, *Genetics and Education* (Harper & Row, 1973), pp. 44–46.

137. Carl Brigham, "Intelligence Tests of Immigrant Groups," *Psychological Review*, March 1930, pp. 158–165. Myrdal, *op. cit.*, p. 148n.

138. Quoted in Lewis Coser, *Men of Ideas*, p.232.

139. Michael Grant, *The Fall of the Roman Empire*, p. 266.

NOTES

140. Edward Gibbon, *The Decline and Fall of the Roman Empire*, Vol. I, p. 477.
141. *Ibid.*, pp. 448, 465, 474.
142. Michael Grant, op. cit., p. 257.
143. *Ibid.*, pp. 257–263.
144. *Ibid.*, p.258.
145. Edward Gibbons, *op. cit.*, Vol. I, p. 715.
146. *Ibid.*, p. 675.
147. *Ibid.*, p. 710.
148. *Ibid.*, p. 719.
149. *Ibid.*, p. 767.
150. *Ibid.*, p. 841. See also pp. 61, 374, 379, 835–865.
151. *Ibid.*, p. 504.
152. *Ibid.*, Vol. II, p. 848.
153. *Ibid.*, Vol. III, p. 314.
154. *Loc. Cit.*
155. *Ibid.*, Vol. pp. 715, 719; *Ibid.*, Vol. II, pp. 8.
156. Charles O. Hucker, *China's Imperial Past* (Stanford University Press, 1975), p. 303.
157. *Ibid.*, p. 356.
158. *Ibid.*, p. 304.
159. *Ibid.*, p. 309.
160. *Ibid.*, pp. 323, 324, 334.
161. *Ibid.*, p. 327.
162. "In many respects, eleventh-century China was at a level of economic development not achieved by any European state until the eighteenth century at the earliest." *Ibid.*, p. 324. See also pp. 336, 349, 351, 352.
163. *Ibid.*, p. 356.
164. *Ibid.*, p. 296.
165. *Ibid.*, p. 362.
166. *Ibid.*, p. 365.
167. Lewis Coser, *Men of Ideas*, pp. 227–233.
168. *Ibid.*, p. 231.
169. *Loc. cit.*
170. John Stuart Mill, *Principles of Political Economy*, ed. W.J. Ashley (Longmans, Green and Co., 1909), p. 950.
171. Lewis Coser, *op. cit.*, p. 150.
172. *Ibid.*, pp. 150–151.
173. *Ibid.*, p. 155.
174. Sidney and Beatrice Webb, *Soviet Communism: A New Civilization?*
175. Arnold Beichman, *Nine Lies About America* (Pocket Books, 1973), p. 177.
176. Lewis Coser, *op. cit.*, p. 237.
177. Arnold Beichman, *op. cit.*, p. 192.
178. Lewis Coser, *op. cit.*, pp. 234–235.
179. *Ibid.*, p. 234.
180. Seymour Martin Lipset and Richard B. Dobson, "The Intellectual as Critic and Rebel: With Special Reference to the United States and the Soviet Union," *Daedalus*, Summer 1972, p. 170.
181. James Burnham, *Suicide of the West* (Arlington House, 1975), p. 104.
182. Ladd and Lipset, *op. cit.*, p. 39.
183. *Ibid.*, Chapter 1.
184. *Ibid.*, p. 123.
185. Frank E. Ambruster, *The Forgotten Americans* (Arlington House, 1972), p. 55n.
186. Earl Warren, *The Memoirs of Earl Warren*, p. 317.
187. Frank E. Ambruster, *op. cit.*, pp. 31–32.
188. James Burnham, *Suicide of the West*, p. 143.
189. Ben Wattenberg, *The Real America*, p. 4.
190. *Ibid.*, p. 15.
191. *Ibid.*, p. 105.
192. *Ibid.*, p. 20.
193. *Loc. cit.*

194. *Ibid.*, p. 188.
195. *Ibid.*, p. 189.
196. *Ibid.*, p. 198.
197. *Ibid.*, p. 192.
198. Everett C. Ladd, Jr., "Traditional Values Regnant," *Public Opinion*, March–April 1978, p. 48.
199. Ben Wattenberg, *op. cit.*, p. 222.
200. *Ibid.*, p. 194.
201. *Loc. cit.*
202. *Ibid.*, p. 125.
203. *Ibid.*, p. 134.
204. *Ibid.*, p. 132.
205. Martin Anderson, *Welfare*, pp. 19–24.
206. *Ibid.*, p. 19.
207. *Ibid.*, p. 20.
208. *Ibid.*, pp. 22–24.
209. U.S. Bureau of the Census, *Social Indicators*, p. 466.
210. Erich Streissler, et al., *Roads to Freedom: Essays in Honor of Friedrich A. von Hayek* (Routledge & Kegan Paul, 1969), p. 7–8.
211. Howard Sherman, *op. cit.*, p. 154.
212. Harry Magdoff, *The Age of Imperialism: The Economics of U. S. Foreign Policy* (Monthly Review Press, 1969), p. 21.
213. "The humanitarians and social reformers particularly need people who can be plausibly classified as helpless victims of causes and conditions beyond their control. And the classification of groups as helpless then actually promotes helplessness, thus serving the psychological, and political aims and possibly also the financial aims of the classifiers," Peter T. Bauer, "Development Economics: The Spurious Consensus and its Background," *Roads to Freedom*, ed. Erich Streissler, p. 19.
214. David Lebedoff, "The Dangerous Arrogance of the New Elite," *Esquire*, August 29, 1978, p. 22.
215. James Burnham, *op. cit.*, p. 78.
216. Daivd Lebedoff, *op. cit.*, p. 24.
217. *Loc. cit.*
218. *Loc. cit.*
219. Michael Meltsner, *Cruel and Unusual*, p. 25.
220. *Ibid.*, p. 26.
221. *Ibid.*, p. 304.
222. *Ibid.*, p. 308.
223. Ronald Dworkin quoted in Irving Kristol, *Two Cheers for Capitalism* (Basic Books, Inc., 1978), p. 192.
224. John Maynard Keynes, *Laissez-Faire and Communism* (New Republic Inc., 1926), p. 99.
225. Arnold Beichman, *Nine Lies About America*, p. 46.
226. James M. McPherson, *The Abolitionist Legacy* (Princeton University Press, 1975), p. 206.
227. James Burnham, *Suicide of the West*, p. 100.
228. Arnold Beichman, *op. cit.*, 127.
229. Robert A. Dahl and Charles E. Lindblom, *Politics, Economics and Welfare*, p. xxvi.
230. *Ibid.*, p. xxviii.
231. *Ibid.*, p. 19. See also p. 73.
232. *Ibid.*, p. 73.
233. *Ibid.*, p. 79.
234. *Ibid.*, p. 245.
235. Max Weber, "Bureaucracy," *From Max Weber: Essays in Sociology*, ed. H. H. Gerth and C. Wright Mills (Oxford University Press, 1958), p. 224.
236. Thorstein Veblen, *The Engineers and the Price System* (The Viking Press, 1954), pp. 142, 144.
237. Peter Meyer, "Land Rush," *Harper's Magazine*, January 1979, p. 49.
238. *Loc. cit.*

NOTES

239. U. S. Bureau of the Census, *Historical Statistics of the United States, Colonial Times to 1970,* pp. 140–141.

240. James Burnham, *Suicide of the West,* Chapter VII.

241. John Stuart Mill, "On Liberty," *The English Philosophers from Bacon to Mill,* p. 1037.

242. Lewis Coser, *Men of Ideas,* pp. 350–352.

243. James Burnham, *op. cit.,* p. 259.

244. U.S. Bureau of the Census, *Historical Statistics of the United States, Colonial Times to 1970,* p. 1141.

245. The Library of Congress, Congressional Research Service, *United States/Soviet Military Balance* (Government Printing Office, 1978), p. 43.

246. *Ibid.,* pp. 43, 45.

247. *Ibid.,* pp. 43–45.

248. "The Equalizer," *Newsweek,* April 17, 1978, p. 37.

249. *Ibid.,* p. 36.

250. *Ibid.,* p. 37.

251. *Ibid.,* p. 37.

252. Roger Freeman, *The Growth of American Government* (Hoover Institution, 1977), pp. 6–7.

253. *Ibid.,* p. 14.

254. Edward Gibbon, *The Decline and Fall of the Roman Empire,* Vol. I, p. 8.

255. *Ibid.,* pp. 10–11.

256. *Ibid.,* p. 15.

257. *Ibid.,* p. 815; *Ibid.,* Vol. II, pp. 317, 793.

258. *Ibid.,* Vol. I, pp. 30–33.

259. *Ibid.,* pp. 107–108, 133, 203, 539; *Ibid.,* Vol. II, pp. 45–46, 100, 203.

260. Michael Grant, *The Fall of the Roman Empire,* pp. 70–71.

261. Edward Gibbon, *The Decline and Fall of the Roman Empire,* Vol. II, pp. 45–46.

262. *Ibid.,* Vol. I, pp. 272, 497, 504, 672, 675, 683, 687, 692, 708, 710, 715, 719–720, 841; *Ibid.,* Vol. II, pp. 21, 46, 131, 805–865; *Ibid.,* Vol. III, pp. 9, 870, 872; Michael Grant, *The Fall of the Roman Empire,* pp. 52–53, 110–111, 158, 252, 257, 258–267, 317.

263. Michael Grant, *op. cit.,* pp. 73–75, 81, 82, 85, 100, 117, 158; Edward Gibbon, *op. cit.,* Vol. I, pp. 381, 542, 953; *Ibid.,* Vol. II, pp. 281, 329, 530.

264. Edward Gibbon, *op. cit.,* Vol. I, p. 518; Vol. II, pp. 147, 299, 346; Michael Grant, *op. cit.,* 92–95, 103.

265. Michael Grant, *op. cit.,* Chapter 6.

266. Edward Gibbon, *op. cit.,* pp. 490, 692, 715, 719; *Ibid.,* Vol. II, p. 8.

267. Roger Freeman, *op. cit.,* p. 6.

268. Quoted in *Ibid.,* p. 15.

269. William Manchester, *American Caesar: Douglas MacArthur, 1880-1964* (Little, Brown and Co., 1978), p. 154.

270. U.S. Bureau of the Census, *Historical Statistics of the United States, Colonial Times to 1970,* p. 1120.

271. *Ibid.,* p. 1141.

272. William Manchester, *op. cit.,* pp. 156–157.

273. *Ibid.,* p. 157.

274. *Ibid.,* p. 174.

275. *Ibid.,* p. 193.

276. *Ibid.,* p. 236.

277. *Ibid.,* p. 243.

278. Michael Grant, *op. cit.,* pp. 297, 307.

279. Telford Taylor, *Munich: The Price of Peace* (Doubleday & Co., Inc., 1979), pp. 197–199.

280. William L. Shirer, *The Rise and Fall of the Third Reich,* pp. 402–403.

281. Harold Willens, "Braking the 'Mad Momentum' Behind the Arms Race," *Los Angeles Times,* June 18, 1978, Part IV, p. 2.

282. Thomas Hobbes, *Leviathan* (Everyman's Library, 1970), p. 110.

283. Lewis Coser, *Men of Ideas,* p. 152.

284. *Loc. cit.*

285. William L. Shirer, *op. cit.*, p. 335.
286. Alexander Hamilton, James Madison, and John Jay, *The Federalist Papers*, p. 157. See also p. 138.
287. *Ibid.*, p. 54.
288. *Loc. cit.*
289. *Ibid.*, p. 53.
290. *Ibid.*, p. 100.
291. *Ibid.*, pp. 101–102.
292. *Ibid.*, p. 54.
293. *Ibid.*, p. 59.
294. Lewis Coser, *Men of Ideas*, p. 151.
295. Alexander Hamilton, *et al.*, *op. cit.*, p. 33.
296. Lewis Coser, *op. cit.*, pp. 31, 5.
297. Alexander Hamilton, *et al.*, *op. cit.*, p. 111.
298. *Ibid.*, p. 110.
299. *Ibid.*, p. 45.
300. *Ibid.*, p. 41.
301. *Ibid.*, p. 80.
302. *Ibid.*, p. 150.
303. *Ibid.*, p. 79.
304. *Ibid.*, p. 54.
305. *Ibid.*, p. 308.
306. *Ibid.*, p. 320.
307. *Ibid.*, p. 321.
308. *Ibid.*, pp. 310–311.
309. *Ibid.*, p. 322.
310. *Loc. cit.*
311. Michael Novak, "A Closet Capitalist Confesses," *Wall Street Journal*, April 20, 1976, p. 22.

INDEX

Ability, 99, 100. *See also* Intelligence; Merit; Skills
Academic paradigm, 154, 215, 336, 337–338
Accountability, 363–364, 365
Administrative agencies, 213, 232–237, 253, 299, 318, 321–322, 323, 369, 379
  Civil Aeronautics Board, 134, 170, 196, 198, 383
  court deference, 302
  Equal Employment Opportunity Commission (EEOC), 235, 251, 252, 253
  Federal Trade Commission, 202, 210, 212, 213
  hybrid powers, 232, 317
  incentives and constraints, 15–16, 134, 142, 146–147, 195–196, 213
  Interstate Commerce Commission, 133, 134, 170, 188, 195, 196, 199, 232
  National Maritime Commission, 233
  partisanship, 236
"Affirmative action," 232, 234, 246, 249–260, 296, 300, 301, 321
  administrative agencies, 250, 252, 253
  Bakke case, 253–255
  Civil Rights Act of 1964, 249, 250, 255, 256, 259
  "Compensation" for the past, 254, 268–269
  Congressional intent, 250, 253, 255–256
  courts, 253–256, 300, 301
  discrimination, 249–260
  Executive Orders, 249
  guidelines, 250
  incentives, 259–260
  inter-ethnic differences, 250–251
  meanings, 250, 253
  minorities designated, 251
  opportunity versus results, 250
  qualifications, 250, 251
  quotas vs. goals, 252
  "representation," 250, 251, 256, 257
  results, 259, 300
  Weber case, 255–256
Africa 227, 267
Age, 78, 192, 251, 257–258
Agnosticism, tactical, 292, 293. *See also* Precisional Fallacy
Agriculture, 14, 219, 222
Agriculture Department, 134
Airports, 189–191
Aluminum Company of America, 209
American Medical Association, 133, 200
American Automobile Association, 11
American Revolution, 12, 379–380
Anderson, Sherwood, 352

Anglo-Saxons, 139, 273. *See also* Law, Anglo-Saxon
Animistic fallacy, 97–98, 390 (note 7)
Antitrust laws, 129, 169, 171, 202–213, 353
  burden of proof, 206, 211, 213
  Federal Trade Commission, 202, 210, 212, 213
  Justice Department, 202
  "predatory" pricing, 169, 211
  Robinson-Patman Act, 202, 210–212, 213, 225
  Sherman Act, 202
  theories, 202, 205, 211
Appomattox, 347
Articulation, 40, 102, 141, 150, 171, 192, 194, 202, 204, 214–217, 220, 222, 288, 334–336, 338, 360. *See also* Indicators of performance; Performance indicators
  advantages, 334–336
  disadvantages, 40, 172, 179, 180–181, 215, 216, 217, 338
  importance in intellectual processes, 334–336
  information loss, 172, 216
  not essential in all social processes, 303, 363–364
  versus accountability, 363–365
Asia, 227
Aspin, Les, 375
Athens, 292
Atlanta, 265
Authentication, 4–6, 8, 9, 148, 150, 271, 309, 336, 360
  consensual, 5–6, 150, 284, 301
  scientific, 5–6, 150
Automobiles, 10, 29, 30, 63, 75, 120, 136, 184–185, 186, 201–202, 226
Axiomatic doctrines, 120, 226, 258, 274, 356, 358

Babbitt, Irving, 352
Bacon, Francis, 335
Bakke case, 253–256, 293
Baldwin, James, 359
Bankruptcy, 9, 64, 170, 218
Banks, 25
Baseball, 208, 347, 364
Bataan, 320, 376
Beard, Charles A., 154, 352
Belgrade, 292
Berle, Adolph A., 387 (note 4)
Bias versus partisanship, 301–302
Bickel, Alexander, 295–296

412

INDEX

INDEX

INDEX

INDEX

INDEX

301.1554   68221
So92k

301.1554   68221
So92k

Sowell, Thomas, 1930-
Knowledge and decisions

DATE DUE	BORROWER'S NAME	ROOM NUMBER

DATE DUE
